Industrial psychology

THOMAS WILLARD HARRELL

Professor of Applied Psychology
Graduate School of Business
Stanford University

Industrial psychology

Revised

RINEHART & COMPANY, INC.

New York

to Margaret

Preface

Industrial psychology provides theory and research methods to personnel management, which is the heart of all management. In this view, industrial psychology is extremely broad. Admittedly the theories are incompletely proved, and the research methods have not yet obtained adequate results with desirably rigorous controls. Nonetheless, the results of the application of psychology to industry and the importance of the problems confronting this discipline explain its tremendous growth.

The concept of motivation is central to the presentation of this book. Psychological methods are being used to select people for jobs in which they can be motivated by their interests and aptitudes to perform effectively. Psychological principles and techniques are being used to train new employees so that they will be motivated to do a good job. The design of new machines is largely an engineering matter, but even here it is becoming accepted that the motivation of employees is important—in that they must be willing to accept a new machine or a new method if their productivity is to be high in the long run. Finally, supervisory practices based on psychological principles are being adopted to motivate the employee on the job.

For the increasing number of teachers who favor class discussion of actual industrial problems, a brief *Casebook in Industrial and Personnel Psychology,* prepared by the present author and Jay T. Rusmore of San Jose State College, has been published by Rinehart & Company, Inc. The problems and role plays in this casebook are articulated with the topics in the text.

A number of research assistants have done library research or have written new drafts of certain sections, entire chapters in some cases. These were Nancy Bay, Charles Braley, Alan Coleman, John Davey, Jerald Haegele, Charles Kessler, Jack Rising, Merritt Robinson, Charles Scarlott, Ellen Uhrbrock, Gerald Weyrauch, and Delbert Williamson. My son, Thomas S. Harrell, drew one of the figures. Valuable suggestions for the revision were made by Dr. Paul S. Burnham and Professor Donald W. Taylor of Yale University and by Professor Robert W. Pitcher of Baldwin-Wallace College. The entire manuscript was read and criticized by Professors Albert Hastorf of Dartmouth College and Jay T. Rusmore.

Again as in the original edition, the assistance of my wife, who suggested many illustrative, editorial, and statistical improvements throughout the manuscript, was indispensable to its preparation.

T. W. H.

Stanford, California
March, 1958

Contents

Figures

Tables

Industrial psychology

1

Introduction

Industrial psychology is the study of people at work in industry and business. It is the study of their aptitudes and their qualifications for jobs. It includes the principles and practices of training in the skills and attitudes for industrial work. Management training is especially important at present. Industrial psychology is concerned with the physical aspects of the work environment as, for instance, lighting and temperature, and their effect on work output and safety. It is the study, to a major degree, of the principles and practices of human relations. It is the study of attitudes and motivation that effect high morale and enthusiasm at work and of the causes of monotony that bring about boredom. It is the study of mental health on the job and of ways of helping back to mental health those people who have become upset and confused. It is the study of the relations between the supervisor and his subordinates and of the factors which lead to industrial strife or to cooperation between management and labor. Industrial psychology is a complicated study of a number of things, but it is always primarily the study of people—as individuals or in groups—in the work situation.

OBJECTIVES

The final objective of industrial psychology must be that of the company in which the psychologist is employed. This objective will be principally one of profit; hence productivity and efficiency are important.

Because productivity of people has often been found to depend on morale, good morale is a primary objective. Because high morale is not always found with high productivity, it must be made clear that high productivity and high morale are separate objectives. High morale necessarily means good mental health; consequently this is another way of stating a fundamental objective—mental health. Thus the objectives of industrial psychology are productivity, morale, and mental health.

WHAT INDUSTRIAL PSYCHOLOGY IS NOT

The rapid growth and great popularity of industrial psychology have led to a number of misconceptions about its meaning. It has been accepted by some as magic. The concept that "ten easy lessons" will teach a supervisor to manipulate people to do his bidding, even when they think that they have made up their own minds, is wrong because there is no such magic.

The extent to which industrial psychology is oversold has often been exemplified by unquestioning acceptance of psychological tests. Tests have been accepted as infallible. Although selection on the basis of psychological qualifications was the earliest major contribution of industrial psychology, the infallibility of tests has been greatly exaggerated. There are other fundamental qualifications that should be used even before a psychological test is considered. When tests are used, they are never infallible; at best, they merely increase the odds that a placement prediction is correct. All placement is a gamble; the outcome is never predictable.

Psychology is not magic. It is an art that applies scientific principles which have been found useful in dealing with people.

SCOPE

In industry, psychology is practiced mainly by line and staff managers, but also by psychologists employed as staff members themselves or, more frequently, staff advisers. When a manager is interviewing, or holding a meeting, or having any contact with people, or making any assumptions about people, he is practicing psychology whether he recognizes it as such or not.

The scope of industrial psychology is therefore the same as the scope of personnel management, that is, the entire process of management's dealings with people at work. Industrial psychology differs only from personnel management in that it emphasizes the scientific and research aspects of people at work and omits many of the routine administrative details.

In 1955 there were approximately 500 industrial psychologists in the United States, as shown by membership in the Industrial and Business Division of the American Psychological Association. Of this number, more than half were employed full time by a single company; the remainder were members of a consulting firm or were college teachers who devoted some of their time consulting with industry.

One way of defining the scope of industrial psychology would be to catalog what psychologists do in industry. Although this is an important part of the scope, it omits the more frequent and more important applications by persons other than professional psychologists.

The main scope of the professional psychologist in industry has included the finding of facts about existing methods and the development of better methods. For example, he has studied the accuracy of the average employment interview and application blank. He has developed new interviewing methods and different application blanks. He has developed tests to accompany the interview and application blank.

Use

Generally, however, the staff and line people, who are not psychologists, are the ones who use these methods—the revised interview, the revised application blank, and the new test. The duties of psychologists in industry are all-inclusive since the problems of people are numerous. The main duties of these psychologists, in order of frequency, have been reported as administration of research, use of statistical methods, test interpretation, test administration, use of occupational analysis methods, interviewing, application of rating scales, administrative duties, administration of questionnaire surveys, use of clinical and personal analyses, labor relations, test construction, education and training, and specific research.[1]* Since this survey was made, there has been a major emphasis on management development with emphasis on the training of managers and prospective managers in human relations. Psychologists have often had the duties of planning and carrying out a part of management development programs. Occasionally their role has been that of an assistant to a president or vice-president. More frequently their services have been rendered on a part-time basis as temporary consultants. They have often served as trainers or conference leaders to instruct on human relations, or leadership, or on how to listen. Frequently, also, they have assisted in the appraisal of managers and prospective managers through the use of interviews and psychological tests.

Definition

Industrial psychology is the study of people as individuals and in groups and of the relationship between individuals and groups. The study of individuals has had the longer history and is more widely recognized as being within the scope of psychology. Finding the qualifications of a person for a job—his work history, his intelligence, his special aptitudes, his nonintellectual personality and his interests—relating these qualifica-

* See list of references at end of book.

3

tions to the requirements of the job, and interpreting the results are well recognized as within the province of industrial psychology.

It is also recognized that the psychologist develops training programs, especially for technical employees, in order to bring about the desired level of skill, including quantity and quality of output and of safety.

Furthermore it is known that on occasions psychologists give questionnaires to employees to find their attitudes toward job, company, and supervisor; and that on other occasions psychologists are called in to counsel with emotionally upset employees.

All these functions emphasize the individual rather than the group. The stress on group behavior has been recent and consequently has had less recognition, but probably, in the long run, it will be even more important than the study of the individual. The study of groups is related to the study of organization, but it is not limited to the study of the formal organization. The importance of the development of group norms is coming to be recognized. The fact that people are motivated by group pressures that are not always the same as that of the logic of economics is becoming apparent. A person may restrict his output and make less money because he wants to be liked by the group, which puts pressure on him to conform.

Important incentives to work are a wise application of fair pay and opportunity for promotion, but there are also the more intangible incentives of being liked by work associates and by superiors and of doing work considered important by each employee. These incentives lead to granting a maximum of participation, so that decisions are delegated to the lowest possible level under skilled leadership. The work group is emphasized, even though this means that changes may come more slowly than management has heretofore wished. Often the faster changes that management has tried in the past have been the causes of great misunderstanding and conflict.

Understanding the relations between and among people is becoming a large part of the function of industrial psychology. It involves the relations of individuals to individuals and of individuals to groups. The supervisor needs to understand his relations to his subordinates. Likewise he needs to understand his relations to his peers and to his bosses. He needs to understand his relations to the union.

PRINCIPLES

There are a number of psychological principles that are basic to an understanding of people in industry. As a matter of fact, the same principles apply to the understanding of people everywhere—in the home, at school, or anywhere else. Since, however, the focus of this book is on industry, industrial examples will be cited.

Causation

The study of the basic elements of the cause of behavior leads to a more cautious and tolerant understanding of people. Behavior is caused by a stimulating situation which acts on a person to behave in some sort of way and may lead to some accomplishment. Therefore, to understand the behavior, one has to understand the stimulating situation as the person sees it. One also has to understand the person. Only by a change in the stimulating situation, or by a change in the person, can one expect a change in the behavior or accomplishment.

There is frequently a temptation to blame the person who does not act as the supervisor wants him to and to expect him to change faster than, in fact, he will. If the necessary time is taken to understand the person and his situation, it often happens that it is the supervisor who changes his point of view.

In a sense, everyone is doing the best he can at any particular time. True, he may be able to do better next time, but he could not, under the circumstances prevailing, have done differently the last time. Therefore, if a supervisor criticizes a subordinate for what he does and expects him to behave differently next time, the odds are not good that there will be a lasting change in behavior in the direction wanted. There will probably be some change. If a man is criticized for smoking on the job, he may cease smoking where the supervisor can see him. He may also form a dislike for the supervisor. Unless he understands why smoking on the job is undesirable, and accepts the reason, a lasting change in the direction desired cannot be expected.

USE OF CAUSATION

The adoption of the principle that behavior is caused and that it is desirable to understand the cause before attempting to change the behavior is fundamental to industrial psychology. This usually makes one slower to act but results in more effective action in the long run. It often makes one realize, after studying the situation and the person, that the behavior should not be changed but is understandable under the circumstances. At other times one recognizes that the situation, which might encompass company policies or supervisory practices, needs to be changed. On other occasions one realizes that the person should be changed through training, or transfer, or in other ways.

While the adoption and understanding of this principle of causation makes the supervisor slower to act, it may help him to understand why many of his fast actions in the past have not accomplished his goal. He will recognize that his wanting a subordinate to act differently is not sufficient reason for the subordinate to change his behavior.

Individual differences

Every person is different from every other, and consequently, within the limits of fairness based on wise policies and regulations, every person should be selected, trained, and treated on the basis of the kind of person he is. The need to know the person has long been recognized as essential to the effective selection and placement of people at work. It is also essential for a supervisor to know his subordinates in order to understand their behavior and to supervise them well. Although the supervisor has to concern himself primarily with the welfare of his work group and of the company, he should also know each subordinate as an individual.

There are dozens of ways in which individuals differ, but five of them will be picked for presentation here. People differ in their physical characteristics, in intelligence and intellectual aptitudes, in interests, in temperament, and in character.[2] These differences are, for the most part, uncorrelated. That is, a short person may be bright or dull, a temperamental person may be short or tall, a thief may be interested in music or in boxing. There are some correlations, but, in general, one may expect any possible combination of these characteristics.

PHYSICAL CHARACTERISTICS

Physical characteristics provide an example of individual differences which are familiar and therefore can furnish an understandable example for less tangible psychological differences. Figure 1-1 shows a distribution of the height of 868,445 American men drafted in World War I. This shows that most men are about average in height, but there are wide differences at the extremes of the curve. These two generalizations apply to all psychological traits: (1) most people are about average, that is, there is a single mode or hump in the curve, rather than two or more; (2) people differ widely on every trait.

It is commonly believed that height often makes an important difference on personality. Managers and salesmen observe that the short man exhibits cockiness in an effort to compensate for his feelings of inferiority. This may be true at times, but there are no statistical data to prove or disprove the extent to which it may be true. In any event, where it is true, one needs to know how the person seems to himself. The point needs to be considered, because a five-foot American male in his own country would be expected to see himself differently from a five-foot Japanese in Japan.

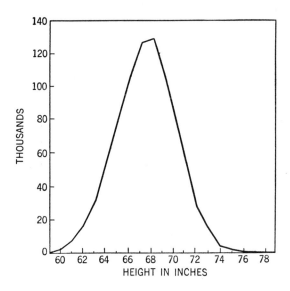

Figure 1-1. Distribution of Height of 868,445 American Men Drafted in World War I. (The lower end of the distribution is curtailed by the rejection of men of very short stature.)

(After Davenport, C. B., and A. F. Love, *Army Anthropology*, Washington: U. S. Government Printing Office, 1921, in Hilgard, Ernest R., *Introduction to Psychology*, New York: Harcourt, Brace & Company, 1953, p. 341.)

INTELLECTUAL FACTORS

Differences in intelligence are distributed in the same way as height. By intelligence is meant ability to learn. A combination of native intelligence and experience is usually tested to measure it. Differences in intelligence are important, since among adults it holds rather constant until senility becomes serious. Figure 1-2 shows the intelligence test results for a large sample of American men who entered the Army during World War II. Again, most men are about average; there are 30 per cent between the scores of 90 and 110. There are some men at the extremes, however, where 8 per cent score 130 and above and 12 per cent are below 70.

The distribution of clerical aptitude and of mechanical aptitude is similar to the curve shown in Figure 1-2. While there is a tendency for the brightest people to have high clerical and mechanical aptitude, and for the dullest to have low clerical and mechanical aptitude, there are many exceptions. One needs to know not only a person's intelligence but also his special aptitudes.

In a work group the range of differences in ability would be less than

7

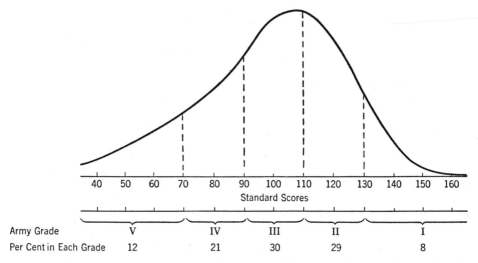

Army Grade	V	IV	III	II	I
Per Cent in Each Grade	12	21	30	29	8

Figure 1-2. Frequency of Occurrence of Scores on the Army General Classification Test (based on 713,000 selectees).

(From *Psychology for the Fighting Man;* Washington: Infantry Journal Press [now Combat Forces Press], 1943. Copyright 1943 Infantry Journal Inc. [now Association of the U.S. Army], and reproduced by permission.)

that shown in Figure 1-2, but it would still be wide, even when careful selection has taken place. Since performance depends at least in part on ability, one should not expect all persons in a work group to perform exactly alike. If they do all perform exactly alike, they are performing at the capability of the slowest member of the group.

INTERESTS

While employees have many interests in common, Strong has found that there are some important differences in interests among successful men in each of forty-four business and professional groups. These interests are changed slightly by working on the job. They become fairly well set at 20 or 25 years of age and change remarkably little over a twenty-year period, whether or not people are working in or out of the job in agreement with their interests. It is, therefore, another responsibility of the supervisor to find out what a person's interest is before selection and placement, or shortly thereafter. Selection and placement of the employee should depend in part on his interests; or the job may be modified to fit his interests. It is useless to expect to change a person's interests.

TEMPERAMENT

Temperament and other nonintellectual personality traits are likewise distributed according to the bell-shaped curve found for physical and intellectual traits. By temperament is meant excitability of response —the degree to which one responds with emotion. Although this depends to some extent on unusual circumstances of a particular day, there are consistencies of response that persist throughout the lifetime of a person.

By character is meant here primarily the same thing as honesty in some situations. This is a narrow definition. It means resistance to stealing, to lying, and to cheating where money is involved. Although this is a very important characteristic in responsible jobs, there is very little information about character of adults that is scientifically proved. More is known about character among children.

Children who were given a chance to cheat on examinations, and who were observed without knowing that they were being watched, showed the familiar bell-shaped curve just a little lopsided toward the high character side. In other words, almost no children cheated all the time, and the great majority of children cheated some of the time.

The extent to which this study of children can be applied to adults is not known, but it probably has some, but not complete, application. It is likely that some men will steal under some circumstances. The situation needs to be considered. Certainly it would be the unusual man who would claim that he has never cheated on an expense account or on his income tax. If their families were starving, most men could be expected to steal.

Consequently, it is desirable to study the situation as well as the person when trying to understand behavior that shows undesirable character. Here business is somewhat unrealistic. Many businessmen assert that if a man steals he should be fired—and no questions asked.

Errors in observation and reporting

Many misunderstandings occur because of errors in observation and reporting. One person sees a person as incompetent, another disagrees. One person sees an event as caused by one thing, and another disagrees. One person clings to a theory, and another discards it. In each of these disagreements the cause is an error on the part of one or both persons in observation or reporting. Presumably we would all like to have good judgment and be accurate observers. The study of the causes of errors may improve our judgment and observation. Furthermore, it may make us tolerant of others who make the same kind of errors.

Everyone looks at the world through colored glasses. These glasses protect the personality. One good description of errors in observation and reporting points out that there are two major causes of the way in which we see things.[3] One set of these is structural, or what's really "out there" in the physical world. The objective measurements of space and the physical properties of light determine structurally what we see. We shall not be concerned with such causes. Another major set of causes of what we perceive is functional, that is, causes that depend on the experience and needs of the person. It is with these functional factors that we shall be concerned in trying to understand some of the characteristic ways in which people make errors. Where children were asked to draw from memory the size of a coin, a quarter, poor children drew it larger than the children of richer parents. This is a distortion due to a functional cause. When ambiguous drawings were shown students, those who were hungry saw food more frequently in the drawings—another instance of functional factors.

The ways in which functional factors distort observation and perception have been outlined in four propositions.[4]

Proposition I: What we see and what we know in its natural state is organized and meaningful.

A company president may see a salesman get in a car at four o'clock in the afternoon and the president may decide that the salesman is quitting work and heading for the nearest bar. Perhaps the president is right, or perhaps he is wrong and the salesman is actually going home for an early supper before returning to work, or is now leaving to make another call on a customer. It is natural for the president to put meaning on the situation, even though he does not have enough information to make a meaningful observation.

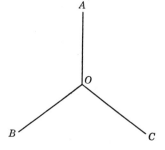

Figure 1-3. What Is Angle AOC?

(By permission from *Theory and Problems of Social Psychology,* by David Krech and Richard S. Crutchfield. Copyright, 1948. McGraw-Hill Book Company, Inc.)

Proposition II: What we see is selective.

When a salesman gets an account he may report that it will bring $100,000 in annual sales. When he loses the same account he may report that it is a $50,000 account. The account has not changed. The salesman has selected what he sees in the account. What we select to see may depend on needs, or on a temporary mental set, or on a mood. A sales-

10

man may be unsuccessful in persuading the first three customers to buy from him on one day. He loses self-confidence and decides that people are no good. On his next call he may see the customer as surly and unresponsive; this, of course, is due largely to his own mood rather than to any structural reasons.

"There are no impartial 'facts.' . . . Data are perceived and interpreted in terms of an individual's needs."[5]

Proposition III: How we see a part of a picture depends on how we see the whole picture.

Figure 1-3 shows that if we see angle AOC as part of a flat surface it is an obtuse angle. On the other hand, in Figure 1-4, angle AOC has become a right angle because it is part of a cube.

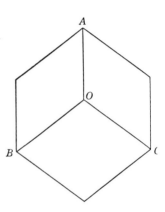

Figure 1-4. What Is Angle AOC?

(By permission from *Theory and Problems of Social Psychology,* by David Krech and Richard S. Crutchfield. Copyright, 1948. McGraw-Hill Book Company, Inc.)

This proposition also applies to our perception of individuals as members of groups. If we have a prejudice against a group of people, we will perceive the acts of an individual member of that group as different from our perception of the same behavior in an individual who is not a member of a group toward which we hold a prejudice.

The opposite application of Proposition III occurs in the assimilation of a prejudice. One salesman encountered a drunken Eskimo who informed the salesman that he was the purchasing agent for his town and wanted to buy something. The salesman, having a low opinion of Eskimos, tried to "brush off" the Eskimo, not believing that he was the purchasing agent. After a while it became clear that, in fact, he was the purchasing agent and was very well educated and intelligent. The Eskimo sobered up rapidly and proved to be a very good customer. The white salesman thought that, had the same drunken behavior been encountered in a white purchasing agent, he would have seen it differently. He

11

would have seen it as merely an accident, rather than as characteristic of his ethnic group, as he initially saw the drunken Eskimo as characteristic of "no-good" Eskimos.

The obvious lesson of Proposition III is that one should judge every person as an individual unless there is evidence for making judgments about the group to which he belongs.

Proposition IV: Events that are close to each other tend to be seen as parts of a common structure.

If you pound on the table and simultaneously the light goes out, someone might half jokingly say that you made the light go out. This confusion is an example of Proposition IV.

A customer may try a new motor oil for the first time. Immediately his motor breaks down and he has to put in new pistons. In anger he tells the service station manager that the oil caused his motor to break down. He really believes it. Actually there was an entirely different reason.

To summarize these four propositions, "all of man's action is shaped by his 'private' conceptions of the world." Consequently, we should try to learn what our own private conceptions are and whether they are based on supportable evidence. Furthermore, we should be tolerant of others whose private conceptions of the world are different from ours. If we know what these conceptions are, we can understand better the way people observe and report.

Attitudes

People often think and act as a result of attitudes rather than of the logic of a situation. The word attitude means a set to action with an emotional overtone. In other words, it is liking or disliking. A like or a dislike prepares us to act favorably or unfavorably, even when we do not realize that we like or dislike the thing in question. If we like the company for which we work, we will tolerate a lot and defend it. If we dislike the company, we will be disposed to criticize and find fault over relatively trivial affairs.

Attitudes are learned, or, usually, they are "caught rather than taught." We learn attitudes from our family, from playmates, and from mass media. We develop attitudes from the way we see things. There is an interaction in that attitudes also determine the way we see things. If a man perceives a supervisor as treating him unfairly, he is likely to develop a hostile attitude toward the supervisor. This hostile attitude may, in turn, lead him to perceive a second act on the supervisor's part as unfair when it actually is completely fair.

The attitudes of rank-and-file employees can be expected to be different from those of managers. We should not expect other people to have the same attitudes as we do; rather, we should expect them to be different.

One should be careful before deciding to attempt to change another's attitude. Maybe the manager's attitude, rather than the subordinate's, is the one that should be changed, or perhaps both should be changed, or maybe neither should be changed. Even if a subordinate has the "wrong" attitude, it may be fruitless to attempt to change it. Some attitudes that are learned in childhood cannot be changed except with the greatest of effort, while others that are held less strongly can be changed relatively easily.

The most popular way of attempting to change attitudes is to give facts. This will work only if the person is open-minded and will accept the facts in the sense in which they are offered. However, the most firmly held attitudes will not be changed by facts.

The best way to change an attitude is to let the person change it himself by expressing it to an understanding listener. If his attitude is wrong, he can see it for himself after he has expressed it and had it played back by someone who is genuinely trying to understand him.

Another way of changing attitudes is to use the group. If one expresses himself and finds that all others have different attitudes, he will frequently change to the popular side.

Motives

Everyone has a similar, but not identical, set of motives. In the discussion of individual differences above we asserted that everyone is different. Now we are saying that everyone is the same, or almost the same, in motivation. Both statements are true. People are the same in some ways and different in others. The term motive means a state of tension which can be relieved by some incentive. Thus hunger is a motive that can be relieved by eating food.

TYPES

Motives are of three general types.[6] There are biological motives which direct behavior to keep the organism alive, such as hunger, thirst, and fear. Second, there are appetites and aversions. By appetite is meant the craving for such things as specific foods. Appetites are based on biological needs but are changed by learning. By aversion is meant the tension of wanting to avoid some unpleasant stimuli such as putrid smells.

Third, there are acquired drives. Important among these is the drive for social approval. Everyone wants to be liked. There is the drive for self-respect; everyone wants to be important. These social motives are the most important for our understanding of behavior in industry today, particularly during prosperity in the United States. The biological drives are generally satisfied, as are the physiological appetites and aversions. It is the acquired drives or social motives which have been least satisfied, primarily because their importance has not been so well understood, and consequently the means of satisfying them at work have not been thoroughly and widely known.

GRATIFICATION AT WORK

All these motives can be gratified at least partially by work. This gratification is achieved often, but not always, through the medium of money as pay. Pay can buy the food and drink to satisfy the biological drives of hunger and thirst. Pay can satisfy our appetites for certain foods and can enable us to move to a neighborhood where we will not find the aversion of an unpleasant dump close by. Pay can at least partly win self-respect by making a person feel important because he receives so much money.

On the other hand, these acquired drives can often be as well satisfied, or better satisfied, by praise and incentives less tangible than pay.

Pay is, then, not a motive in itself, but it serves in important ways to satisfy one or more basic motives. Security often means a steady job, or the promise of motives being gratified in the future, and especially late in life, when one expects to have to quit work. It is not a separate motive.

Fear is a motive that has often been used to attempt to motivate employees. Its use has decreased greatly in the United States. Now no one will admit that it should be used as a conscious part of personnel policy, or at least only as a last resort. When fear is so used, the employee who is not performing adequately is warned that he will have to be fired if he does not improve his performance. There is no evidence that this is usually effective in improving performance, but the supervisor feels better because he thinks that he has "done his duty." Fear is easier to inspire in an employee than the positive motives of social approval and self-respect. Fear often disorganizes and frustrates people so that they are incapable of their best performance. Just as a golfer cannot play his best game if he is tense, employees cannot generally perform well if motivated by fear. Furthermore, the behavior that occurs when people are fearful is often less predictable than that which results from the positive motives.

Even where a supervisor does not consciously use fear to motivate employees, there is often present a fear, or anxiety, or insecurity among

14

employees. In a new job, employees are frequently worried about whether they can meet standards. The supervisor should try to prevent rather than to induce fear.

Frustration

Where one cannot overcome a barrier, behavior sometimes becomes frustrated. Frustrated behavior is behavior without a goal.[7] Frustrated behavior is harder to understand than motivated behavior, but the rewards of understanding it are usually greater. The frustrated person is in greater need of understanding and can profit more from it. Whereas motivated behavior is flexible, and a person is learning when he is motivated, the opposite is true of frustrated behavior. There the person is inflexible, stubborn, unreasonable, and he is not learning. It is desirable to be able to recognize frustrated behavior and to attempt not to be frustrated oneself when it is encountered. At times the supervisor should attempt to help others to shift from frustrated to motivated behavior.

Four types of frustrated behavior will be outlined and exemplified. *Aggression* "means trying to injure or hurt the person, group, or object that is acting as the barrier, or as the cause of conflict."[8] One manager stated that there were people in his organization who when meeting a person for the first time would react, "You're wrong! What's your idea?" This is aggression.

A salesman told of a customer who was always critical of the product or service. No matter how hard he tried, the customer was never satisfied. The salesman had given each customer a bottle of whisky each year as a Christmas present. This Christmas the salesman decided that he would give a present to the wife of each customer instead of to the customer. This frustrated customer was married to a woman of an ethnic group which was not accepted socially in the community in which she lived. The present was magic. The customer was not so critical after that. This demonstrates that one needs to get to the cause of frustration to cure it, rather than attempt to deal logically with the symptoms or, in this case, the complaints.

Resignation is a type of frustration wherein one gives up. The salesman who fails to persuade a customer to buy in several attempts, may quit trying, and may adopt the attitude, "What's the use?" Two other types of frustrated behavior are regression and fixation. *Regression* means behavior that is childlike, where one's effectiveness is lessened. An unreasonable generalization can be an example. *Fixation* is behavior that is repeated over and over without accomplishing anything. Unreasonable stubbornness is an example.

15

Whatever the type of frustration, the supervisor should attempt to understand the employee's behavior or, better yet, help him to understand himself so that he becomes motivated.

Morale

Morale is a combination of attitudes. Employee morale means the extent to which the employee has satisfaction with his job, his immediate supervisor, and the company.[9] Working companions, home conditions, and many other factors influence morale. A supervisor can usually, but not always, tell when an employee's morale is getting low by changes in his behavior. An employee may change by complaining more, or he may become silent and not talk as much. Production may suffer, but this, by no means, always happens. It is an important part of the supervisor's job to keep in touch with his employees so that he will know the state of their morale, not in a formal, or prying way, but in a friendly, normal fashion.

Types of leadership

AUTOCRATIC

There are three main types of leadership. One is autocratic, in which the leader leads by fear and force. He makes all the decisions, telling subordinates not only what to do but also how to do it.

LAISSEZ-FAIRE

A second type of leadership is *laissez-faire,* which means, literally, "let (people) do, or make (what they choose)"—or no leadership. Here the leader is a leader in name only.

DEMOCRATIC

A third type of leadership is democratic; this is more difficult to define than the other two partly because of its political connotations, which do not completely apply to its use in business. In democratic leadership in business the leader delegates to his immediate subordinates a large amount of participation. This means that he delegates the making, under his leadership, of decisions within his area of freedom. The leadership of the democratic leader consists in large part in being an effective conference leader. It also includes the same attitudes and skills in dealing with individuals that are present in effective conference leadership.

The democratic leadership of a business organization must be limited by qualifications. One qualification is the concept of area of freedom already mentioned. One cannot delegate what one does not have, and consequently a supervisor cannot lead a problem-solving conference about a problem that is not within his area of freedom. A supervisor's area of freedom needs to be defined carefully. One's boss may have taken something out of what might be expected to be a part of the area of freedom. This would decrease the area of decision-making that could be delegated. Company policy might likewise decrease the area, as might union contracts, and custom. Another qualification is that emergencies sometimes call for prompt decisions that cannot be made democratically.

Democratic leadership in industry is different from that in politics not only in that smaller groups (only the immediate work group at each level) are involved, but also in that voting is to be avoided in the industrial process. The goal is to achieve unanimity. While this cannot always be reached, it can still be sought by carrying out a discussion to reach a satisfactory agreement. Voting in industry often causes a split by polarizing the group into two cliques, and the minority is left unhappy.

Democratic leadership in industry has been shown to obtain better acceptance of decisions. It does not necessarily produce better decisions. It appears to take more time, but in the long run it saves time because cooperation is better. Often, but not always, productivity as well as morale is higher under democratic leadership.

SUMMARY

Industrial psychology is the scientific study of people at work. It includes certain principles of understanding people and the applications of certain techniques to dealing with people. It is a broad study which includes three major parts. (1) Knowledge of individual differences is used in the selection, placement, promotion, and rating of employees. (2) Human engineering is the study of the man-machine system for the purpose of having the design of machinery intelligently based on the capabilities and limitations of people's behavior. This part of industrial psychology also includes the work environment as a source of stimuli to employees. (3) Human relations is the understanding of individual and group behavior at work. This behavior is stimulated by motives and attitudes. It includes the relations of supervisor to subordinates, and of labor unions to management.

RECOMMENDED READINGS

Ruch, Floyd L., *Psychology and Life,* 4th ed., Chicago: Scott, Foresman and Company, 1953. Anyone who has not had a course in introductory psychology will find this book worth while. It is the most popular psychology book ever written.

Fryer, Douglas H., and Edwin R. Henry (eds.), *Handbook of Applied Psychology,* Vols. 1 and 2, New York: Rinehart & Company, Inc., 1950. This is the standard reference work for applications of psychology generally, as well as for specific applications to industry. The majority of industrial applications are summarized in Volume 1, but the administration of consulting psychology in industry is described in Volume 2.

Blum, Milton L. (ed.), *Readings in Experimental Industrial Psychology,* Englewood Cliffs, N. J.: Prentice-Hall, Inc., 1952; and Karn, Harry W., and B. von Haller Gilmer (eds.), *Readings in Industrial and Business Psychology,* New York: McGraw-Hill Book Company, Inc., 1956. These are the latest standard books of readings which reprint classic studies. The two books cover essentially the same topics, and in some instances include identical articles. Only one of them, consequently, need be read.

2

Occupational information

INTRODUCTION

Systematic, accurate occupational information is necessary for the successful execution of personnel actions based on psychological methods. Before the right employees can be recruited, selected, or placed, it is necessary to know the jobs that are to be done. Realistic training needs can be shown only by a careful study of what has to be done on a job. Fair pay must be based on the requirements of a job and their relation to those of other jobs.

The need for systematic occupational information has become recognized, and a majority of American companies are obtaining it. Four of five companies responding to a national survey were making job analyses in 1953; this was an increase from two out of three in 1947.[1]

In an organization with only a few employees, duties are so well known that occupational information does not generally need to be written. In medium-sized and large organizations the diversity of work and changes in work processes require a written statement of what each employee is expected to do. For even a relatively small organization the industrial psychologist usually needs a description of any job about whose personnel he is consulted.

Definitions

A job description that tells what the employee does is the heart of occupational information. Job analysis is the method of obtaining the information that makes up a job description. Information in job descriptions leads to setting up hiring specifications, job families, physical demands of jobs, worker characteristics, training standards, and provides the basis for job evaluation for setting pay.

Accepted definitions of the terms "position," "job," and "occupation," are[2]

A *position* is a group of tasks performed by one person. There are always as many positions as there are workers in a plant or office.

19

A *job* is a group of similar positions in a single plant, business establishment, educational institution, or other organization. There may be one or many persons employed in the same job.

An *occupation* . . . is a group of similar jobs found in several establishments.

Occupational information and psychology

Occupational information is the product of several professional groups. Much of the occupational information that we have has been accumulated by industrial engineers, although psychologists have occasionally obtained such information or, more frequently, have had a hand in developing the methods by which the information is gathered. The participation of psychologists in securing such information has been outstanding in the United States Employment Service and in other government services. When the information is to be used for employment purposes, the participation of a psychologist is especially desirable.

As in personnel methods in general, the psychologist's most important role in occupational information has been in research. He has been particularly active in making studies to improve methods by simplifying them, as, for example, in job evaluation.

After a job has been analyzed by studying one position, it is necessary to study a number of other persons on the same job to ensure that the final analysis is representative of those who perform the job. One person's duties may not be typical of the job.

A different emphasis on the content of a job analysis and a different method of collecting the information has been employed in the Critical Incident Technique.[3] The emphasis in this method is on those requirements for the job that make for failure or for outstanding success. While such extremes of job performance are found in any system of job analysis, they are made much more explicit in the Critical Incident Technique. In this technique, information is collected through the supervisor. A supervisor is given a form on which to keep a historical record of incidents that occur on the job that show outstanding success or failure.

The Critical Incident Technique has been used a few times, but there is no direct objective comparison between it and other job analysis methods. It was originally formulated for the study of United States Army Officers. It has been used a few times in industry.

JOB DESCRIPTION

The job description is the heart of occupational information. It describes what is done on the job. It summarizes and gives typical duties, it lists machines, if any, that are used, and it describes processes.

BRANCH MANAGER

Directly responsible to the District Manager, through the Assistant District Manager in charge, for securing a maximum proportion of the available business in the Branch consistent with cost, employee relations, and public good will.

The duties and responsibilities of the position are to:

1. Direct sales plans and solicitation efforts of Branch personnel and the activities of District staff members when the latter are working within the Branch.

2. Personally solicit key accounts and assist Branch personnel with solicitation problems.

3. Keep currently conversant with, and analyze, matters pertaining to competitive activities and economic conditions and recommend sales programs or changes in policy to effectively meet these.

4. Negotiate proposals for the acquisition and construction, lease renewal and modernization of dealer outlets and strengthen resale representation.

5. Supervise dealer activities and merchandising programs.

6. Assist and guide Distributors to secure full sales coverage and assure proper operating practices; make recommendations for conversions, the appointment of new Distributors or replacement of Distributors.

7. Supervise activities of Heating Oil Distributors, Marine Dealers, Airport Dealers, and Distributors of Liquefied Gases under prescribed policies.

8. Train the selling, plant clerical and delivery organization; coordinate activities and impart sales and specialized knowledge to sales outlets and employees.

9. Develop and appraise the performance of Branch personnel; recommend reclassification, personnel changes, and wage or salary adjustments; foster employee morale.

10. Efficiently use manpower, equipment, and facilities and control operating costs.

11. Supervise Branch accounting and clerical activities and control inventories and stock losses.

12. Maintain plant facilities in a safe, efficient, and presentable condition; train employees in safety practices.

13. Administer the Company's credit and collection policies.

14. Maintain the standard of service required to keep the trade satisfied and complaints at a minimum.

15. Promote and maintain good public relations.

16. Provide fair and equitable treatment to all employees through local administration or recommendations to the District Manager and carry out the industrial relations policies of the Company.

17. Conduct Branch affairs within general or specific policy rulings and make all decisions affecting operations within limits of authority delegated.

(For Authority and Relationships see the *Guide for Branch Managers.*)

Figure 2-1. Job Description of a Branch Manager.

ENGINE LATHE OPERATOR, FIRST CLASS

Job Title... Schedule No...

Indicate the amount of each characteristic required of the worker in order to do the job satisfactorily by putting an X in the appropriate column. Following are the definitions of each level:

O—The characteristic is not required for satisfactory performance of the job.

C—A medium to very low degree of the characteristic is required in some element or elements of the job.

B—An above-average degree of the characteristic is required, either in numerous elements of the job or in the major or most skilled element.

A—A very high degree of the characteristic is required in some element of the job.

When in doubt between A and B, rate B; when in doubt between B and C, rate B; when in doubt between C and O, rate C. If some characteristic not on this list is required, write it, rate it, and define it briefly at the bottom of the form.

AMOUNT				CHARACTERISTICS REQUIRED	AMOUNT				CHARACTERISTICS REQUIRED
O	C	B	A		O	C	B	A	
—	X	—	—	1. Work rapidly for long periods.	—	—	X	—	7. Dexterity of hands and arms.
—	X	—	—	2. Strength of hands.	X	—	—	—	8. Dexterity of foot and leg.
—	X	—	—	3. Strength of arms.	—	—	X	—	9. Eye-hand coordination.
—	X	—	—	4. Strength of back.	X	—	—	—	10. Foot-hand-eye coordination.
—	X	—	—	5. Strength of legs.	—	X	—	—	11. Coordination of both hands.
—	X	—	—	6. Dexterity of fingers.	—	X	—	—	12. Estimate size of objects.
					—	X	—	—	13. Estimate quantity of objects.

A sample job description is shown in Figure 2-1; it is for a Branch Manager of an oil company, and tells what is expected of him. This description shows how specific are the duties for a particular job.

Uses

Job descriptions are basic for successful personnel procedures in medium- or large-sized industrial companies. Recruitment and selection of employees, transfer, training, and pay setting all require accurate job descriptions. Recruitment of employees, selection, transfer, and placement of employees all require separate procedures, but the occupational

O	C	B	A	CHARACTERISTICS REQUIRED	O	C	B	A	CHARACTERISTICS REQUIRED
—	—	X	—	14. Perceive form of objects.	—	X	—	—	33. Attention to many items.
—	X	—	—	15. Estimate speed of moving objects.	—	X	—	—	34. Oral expression.
—	X	—	—	16. Keenness of vision.	X	—	—	—	35. Skill in written expression.
—	X	—	—	17. Keenness of hearing.	—	X	—	—	36. Tact in dealing with people.
X	—	—	—	18. Sense of smell.	—	X	—	—	37. Memory of names and persons.
X	—	—	—	19. Sense of taste.					
—	X	—	—	20. Touch discrimination.	—	X	—	—	38. Personal appearance.
—	—	X	—	21. Muscular discrimination.	—	X	—	—	39. Concentration amidst distractions.
—	X	—	—	22. Memory for details (things).					
—	X	—	—	23. Memory for ideas (abstract).	—	X	—	—	40. Emotional stability.
—	X	—	—	24. Memory for oral directions.	—	X	—	—	41. Work under hazardous conditions.
—	X	—	—	25. Memory for written directions.					
					—	X	—	—	42. Estimate quality of objects.
—	X	—	—	26. Arithmetic computation.	—	X	—	—	43. Unpleasant physical conditions.
—	X	—	—	27. Intelligence.					
—	X	—	—	28. Adaptability	—	X	—	—	44. Color discrimination.
—	X	—	—	29. Ability to make decisions.	—	X	—	—	45. Ability to meet and deal with public.
—	—	X	—	30. Ability to plan.					
—	—	X	—	31. Initiative.	X	—	—	—	46. Height.
—	—	X	—	32. Understanding mechanical devices.	X	—	—	—	47. Weight.
									48. _____
									49. _____
									50. _____

Definitions for additional characteristics:

Figure 2-2. Worker Characteristics Form.

(U.S. Dept. of Labor, U.S. Employment Service, *Training and Reference Manual for Job Analysis,* Washington: U.S. Government Printing Office, June, 1944.)

information needed for a sound decision in each action is essentially the same. Recruitment means obtaining prospective employees with appropriate qualifications. Selection means choosing the right person to be hired from a group of applicants. Placement means assigning the right person, from a group already selected for the employ of the company, to a specific job, in terms of how his qualifications match its requirements. Transfer from one job to another also depends on a knowledge of the requirements of the new job as well as of the qualifications of the people being considered. The job description provides information on which judgments can be made about the qualifications required in a job.

Selection

The use of information from a job description for selection purposes is exemplified in Figure 2-2, which shows the characteristics required for Engine-Lathe Operator, First Class. This Worker Characteristics Form can be used with a series of aptitude tests by an employment interviewer to determine whether an applicant has the necessary qualifications to be an engine-lathe operator.

It is necessary to know exactly what a prospective employee will be required to do in order to determine the characteristics on which recruitment will be based. An extreme example of failure to do this occurred during World War II. Officers who were training radar operators complained that the men they were receiving did not have the proper qualifications. This was in the early days of radar, when it was still a military secret. It was, in fact, so secret that the personnel officers responsible for placing soldiers were not allowed to know what was required of a radar operator. It was not surprising, therefore, that many placements were failures.

That job descriptions do provide information that will predict the aptitudes actually required to perform various jobs has been demonstrated by the United States Employment Service.[4] The job descriptions for the following ten jobs were studied: accounting clerk, cabinet maker, central office operator (tel. & tel.), coil assembler, cylinder pressman, structural draftsman, packer, hand sewer, sheet metal worker, and survey worker (clerical). Analysts then rated the aptitudes needed for success in each job in terms of its job description. The aptitudes considered were intelligence, verbal, numerical, spatial, form perception, clerical perception, eye-hand coordination, motor speed, finger dexterity, and manual dexterity. These aptitudes are the factors measured by the Employment Service General Aptitude Test Battery. Workers on each of the ten jobs had been given the GATB. The correlation was .44 between analyst's ratings of the aptitudes needed for success on the job and the aptitude scores obtained by the workers on that job.

Training

Training can be accomplished more intelligently when it is based on a good job description. Minimum training standards can be obtained from such information. For example, radio operators have to receive messages at the rate of twenty-two words per minute; therefore that rate should be the training standard rather than a standard that is above or below the actual requirements of the job.

24

Job Title_____ Occupational Code_____

Dictionary Title _____

Firm Name & Address_____

Industry_____ Industrial Code_____

Branch_____ Department_____

Company Officer_____ Analyst_____ Date_____

PHYSICAL ACTIVITIES		WORKING CONDITIONS	
X 1 Walking	X 17 Pushing	X 51 Inside	O 68 Cramped
O 2 Jumping	O 18 Pulling	O 52 Outside	Quarters
O 3 Running	X 19 Handling	O 53 Hot	O 69 High Places
O 4 Balancing	X 20 Fingering	O 54 Cold	X 70 Exposure to
O 5 Climbing	X 21 Feeling	O 55 Sudden	Burns
O 6 Crawling	X 22 Talking	Temp.	O 71 Electrical
X 7 Standing	X 23 Hearing	Changes	Hazards
X 8 Turning	X 24 Seeing	O 56 Humid	O 72 Explosives
X 9 Stooping	O 25 Color Vision	O 57 Dry	O 73 Radiant
O 10 Crouching	O 26 Depth	O 58 Wet	Energy
O 11 Kneeling	Perception	O 59 Dusty	O 74 Toxic
O 12 Sitting	O 27 Working	X 60 Dirty	Conditions
X 13 Reaching	Speed	O 61 Odors	X 75 Working
X 14 Lifting	28	X 62 Noisy	with Others
X 15 Carrying	29	X 63 Adequate	X 76 Working
O 16 Throwing	30	Lighting	Around
		X 64 Adequate	Others
		Ventilation	O 77 Working
		O 65 Vibration	Alone
		X 66 Mechanical	78
		Hazards	79
		O 67 Moving	80
		Objects	

Details of Physical Activities:

Stands (100%); stoops and turns while operating machine (80%); occasionally walks about 10 feet, lifting and carrying chucks and materials not over 30 lbs. (5%); pushes hand truck to transport loads up to 300 lbs. about 75 feet (5%); using both hands, manipulates lathe control handwheels to set controls to fine (1/64-inch) etched gradations (30%); visually and tactually examines finishes on machine parts (5%); stoops to read vernier and other fine-etched gradations (30%); orally instructs learners (15%).

Details of Working Conditions:

Inside (100%); noisy from operating machines (100%); dirty and greasy from machine equipment (70%); works with learners (15%) and around other machine shop employees without direct contact (100%); adequate light and ventilation (100%).

Details of Hazards:

Liable to cuts and bruises from machine operations; frequent minor cuts since gloves cannot be worn (70%); subject to first-degree burns from accidental ignition of inflammable magnesium alloy materials (20%); possibility of hernia and strains from pushing hand truck (5%).

Figure 2-3. Physical Demands Form.

(U.S. Dept. of Labor, U.S. Employment Service, *Training and Reference Manual for Job Analysis,* Washington: U.S. Government Printing Office, June, 1944.)

25

RAYTHEON MANUFACTURING COMPANY

DICTIONARY OCCUPATIONAL TITLE CODE*	TITLE	INDUSTRIAL DESIGNATION
0–48.01	Detailer II	(Profess. & Kin.)
0–48.04	Draftsman, Aeronautical	(Profess. & Kin.)
0–48.05	Draftsman, Architectural	(Profess. & Kin.)
0–48.08	Draftsman, Construction	(Profess. & Kin. Petrol. Refin.)
0–48.11	Draftsman, Electrical	(Profess. & Kin. Elec. Equip.)
0–48.12	Draftsman, Heating and Ventilating	(Profess. & Kin.)
0–48.16	Draftsman, Marine	(Profess. & Kin.)
0–48.18	Draftsman, Mechanical	(Profess. & Kin.)
0–48.21	Draftsman, Mine	(Profess. & Kin.)
0–48.22	Draftsman, Plumbing	(Profess. & Kin.)
0–48.23	Draftsman, Refrigeration	(Profess. & Kin.)
0–48.25	Draftsman, Structural	(Profess. & Kin.)
0–48.31	Tracer IV	(Profess. & Kin.)
0–48.99	Chassis—Draftsman Apprentice	(Auto. Mfg.)

Drafting Occupations Not Involving Extensive Knowledge of General Mechanical or Structural Principles and Methods.

0–48.06	Draftsman, Commercial	(Profess. & Kin.)
0–48.13	Draftsman, Landscape	(Profess. & Kin.)
0–48.26	Draftsman, Topographical	(Profess. & Kin.)

Occupations Involving Knowledge, Training, or Skill in the Preparation, Interpretation, or Use of Drawings, Blueprints, or Maps, and Requiring a High Degree of Perception of Form for Structural or Graphic Visualization, and General Knowledge of Mechanical or Structural Principles and Methods.

0–46.10	Experimental Man II	(Wood. Box)
0–46.11	Fixture Designer	(Furn.)
0–46.12	Furniture Designer	(Furn.)
0–46.87	Bank-Note Designer	(Gov. Ser.)
0–46.88	Industrial Designer	(Profess. & Kin.)
0–46.94	Jewelry and Flatware Designer	(Jewelry)
0–46.95	Memorial Designer	(Stonework)
0–46.98	Toy Designer	(Toys & Games)
0–48.41	Tool Designer	(Profess. & Kin.)
0–48.42	Die Designer	(Mach. Shop)
0–48.99	Lay-Out Man, Tool Design	(Auto. Mfg.)
0–48.99	Motor and Chassis Tool Checker	(Auto. Mfg.)

*United States Department of Labor, United States Employment Service, *Dictionary of Occupational Titles*, Washington: United States Government Printing Office, 1939.

Figure 2-4. Job Family Showing Occupations Related to Mechanical Draftsmen.

(Harvard University and Lindberg, Ben A., *Cases in Personnel Administration*, Englewood Cliffs, N. J.: Prentice-Hall, Inc., 1954, p. 418.)

Job satisfaction

The information in a job description can be used to reduce monotony and raise job satisfaction. The description can be studied to determine whether the job is so repetitious as to suggest extreme monotony; if it is, some variety might be given to the job by the addition of other duties or by a rotation system of equally monotonous but different jobs.

Physical demands

The study of the physical demands of jobs became common after World War II in order to place partially disabled persons. The physical demands for Engine-Lathe Operator are shown in Figure 2-3. These demands are compared with the qualifications of an applicant.

Job families

Job families can be established from the information in job descriptions. A job family is a group of jobs that are related by the requirements of the job but not necessarily by the industry in which the jobs are located. The relationship lies in the traits required to perform the job. Job families were first used in the conversion of peace-time industry to the wartime industry of World War II and were a useful device for employment offices in that tight labor market. One example of how they were found useful for recruiting for a growing electronics company is shown in Figure 2-4. There were not enough mechanical draftsmen available to meet the needs of the Raytheon Manufacturing Company, but, by using a job family in which mechanical draftsmen were members, it was possible to find persons in related jobs who could be satisfactorily trained to do the drafting necessary. As shown in Figure 2-4, certain other draftsmen, or even designers or persons qualified in other related jobs could be sought.

JOB ANALYSIS

A job description is obtained from a job analysis. Job analysis means the careful determination of what workers do on a job, as determined by a trained analyst. Fifteen or twenty other items of information in addition to the statement of duties are customarily included in the analysis. The exact list of these other items varies with the judgment of the person planning the study and with the purpose to which the information is put. Several items of identification, such as the name of the plant, industry, department, job titles and alternative titles, and number of persons working at the job, are usually included. These items of identification can be obtained from the personnel department.

PART A—Identifying Information

1. Name and Serial No. _____
                                Last Name   First Name   Middle Initial Serial No.
2. Job Title or M.O.S.: _____
4. Alternate Titles: _____
5. Organization: _____
6. Name of Air Base: _____

PART B—Work Performed

Duty Summary   % of Time   Importance Rating

Duty #1

PART C—Equipment, Tools, and Materials

(Include: purpose, uses, characteristics, frequency of use, and other information)
1. Equipment Used:
2. Tools Used:
3. Materials Used:
4. Equipment and Materials Worked Upon:

PART D—Skills and Knowledges

List the broad and specific skills and knowledges required in this job.

PART E—Job Characteristics

2. Work Site Description: Outside_____ Inside_____ Both_____
       Description:

3. Work Hazards and Dangers

PART F—Supervision

1. Supervision Received:
       Rank and title of supervisor_____
       Nature of his supervision: Close _____
                          General _____
                          Inspections _____
2. Supervision Given:
       (None_____)

No.	Rank	Job Title
-------------	--------------------	--------------------
-------------	--------------------	--------------------
-------------	--------------------	--------------------

PART I—Comments

(Opinions, recommendations, additional information)

Figure 2-5. Part of a Thorough Job Analysis Form.

(Rupe, Jesse C., "Research into Basic Methods and Techniques of Air Force Job Analysis—I," *Technical Report 52–16,* San Antonio: Human Resources Research Center, Lackland Air Force Base, December 1952, pp. 57–64.)

To determine exactly what the worker does is the primary purpose of job analysis. The analysis also ascertains why the work is done, how it is done, and the skill involved. Also included are minimum and desirable qualifications of training and experience, working conditions, physical requirements, number of persons supervised, supervisor and character of supervision received, relationship to other jobs (listing of jobs from which employees are usually recruited and to which employees can be promoted), tools and processes used, qualifications found desirable for placement on the job including intelligence and dexterity.

Part of a thorough job analysis form which has been used for research purposes by the United States Air Force is shown in Figure 2-5.

Kinds

Job analysis has most frequently been done by having an analyst observe directly the employee at work, but in some companies a questionnaire rather than direct observation has been used.[5]

These two methods, observation and questionnaire, have been studied along with three others: a group interview with workers, an individual interview, and a technical conference with a group of experts on the particular job in question.[6] The purpose of the research was to find which of these job analysis methods yields the most information and which is most practical in terms of time and, therefore, expense. The individual interview with the employee was the best in terms of taking the least time and therefore being the least expensive of the three methods which obtained complete information. Just as much information was obtained by observation and by the technical conference, but these methods were more expensive.

JOB EVALUATION

Job evaluation is a method for determining the relative worth of jobs within a company. It does not determine the absolute pay for a job. This is set by custom or collective bargaining or both. The reason advanced for the use of job evaluation is to provide a fair basis for differences in pay between one job and another within a company. Management has emphasized the use of job evaluation more than have unions, although unions generally recognize that there is a place, but a less important one, for the method.

Gomberg, once organized labor's most articulate spokesman on personnel procedures, has expressed several reservations about the use of job evaluation.[7] One is that the range of pay from janitor to corporation president does not depend on a scientific scale. He admits that job evaluation can rank jobs according to their relative pay, but he points out that it cannot set scientifically the absolute amount of pay. He also states that the decision about relative weights for different factors of the job may be a matter of judgment. For example, one might give hazard on a job a maximum weight of 30 as compared to a maximum of 60 points for skill. Gomberg points out that such a decision might be in error. To generalize, any decision about weights is a matter of judgment and not one of science.

Both of these reservations about job evaluation are sound, but it is still desirable to reduce inequities in pay between one job and another in a company.

Steps

There are several steps in job evaluation. It begins with job standardization to ensure that the same job will be done in the same way in a company. Next there is a job description based on a job analysis. After this comes the evaluation itself, which consists of one of several definite procedures that will be discussed at greater length later. The evaluation results are converted into money values after the community level, or industry level, or both, of pay, for at least some jobs, have been considered. In unionized companies, negotiation will take place before the formula is accepted for setting pay.

One of the most important points in obtaining employee acceptance for a job evaluation system is to obtain the confidence of the employees. They are frequently mystified by the technical procedures of graphs and the like. When a company is unionized, it is necessary to have union acceptance. Whether or not the company is unionized, employee participation should be sought. A joint labor-management committee on job evaluation is common.

The difficulties encountered in establishing a joint union-management job evaluation program—and there are many—are more than offset by the many benefits that accrue to both sides. Not the least of these has been management's ability, as a result, to enlist the active support of employees and their chosen representatives, and to eliminate the grievances arising from an arbitrarily imposed wage system.[8]

Full cooperation between union and management in job evaluation is rare, but it did occur in one company. This company took time to overcome union resistance and to persuade the workers that the plan was desirable. Job evaluators were selected and trained from within the company. This careful program was "satisfactory to both union and management." A different attempt, where management sought to impose a job evaluation system without securing employee cooperation and participation, was clearly a failure.[9]

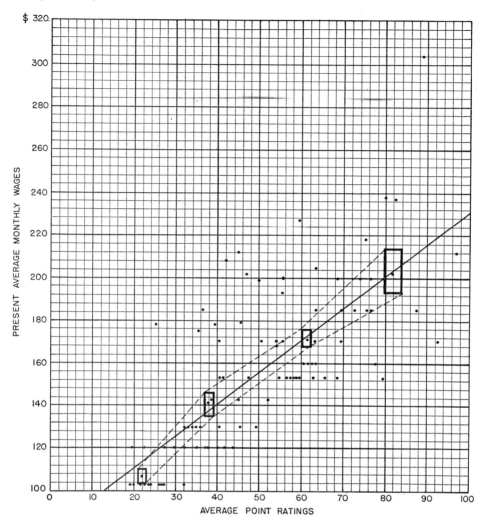

Figure 2-6. Wages and Job Ratings.

(Jones, Alice May, "Job Evaluation of Nonacademic Work at the University of Illinois," M.A. Thesis, University of Illinois, 1946.)

Results

Employees evaluated their own jobs in one organization.[10] The same jobs were evaluated by a specialist in the personnel department, by supervisors, and by the employees themselves. Agreement among the three types of raters—employees, supervisors, and personnel man—was rather high. Ratings by supervisors were higher than those by employees, but the ratings by employees were higher than those by the personnel man. This experience suggests that employees are capable of evaluating their own jobs fairly. Their participation led to greater confidence in pay rates.

The results of this evaluation are shown in Figure 2-6. This figure shows the straight line of best fit between pay and point ratings. It was not expected that the points would all be exactly on the line. The existing wage scale was close to the relative standings of the jobs with a few exceptions as shown in Figure 2-6, but the exceptions were important enough to justify making such a study. Some recommendations for pay changes were made where wages were far below the line of best fit. As a rule, wages should be raised where indicated, but the correct action is less clear when a wage is too high for the value of the job. Where possible, it would be desirable to transfer overpaid persons to higher-rated jobs where they will deserve their present rate of pay. Bad morale could certainly be expected if a person's pay were reduced as the result of such a survey.

The curve of best fit between pay and evaluation, as in Figure 2-6, does not have to be a straight line, but, when it approximates a straight line as in this instance, it is believed to be more satisfactory to make the curve a straight line for the sake of simplicity.

Management has found it desirable to find the average level of wages in the community for five or six jobs which are common to the company and to the community. These are called "bench jobs." A straight line of best fit is drawn through coordinates of these jobs, with pay on one coordinate and evaluation results on the other. Then management negotiates to reach agreement with the union on pay for the bench jobs. Pay for all other jobs falls along the line established by the bench jobs. Sometimes a union, because of custom or for some other reason, will force a decision to give one job more pay than its evaluation requires.

Methods

There are four main methods of job evaluation, and various modifications of them. These are the Point System, the Factor Comparison System, the Classification System, and the Ranking Method. Results are essentially the same regardless of the method. The point plan is the most popular; as a matter of fact, it is used more often than the other three systems together because of its simplicity and perhaps because of its apparent precision.[11] In the Point System a series of factors is selected which will include the requirements of the jobs to be evaluated. A numerical weight, between a minimum and a maximum, is set for each factor. The range may, and usually does, vary for at least some factors. The minimum amount of each factor necessary for the successful operation of the job is rated. Examples will be given of the Point System and the Factor Comparison System. The Classification System consists in putting jobs into several grades established on the basis of a study of the job descriptions. A crude classification would be Unskilled, Semi-skilled, and Skilled. In the Ranking Method the jobs are arranged in the order of their value as determined by a line or staff supervisor.

A larger number of factors than necessary has often been used in a job evaluation system. For example, a widely used system of the National Electrical Manufacturers Association requires ratings on eleven factors: education, experience, initiative and ingenuity, physical demand, mental and visual demand, responsibility for equipment, responsibility for material, responsibility for the safety of others, responsibility for the work of others, working conditions, and unavoidable hazards.[12] A study of the job evaluations in seven companies showed that two or three factors would explain the results adequately.[13] The important factors vary slightly from one company to another, but there is substantial agreement. In four of the seven companies, skill demands accounted for almost all the evaluation. In the three other companies, experience, or learning time, was most important. With workers paid by the hour, job characteristics are of some importance, and, with salaried jobs, supervisory demands are important.

These results suggest that job evaluation would be substantially as accurate if simpler methods using fewer factors were employed. The factors established by observation are always more numerous than the independent factors defined by the statistical process of factor analysis. The simpler methods have not been widely used because managers are believed to have more faith in a larger number of factors. These factor analyses, like all factor analyses, do not prove that the resultant factors and their weights are the most valid representation of the true facts. They only demonstrate a simpler explanation for the original data. If the original data were wrong, the outcome is just as wrong. Here the original data depend in large part on human judgment regarding the pertinent factors and their weights.

A "simplified" job evaluation system was compared with the National Electrical Manufacturers Association system and was found to be not only simpler and therefore cheaper, but also more reliable.[14] The items rated on the two methods are shown in Figure 2-7. Experienced analysts rated forty jobs by the "simplified" and by the NEMA system. Because of the time required, not all analysts rated each job. The reliability coefficient of the "simplified" system was .98; of the NEMA, .94.

It may be that a different rating system is better for office jobs and for high-level supervisory jobs than for factory production jobs. What-

33

ITEMS RATED FOR JOB EVALUATION

Simplified System	National Electrical Manufacturers Association System
General Schooling	Education
Learning Period	Experience
Working Conditions	Initiative and Ingenuity
Job Hazards	Physical Demand
	Mental or Visual Demand
	Responsibility for Equipment
	Responsibility for Material
	Responsibility for Safety of Others
	Responsibility for Work of Others
	Working Conditions
	Unavoidable Hazards

Figure 2-7. Items Rated on Two Systems of Job Evaluation.

(Lawshe, C. H., and R. F. Wilson, "Studies in Job Evaluation 6, The Reliability of Two Point Rating Systems," *Journal of Applied Psychology*, 1947, **31**, 355–365. Reprinted by permission of American Psychological Association.)

ever the need, it appears that only a few factors of a job need be rated to give just as much accuracy as a more complicated system.

RELIABILITY OF JOB EVALUATION

A number of studies have been made to show the reliability, that is, the consistency, of job evaluations. In a study of eight companies an abbreviated scale made up of three factors, experience, hazards, and initiative and ingenuity, obtained essentially the same results as a more elaborate system.[15] Three of the companies had used the NEMA procedure, which has been most widely employed. The scale was based on a thorough statistical study of the variables present in various systems.

A Job Description Check List was shown to be reliable in evaluating office jobs.[16] The five operations most important in a job was the optimum number to be rated. More or less than five operations gave less reliable results.

Occupational information

Rated by _____   Job _____

Date _____   Department _____

FACTORS	CHECK THE CORRECT ITEM FOR EACH FACTOR				
1. EDUCATION	College 5	High School 4	Elem. Math. 3	Add. & Sub. 2	Read & Write 1
2. EXPERIENCE	Over 12 mo. 15	9 to 12 mo. 12	6 to 9 mo. 9	3 to 6 mo. 6	0 to 3 mo. 3
3. LEARNING PERIOD	Over 3 yr. 10	1 to 3 yr. 8	6 mo. to 1 yr. 6	3 to 6 mo. 4	1 to 3 mo. 2
4. MENTAL EFFORT	Very High 5	High 4	Average 3	Below Avg. 2	Slight 1
5. MECHANICAL ABILITY	Very High 5	High 4	Average 3	Below Avg. 2	Slight 1
6. PHYSICAL EFFORT	A, B, C, D 10	E, F, G 8	H, I, J 6	K, L 4	M 2
7. CONDITIONS	A 5	B, C 4	D, E 3	F, G 2	H, I 1
8. HAZARDS	Very High 10	High 8	Average 6	Below Avg. 4	Slight 2
9. RESPONSIBILITY (EQUIPMENT)	Over $50M 5	$25M to $50M 4	$10M to $25M 3	$1M to $10M 2	Less $1M 1
10. RESPONSIBILITY (MEN)	Over 16 5	11 to 15 4	6 to 10 3	2 to 5 2	1 1
11. RESPONSIBILITY (MATERIALS)	Over $50M 5	$25M to $50M 4	$10M to $25M 3	$1M to $10M 2	Less $1M 1
12. COMPLEXITY	Very High 5	High 4	Average 3	Below Avg. 2	Slight 1
13. EFFECT ON SUBSEQUENT OPERATIONS	Very High 5	High 4	Average 3	Below Avg. 2	Slight 1
14. ATTENTION TO ORDERS	Very High 5	High 4	Average 3	Below Avg. 2	Slight 1
15. KNOW OTHER OPERATIONS	Very High 5	High 4	Average 3	Below Avg. 2	Slight 1
16. COORDINATION	Very High 5	High 4	Average 3	Below Avg. 2	Slight 1

PRESENT HOURLY RATE _____   _____

Figure 2-8. Job Work Rating Sheet—Le Tourneau Plan.

(Kimmel, W. W., "Evaluate Jobs and Pay Accordingly," *Factory Management and Maintenance,* 1945, **103,** No. 8, 144–151.)

An example of a Point System has been developed at R. G. LeTourneau, Inc., and it is shown in Figure 2-8. Each of sixteen job characteristics is rated and assigned a point value. For example, if the job is judged to require college graduation, 5 points are given; if the minimum education requirement is to read and write, only 1 point is given. In addition, if the minimum learning period necessary is judged to be over three years, 10 points are given, but, when the learning period is between three and six months, 4 points are given. After the ratings are made on each of these sixteen characteristics, the total number of points is added to give the evaluation for the job.

FACTOR COMPARISON SYSTEM

The Factor Comparison System is similar to the Point System in that each job is compared for a number of factors. Key jobs are selected whose pay, it has been agreed, is relatively fair, and whose pay covers the entire range of pay of the jobs to be evaluated. A group of evaluators, using job descriptions in making their decisions, compare each of the key jobs on each factor.

The pay for the key jobs is broken down into the amount of money deserved for each factor. For example, the job of janitor might be a key job which is being paid $2.00 per hour. This sum would be divided among the factors being used. Then the jobs to be evaluated would be ranked with the key jobs on each factor, and the money value of each factor for each job would be estimated. Finally the total money value for the job would be obtained by adding the values for each factor.

Analysis of the important factors present in the evaluation of jobs by the Factor Comparison System has shown that there are really few important factors, as in the case of the Point System.[17] Key jobs in a paper mill were ranked on each of five characteristics: mental requirements, physical requirements, skill requirements, working conditions, and responsibility. One factor, skill demands, accounted for 98 per cent of the variability found among the five rated characteristics; job characteristics accounted for the remaining 2 per cent of the variability. Hence it would appear that evaluation of skill demands, and possibly of job characteristics, would be preferable to evaluating the five characteristics.

Use of job evaluation

Job evaluation has continued to become more popular in the United States. In 1953 two-thirds of all companies were using some system.[18] Like most personnel procedures, job evaluation is performed less frequently in smaller companies than in larger ones. Job evaluation is being used increasingly for salaried employees, for supervisors, and even for executives. A large number of companies have described systems of job evaluation which, they report, have been helpful in setting fair pay.

OCCUPATIONAL CLASSIFICATION

Two ways of classifying the 30,000 to 35,000 occupations are discussed: by socioeconomic groups, and by intelligence.

Socioeconomic groups

A classification of occupations according to socioeconomic groups in the United States is[19]

1. Professional Persons
2. Proprietors, Managers, and Officials
3. Clerks and Kindred Workers
4. Skilled Workers and Foremen
5. Semi-skilled Workers
6. Unskilled Workers

This is a classification by type of work as well as by socioeconomic groups. The order is from high to low socioeconomically, although the economic status of some white-collar occupations is being supplanted by some blue-collar ones.

Intelligence

Intelligence test scores are another basis for the classification of occupations. The most comprehensive data have come from United States Army sources. A classification of occupations by intelligence is shown in Table 2-I. These results show some agreement with the socioeconomic grouping above to the extent that the professions have the highest scores and unskilled workers the lowest. As one descends the socioeconomic scale, the average intelligence test scores are lower, but the range of scores is greater. Thus, although only 2 per cent of accountants have a score as low as that of the average truck driver, there are 64 per cent of truck drivers with scores as high as the lowest accountant.

ORGANIZATION CONTROL

Occupational information is being used more and more in the selection and promotion of supervisors and managers. Two studies have been reported which show how the supervisory organization can be controlled more effectively by a thorough knowledge of jobs and men. Supervisors

TABLE 2-1

Mean GCT Standard Scores and Range of Scores
of 18,782 AAF White Enlisted Men by
Civilian Occupation

OCCUPATION	M	RANGE
Accountant	128	94–157
Lawyer	128	96–157
Engineer	127	100–151
Public Relations Man	126	100–149
Auditor	126	98–151
Chemist	125	102–153
Reporter	125	100–157
Chief Clerk	124	88–153
Teacher	123	76–155
Draftsman	122	74–155
Stenographer	121	66–151
Pharmacist	121	76–149
Tabulating Machine Operator	120	80–151
Bookkeeper	120	70–157
Manager, Sales	119	90–137
Purchasing Agent	119	82–153
Manager, Production	118	82–153
Photographer	118	66–147
Clerk, General	118	68–155
Clerk-Typist	117	80–147
Manager, Miscellaneous	116	60–151
Installer-Repairman. Tel & Tel	116	76–149
Cashier	116	80–145
Instrument Repairman	116	82–141
Radio Repairman	115	56–151
Printer, Job Pressman, Lithographic Pressman	115	60–149
Salesman	115	60–153

Continued

38

TABLE 2-I (continued)

OCCUPATION	M	RANGE
Artist	115	82–139
Manager, Retail Store	114	52–151
Laboratory Assistant	113	76–147
Tool Maker	113	76–143
Inspector	112	54–147
Stock Clerk	112	54–151
Receiving and Shipping Clerk	111	58–155
Musician	111	56–147
Machinist	110	38–153
Foreman	110	60–151
Watchmaker	110	68–147
Airplane Mechanic	109	66–147
Sales Clerk	109	42–149
Electrician	109	64–149
Lathe Operator	109	64–147
Receiving & Shipping Checker	108	52–151
Sheet Metal Worker	108	62–153
Lineman, Power and Tel & Tel	107	70–133
Assembler	106	48–145
Mechanic	106	60–155
Machine Operator	105	42–151
Auto Serviceman	104	30–141
Riveter	104	50–141
Cabinetmaker	104	66–127
Upholsterer	103	68–131
Butcher	103	42–147
Plumber	103	56–139
Bartender	102	56–137
Carpenter, Construction	102	42–147
Pipe Fitter	102	56–139
Welder	102	48–147
Auto Mechanic	101	48–151
Molder	101	48–137

Continued

39

TABLE 2-1 (continued)

OCCUPATION	M	RANGE
Chauffeur	101	46–143
Tractor Driver	100	42–147
Painter, General	98	38–147
Crane Hoist Operator	98	58–147
Cook and Baker	97	20–147
Weaver	97	50–135
Truck Driver	96	16–149
Laborer	96	26–145
Barber	95	42–141
Lumberjack	95	46–137
Farmer	93	24–147
Farmhand	91	24–141
Miner	91	42–139
Teamster	88	46–145

Harrell, T. W., and M. S. Harrell, "Army General Classification Test Scores," *Educational and Psychological Measurement,* 1945, **5**, 229–239.

were transferred to bring about a better fit between job demands and qualifications of men.[20] In both instances a thorough job description of each supervisory job was broken down into what were considered the essential elements for a supervisor or a manager. One analysis concluded that there were six important elements:

(1) plans an activity,
(2) decides to do, or not to do, a certain thing,
(3) organizes a group of persons to carry out the plans that have been decided upon,
(4) communicates the program to the organization,
(5) leads the organization toward the established goal, and
(6) analyzes the progress toward the goal.[21]

These six elements were rather highly correlated, the median intercorrelation being .73.

Each job was rated for the amount of each of the six elements required. Each manager and supervisor was rated for his qualifications on the six elements. Figure 2-9 shows a comparison of the qualifications of three candidates with the requirements of the job of General Foreman.

Mr. Brown possessed much better qualifications than his current fore-man's job required, and therefore he was considered first for the position of General Foreman. Mr. Black's job was better suited to his qualifications, but he was slightly better than his job requirements. Mr. White was not quite up to the requirements of his current job, but this job fitted better the requirements of the General Foreman's job than the requirements of the jobs of the other two candidates did. Which one of the three would you choose?

In the other study an over-all point rating was made of the jobs of each of twenty-six supervisors in a branch plant. This was based on the elements of job knowledge, intelligence, skill in handling people, and versatility. Next each supervisor was rated on the same scale. The rating for the job was compared with the rating for the man holding the job. The job was bigger than the man in fifteen instances; the man bigger than the job in eleven. Where the difference was great between personnel and job, a change was made in either the personnel or the job, or both. Some men were promoted, some transferred, some fired. The results after

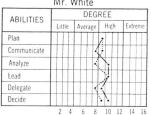

Figure 2-9. Comparison of the Qualifications of Three Candidates with Requirements of One Job.

(Rothe, H. F., "Matching Men to Job Requirements," *Personnel Psychology,* 1951, **4,** 291-301.)

41

the changes were made show that the differences between job and personnel had been reduced sharply. There was much better placement.[22]

SUMMARY

It is necessary to have detailed information about a job before applying psychological principles and techniques to people on the job. This has proved true for selection, placement, transfer, promotion, training, rating performance, and fair payment. Occupational information can also probably be useful for some of the decisions that are made about safety, design of equipment, work methods, leadership, and morale.

Occupational information has been gathered by several professional groups, psychologists being one. Since psychologists have needed the information, they have incidentally made a few improvements in the way it is collected.

Job evaluation not only assures fair pay on a relative basis within the company, but also assures fair pay in comparison to community rates.

Job evaluation is to some extent arbitrary, or at least depends in important ways on judgment that may be in error. How can it ultimately be decided how much money is to be paid for danger, for example? How to find the right answer in any ultimate sense is unknown.

The advantage of a system of job evaluation is that it is fair to the employees in that the jobs of all are judged on the same scale.

RECOMMENDED READINGS

Shartle, Carroll L., *Occupational Information,* 2nd ed., Englewood Cliffs, N. J.: Prentice-Hall, Inc., 1952. This book details the development and application of occupational information in industry, government, and vocational guidance.

Otis, Jay L., and Richard H. Leukart, *Job Evaluation,* 2nd ed., Englewood Cliffs, N. J.: Prentice-Hall, Inc., 1954. The techniques of job evaluation are given in detail as a basis for sound wage administration.

3

Individual differences and their evaluation

INTRODUCTION

Differences in temperament, physical skill, mental ability, and behavior are easily recognized. It seems natural, therefore, that the first problem studied in industrial psychology was that of individual differences, which has been studied more than any other problem. The new emphasis on human relations and clinical understanding in industrial psychology is not inconsistent with the continued exploration of individual differences. Many problem employees are problems because of improper placement. Poor employee relations are often the result of selecting the wrong man as a supervisor. The study of individual differences will remain, therefore, a central problem in industrial psychology, although other considerations increase in importance.

PERSONALITY

Individual differences can be grouped into broad classifications in terms of personality. Personality has been defined as "the most adequate conceptualization of a person's behavior, in all its detail, that the scientist can give at a moment in time."[1] Several important implications are included in this definition. First, personality is a theoretical interpretation derived from all a person's behavior. Secondly, it is not static, but is subject to change.

The definition quoted has significant values for the industrial psychologist. All individual behavior contributes to personality. This suggests that individual differences are important, not only in terms of comparison with other persons, but also in understanding the personality of the individual. Since personality is a theoretical interpretation, differences in interpretation should be expected and recognized. A final significant value in the definition of personality is that personality and behavior are capable of change and adjustment. This means that the objective of industrial psychology—to improve the adjustment and satisfaction of the individual—is realistic and obtainable.

The various determinants of personality have been classified in many ways. McClelland has classified them into four basic theories to facilitate understanding, describing, and predicting behavior. These theories will also aid in classifying individual differences.

Traits

"A trait is the learned tendency of an individual to react as he has reacted more or less successfully in the past, in similar situations, when similarly motivated."[2] Trait psychology endeavors to explain recurrent responses and consistencies in behavior. In terms of this definition a trait is a function of heredity, learning, similar situations, and similar motivation. Mechanical aptitude, for example, is a trait of great importance in some industrial situations. The nature of various traits, and individual differences in them, will be discussed in detail later in this chapter.

Schema

McClelland uses this term to refer to the individual's beliefs, frames of reference, major orientations, role perceptions, ideas, and values. The word *attitudes* has been more widely used to describe these determinants of behavior, and this more familiar term will be used later, in Chapter 11, in defining and exploring individual differences in this area.

This theory seeks to explain behavior partially in terms of responses primarily patterned by culture. Three major types of cultural influence have been suggested. The individual's system of beliefs, concerning such areas as religion, government, and pleasure, are derived partly from his environment and partly from cultural emphases on aspects of it. A second type of cultural influence results in the perception of various roles. The individual reacts in certain situations in a culturally accepted way. Others in the same situations are similarly expected to react in a definite way. A boss, for example, is expected to behave in a certain way as compared with a subordinate. The third type of cultural influence is termed the socialization procedure. It is concerned primarily with the effects of early childhood experiences on later behavior.

Motives

This theory deals with the inner drives, physiological and social, which prompt certain types of goal-directed behavior. Examples of such behavior include actions to satisfy hunger or the need for social approval. Because of its importance in industrial psychology, this aspect of behavior will be the subject of Chapter 10.

44

Several characteristics of motives will be mentioned here to permit a better appreciation of this theory of personality. Motivation prompts all behavior in an effort to satisfy various needs. Motives are persistent, and often the individual is not aware of them. Usually, various responses are learned to gratify most physiological drives.

Self-schema

The final theory used by McClelland to interpret behavior is self-schema, which refers to the observation of one's own behavior and the resulting picture of the self. It is a picture analogous to that which another person might form of a personality. When the individual's ego, for example, is involved in a situation, self-schema enters independently with traits, attitude, and motives to determine specific acts.

Summary

Personality is a function of all behavior of an individual. It is a changing function commonly interpreted differently by the self and by others. The trait concept was developed to explain the *how* of behavior characterized by recurrent responses and consistencies. The attitude concept was developed to handle the problem of *what* the person has acquired from cultural influences. The motive concept seeks to answer the question *why* people behave as they do. These three concepts, plus the self-schema idea, may prove useful in understanding, describing, and predicting behavior.

INDIVIDUAL DIFFERENCES IN VARIOUS TRAITS

Traits have been defined as recurrent or consistent responses when situations and motivation are similar. Learning also has a definite effect on traits. Several problems in studying traits are inherent in the theories presented above. When are situations really similar? How can the existence of similar motivation be determined? Are degrees of learning comparable? Such questions pose formidable problems. Industrial psychologists have, with all available means and to the best of their ability, attempted to answer these questions in the study of various traits, but complete solution in a given study is highly improbable.

A final problem is that of finding some means of grouping traits. One method is to classify primarily habitual motor responses as expressive traits and all other responses as performance traits. This division seems objective and convenient.

Expressive traits

This group of traits consists primarily of regular habitual motor responses to recurrent problems. Traits which are not strictly motor responses, however, such as physique traits, are included. Perceptual traits, which are influenced by other determinants of personality, are also included. Finally, age and sex make differences that are given great weight in industry. The classification of such traits as expressive is more convenient than precise.

PHYSIQUE TRAITS

Differences in physique are obvious and are easily measured. Height, weight, and muscularity factors often have importance in the selection of men for certain types of industrial work. Some attempts have been made to relate various physique traits to personality. Fat people, for example, are often thought to be jolly people. Such coincidences are common, but physique traits, in themselves, generally have failed to prove satisfactory for the appraisal of personality.

MOVEMENT TRAITS

Differences in posture, poise, and movements with hands or legs are considered under movement traits. Once again, the existence and nature of individual differences in movement traits are well known. Coordination of fingers, hands, and feet are important in many industrial jobs, for example, sewing-machine operators.

PERCEPTUAL TRAITS

The various ways in which individuals perceive the world and generally approach life's problems represent the subject matter of perceptual traits. The study and interpretation of such traits are commonly a clinical undertaking involving projective measures such as the Rorschach ink blot test. This test determines what one perceives in a picture which has no essential objective meaning. The significant portion of the response is what one perceives beyond what "is there." Through the use of trained industrial psychologists, industry may eventually find valuable application for such testing procedures.

STYLE TRAITS

Various forms of individual expression, such as talking, composing, and singing, are generally characterized by a style peculiar to the individual. Individual differences in expressive style can be important in jobs such as advertising and public relations. There seems to be little relation between such style traits and other aspects of personality.

AGE

Age is a difference among people in industry that is often considered important. People over 40 years of age usually have difficulty finding employment when the labor supply is large. A 1944 publication stated that 66.1 per cent of a sample of American companies had no maximum hiring age for men.[3] Probably this was due largely to the labor shortage during the war. Newspaper advertisements for responsible positions are often restricted to applicants no more than 35 or 40 years old. The basis for choosing persons under 40 years is the belief in psychological differences accompanying age. There is a common belief that older persons cannot learn so well, but, in fact, up to ages 60 and 70, differences in ability to learn and in intelligence are customarily slight. Tests have shown that abilities of older workers are comparable to those of younger ones in speed tasks which involve neither precision nor complex mental processes, but that the older groups do not do so well with tasks involving the abstract and complex.[4] Many older people are stubborn; this is not true of all of them, but only of those who have been seriously frustrated.

SEX

Discrimination against women in industry is based on cultural influences as well as physiological reasons. Because of cultural influences, women are often considered unfit for jobs which they are equipped, both physiologically and psychologically, to perform satisfactorily. During peace time, women are often kept out of certain jobs because of prejudice. American experience in World War II proved that women can effectively perform many of the jobs that had been hitherto barred to them because of their sex. In 1956 almost one woman in three in the United States was employed outside the home.

Men and women are very similar in mental abilities. They are identical in average I.Q. Women apparently are better than men in memory work. They have had more success than men in jobs involving details and routine work. Perhaps woman's lower level of aspiration, because of her minority status in industry, is more important here than different abilities.

Performance traits

Individual differences in performance traits are of considerably greater importance to industry than differences in expressive traits. Performance traits involve consistent responses in physical, intellectual, and nonintellectual work situations. The responses required are generally more complex than those prompted by expressive situations. Individual differences in various performance traits have been tested and measured in both laboratory and field situations. This section deals with such studies under the broad headings of physical performance traits, intellectual abilities, and nonintellectual traits.

Industrial Psychology

PHYSICAL PERFORMANCE TRAITS

The tendency of increasing industrial mechanization and automation to minimize the importance of individual physical performance differences is generally apparent. In spite of this tendency there are many industrial jobs today in which physical performance differences are important. Such differences are also important considerations in the establishment of some incentive wage and promotion plans.

An appreciation of the distribution and range of individual differences in several industrial situations can be gained from Figures 3-1 and 3-2. In Figure 3-1 the results of a performance study of knitting-machine operators are shown. In terms of pounds knitted, the best worker was approximately 2.5 times better than the poorest. Figure 3-2 shows the performance differences for a group of semiautomatic-lathe operators. The output of the best operators was almost twice that of the poorest. One feature of Figure 3-2 is the grouping of large numbers of operators in the intermediate output brackets. This may be partially accounted for by the fact that premium pay began to be earned at 60 units of output per hour. Operators in the intermediate brackets may have been satisfied at those output levels.

The ratios of the least efficient to the most efficient individual in various occupations are shown in Table 3-I. These ratios show a wide

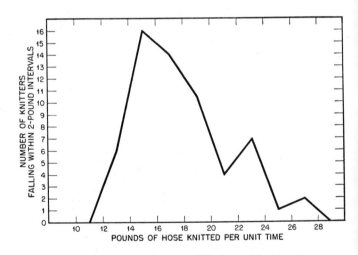

Figure 3-1. Distribution of Poundage Output of Knitting Machine Operators.

(Hull, Clark L., *Aptitude Testing,* Yonkers, N.Y.: World Book Co., 1928, p. 27. Reference to Pollock, Howard, "The Application of Vocational Ability Tests in the Hosiery Industry," B.Ph. Thesis, 1921, University of Wisconsin.)

48

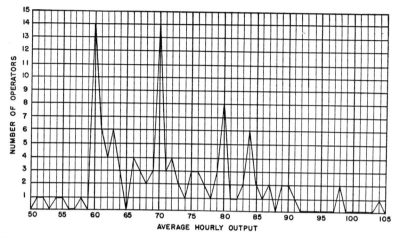

Figure 3-2. Difference in the Performance of Operators Working on Semi-automatic Lathes.

(Reprinted by permission from Barnes, R. M., *Motion and Time Study,* 2d ed., New York: John Wiley & Sons, Inc., 1940.)

TABLE 3-1

Ratio of the Least Efficient to the Most Efficient Individual Actually Engaged in a Variety of Gainful Occupations

OCCUPATION	CRITERION	RATIO OF POOREST TO BEST WORKER
Heel trimming (shoes)	No. pairs per day	1:1.4
Loom operation (silk)	Per cent timeloom in operation	1:1.5
Hosiery maters	Earnings	1:1.9
Loom operation (fancy cotton)	Earnings	1:2
Bottom scoring (shoes)	No. pairs per day	1:2
Knitting-machine operators	Pounds women's hose per hour	1:2.2
Polishing spoons	Time per 36 spoons	1:5.1

Hull, Clark, L., *Aptitude Testing,* Yonkers, New York: World Book Company, 1928, p. 35.

49

range from 1:1.4 for heel trimming to 1:5.1 for polishing spoons. Differences such as these cannot always be ascribed to physical performance abilities. The degree of learning or training has already been cited as an important factor in trait differences. In the occupation of polishing spoons, the wide difference in efficiency was due primarily to training differences. The differences shrank considerably when systematic training was introduced. This does not mean that equivalent experience and training will eliminate variations in individual performance. As a matter of fact, the same amount of training in some tasks actually has the effect of increasing individual differences.

The preceding examples have dealt with actual industrial situations in which the control of variable elements is limited. Laboratory studies offer the advantage of better control of variables influencing trait differences. Table 3-II presents the data from laboratory studies in which the effects of the variables of motivation and training were minimized. The performance required in each instance was similar to that required in an actual work situation. These studies bear out the earlier statement

TABLE 3-II

Ratios of Differences in Human Capacities

TRAIT OR ABILITY	RATIO
Speed of inserting bolts	1:2.09
Upper limit of audibility	1:2.09
Stringing disks	1:2.12
Vital capacity (age and height constant)	1:2.13
Tapping	1:2.20
Simple reaction time	1:2.24
General intelligence (Binet M. A.)	1:2.30
Simple learning	1:2.42
Memory span	1:2.50
Card sorting	1:2.50
Latent reflex time	1:2.50
Vital capacity (only age constant)	1:2.75
Intelligence quotients (Otis)	1:2.86
Swiftness of blow	1:2.93
Hard learning	1:3.87

Adapted from Wechsler, David, *The Range of Human Capacities,* Baltimore: The Williams & Wilkins Company, 1935.

that equivalent experience and training will not eliminate differences in individual performance.

No thorough study has been made of the different abilities of an individual for a variety of industrial jobs. Some indication of the possible range of an individual's ability in various traits can be gained from a study of high-school students. On a group of psychological tests the average student was almost three times as good on some traits as on others.[5]

INTELLECTUAL ABILITIES

Mental functions have generally been measured by intelligence tests. Such tests evaluate the performance of an individual on a variety of new tasks. The results of these tests are normally considered indicative of intellectual abilities.

A knowledge of mental abilities can be of value in selecting personnel for various jobs. A study of minimum intelligence levels for several different occupations revealed that excellent laundry workers had an average mental age of 9 years; successful barbers and high-grade domestic workers had a mental age of 8 years.[6] In some routine jobs, turnover is excessive if the employee's intelligence is too high or low. In other jobs, such as that of an accountant, a high degree of several mental abilities is indispensable for successful work. The measurement of mental abilities, as well as other personnel test methods, will be discussed in detail in Chapter 6. An introduction to the subject will be given here.

Ability-test scores, for a large number of unselected cases, when plotted on an arithmetic scale, usually result in a chance or bell-shaped distribution. This means that the plotted test scores for a large group of people will tend to pile up somewhere close to the middle and taper off toward the ends. The scores shown in Figure 1-3 in Chapter 1, from the intelligence test given in the Army during World War II, are an example of this chance distribution.

CORRELATION. The correlation method is an important one for relating individual differences on two or more variables. The coefficient of correlation is a measure of agreement between two variables, such as the variable of mechanical-aptitude test scores with the variable of job performance ratings by a supervisor of airplane mechanics. The correlation coefficient, if perfect and positive, is +1.00. Such a coefficient would mean, for these two variables, that the airplane mechanic rated the best made the highest test score; the mechanic rated the second-best made the second-highest test scores; and so on, down to the mechanic rated the worst, who made the lowest test score. If there were no correlation

51

between the variable measures, the coefficient would be exactly 0. If the correlation were perfectly negative, that is, if the mechanic rated the worst made the highest test score, the coefficient would be −1.00.

A coffiecient of correlation of −1.00 is as predictive as a coefficient of +1.00. They both are perfect in predicting from one variable what the other variable will be. Thus it is the size of the coefficient of correlation and not its sign which shows its predictability and therefore its usefulness.

An explanation of the exact statistical meaning of the coefficient of correlation and the method of computing it are beyond the scope of this book, but it is intended here to present some of the elements of the meaning of coefficients of correlation. These coefficients are the most frequently used methods of presenting data in industrial psychology.

The coefficient of correlation is not identical with percentage relationship except at the extremes of +1.00, −1.00, and 0.00. The ultimate meaning of the coefficient of correlation is a trigonometric function. A coefficient of correlation is converted to percentage by squaring the value; when squared, it becomes a coefficient of determination. A coefficient of correlation of .70 means, therefore, that only 49 per cent of the variance present in one variable is explained by the variance in the other. Fifty-one per cent of the variance is therefore unexplained when a coefficient of correlation of .70 is found.

The size of coefficients of correlation in industrial psychology is closer to zero as a rule than to 1.00. The reason is undoubtedly that our tests and other measures of people are not perfect and therefore cannot give perfect prediction of work success, accident records, or other practical yardsticks. Even more important in explaining the low values found is that the yardsticks of work success are not perfectly accurate, and as a rule they are even less reliable than are the psychological tests.

The magnitude which a coefficient of correlation must attain to be useful depends on the situation. The number of people studied is important because it shows how stable the coefficient is in terms of how much it would be expected to change if more people were studied. The number of people from which one has to draw is also important. For example, one might find a coefficient of correlation of .60 between a test and a measure of work success, but, if the supply of labor is so tight that every applicant has to be hired, this correlation is useless for practical purposes.

In practice a correlation of .60 is about as high as is found between a psychological test and a measure of work success. As a rule, it takes more than one test to obtain a correlation as high as .60, and even then it is exceptional. Correlations as low as .30 can be of some value if there are enough cases to show that the relationship is not simply due to chance, and if the labor supply is plentiful enough so that one can be highly selective. A correlation of .30 between a test and a measure of job success combined with a correlation of .15 between another test and the measure of job success, where the two tests are independent of each other (correlate practically zero), could be useful to the prediction of success if there were 200 or more employees in the population studied.

The correlation procedure can be used with more than two variables in a single problem. It is possible to determine the degree of relationship between a measure of success on the job, for example, number of over-alls sewed per day, and two psychological tests, for example, coordination and space relations. Coordination may show a significantly positive correlation with this measure of success on the job. There are abilities other than coordination that undoubtedly account for the total pattern of aptitude in operating a sewing machine. A space-relations test may also show a significantly positive correlation with success in sewing over-alls. The question then arises how the two test scores can be combined for maximum selection efficiency. The most exact method is that of multiple correlation.

In multiple correlation it is necessary to obtain the correlation of each variable with every other variable in the problem. In the sewing-machine example it would be necessary to obtain three correlations; one each for the two tests and the job success measure, and one between the tests. From these correlations the most efficient weights for the tests can be found by means of the multiple correlation process.

FACTOR ANALYSIS. Factor analysis is, in a sense, an extension of the multiple correlation procedure. The analysis starts with a set of coefficients of correlation between every pair of variables under study. The final result is a set of factors, or least common denominators, which explain all the correlations except those resulting from chance errors. The detailed methods of factor analysis are too technical for presentation here.

Factor analyses are reported for fundamental abilities and traits on a performance rating later in this chapter; for personnel tests in Chapter 5; for interest tests in Chapter 6; for the elements of a job as evaluated in Chapter 2. The results of the analyses are in each instance a simplification and clarification of the psychological measurements analyzed.

ABILITY FACTORS. Mental abilities have been measured mainly by the use of I. Q. tests. These tests are composed of several separate mental factors. Different tests use varying mixtures of these factors, depending on the test objectives. The mixture used in any given test can only be determined through detailed study. I. Q. tests have been studied in rela-

53

tion to success on a number of jobs. They have also been given to determine the mental level of a great number of occupations. Determination of the separate mental ability requirements for an occupation would be more helpful to industry. A few such studies have been performed, and this is currently a live field of research.

The usual factors which make up various I. Q. tests, and the tasks that measure them, are as follows:

Verbal factor, measured well by vocabulary.

Numerical factor, measured by speed and accuracy in addition, subtraction, multiplication, and division.

Perceptual speed factor, measured by discriminating small differences in visual designs.

Reasoning factor, measured by figuring out relationships. It is found in many verbal and numerical items, suggesting the existence of some general factor which, no doubt, exists.

Spatial factor, measured by the ability to imagine the way objects are arranged in space. There may be a visualization factor separate from this which requires the imaginary manipulation of objects in space. This may have been confused with the space factor.[7]

The only other factor that has been very clearly demonstrated is one for memory. There are several other fairly well-established factors.[8] One of these, a *mechanical-experience factor,* is important in the understanding of tests for mechanical ability. Tests for mechanical ability consequently measure experience as well as abilities.

Another fairly well-established factor that could be important to industrial selection is *judgment.* I. Q. tests have been criticized because they fail to measure common sense or judgment. This criticism appears to be justified because such a factor has been found in a study of pilots. It is a factor separate from those commonly measured by I. Q. tests. The judgment factor appeared to be present in "items in the form of verbally described predicaments such as those a service man might encounter, each with five more or less plausible solutions, one of which was regarded as the wisest under the circumstances." Analysis of such tests showed significant loadings in the verbal factor, in general reasoning, and in the mechanical-experience factor. (Knowledge of common tools and material was apparently useful to the examinee in this kind of test.) Judgment emerged as a common factor in addition to the other factors mentioned.

A sample item that possessed this judgment factor follows.[9]

A bomber squadron is over enemy territory on its way to bomb an oil refinery when one of the observers notices an advanced enemy airdrome. He notifies the squadron leader. It would be best for the leader to

    A. Order the bombers in the squadron to continue as planned and report the location of the enemy airdrome on arrival at their base.

    B. Order the squadron to circle the airdrome while he radios its position to his base.

    C. Order half the bombers in the squadron to bomb the enemy airdrome and the other half to carry out the mission against the oil refinery.

    D. Order all the planes in the squadron to bomb the enemy airdrome and return to their base.

    E. Order the squadron to continue as planned while he returns to his base to report the location of the enemy airdrome.

SPECIAL APTITUDES. The special aptitudes important in industry shade into the mental abilities. Mechanical and clerical aptitudes are referred to most often in industry. These appear to be composed almost entirely of combinations of the above-mentioned mental factors.

Mechanical aptitude, aside from mechanical knowledge, is primarily the space ability, the ability to deal in space relationships.[10] Space ability is important in visualizing how objects can be taken apart and put together again. It is essential in repairing machines and in trouble shooting. Reasoning is also important in mechanical aptitude. As used above, mechanical aptitude refers to the aptitude for work of medium difficulty, such as the repair of machines rather than the invention of machines.

Manual dexterity and finger dexterity are important in some routine jobs but are essentially independent of mechanical aptitude. In fact manual dexterity is largely independent of finger dexterity. A person may score high in one and low in the other about as often as he may score high in both or low in both.

Clerical aptitude is made up of the verbal, numerical, and perceptual speed factors. The exact pattern of factors required depends on the precise nature of the job.

One or more visual factors are important in some inspection jobs.

NONINTELLECTUAL TRAITS

Nonintellectual personality and interest traits are extremely important in some jobs. In the jobs of executives and salesmen they appear to be of particular importance. Furthermore, emotional or personality difficulties are often the cause of much of the turnover, even for routine jobs.

Turnover resulting from discharge was analyzed for 4000 cases among seventy-six companies, and the results are given in Table 3-III. Table 3-III shows that personality and character traits are eight times more important than lack of specific skills in the reasons given for discharge of clerical employees.

In spite of the importance of personality traits, relatively little has been done to measure those traits of particular importance to industry.

TABLE 3-III

Reasons for Discharge of Office Employees

CHARACTER TRAITS		LACK OF SPECIFIC SKILLS	
Carelessness	14.1%	Shorthand	2.2%
Noncooperation	10.7	Typewriting	1.6
Laziness	10.3	English	1.6
Absence for Causes		Dictaphone	1.3
Other than Illness	8.5	Office Machines	.9
Dishonesty	8.1	Bookkeeping	.6
Attention to Outside		Spelling	.6
Things	7.9		
Lack of Initiative	7.6		
Lack of Ambition	7.2		
Tardiness	6.7		
Lack of Loyalty	3.5		
TOTAL	84.6%	TOTAL	10.1%

Unclassified 5.3%

Bixler, Harold R., "Reconversion Problems," *The Personnel Journal*, 1945, **2**, 130–138.

A number of studies relating personality or nonintellectual factors to occupational success in sales and executive positions have been made. These studies are only a beginning in this vast area, and much remains to be done.

There is no agreement about what are the important nonintellectual or personality traits. It is difficult to reach agreement on the definitions of such traits as honesty, integrity, initiative, and ambition. Until it is decided what should be measured, the understanding of personality must remain in a primitive state.

In one popular theory, personality is interpreted in terms of abnormal traits. The most common types of mental disease have been classified, and the discriminating symptoms of each disease have been listed. Although the industrial psychologist is primarily concerned with "normal" personalities, it is possible to obtain scores on the extent to which an employee is "normal," and these may be of some value. One such attempt is the Minnesota Multiphasic Personality Inventory, which investigates a representative set of traits.[11] By comparing the answers given to 550 questions with those provided by a "normal" personality group, the psychologist is able to evaluate an individual's personality fairly well. Graduate training in clinical psychology is necessary for the interpretation of the test scores. The validity of the inventory is indicated by the fact that, in one study, 60 per cent of new psychiatric admissions were positively predicted. The inventory is being tried in industry, but it has not yet been validated there.

Personality characteristics are assessed on the basis of scores on nine clinical scales. The scales are based on clinical cases that were classified according to conventional psychiatric nomenclature. A brief description of these scales follows.

a. Hypochondriasis. Unduly worried over health; immature in approach to adult problems.
b. Depression. Lack of self-confidence, tendency to worry, narrowness of interests, and introversion.
c. Hysteria. Under stress, likely to become overtly hysterical and to solve the problems confronting him by the development of physical symptoms.
d. Psychopathic Deviate. Absence of deep emotional response, inability to profit from experience, and disregard for social mores.
e. Masculinity-Femininity. Extent to which one's interests are similar to those of one's own or the opposite sex.
f. Paranoia. Suspicious, oversensitive, feelings of persecution.
g. Psychasthenia. Unreasonable fear of things or situations as well as overreaction to more reasonable stimuli.
h. Schizophrenia. Bizarre and unusual thoughts or behavior.
i. Hypomania. Overproductivity in thought and action.

INTERESTS

People differ in interests in such a way as to make for extremely important variations in work performance and industrial success. The permanence of interests after adolescence is noteworthy.[12] Successful persons in the same occupation have, to a large extent, the same interests. The occupations for which separate interest scales have been developed are shown in Figure 3-3. These occupations are mainly professional and managerial. The occupations are arranged in groups in the figure according to the similarity of interests of the occupations within the group as determined by a factor analysis. The occupational interest groups can be described as: Group I, Biological Sciences; II, Physical Sciences; IV, Technical; V, Social Service; VIII, Business Detail; IX, Business Contact; and X, Verbal-Linguistic.[13]

The interests of Production Manager, Certified Public Accountant, and President Manufacturing Concern do not fall within any of the above groups. Separate scales have been developed for each of these occupations, but they are quite distinct from each other. Top executives do not have interests in common. Their interests are specific to their job, they do not form a general management factor.[14]

57

GROUP	OCCUPATION	GROUP	OCCUPATION
I	Artist	V	Y.M.C.A. Physical Director
	Psychologist		Personnel Manager
	Architect		Public Administrator
	Physician		Vocational Counselor
	Psychiatrist		Y.M.C.A. Secretary
	Osteopath		Social Science Teacher
	Dentist		City School Superintendent
	Veterinarian		Minister
II	Physicist	VI	Musician, Performer
	Chemist		Music Teacher
	Mathematician		
	Engineer	VII	Certified Public Accountant, Partner
III	Production Manager	VIII	Senior Certified Public Accountant
			Junior Accountant
IV	Farmer		Office Worker
	Carpenter		Purchasing Agent
	Printer		Banker
	Mathematics-Science Teacher		Mortician
	Industrial Arts Teacher		Pharmacist
	Vocational Agriculture Teacher		
	Policeman	IX	Sales Manager
	Forest Service Man		Real Estate Salesman
	Army Officer		Life Insurance Salesman
	Aviator		
		X	Advertising Man
			Lawyer
			Author-Journalist
		XI	President, Manufacturing Concern

Figure 3-3. Occupations for Which Scales Have Been Standardized for the Strong Vocational Interest Test for Men.

(Strong, E. K., Jr., *Report on Vocational Interest Test for Men*, Stanford, Calif.: Stanford University Press, n.d.)

58

EVALUATION OF EMPLOYEES
Purpose

From the point of view of both management and the employee, it is desirable to evaluate the differences between individuals in industry. Industrial workers often do not have an opportunity to know their success on the job except in terms of the pay check. Management owes it to the worker, as well as to itself, to spend some effort in determining whether each man is succeeding on the job. Almost everyone is interested to know whether he is succeeding and to what extent.

Management has several reasons for evaluating the success of employees. Many pay systems depend in part on evaluating employees. Pay is often based on measured output or on rated merit. If promotions are to be made on the basis of merit, a system must be employed which will designate the person meriting promotion. If transfers are to be made on the basis of merit, it is necessary to evaluate the qualifications of a man in relation to the prospective job. Measuring proficiency or evaluating the worker is also desirable in order to develop ways in which employee performance can be improved through training. Finally, when employees must be laid off on the basis of relative merit, it is necessary to have an evaluation of their success on the job.

Criterion

An evaluation of employees is essential to the determination of the effectiveness of existing methods of personnel selection. Preferably, such an evaluation, or criterion of success, should be objective, as, for example, the number of yards of cloth woven or the number of bricks laid per hour. Often, however, there is no trustworthy objective measure and a more subjective approach to rating must be used.

Obtaining a reliable and valid criterion, or measure of work success, is often the most difficult step in improving selection procedures. Statistical reliability is essential in any vocational criterion because, if a thing does not agree with itself, it cannot agree with anything else. Reliability means accuracy in the sense that the measure is internally consistent. If the production records of weavers are not reliable—if their production records are not relatively the same from one week to another so that those who are high in one week are high in another—it is not possible for their production records to agree with any test score or other predictor.

The production record may be reliable and still be worthless as a criterion unless it is a valid measure of the competence of the employee. Whether the criterion is an objective measure or a subjective rating, it must reflect what is important in the performance of the job.

TABLE 3-IV

Merit Rating (Performance Appraisal Plans) by Class of Employee and Size of Company

	COMPANIES WITH MERIT RATING PLANS FOR	
	NONSUPERVISORY SALARIED	HOURLY
SIZE OF COMPANY	EMPLOYEES	EMPLOYEES
1000 or more employees	62%	46%
Less than 1000 employees	46	35

Adapted from National Industrial Conference Board, Studies in Personnel Policy No. 145, *Practices in Factory and Office,* New York, 1954, pp. 15, 69.

About half the companies have a merit rating program for rank-and-file employees, as shown in Table 3-IV. These plans are more frequently in effect in large companies and for salaried employees.

Ratings

There are frequently several traits which could be rated. For example, leadership, character, cooperation, judgment, personality, and appearance have been employed in many merit rating programs. A survey of rating forms reveals that the number of personal traits included in an employee rating program may vary greatly. The greatest number on any single form has been nineteen, and the average, ten.[15] Sometimes as few as two traits are rated. The selection of the most meaningful traits to be used in a merit rating program is of central importance. One writer has suggested that traits to be included on the merit rating form should be selected on the basis of "observability, universality and distinguishability."[16]

Observability refers to the opportunity of the rater to study and evaluate a trait in an employee as it pertains to the performance of his job. For example, does the weaver display an adequate knowledge of the operation and maintenance of his looms?

Universality means that a trait should be essential to all the jobs being rated. If a particular trait, for example, initiative, is not important to all jobs on which it is rated, then it will not serve as a valid measure of relative job performance.

Distinguishability suggests that the criteria included should be mutually exclusive and should not overlap or create an ambiguous interpretation in the mind of the rater. The terms "leadership" and "personality" are illustrative of this common problem.

The success of a rating plan depends less on the method, or rating form, than on three important fundamentals.[17] One of these is that rating must be taken seriously by line officials rather than be made the primary responsibility of the personnel department. If the boss wants it done and done right, the rating will probably be taken more seriously than if it is considered merely another form to fill out for the personnel files. The influence of the line can be shown in several ways on the success-of-performance rating. One of the possible effects is for the line manager to review the ratings, to refer to them, so that if a supervisor makes an obviously erroneous rating he will be held responsible for making a serious mistake.

The second fundamental of successful rating is that the rater know the performance which is being rated. All elements of the job being rated should be thoroughly understood by the rater. Supervisors often think that they know a man's worth, when actually their "knowledge" is highly unreliable. The demonstration of the unreliability is shown clearly in cases where a man has been performing the same job in the same way under two supervisors. The disagreement between the two supervisors concerning the performance of the subordinate is often great.

A third fundamental is training of raters. There is no method that by itself will assure accurate ratings. Unless raters have been thoroughly trained, ratings will not be accurate. In addition to initial training, it is also necessary to continue training and to check up on ratings if they are to be effective. However, in one survey of sixty companies using formal evaluation programs, results showed that thirty-two of them provided no training whatsoever for raters, while nineteen other firms supplied only four hours or less.[18]

One phase of an effective training program might be to have ratings made in conference or under supervision. On occasion, ratings are thought to be extra paper work, not particularly important and only a nuisance. If time on the job is allotted to the rating procedure, it will assume more importance and will be done more carefully. By having a conference after their judgments have been independently made, supervisors can ask questions and can arrive at a more uniform understanding of the traits to be rated.

The paramount point to get across in training raters is the purpose of the ratings. As mentioned above, the purpose of rating is to have valid discriminating judgments regarding the occupational competence of workers. Fulfillment of this purpose means that the raters must be honest and not lenient or frivolous in making ratings. The raters should be impressed, not only immediately before they make a rating, but throughout the rating period, with the necessity of making careful observations. The rater should be on the alert to note and to record any evidence of outstanding accomplishment, whether at the superior or at the inferior end of the scale. The sources of error in rating cannot be completely overcome, but it is possible by careful and continuous training to rate so that the best employees are separated from the poorest ones.

SOURCES OF ERROR IN RATING

The accuracy of subjective measures of success on the job has been the object of much critical study. The errors and inconsistencies humanly inherent in merit rating must be fully understood and appreciated if the results are to be evaluated skillfully and used effectively. The purpose of ratings is to have discriminating judgments that are valid concerning the occupational competence of workers. However, in practice, difficulties frequently arise which may materially lessen the value of the ratings. Excessive lenience is one of the most common defects encountered among raters. The problem of leniency arises when supervisors tend to concentrate their ratings among the highest categories and to

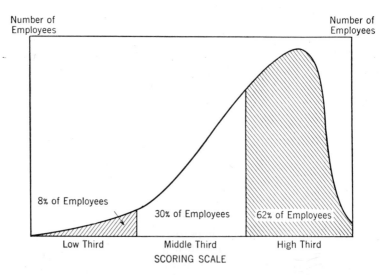

Figure 3-4. Distribution of Performance Scores Obtained on Graphic Scale Report Form.

(Blum, Milton L., *Industrial Relations Memos,* No. 119, Sept. 22, 1950, Standard Oil Company of New Jersey. Reproduced by permission from *Readings in Experimental Industrial Psychology,* Milton L. Blum, p. 393. Copyright, 1952, by Prentice-Hall, Inc., Englewood Cliffs, N. J.)

avoid labeling workmen below average or unsatisfactory. Leniency is further heightened when the final ratings are to be discussed by the rater with each employee. Higher ratings may be given to avoid the possible arguments and almost certain discontent which arise from a low evaluation of an individual's job performance. A typical example of this is shown in Figure 3-4. Almost two-thirds of the employees were rated in the upper third of the scale.

A second source of error stems from the tendency of many raters to avoid giving either very high or very low scores. Thus ratings will tend to cluster near the middle of the scale. This is referred to as the error of "central tendency."

Another fundamental difficulty often found in ratings is called the "halo effect." This may be defined as the tendency to rate employees on several traits according to the general impression the rater has of the employee. Thus a foreman who has a favorable impression of a worker may rate the man very highly on most traits rather than evaluate each characteristic separately. A machinist who is rated "excellent" on his knowledge of the job may receive equally high scores on other traits such as initiative or cooperation when in fact a much lower rating is deserved. The halo error further emphasizes the problem a rater must face in attempting to appraise accurately and critically each trait independently and without reference to the other personal attributes the individual possesses.

Types of rating scales

Rating scales can be classified in any one of several different ways. The purpose of the rating is a determining factor. It may be to compare employees with each other or to compare them with job standards.[19] If employees are compared, this may be done by ranking them one with another, or by grading them on a scale first and comparing the results later. When employees are to be compared with job standards, it is first necessary to consider the requirements of the job from a job description and then to compare the employee's performance with each element of the job.

Ratings have serious limitations, but they can provide useful information. Ratings are personal judgments and are therefore susceptible to all the sources of error present in such judgments. For that reason they have been criticized by many labor leaders and by many business executives. The business managers who defend rating systems do not think that they are perfect but that they are better than the judgments that would be made and used without some systematic procedure.[20]

There is no perfect method, or no one best method, of rating. Although the search has been long, there is no prospect that a perfect method will be found; therefore a company should select a method which suits its needs.[21] However, a number of different rating systems have been tried. Those which will be described briefly are rank order, forced distribution, graphic, field review, critical incident, and forced choice.

The rank-order method of rating works well when ten or fewer persons are to be rated. In this method the rater assigns a rank to each person, such as, first, second, third. Rank-order rating is simple in application and is easy to understand; however, when there are a large number of persons to be rated, this method becomes too difficult to be practicable.

FORCED DISTRIBUTION

Forced distribution is a system in which the rater is required to put only a certain percentage of employees in a certain rating. In this system employees have been rated on only two basic characteristics, job performance and promotability, although the number of characteristics could vary. The rating is limited to two traits in an effort to minimize the problem of "halo effect" which is introduced when several traits must be scored. According to Tiffin, "most production men will agree that job performance is the basic factor in determining any employee's value to the company, and that the other things such as cooperation, personality, etc., are worth considering only insofar as they contribute to job performance."[22]

In evaluating employees the scoring is based on a five-point scale. The supervisor is requested to distribute his ratings by placing approximately 10 per cent in the highest group, 20 per cent in the next highest, 40 per cent in the middle, 20 per cent in the lower group and 10 per cent in the lowest category. The forced-distribution system helps avoid the human errors of leniency and central tendency which are frequently present in other performance-rating plans.

Promotability, the other characteristic evaluated by this method, is rated on a three-point scale with word descriptions, such as: very likely promotional material; may or may not be promotional material; very unlikely to be promotional material.

The job performance rating and the promotability rating are kept separate and are not combined to form a single over-all employee evaluation.

GRAPHIC

The graphic method of rating is the most common rating procedure used in industry today. The rating is indicated by making a check along

FORM 1060

OLIVER IRON MINING COMPANY

RATING – NONSUPERVISORY EMPLOYEES

File No.

INSTRUCTIONS TO RATER:	
Read the rating factors and definitions carefully. Rate all employees of a given classification on one factor at a time: i.e., rate all employees engaged in similar work on quality and then rate all of them on quantity. Use the number on the graduated scale corresponding to your evaluation of the individual as his rating on the factor being considered.	District:_____ Mine:_____ Name:_____ Check No:_____ Date:_____ Occupation:_____ Rated By:_____ Position of Rater:_____

FACTORS	POOR (1) 1 2 3 4 5	BELOW AVERAGE (2) 6 7 8 9 10	AVERAGE (3) 11 12 13 14 15	ABOVE AVERAGE (4) 16 17 18 19 20	EXCELLENT (5) 21 22 23 24 25	SCORE
QUALITY	Often unsatisfactory	Usually acceptable	Consistently satisfactory	Sometimes superior	Consistently superior	
QUANTITY	Consistently below established standard	Frequently below established standard	Meets established standard	Frequently exceeds standard	Consistently exceeds standard	
VERSATILITY	Competent only on his own job	Can do closely related jobs	Can do several related jobs	Acceptable performance on unrelated jobs	Can do several unrelated jobs well	
COOPERATION	Unwilling to work with or assist others	Seldom works with or assists others	Generally works well with and and assists others	Quick to volunteer to work with and assist others	Inspires good team work	
RESOURCEFULNESS	Needs help to handle any irregularities	Seldom able to handle Irregularities alone	Occasionally devises ways and means of meeting unusual situations	Usually finds ways and means of meeting emergencies alone	Anticipates and successfully meets emergencies by ingenious planning	
DEPENDABILITY	Frequently undependable	Occasionally undependable	Dependable in most respects	Dependable in all respects	Highly dependable — inspires others	
HEALTH	Distinctly handicapped by lack of vigor	Often lacks needed energy and endurance	Efficiency seldom impaired	Consistently vigorous	Unusual energy and endurance	
SAFETY	Careless of his own and others' safety	Sometimes fails to see or report unsafe practices and conditions	Careful. Protects others. Allows for unusual incidents	Observes visible hazards and suggests need of improvements	Quick to sense possible hazards and takes steps to get them corrected	

Use other side of this sheet for additional information, if any.   TOTAL INDUSTRIAL SCORE

Figure 3-5. A Graphic Rating Form.

(Dooher, M. Joseph, and Vivienne Marquis (eds.), *Rating Employee and Supervisory Performance,* New York: American Management Association, 1950, p. 170.)

a horizontal line. Appropriate descriptive phrases to help guide the rater are frequently written underneath the line. A separate line is included for each characteristic to be evaluated. Figure 3-5 shows a typical graphic rating form. This method is simple to understand and relatively easy to use; its validity, however, may be impaired because of excessive lenience among raters. The "halo effect" may also prejudice the accuracy of graphic scale ratings.

FIELD REVIEW

The field review provides a different approach to the intelligent evaluation of employee performance. A representative of the personnel department cooperates with the supervisor in developing the rating. The personnel specialist literally goes "into the field" and conducts informal interviews with supervisors and foremen at their place of work. Each employee in the department is evaluated, and the supervisor is encouraged to talk freely and to amplify his opinions regarding the performance characteristics of his subordinates. The personnel specialist may memorize a list of pertinent questions, or he may rely on a "patterned interview" form so that the analyses of the employees will be as uniform and as consistent as possible. As the interview progresses, the personnel man takes notes and asks leading questions regarding each employee, such as, "What is he doing well?" "In what ways has he impressed you?" "What are his weaknesses?" "Do you feel he is worthy of promotion?"

After the interview with the supervisor has been completed, the personnel representative returns to his office, studies and reviews his notes on each employee, and drafts a tentative summary rating. He then may confer with the supervisor, discuss the rating, and solicit any suggestions, additions, or corrections. The final rating is then drawn up. The supervisor remains fully responsible for the rating, but the details surrounding its preparation are handled by fully trained representatives of the personnel section.

A plan of this type has been in operation for several years at Gimbel Brothers department store in New York City.[23] The executives at Gimbels have stressed two elements which are essential if the field-review method is to operate successfully: "Highly competent personnel analysts and strong line support including full backing by top management."

Field review has several significant advantages. Supervisors appear to prefer oral rating interviews to the usual written procedure. Management becomes better acquainted with the performance and development of each employee, and the results of rating are expertly prepared, regularly reviewed, and effectively used.

PERFORMANCE RECORD

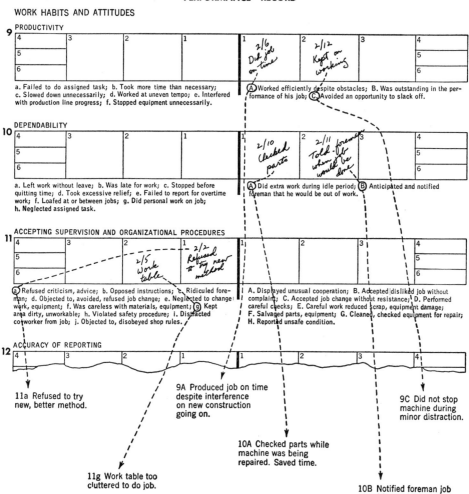

Figure 3-6. An Illustrative Section of the Critical Incident Performance Record.

(Flanagan, John C., and Robert K. Burns, "The Employee Performance Record," *Harvard Business Review*, 1955, **33,** No. 5, 99.)

CRITICAL INCIDENT

The critical-incident technique is one of the newly developed methods which lends greater objectivity to employee evaluation. It was developed as a result of the criticism of many merit rating plans for the highly subjective nature of the traits measured. This criticism prompted research personnel to seek new methods of employee evaluation based on objective criteria which are easily observed and recorded.

In this method a large number of factual incidents regarding workmen are collected for each job to be rated. Such incidents might include: quarreling with fellow workers, calmness during an emergency situation, willingness to work overtime during peak periods, declining to accept additional training or responsibility. These incidents are then analyzed and evaluated to determine which are critically associated with success on the job and which are found in substandard or unsuccessful employee performance. A scientifically constructed rating scale may then be developed which contains factual elements important to success on the job. Supervisors and foremen may then observe and record these incidents as they take place and hence appraise the relative merit of their workmen more objectively. Part of a sample critical-incident rating form is shown in Figure 3-6.

An attempt has been made to overcome some prominent sources of error in observation and reporting in the design of the critical-incident method. Flanagan suggests these principal difficulties among raters: "Supervisors have complex aims or goals; they forget; they don't notice; they don't always know what is important; they are busy; they need standards."[24] A rating system which is successful must overcome these limitations. The critical-incident technique contributes toward the solution of some of these problems. The system provides a set of standards which guide the rater. It has been suggested that supervisors make frequent brief notes on the daily incidents they observe so that memory need not be relied upon when the complete periodic rating is to be drawn up.

FORCED CHOICE

The forced-choice method of rating presents another attempt to overcome the familiar problems of personal bias and lack of objectivity in employee evaluation. This plan forces the rater to choose from a group of several short statements describing job proficiency or personal characteristics the one statement which most accurately describes the employee being rated. At the same time the rater also selects from the same block of statements the one which least accurately portrays the individual. Figure 3-7 contains a portion of a forced-choice rating scale.

This "most-least" selection procedure is repeated until all the blocks of statements have been evaluated by the rater. Two of the statements are complimentary, and the remaining two are uncomplimentary. The fifth statement is neutral. It is the selection of the pairs of statements

---

EMPLOYEE PERFORMANCE REPORT

20.   A   Gets along well with co-workers and supervisors.
       B   Is absent from work a great deal.
       C   Is dependable.
       D   Is impartial in his dealings with others.
       E   Is interested in the job.
       F   Knows less than the average employee about the work.

21.   A   Can put on steam in an emergency.
       B   Causes trouble among fellow workers.
       C   Exercises good judgment.
       D   Follows instructions very accurately.
       E   Is anxious to accept any assignment.
       F   Needs more supervision than the average employee.

Figure 3-7. Part of a Forced-Choice Performance Report.

(Employee Relations Dept., Standard Oil Company [New Jersey], "Employee Relations Research in Standard Oil Company [New Jersey] and Affiliates," No. 1, Vol. II, New York: Standard Oil Company [New Jersey], 1955, A-86.)

which is the crucial problem in the development of a forced-choice rating scale. Six basic steps have been outlined for constructing a forced choice scale:[25]

1. Collection of brief essay descriptions of successful and unsuccessful employees.
2. Preparation of a complete list of descriptive phrases or adjectives culled from these essays, and the administration of this list to a representative group of employees.
3. Determination of two indices for each descriptive phrase or adjective—a preference index and a discrimination index.
4. Selecting pairs of phrases or adjectives such that they appear of equal value to the rater (preference index) but differ in their significance for success as an employee (discrimination index).
5. Assembling of pairs so selected into tetrads.
6. Item selection against an external criterion and cross validation of the selected items.

The forced-choice system is predicated upon the fact that some statements are both preferential and discriminating regarding an individual, while other statements carry preference value but do not discriminate the successful worker from the unsuccessful one. Thus, in one prominent industrial application of this method of rating, each group of statements contained: (1) a favorable statement that had been found to differentiate between high- and low-proficiency foremen, (2) a favorable statement that did not differentiate, (3) a differentiating unfavorable statement, (4) a nondifferentiating unfavorable statement, (5) a neutral statement intended to apply to almost anyone in the group.[26]

In selecting two statements from each group, the ones that "most" and "least" describe an employee, the rater is not able to introduce personal bias into the rating since he does not know which of the statements is indicative of successful performance. The rater does not know how high or low he is rating the employee because the scoring key is not released to the people actually performing the rating. This virtual elimination of personal bias lends greater over-all objectivity to the method. Errors of leniency, halo, and central tendency are avoided, and the precise nature of the blocks of descriptive statements forces the rater to appraise each individual carefully in terms of specific job performance and personality characteristics.

There are, however, some limitations to the forced-choice method which may tend to minimize its usefulness to industry. Each application is a unique one and must be custom-tailored to the firm involved. The blocks of statements which describe successful and unsuccessful job performance relate to a particular company and a particular management's interpretation of personal success or failure. Thus the forced-choice method is costly in actual use because each job requires comprehensive research and analysis to determine which personal characteristics discriminate an effective employee from an ineffective one.

The rating results are not adaptable to employee counseling and training because the rater does not know how he is evaluating the individual. This difficulty was avoided in one company by having the supervisor fill out a "performance summary report" in addition to the forced-choice rating.[27] This summary report is retained by the rater and may be used for a discussion or counseling interview with each employee. The method, therefore, is probably better adapted to medium- and large-sized firms which have a fairly large and stable work force and which are better able to assume the costs of initially installing the system.

Results of rating

Several studies demonstrate the reliability of ratings, but few confirm their validity. Reliability means accuracy in the sense that the rating method is internally consistent; that is, two ratings of a workman by

26 *Industrial Relations Memos,* No. 119, p. 9.
29 IBID., p. 19.

competent independent raters should produce substantially the same result.

Validity of a rating means that it accurately measures the traits it was designed to measure. Hence employees who are high in quantity of production or quality of work should, in fact, be rated highly if the ratings are valid. Few studies of validity have been made, probably because there would be little reason to use subjective rating if a more objective measure of success on the job were available.

RELIABILITY OF GRAPHIC METHOD

In ratings at the Atlantic Refining Company the average reliability for a single trait as determined by comparing two raters showed a coefficient of correlation of .78. Under such circumstances, this is higher than the usual reliability for the graphic method, which ordinarily has been only .55.[28] The reliability of the graphic method can be increased by increasing the number of raters. In industry it is not practical ordinarily to have more than one main rater, the immediate supervisor. It is a loss, rather than an advantage, to increase the number of raters by including persons who are unqualified to rate because they lack opportunity to observe.

NUMBER OF TRAITS

Recent trends in rating appear to favor the use of fewer traits than were formerly included. As noted above, one writer has advocated that only two traits, job performance and promotability, are all that need be rated. This proposed simplification was based on a factor analysis of more complicated merit ratings in which twelve traits collapsed upon analysis into these two. The simplification fits in with the uses to which management actually puts ratings. Evaluating performance and deciding whether or not a man is good material for promotion are the main uses of ratings.

The factor analysis yielding two factors, performance and promotability, came from a rating study based on twelve supposedly independent traits.[29] These were:

1. Safety
2. Knowledge of job
3. Versatility
4. Accuracy
5. Productivity
6. Over-all job performance
7. Industriousness
8. Initiative
9. Judgment
10. Cooperation
11. Personality
12. Health

The ability-to-do-the-job factor was more important statistically than promotability.

Ratings of Radio Corporation of America employees were analyzed into six factors from a scale that started with fourteen traits.[30] The persons rated were field engineers. The fourteen traits on the scale were "Personality, Personal Appearance, Punctuality, Thoroughness, Efficiency, Resourcefulness, Dependability, Cooperation, Job Attitude, Technical Ability, Sales Ability, Organizing Ability, Judgment, and Desire for Self-Improvement." The six factors that came out of the analysis were "Attendance to Detail, Ability to do the Present Job, Sales Ability, Conscientiousness, Organizing or Systematic Tendency, and Social Intelligence."

When the two analyses of ratings are reviewed together, it appears that different factors emerged in each instance, but in each analysis the number of separate factors was smaller than the number of traits the originators of the scale thought were independent. Consequently, it appears that ideally it would be advisable to make a statistical analysis of the ratings after a scale is tentatively accepted, as well as to base the traits on a job analysis to begin with. No doubt, it will not be practical to have a different set of traits for each occupation, but several related occupations could be grouped into a single scale.

The employment of a greater number of traits to be rated looks more refined and is in a sense more specific. However, when the specific traits collapse into more general traits, there seems to be no justification for continuing the rating of specific traits. Training might make the raters' judgments more specific for supposedly separate traits.

DISCUSSION OF RESULTS

Ratings should be discussed privately with each employee if maximum benefit is to be obtained from the program. The individual workman may be unaware of his shortcomings in certain areas. Improvement can hardly be expected if the man is not told of his deficiencies. Workers are interested in how they are getting along on the job and how they stand in their supervisor's estimation. One survey, however, reported that 76 per cent of a group of employees indicated that their ratings were never discussed with them.[31]

Supervisors and raters often dislike telling the employee his rating and explaining the basis used for evaluating each trait. Arguments and disagreements may easily arise unless the interview is skilfully conducted. Some supervisors lack the ability to explain clearly and effectively what the rating procedure is and how it is used by the company. Others do not wish to discuss ratings with employees who have received low scores or with employees who are problem cases.

A few companies do, however, include an employee conference with the rater as an integral part of the evaluation program. Such a plan is in operation at the East Springfield works of the Westinghouse Electric Company.[32] At this plant, rating personnel receive training in the techniques of interview and discussion and hence are better able to conduct satisfactory employee conferences. During each interview the more favorable elements of the rating are discussed first, then the adverse items are brought forward, and the discussion is closed by reviewing the employee's strong points and urging him to improve the weaker ones.

MERIT RATING AND SENIORITY

Management's desire to use the results of merit rating rather than strict seniority as a basis for determining promotions and salary increases has often met with considerable union opposition. The labor position was summarized by one union official as follows: "Our reason for rejecting most merit rating plans is not because we don't want to give management the opportunity to reward workers in accordance with their output, but because we say if there is an objective method of measuring output, then key the wage rate to the output."[33]

The union clearly prefers objective measures, such as productivity or seniority, to the more subjective and arbitrary rating of personal characteristics. The principle of seniority is firmly established, and subjective employee evaluation is viewed as a supplemental device for appraising worker performance. In a survey of employee attitudes toward merit rating, workers were asked how much weight should be given to merit rating in deciding who is to be promoted. Fifty-two per cent thought that no importance should be attached to ratings, while another 42 per cent believed that ratings should count only 25 per cent toward deciding who to promote.[34]

There are several examples of rating methods which have been worked out satisfactorily with unions; in addition, to be successful, management should enlist the cooperation of the workers.

Ideally, ratings would be approved by those on whom the ratings are made. It is at least desirable for employees to understand the ratings, for the ratings to be simple, and for the employees to have a chance to see them.

An example of union-management cooperation in applying a rating plan has been reported for Air Associates, Inc.[35] There was so much trouble between management and labor in this company that it was taken over by the Army. Changes in personnel practices, job evaluation, and merit rating were given credit for a tremendous improvement in morale and for decreasing unit costs. The form used in the merit rating is shown in Figure 3-8. This form is filled out by the foreman and shop

73

EMPLOYEE RATING SHEET

NAME.. BADGE NO........................... DATE................................

Dep't........................... JOB TITLE .... Grade................................

FACTOR

QUALITY OF WORK

25	21	18	15	12	9	6	3
Rejects and errors consistently rare		Work usually good. Errors seldom made		Work mostly passable. Must be checked		Frequent errors and scrap. Careless	

QUANTITY OF WORK

25	21	18	15	12	9	6	3
Output unusually high. Exceptionally fast		Output above average. Usually works fast		Output just average. Seldom makes more		Output below average. Slow producer	

ADAPTABILITY

15	13	11	9	7	6	4	2
Learns very quickly. Changes met easily		Adjustments made with little trouble		Detailed instructions required for changes		Requires repeated instructions. Learns slowly	

JOB KNOWLEDGE

15	13	11	9	7	6	4	2
Makes most use of knowledge and experience		Well-informed on jobs. Rarely needs help		Knows job fairly well. Requires average supervision		Knowledge limited. Little desire to improve	

DEPENDABILITY

10	8	6	5	4	3	2	1
Marked ability to follow any fair job		Does task faithfully. Needs some follow-up		Generally requires checkup on work		Requires frequent checking or watching	

ATTITUDE

10	8	6	5	4	3	2	1
Exceptionally good team-worker. Cooperates		Usually willing to co-operate with others		Reacts to changes with some reluctance		Cooperates if required to do so. Disgruntled	

TOTAL................................

FOR THE MANAGEMENT... Present Rate...........................

Increase Granted...........................

FOR THE UNION... New Rate...........................

Figure 3-8. Employee Rating Sheet.

("Rate Jobs and Establish Wage Brackets. Case of Air Associates, Inc.," *Factory Management and Maintenance,* August, 1944, **102**, 2, 97–104.)

EMPLOYEE RATING FORM

NAME............................... CLOCK NO.................. DEPT.................

TYPE OF WORK................................. CLASS..................

GRADING OF EMPLOYEES

Quality of Work: Consider the amount of scrap and the care and accuracy with which he worked. Poor 1–9; Average 10–18; Excellent 19–27. ....

Quantity of Work: Consider the speed and the amount of work accomplished. (To be estimated by foremen for *all* men.) Poor 1–6; Average 7–12; Excellent 13–18. ....

Dependability: Can you rely on him to do his best at all times? Trust him to do as instructed? Poor 1–4; Average 5–8; Excellent 9–12. ....

Attitude: Consider his attitude toward his job; his fellow workmen; his foreman; and the company. Poor 1–4; Average 5–8; Excellent 9–12. ....

Initiative: Does he use his own head? Does he have a self-starter? Is he able to do his work without being told? Poor 1–3; Average 4–6; Excellent 7–9. ....

Judgment: Does he foresee scrap? Can he be trusted to choose the better of optional ways to do his job? Poor 1–2; Average 3–6; Excellent 7–8. ....

Ease of Learning: How quickly does he grasp and understand new ways to do his old job, or new jobs? Poor 1–2; Average 3–5; Excellent 6–7. ....

Attendance: (*Not* to be *graded* by the foreman.) Maximum is 7. ....

TOTAL POINTS ....

Remarks...

....

Signed................................... Date..................

Figure 3-9. Employee Rating Form.

("Union Contracts Rate Employees," *The American Machinist,* 1941, **85,** 913–914.)

steward together. If they fail to agree, a joint committee settles the rating. The joint rating system is used as a basis for making transfers or filling higher vacancies. The union is the CIO (now CIO/AFL) United Auto Workers. The extent of union participation here is unusual.

A second case of union-management cooperation in rating employees is that of the Cummins Engine Company.[36] The labor agreement provides for pay to be determined in part by the results of ratings. The rating form used is shown in Figure 3-9. The union is given a copy of each completed rating form. Seniority also plays a part in wage determination, in that for each year of service one point is added to the total of the rating.

One company that has found an employee rating system useful is the Scovill Manufacturing Company.[37] The key point in explaining the success appeared to be that the supervisors were carefully trained in rating before the method was started, and they continued to have follow-up training. It may likewise have been important to the success of the rating system that the employees had been persuaded that the plan was fair.

SUMMARY

Individuals differ in many ways that are important to industry. While the relative contributions of heredity and environment are not fully known, there is still plenty of evidence that by the time a man enters the labor market his personality has become stabilized to the point that his behavior is predictable in many ways.

People differ in intellectual traits that are important for many jobs. Intelligence, or the ability to learn, is a combination of a general factor and several group factors. Somewhat correlated with, but also to some extent independent of, intelligence are mechanical ability and clerical ability. Mechanical ability is essentially a space-relations factor, or the ability to visualize correctly how objects can be taken apart or fitted together. Clerical ability is made up mainly of a perceptual speed factor, and many clerical jobs also require a high order of verbal and numerical factors, which are part of intelligence.

Interests differ in that men who are successful in one occupation or profession have interests that are different from men in other occupations. For the most part, a man's interests stay the same from age 20 to age 40 and probably beyond that age.

Nonintellectual traits of personality are believed to be crucial to outstanding success and to failure in some industrial jobs. There is, however, no agreement on what are significant personality traits.

Individuals differ on the job in quantity and quality of production by large amounts. These differences in output cannot generally be measured adequately. The appraisal of performance is generally made by a subjective rating. Many methods of rating have been tried. No single one has yet emerged as outstandingly preferable.

The forced-choice method gets away from the leniency of rating that is fatal to valid results in many systems. This method, however, is expensive, and it is not liked by the raters because they do not know what ratings they are making.

The field-review method has much to recommend it. Here a personnel specialist interviews the immediate supervisor and any other competent raters. Since people will talk more frankly than they will write, a fair appraisal will emerge if there has been proper training for all concerned.

RECOMMENDED READINGS

Dooher, M. Joseph, and Vivienne Marquis (eds.), *Rating Employee and Supervisory Performance,* New York: The American Management Association, 1950. A manual of merit rating techniques which gives in detail the major methods that are being used today in American business.

Edwards, Allan L., *Statistical Analysis,* rev. ed., New York: Rinehart & Company, Inc., 1958. The correlation method, which is used often in the presentation of results reported in industrial psychology, is given clearly and in detail, with examples.

McClelland, David C., *Personality,* New York: William Sloane Associates, 1951. A balanced and comprehensive view of the theory of personality is given.

4

Selection by interview
and application blank

That individuals differ in their ability to perform different types of activities is well known, and it has been indicated in the preceding chapter. Because of these large differences in human abilities the problem of proper selection becomes a very important one for modern industry. How to find the capabilities of the employee before hiring him is the subject of this and the following two chapters. This chapter is concerned with the interview and the application blank, the next two chapters with personnel tests.

Evaluation of individual differences for industrial selection

Individual differences are due to the interaction of heredity and environment. The relative contribution of heredity and environment remains controversial, and it must be decided in terms of the specific trait. For the purposes of industrial psychology it is usually not necessary to answer the question whether differences are due to heredity or environment. Management is more interested in defining the differences that presently exist in the individual and in trying to determine whether they will continue to exist after employment.

Certainly the most common methods for evaluating individual differences for industrial selection are the interview and the application blank. Personnel testing is an important method for determining individual differences, although it is used much less often.

INTERVIEW
Use

The personal interview along with the application blank continues to be used by almost every employer. There is practically a universal desire to want to see and to talk with anyone who is being considered for what seems to the employer an important job. Almost everyone has optimistic faith in his ability to size up people unless he has made a careful follow-up study of his batting average in appraising people, and only a very small number of employers bother to do this.

A recent survey of 325 companies indicated that over 98 per cent of them used selection interviews.[1]

Definition

The interview is a conversation with a purpose.[2] There are three purposes that may be served: obtaining information, giving information, and motivation. The employment interview should serve each of these three purposes. It should provide an appraisal of personality by obtaining relevant information about the prospective employee's background, his training, work history, education, and interests. The interview should give information about the company, the specific job, and the personnel policies. It should also establish a friendly relationship between the employer and applicant and motivate the satisfactory applicant to want to work for the company.

Obtaining information has been the primary objective of the interview rather than giving information or motivating the prospective employee. Customarily the interview is used in conjunction with the application blank. When this is the procedure, the answers to any duplicated questions should be studied for serious inconsistencies. The interview should also supplement the blank to obtain additional information about areas in which there is an interest in a fuller answer.

Advantages

Often abilities and traits important to the employer cannot be adequately measured by tests and other techniques. Many psychologists are of the opinion that the interview can be a better means of appraising personality than a paper and pencil test.[3] A recent test shows that a set of behavioral characteristics can be reliably rated during the employment interview.[4] The appraisal of personality is the main purpose of the interview; however, such an appraisal is difficult and the results often unreliable. A major difficulty is the failure to recognize its limitations.

On the positive side, it is possible to determine from an interview whether or not the candidate is good looking and how he reacts in conversation. Good looks can also be judged from a photograph, but less accurately than face to face because of the unreliability of photographs and because the interview affords an opportunity to show facial animation. The personality traits that can be demonstrated in an interview are responsiveness, alertness in conversation, manners, presence, and poise. The interviewer needs to be trained and skilled to determine other important personality traits such as loyalty and responsibility.

The individual is a combination of many abilities and traits which interact with each other. What the interview should evaluate is the applicant's motivation, personality make-up, and the influence of environmental and emotional problems upon him.

Limitations

The interviewer cannot judge from a man's face such personality and character traits as honesty. A shifty gaze does not necessarily mean dishonesty. There is no evidence to support popular notions that personality and character traits agree with the contour of the face, the height of the forehead, the jut of the jaw, the closeness of the eyes, and the like.

Interviewers frequently form unwarranted impressions of an interviewee on the basis of similarity to some other person who is liked or disliked. Stereotyping of the individual and the often unconscious effect of personal bias are two of the most common pitfalls of the interview. Many employment interviewers have no special immunity to these weaknesses.

HALO

Halo effect, the tendency to judge the total worth of the person on the basis of one of a few specific characteristics, is closely connected to stereotyping and is also dangerous. The interviewer is apt to like one or more traits, not necessarily connected to job success, and transfer his favorable impression to his final evaluation of the applicant. A negative or inverse halo effect is also possible in the untrained interviewer and is equally dangerous.

Recognition of human errors in judgment is a step toward more objective interviewing. Training interviewers to escape these common pitfalls would improve the interviewing technique. The recognition of this effect of conditioning on the part of the interviewer can make him more careful to offset it.

Finding interests

The interviewer usually wants to determine vocational interests, although these are sometimes measured by tests. One approach to the determination of interests in the interview is to ask the applicant just what he wants to do, what he is interested in getting out of a job. His responses and enthusiasm often reveal his interests well. The strength of the applicant's interests can be tested to some extent by explaining the disagreeable features of a job. For example, one company when selecting salesmen neglected to tell them that they would have to carry merchandise in an automobile, unload it at stores, and set up displays. This phase of the work was so disagreeable to many of the salesmen once they were on the job that they quit. A complete description of the job should be presented so the interviewer will learn whether the applicant is really interested in the kind of work that is available. Because many college-trained graduates are inexperienced and find it difficult to visualize job duties, there is a growing tendency among some employers to employ during vacation periods as a selection device. This allows both employer and applicant a chance to look each other over more closely and gives the future permanent employee a chance to understand the nature of the job and his duties.

Reliability

There is a wide margin of error in the ordinary employment interview. One study, illustrated in Table 4-I confirms this. Twelve sales managers rated fifty-seven applicants for sales jobs. Each interviewer conducted the interview in the way he saw fit. At the end of each interview the sales manager rated the applicant according to his over-all suitability. The ratings were placed in rank order from 1 to 57 for the job of salesman. Table 4-I reveals the low agreement among the sales managers. The most extreme case was candidate C, who was ranked first by one interviewer and last by another. Although this is the most striking disagreement, others are almost as bad.

Another study of the reliability of employment interviewing had six

TABLE 4-I

Twelve Interviewers' Rankings of Job Applicants for Sales Positions

| | INTERVIEWER | | | | | | | | | | | | |
APPLICANT	1	2	3	4	5	6	7	8	9	10	11	12	RANGE
A	33	46	6	56	26	32	12	38	23	22	22	9	6–56
B	36	50	43	17	51	47	38	20	38	55	39	9	9–55
C	53	10	6	21	16	9	20	2	57	28	1	26	1–57

Adapted from *Vocational Psychology and Character Analysis,* by H. L. Hollingsworth, copyright 1929 by D. Appleton and Co. Reprinted by permission of Appleton-Century-Crofts, Inc.

sales managers appraise thirty-six candidates.[5] There was also a large amount of disagreement here. When each of the six interviewers ranked a candidate as to whether he was in the better or the worse half of the group, twenty-eight of the thirty-six applicants were placed in the worse half by some interviewer and the better half by another. Whether a man would be hired, then, depended a great deal on which sales manager interviewed him.

A third study of interviewing error had six sales managers and a psychologist interview twelve candidates for a job as truck salesman.[6] When the judgment of each interviewer was compared with the group judgment, the coefficient of correlation was only .47, which is decidedly below the demands for a satisfactory reliability coefficient.

In the three studies mentioned, the employment interview had several possible defects that can be corrected. First, the fact that the interviewers were experienced sales managers does not mean that they were satisfactory interviewers. There was also a lack of job specifications, of plan to the interview, and of interview training, and there was no definite system for recording the different components that made up the rating.[7] Haphazard interviewing by untrained persons fails to obtain the objective analysis necessary for predicting future job success.

Ways to improve interview

The employment interview can be made satisfactorily accurate if it is carried out with sufficient care. Interviewers need to be trained in definite procedures and to have supervised practice. The interviewer must maintain an objective attitude toward the applicant. The traits to be measured should correlate highly with future job success.

An Employee Evaluation Form for Interviewers which is useful for employment interviewing is shown in Figure 4-1. A manual has been prepared as an aid in the training of employment interviewers, and it is directly connected to the use of this form.[8] In using this form the interviewer begins with work experience, goes on to training, and then to personal history. Only those items on the blank are completed that apply to the job under consideration.

Interviewing techniques

PATTERNED INTERVIEW

The possibility of obtaining good results with a careful interview has been most clearly shown by McMurry in what he calls a "patterned interview." By this is meant that the interview had a definite plan, as described below. The patterned interview in combination with an appli-

EMPLOYEE EVALUATION FORM FOR INTERVIEWERS

NAME Carter, John W.   JOB CONSIDERED FOR Engine Lathe Operator

INTERVIEWER Q.R.C.   DATE 2/3/43

INSTRUCTIONS: Rate the adequacy of the applicant's work experience, training, and manner and appearance only as they apply to the job for which he is being considered. For your aid in writing interview summary, mark a check (✓) in box before question items to which answers are favorable and a cross (✗) where responses are unfavorable. Mark only those items which have a bearing on the requirements of the particular job in question. Place a check (✓) on each line to indicate your estimate of how well the applicant satisfies the requirements of the factor considered. Note brief facts which substantiate your decision in space below each line.

I PREVIOUS EXPERIENCE

A ☑ Similar job duties?
B ☑ Required hand and machine tools?
C ☑ Same type materials?
D ☑ Similar working conditions?
E ☑ Same degree of supervision?
F ☑ Shown development on the job?

Below Average | Average | Above Average ✓

2 yrs. - Le Blonde 24" - turning down rough surfaces on crank shaft. O.D. tolerance .009
3 yrs. - South Bend - job shop - turning down punches and similar job work. Sets up, grinds tools, works from prints.

II TRAINING

A ☑ Sufficient formal school education?
B ☒ Best liked or least liked subjects related to job requirements?
C ☑ Required mechanical, mathematical or other specialized training?
D ☑ Required "on the job" training?
E ☐ Any special training since leaving regular school?

Below Average | Average ✓ | Above Average

Finished 3 yrs. H.S. - one year machine shop course. Disliked most school subjects - math especially. Enjoyed machine shop course - liked to work with his hands. Probably had difficulty passing subject. Extensive all around training in job shop lathe work - has plugged some of the gaps in school training

III MANNER AND APPEARANCE

A ☑ Favorable, unfavorable mannerisms? (gestures, facial expressions, speech)
B ☑ General appearance satisfactory? (features, poise, dress, personal hygiene)

Below Average | Average | Above Average

Rugged, used to hard work

INTERVIEW SUMMARY

Well qualified by previous experience and training for engine lathe job. Should be able to take over assignment here with little or no adjustment. Should reach normal job productivity in a few days. Appears to be a good solid citizen with steady living habits. All home and family ties located in this area. Has good motivation for taking work here - This is sufficiently strong to counteract the considerably higher rate he is now receiving in a crowded war production center.

Good candidate but apparently has very little potentiality for upgrading to supervisory capacity.

OVER-ALL RATING FOR SPECIFIC JOB
Considering all the facts you have learned about the applicant, how well is he fitted for this job in comparison with other men already doing this work in the plant?

✓ Above Average
___ Average
___ Below Average

TEST RESULTS

Test	Score	Percentile
Intelligence	68	40
Mechanical Comp.	46	65
Tool Dexterity	6'21"	70

Figure 4-1. Part of an Employee Evaluation Form for Interviewers.

(Fear, Richard A., and Byron Jordan, *Employee Evaluation Manual for Interviewers,* New York: The Psychological Corporation, 1943, Appendix.)

83

PATTERNED INTERVIEW FORM—SALES POSITION

SUMMARY

Rating: | 1 | 2 | 3 | 4 | Interviewer_____ Date_____

Division_____Territory_____

Comments_____ In making final rating, be sure to consider not only the man's sales ability and experience but also his stability, industry, perseverence,

ability to get along with others, loyalty, self-reliance, competitiveness, and leadership. Is he mature and realistic? Is he well motivated for this

work? Are his living standards and his domestic situation favorable to this work? Does he have sufficient health and physical reserve?

Name_____Telephone Number_____Is it your phone?_____

Present Address_____City_____State_____
              Is this a desirable neighborhood? Does it appear consistent with income?

Date of your birth_____Age_____Do you own a car? ☐ No, ☐ Yes; Make_____Age_____
                                    Will his car be satisfactory for this work?

What do you use your car for?_____
                            Will this interfere?

Have you served in the Armed Services of the United States since 1940? ☐ No, ☐ Yes; Which branch?_____

If rejected or exempted, what were reasons?_____

Why are you applying for this position?_____
                           Are his underlying reasons practical? Does he have a definite goal?

Are you employed now? ☐ No, ☐ Yes; (If yes) How soon available?_____

WORK EXPERIENCE. Cover all positions. This information is very important. Interviewer should record last position first. Every month since leaving school should be accounted for. Experience in Armed Forces should be covered as a job.

LAST OR PRESENT POSITION

Company_____Address_____From_____19___To_____19___
                                   Do dates check with application?

How was position obtained?_____Superior_____Title_____
         Was he trying to get into sales? Did he show self-reliance in getting this job? Have there been changes here?

Nature of work at start_____Earnings at start_____
        Did this work require energy and industry?   Salary or commission?

Nature of work at leaving_____Earnings at leaving_____
        Did this require steady industry? Was salesmanship used? Any indication of favorable motivation? Progress? Salary or commission?

How did you plan your work?_____How did you get your contacts?_____
              Was he on top of his job?   Was he on his own?

Was there anything you especially liked about the position?_____
                      Has he been happy and content in his work?

Was there anything you especially disliked?_____
                  Did he get along well with people? Were his dislikes justified?

How much time have you lost from work?_____Reasons_____
            Is he regular in attendance on the job?

Reasons for leaving_____Why right then?_____
        Are his reasons for leaving reasonable and consistent?   Do they check with records?

Part-time jobs during this employment_____
           Does this indicate industry? Ambition? Lack of loyalty? Will this interfere with the job under consideration?

NEXT TO LAST POSITION

Company_____Address_____From_____19___To_____19___
                                     Do dates check with application?

Figure 4-2. Part of a Patterned Interview Form—Sales Position.

(McMurry-Hamstra and Co., Sales Personnel Forms, Chicago: The Dartnell Corp., 1952.)

TELEPHONE CHECK ON SALES APPLICANT_____

Name of Applicant

_____

Person Contacted   Position

_____

Company   City and State   Telephone Number

1. I wish to *verify* some of the information given to us by Mr. (name) who has applied for a position with our firm. Do you remember him? What were the dates of his employment with your Company?   From_____19____To_____19_____
   Do dates check?

2. What was he doing when he started? _____
   Did he exaggerate?

   When he left? _____
   Did he progress?

3. He says he was earning $_____ per_____when he left. Is that right?   ☐ Yes,   ☐ No; $_____
   Did he falsify?

4. How much of this was salary? $_____

   How much commission? $_____

5. How was his attendance? _____
   Conscientious?   Health problems?

6. What type of selling did he do? _____
   To whom?   How did he get his contacts?

7. How did his sales results compare with others? _____
   Industrious?   Competitive?

8. Did he supervise anyone else?   ☐ No,   ☐ Yes; How many?_____
   Does this check?

   (If yes) How well did he handle it? _____
   Is he a leader or a driver?

9. How closely was he supervised? _____
   Was he hard to manage?

10. How hard did he work? _____
    Is he habitually industrious?

11. How well did he get along with other people? _____
    Is he a troublemaker?

12. What arguments did he have with customers? _____
    Does he like selling?   Can he control his temper?

13. What did you think of him? _____
    Did he get along with his superiors?

14. Why did he leave? _____
    Good reasons?   Do they check?

15. Would you rehire him?   ☐ Yes,   ☐ No; Why not?_____
    Does this affect his suitability with us?

16. Did he have any domestic or financial difficulties that interfered with work?   ☐ No,   ☐ Yes; What?_____
    Immaturity?

17. How about drinking or gambling?   ☐ No,   ☐ Yes; What?_____
    Immaturity?

18. What are his outstanding strong points? _____

19. What type of saleswork do you feel he would do best? _____

20. What are his weak points? _____

Checked by_____Date_____

Figure 4-3. Telephone Check on Sales Applicant.

(McMurry-Hamstra and Co., Sales Personnel Forms, Chicago: The Dartnell Corp., 1950.)

cation blank and a careful reference check was much more accurate than less standardized interviews.[9] The patterned interview was designed by McMurry to measure the personality traits that are wanted among all employees. Such traits are "(1) stability, (2) industry, (3) ability to get along with others, (4) self-reliance, (5) willingness to accept responsibility, (6) freedom from emotional immaturity, and (7) motivation." A part of the form used in the patterned interview is shown in Figure 4-2. The basis for this approach is that an applicant's future behavior can be judged by his past performance. If he has been industrious in the past, he will probably be industrious in the future. If he has been unstable in the past, he will probably be unstable in the future.

The patterned interview contains no questions relating to job skills. Rather, it is designed to appraise only personality, motivation, and interests. The applicant's suitability in regard to job competence and knowledge is evaluated through such means as school and work records, reference checks, and tests. More of the valuable interviewing time can thus be spent on appraising the applicant as a personality with less duplication of information that may be secured elsewhere. Interview forms for specific jobs should vary in details and points of emphasis. The main areas mentioned above, however, remain the same.

A check of names given as references by the applicant is often made on the telephone. Questions asked on a thorough check are shown in Figure 4-3. Greater frankness is secured by telephone than through the usual letters of reference, which typically do not state anything unfavorable.

RESULTS. The most convincing demonstration of the validity of the patterned interview procedure was made at the Link-Belt Ordnance Company in Chicago. The interviewing was done by three members of the company, the personnel manager, the employment manager, and an employment interviewer, all of whom were specially trained. Their training consisted of "ten hours in the theory of personality, followed by another ten or fifteen hours of supervised practice with actual applicants." Applicants were interviewed for various factory jobs, and it was not necessary to consider the occupations separately in the personality appraisal.

Of the seventy employees who were clearly unpromising, 60 per cent left in a month or less; whereas only 9 per cent of those who seemed worth while or marginal to the interviewer left within a month. Less than 2 per cent of the unusually promising candidates left in such a short time. Variations in length of service correlated .43 with interviewers' judgments.

The correlation between supervisors' ratings and interview judgments is higher in another study than the one just given between turnover and

TABLE 4-II

Comparison of Initial Interview Score
with Success Rating

(Men and Women Combined)

INTERVIEW SCORE	SUCCESS ON THE JOB RATING				
	VERY POOR	BELOW AVERAGE	ABOVE AVERAGE	OUT-STANDING	TOTAL
Unusually outstanding			2	6	8
Good		13	88	8	109
Marginal	4	176	75	3	258
Unpromising	23	8	1		32
TOTAL	27	197	166	17	407

Adapted from McMurry, Robert N., and Dale L. Johnson, "Development of Instruments for Selecting and Placing Factory Employees," *Advanced Management,* September 1945, pp. 113–120.

interviewers' ratings. The comparison with supervisors' ratings is shown in Table 4-II. The coefficient of correlation is .68 between interviewers' judgments before hiring and success rating by supervisors eighteen months after the men have been on the job. This is outstandingly good. Two additional studies in separate companies demonstrated good validity for the patterned interview.

All these successful applications of a patterned interview are alike in that there is a definite plan to the interview and a specific system of recording results. Each depends on trained interviewers. To use the employment interview to advantage the interviewer must be trained for several weeks. Training will produce closer agreement among interviewers' judgments.[10] The use of rating scales for recording results makes the interviewing definite and the interviewers' judgment more pointed and specific. A standardized form also reduces interviewer bias and minimizes misunderstandings through the use of more carefully worded questions.

NONDIRECTIVE

Another interviewing technique that merits study is the use of nondirective questioning. Basic to this procedure is the minimum use of direct questions. Questions that can easily yield yes or no answers are avoided, and instead broad general questions are substituted. Questions such as "What did you like about your last job?" and "What sort of work interests you most?" often have more success in revealing the applicants' real personality. It is felt that, the more the applicant is allowed the freedom to talk about himself without the limiting nature of direct questioning, the more he will reveal his personality as it really is and not as he thinks the interviewer wants it to appear.

STRESS INTERVIEW

The stress interview in which pressure is purposely put on the applicant may have some value for jobs where emotional balance is a key requirement. This procedure, like many procedures of industrial psychology, was developed originally in the military service. It involves putting the candidate under relatively severe emotional strain in order to test his responses. It often is characterized by the rapid firing of questions by several seemingly unfriendly interviewers. The stress interview was used in the selection of spies for the United States Office of Strategic Services during World War II. Although it was believed to be very useful, there has never been any statistical proof that it is valid.

The stress interview would appear to be worthy of study for management and sales positions where resistance to stress is important. It has been reported it has been used by one business company and by several civilian government agencies, but again there is no proof of its validity. It seems more plausible than pencil and paper tests, but it is obviously much more expensive.

GROUP INTERVIEW

The group interview is a relatively new procedure which offers some promise for the appraisal of leadership, but it has not been validated as yet. Several job applicants are placed in a leaderless discussion and observers sit in the background to evaluate the performance of the applicants. The procedure has been to assign a topic for discussion, but to have it leaderless, at least in the beginning. One of the key points on which the observers focus is who, if anyone, assumes leadership, how this is done, and how it is accepted by other members of the group. This method deserves more study to determine whether it is useful in selecting supervisors.

Training

There are several skills in which an employment interviewer should be trained. He needs to be able to establish rapport, encourage the interviewee to talk, know how to ask questions, and listen. It is his job to establish rapport—a relationship of mutual confidence and free expression. The best way for the supervisor to put the applicant at ease is to be at ease himself. The candidate will be made to feel free to talk if he is started off with a subject that is of interest to him. While such a subject is often irrelevant to the main purpose of the interview, it is chosen simply to start a person talking. Such topics are numerous, and they depend, of course, a great deal on the applicant, although there are several topics of general interest. The weather is usually a safe opening, or current sporting events.

Frankness and sincerity are more effective than a clever attempt to trick a person into talking.[11] It is best for the interviewer to take the interviewee into his confidence and tell him the purpose of the interview, whether it is to find out his background of experience, or to find what he knows about a situation that has led to a grievance. It is true that on occasions an interviewer, by being clever, could learn something he wished to know by outsmarting the interviewee, but such action is likely to have an unfortunate rebound, either with this interviewee during the current session, at a later session, or through antagonism built up and transmitted to other interviewees. If you want people to talk, you have to make them want to talk rather than force them to do so.

After the purpose of the interview has been set forth by the interviewer, he should ask questions. When the interviewee answers the questions, the interviewer should not only listen but also be attentive and express interest. If the interviewer does not give his complete attention to the applicant, he will very likely lose his cooperation. The interviewer should not interrupt, as this will reduce cooperation. The level of questions that the interviewer uses should not be "over the head" of the applicant. The interviewer should maintain a friendly, sympathetic attitude toward the candidate at all times.

Even if what the interviewee says is obviously untrue or prejudiced, the interviewer should not argue with him, for it is the rare person who will retract a statement after he has expressed himself, and usually an argument only puts a man on the defensive and creates some antagonism. A defensive attitude on the part of the applicant will discourage the free flow of information and reduce the interview's effectiveness. If there is any doubt in his mind, the interviewer should attempt to restate in his own words what the interviewee has told him. The interviewer should be attentive not only to what the applicant says but to what he does not say, as, for instance, when an applicant does not give the reason for leaving previous employment or does not explain some time gap in his work history. While an interview form is often followed and its use should be encouraged, the questions put to the applicant should not be asked in an impersonal, mechanical fashion. Rapport can be more easily maintained if the interview form is used in a more flexible manner, as a guide instead of as a set and limiting form to be followed through "to the letter." Leading questions should not be used.

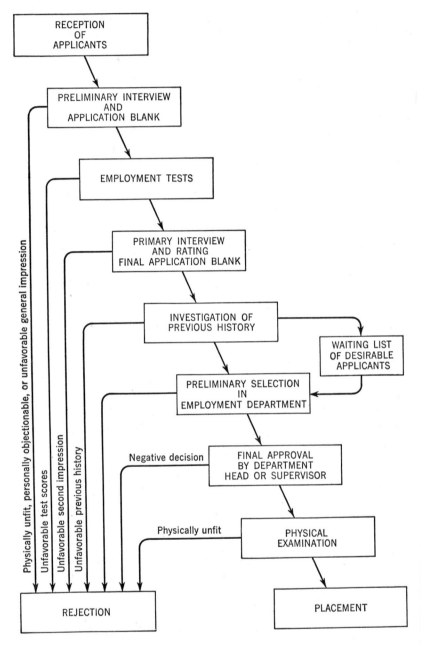

Figure 4-4. Flow Chart of Selection Procedures.

(Uhrbrock, Richard S., "Mental Alertness Tests as Aids in Selecting Employees," *Personnel,* 1936, **12,** 231. Reprinted by permission of the American Management Association, Inc.)

Phasing the interview

The use and phasing of the interview with other selection procedures, illustrated in Figure 4-4, is sound. This is the "successive hurdle" type of selection process. It adds organization and objectivity to the selection procedure. Because of the practical limitations of time, a selection form such as that in Figure 4-4 will make maximum use of time. A set procedure to be followed also reduces confusion in the applicant's mind. It should be noted that there are three interviews in the procedure shown in the form.

Summary

The bulk of employment interviews in industry have to be short because of practical limitations. Because of this limitation many college students are interviewed in a two-part program: first, a short interview on the campus, and, later, intensive interviewing during a visit to the company. Whatever the time limitations, termination of the interview should not be abrupt. The applicant often feels most at ease just before he is leaving, and freedom of his expression should not be suppressed. Whether the applicant is to be hired or not, the interviewer should leave in the applicant's mind a favorable impression of the company. From the establishing of good rapport at the beginning to the parting words, good company public relations should be maintained by the interviewer.

Much work remains to be done to increase the effectiveness of employment interviewing. More research is necessary. We still have a shortage of skilled interviewers. In many job areas definite personality requirements have not been established. More work in these areas would certainly help to increase the validity of the employment interview. More thought should be given to aims and methods. Although much work remains to be done and many interviewing practices are followed, the interview remains the most popular method of employee selection today.

APPLICATION BLANK

The application blank and the employment interview are the two most widely used selection methods, and they are often used in combination to supplement each other. A recent survey showed that 99.5 per cent of the companies participating used application blanks.[12] Application forms vary from small 3 by 5 cards to many-paged folders containing hundreds of questions about the applicant's history. The main items of information requested on application blanks are "name, address, age, marital status and dependents, schooling, experience and references . . ."[13] Other items on application blanks vary considerably from one company to

APPLICATION FOR SALES POSITION
(All information treated confidentially)

Date_____

Name_____   Home telephone number_____
(Please print plainly)

Present address_____   How long have you lived there?_____
No.   Street   City   State

Previous address_____   How long did you live there?_____
No.   Street   City   State

Business address_____   Business telephone number_____
No.   Street   City   State

Sex: ☐ M, ☐ F; Date of birth_____19_____   ☐ Married; Date_____19___   No. children____ Their ages____

Height_____ft._____in. Weight_____lbs.   ☐ Single, ☐ Engaged, ☐ Separated, ☐ Widowed   No. other dependents____Ages____

Are you a citizen of the U. S.?   ☐ Yes,   ☐ No   ☐ Divorced; Date_____19___   Soc. Sec. No._____

Position applied for_____ Earnings expected $_____

Why are you applying to this Company?_____

Who referred you to this Company?_____

Have you ever applied to, or been
employed by, this Company?_____ If so, when?_____ Where?_____

Names of relatives employed by this Company_____

	EDUCATION							
Type of School	Name of School	Courses Majored In	Check Last Year Completed				Graduate? Degrees Received	Last Year Attended
Elementary			5	6	7	8	☐ Yes, ☐ No	19
High School			1	2	3	4	☐ Yes, ☐ No	19
College			1	2	3	4		19
College			1	2	3	4		19
Graduate School			1	2	3	4		19
Business or Trade School			1	2	3	4		19
Corresp. or Night School			1	2	3	4		19

	JOBS WHILE IN SCHOOL				
	Name of Employer	Your Job	Your Salary	Dates	Hours Per Week
				From To	
1.					
2.					
3.					

Scholastic standing in H. S._____ In College_____

EXTRACURRICULAR ACTIVITIES (athletics, clubs, etc.)
(Do not include military, racial, religious, or nationality groups)

In high school_____   In college_____

Offices held_____   Offices held_____

Principal source of your spending money while in H. S. and College_____

Part of College expenses you earned: ☐ None, ☐ 0-25%, ☐ 25-50%, ☐ 50-75%, ☐ More than 75%_____

What languages other than English do you speak?_____

Figure 4-5. Part of an Applicant for Sales Position.

(McMurry-Hamstra and Co., Sales Personnel Forms, Chicago: The Dartnell Corp., 1950.)

another and from job to job. Special requirements should dictate the specific form of the blank. Not only do application blanks serve as sources of preliminary information, but also they aid in the interview by opening up areas of interest and discussion.

The soundness of using personal history items from an application blank is unquestioned, provided that they are the proper items. With individuals as with nations, "we can only judge the future by the past." The most certain predictor of job success is a person's demonstrated capacity to succeed on a very similar job.

In practice the use of the application blank usually falls far short of its promise. For one thing, some applicants exaggerate their capabilities. For another, the right questions are not always asked, and wrong or useless questions are substituted. The personnel man often does not know how to evaluate the information that is in front of him. To do these things properly requires a study of the particular situation.

The majority of items contained in application blanks can be answered by a short one- or two-word statement or a simple yes or no. An example of a careful application form appears in Figure 4-5.

Uses

SALESMEN

The most impressive use of application blanks, wherein the information was shown to be definitely predictive of success, has been with salesmen—especially life insurance and department store salesmen. In the Aetna Life Insurance Company, for example, several items of personal history were found to be useful for selecting agents.[14] College applicants were more successful if they had completed college and joined the company before they were 25 years of age. For applicants older than 30, dependents constituted a favorable item. Applicants in this age range who were married and had one or two dependents in addition to a wife succeeded more frequently than a single person, or than a man who was separated from his wife or divorced. Insurance agents who had the highest scores on such personal data items and on the Strong Vocational Interest Test sold almost twice as much life insurance in a year as agents who had the lowest scores on the personal data and interest test.

BAUSCH AND LOMB

Certain personal history items were found to be associated with turnover at the Bausch and Lomb Optical Company.[15] Men who stayed longer on the job were over 30 years of age, had more than one dependent, had completed less than ten years of school, and were married.

SCHOLARSHIP

Scholarship is frequently associated with executive success. There was a tendency for the men with the highest scholarship in college to make the highest salaries with the Bell Telephone System.[16] This tendency is shown in Table 4-III. The high-scholarship men showed a continually increasing salary advantage throughout the years.

"Thirty years after graduation the median salary of the men in the first tenth of their college classes is 155 per cent [of the class median], that of the men in the lowest third of their classes is 79 per cent of this median." Successful executives in the Bell Telephone System, in addition to high scholarship, had "campus achievement, early graduation, and immediate employment in the Bell System."[17] College scholarship was the most important of these items for success in the business.

School achievement was associated with the success of 150 executives employed by a number of companies, as illustrated in Table 4-IV. This group was made up of three salary classifications: top group, averaging $80,000 per year; middle group, averaging $12,000; and lower group, about $4,000. Scholarship and a college education set apart the two upper groups from the lower one. There is little difference in scholarship and college graduation between the two top earnings groups. College education and high scholarship take the place of an intelligence test and a test of motivation, and intelligence and motivation probably exceed the value of the information obtained in college.

TABLE 4-III

College Scholarship Compared with Salaries after Five Years Following Graduation

COLLEGE SCHOLARSHIP RANK	LOWEST THIRD SALARY GROUP	MIDDLE THIRD SALARY GROUP	HIGHEST THIRD SALARY GROUP
Highest third	25%	27%	48%
Middle third	37	39	24
Lowest third	47	31	22

Adapted from Gifford, Walter, "Does Business Want Scholars?" *Harper's Magazine,* May, 1928, p. 672.

TABLE 4-IV

Executive Level Compared with
School Achievement

EXECUTIVE LEVEL	STOPPED WITH GRADES	STOPPED WITH HIGH SCHOOL	WENT TO COLLEGE	UPPER THIRD OF CLASS
Top third	10%	18%	72%	68%
Middle third	8	16	76	66
Lowest third	32	48	20	32

Starch, Daniel, *How To Develop Your Executive Ability,* 2nd ed., New York: Harper & Brothers, 1943, pp. 22–3.

PHYSIQUE

Executives have been found to be taller and heavier than nonexecutives.[18] Contrary to some opinion, business leaders are usually college graduates and have not often benefited by "family pull" in the business.[19] The leaders of management come from the homes of professional people, managers, and business people.[20]

Weighted blank

On the basis of the principle that certain data of an applicant's personal history are indicative of future job success, a weighted application blank is sometimes used. The major uses have been with insurance and department stores salesmen mentioned above. For instance, if being under 28 years old is an advantage, it is weighted high; if a handicap, it is weighted low. If a college education is unnecessary, it is given a low weight value; if college graduates are successful in the particular work, such education is given a relatively high weight. Although no application blank can be successfully weighted for jobs in general, weighted application blanks for particular jobs have been found highly promising.[21]

SUMMARY

Personality traits are customarily evaluated in industry by casual methods of observation, and their accuracy is often unchecked. Such observations are made in daily contacts on the job and in selection interviews.

The ordinary selection interview and appraisal from an application blank have a very high margin of error. It is possible to improve the accuracy of the selection interview by careful planning, training of the interviewer, and skillful execution. The results of the interview should be closely geared to the findings from an application blank, each supplementing the other. A check of former employers should be made by conversation and not by letter.

Selection and placement can be improved by first defining the traits indicative of job success, and then deciding on the best method of evaluating them—test, interview, application blank, or other procedure. The method of appraisal should be carefully planned, and its execution ordinarily requires detailed training. Results of selection and placement procedures should be followed up from time to time to determine their effectiveness. Revisions in the procedures should be made if necessary. While the interview and application blank are the two most widely used tools for appraising an individual, the results obtained reflect a need for more effective research.

RECOMMENDED READING

Bellows, Roger M., and M. Frances Estep, *Employment Psychology: The Interview,* New York: Rinehart & Company, Inc., 1954. A relatively nontechnical presentation of the uses and limitations of the employment interview.

McMurry, Robert N., *Tested Techniques of Personnel Selection,* Chicago: The Dartnell Corporation, 1955. The use of the patterned interview, coupled with the application blank and other selection procedures, is explained.

5

Personnel tests

INTRODUCTION

INTRODUCTION

Psychologists have expended greater effort on personnel tests than on all other problems in industrial psychology combined. Their efforts have been devoted both to the development of psychological tests and to research on the application of tests to personnel within industry. The area is so vast, however—in excess of 60 millions currently employed, and with a constant inflow and outgo in the labor market—that only a small sample of jobs and employees has been explored, although the literature seems voluminous. In these chapters only illustrative studies are presented; it is not proposed to examine the entire range of available materials.

Value

There is some disagreement about the value of personnel tests. This is understandable in view of the diversity in jobs, the heterogeneity of the worker population, the possibilities for variation in administration and sometimes in scoring the tests, and in the statistical measures which may be used for reporting as well as interpreting results.

Use

Tests are used in industry by only a minority of companies. In 1953 only 24 per cent of reporting firms used tests for employment with hourly workers, and 39 per cent with salaried workers.[1] This, however, represents a substantial increase over earlier years, as shown in Figure 5-1.

As with the majority of systematic personnel procedures, the use of psychological tests is greater among the larger companies. Here the relationship between size of company and use of tests is closer than with the majority of procedures. Results of one study are shown in Table 5-I.

The trend is to shorter tests, because they allow more tests to be used in the same time, although such tests sustain some loss in reliability. Thus one interest inventory has forty-three items, compared with the 400 on the Strong Vocational Interest Blank. The Short Employment

Tests, a battery of three tests—verbal intelligence, numerical skill, and clerical speed and accuracy—take only five minutes each. One early study of these tests showed substantial correlation with job level of 177 clerical workers with an arithmetic test validity of .49 exceeded only slightly by the validity of the entire battery.[2] Correlation between merit ratings and test scores were less favorable: arithmetic .21, and clerical aptitude .23. It seems likely there will be increased emphasis on shorter tests as more organizations come to use tests, if only for the savings in time, manpower, and costs.

Status of intelligence tests

A group of psychologists were asked to give their opinion of the status of intelligence tests in industry.[3] A majority, specialists in the use of personnel tests, believed that intelligence tests met the practical need of classifying people better than this could be done without the use of tests. It was admitted by the majority that there is considerable error in comparing the test scores of people having a small amount of schooling with those who are better educated. Three false impressions on the part of the public were held to be common. The most widespread of these was an exaggerated belief in the accuracy of intelligence-test scores in predicting job success. There was also a mistaken belief that the intelligence test measures all aspects of ability. A third false impression led to extremes in the evaluation of the intelligence test—it was either wonderful or it was useless, when in fact it is somewhere in between. Despite the passage of more than ten years since this survey, it appears that only slow progress has been made in changing these ideas.

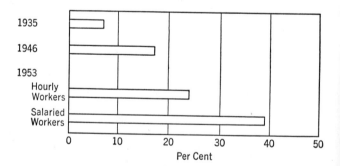

Figure 5-1. Per Cent of Firms Using Psychological Tests.

(Adapted from National Industrial Conference Board, Studies in Personnel Policy No. 86, *Personnel Activities in American Business* (Revised), New York, 1947, Table 36, p. 32, and No. 145, *Personnel Practices in Factory and Office* (5th ed.), New York, 1954, Table 12, p. 12, and Table 211, p. 69.)

TABLE 5-I

Use of Psychological Tests According to Size of Company

SIZE OF COMPANY (NUMBER OF EMPLOYEES)	PER CENT OF COMPANIES IN OWN SIZE GROUP WHO USE TESTS		
	1947	1953	
		FOR HOURLY WORKERS	FOR SALARIED WORKERS
Under 250	2.4	15.2	25.6
250–999	11.1	28.3	38.8
1000–4999	31.0	43.0	57.9
5000 and over	48.1	52.5	65.9
Not reported	13.2	—	—
TOTAL	16.8	31.8	43.1

Adapted from National Industrial Conference Board, Studies in Personnel Policy No. 86, *Personnel Activities in American Business* (Revised), New York, 1947, Table 32, p. 32, and No. 145, *Personnel Practices in Factory and Office* (5th ed.), New York, 1954, Table 12, p. 12, and Table 211, p. 69.

Views of labor unions

The attitude of organized labor toward psychological testing has not been widely expressed. Union reaction probably ranges from unenthusiastic acceptance to strong hostility. It seems only likely that psychologists and their work may be suspect, since they have almost always been paid by management. This was expressed in a labor newspaper editorial: "Workers don't know it yet, but only their unions are standing between them and a humiliating new kind of tyranny—'personality testing' by scientific charlatans who are getting rich by bamboozling big employers."[4] In one case union antagonism to testing was attributed to a belief that management used the tests as a shield for discriminating against union sympathizers.[5]

Views of employees

Workers themselves probably are generally favorable to employment testing, although many are opposed. Sixty-seven per cent of a group of employees thought that employment tests were to the advantage of both employer and employee, and slightly more than half the subjects placed after a testing program felt more secure in their jobs and were more satisfied because they had been placed after testing.[6] Nineteen per cent of this sample did not like taking employment tests, and 29 per cent stated that they would not apply if they knew they would have to take an employment test.

Steps in a test program

Care must be taken, however, in testing present employees, to explain the purposes of the program, and the policy that no one will have his job or prospects jeopardized because of test results should be stated and carried out. To the extent possible, testing should be optional with the employee. Good rapport is essential if realistic results are to be obtained, for many employees resist a new procedure and any process which they think may tend to reflect on their abilities and to expose them to further competition.

Individual test results should be confidential. Generalized results may be publicized, but anonymity should be safeguarded by the use of keyed or coded substitutes for names and other identifying data.

People are usually interested in knowing their own test scores and how they compare with others. It is generally advisable to inform an individual of his own results and of how he compares with the average. Secrecy is likely to lead to the suspicion that test results are being used for purposes of discrimination against individuals. Besides being of personal interest to the subject, knowing his test result and his areas of strength or weakness may be useful in his future decisions about jobs or tasks or training. Care must be taken to communicate the results to the subject in language that is nontechnical and meaningful to him.

A hard-and-fast rule cannot be made about giving individual scores of a supervisor's group to the supervisor. He should be given only generalized information about his men, with no possibility of his identifying the test results of individual members. Identified results should, except under most unusual circumstances, be given only with the subject's consent.

PURPOSES OF PERSONNEL TESTS IN INDUSTRY
Selection

The general purpose of personnel tests in industry is to improve the selection or placement of employees. Jobs require many traits in varying degrees, but for the sake of simplicity the present discussion will speak of attempts to measure a single trait. There is a rather general misconception that, when a psychologist first devises a test to measure a specific trait, it will measure that trait. That is a serious error, because at that stage it still remains to be seen whether the test in question actually measures what the test author intends. Unfortunately, from the standpoint of simplicity, there is a further complication. In one situation a test may measure what it purports to measure, but in a second situation which appears to be similar to the first the test will not be useful. To state a possible example, a test which in one situation may pick good airplane mechanics may prove to be of no value in another. The reasons for such an apparent paradox are several. Aside from faulty test administration, one prominent reason could be the quality of the prospective employees. Where the test worked, the prospects might have varied all the way from mechanical whizzes to men who were all thumbs and had no aptitude as mechanics—the range of talent might have been great. In contrast, in Company B, where the test did not show validity, the reason could be that all the prospects were so good that no test was needed—the range of talent was small.

EACH COMPANY MUST VALIDATE

Another situation in which the same mechanical-aptitude test might prove useful for picking airplane mechanics for Company C and useless for Company D would be one in which the jobs differed. The same job title is sometimes applied to jobs that actually require an entirely different pattern of abilities. Company C might be repairing conventional airplane engines, Company D might be repairing jet planes.

The situation at present is such that each company must test the test to be sure that it will be useful for its needs. Perhaps with greater knowledge of jobs and abilities some of this work will be reduced. Although the broad outlines of testing tests are fairly simple, the statistical methods are so complex and the possible errors and accidents are so numerous that it is necessary for a company establishing a sound personnel test program to use the services of a psychologist, either on a full-time or on a consulting basis. After the program has been installed, the services of the psychologist are not so essential, although some continual or periodic follow-up is necessary if changes have occurred in the labor market or in the occupational structure.

Other purposes

A valid testing program for selection and placement will bring a number of advantages to management. It will improve the matching of traits and job demands. Training expense will be decreased because the number who will fail to complete training will be reduced and the training time required by those selected will also be reduced. The incidence of failures on the job will be reduced. Some weaknesses can be spotted which can be corrected through training. Costs can be reduced for selection, placement, and training. Morale will be improved through the increased job satisfaction of correctly placed employees. Turnover will be reduced. Productivity can be raised.

Illustrations will not be given to support all these benefits, but, to show that they are of more than academic consideration, one case is presented. During World War II, from a battery of fifteen tests used at Army Ordnance schools five tests were selected to screen out personnel who would be allowed to drop the first four weeks of a twelve-week training course.[7] These "skipped" students achieved substantially higher final grades, on the average, than the typical students who took the twelve-week course—85.01 versus 80.97. Allowing these students to skip one-third of the course reduced training costs and returned the trainees to useful work more rapidly.

Testing drew better applicants in one company. After a testing program had been installed in this company (with three plants), applicants showed a substantial improvement in scores over old employees.[8] Four tests were used in two of the plants, and three tests in the third. In one plant the first group hired under testing had less favorable scores than old employees on two of four tests, and more favorable scores on two tests. Three months after the testing began, applicants showed superior scores over old employees and over the first applicants on three of the four tests. In another plant, applicants were superior to the criterion group, old employees, on all three tests used in that plant.

REDUCTION IN TURNOVER

In adopting a testing program a company would also be interested in ease of administration and scoring and in costs, both cost of the test itself and costs of administration, scoring, and interpretation of results. The costs of selection and training are often high. It was estimated in 1952 that training a bank clerk cost at least $500.[9] The average cost of training mechanics' helpers in a large food corporation was earlier estimated at $675, the major portion being due to substandard production by the trainee and the loss of productive time by the trainer.[10] It is obvious that a few dollars spent on testing may save many dollars by eliminating in advance the major portion of applicants most likely to be unsuccessful in training or employment.

TABLE 5-II

Retention and Reward of Clerical Employees
Compared to Test Scores

	SUBJECTS STUDIED		RETAINED BEYOND 90-DAY PERIOD	
GROUPS	NUMBER	PER CENT OF TOTAL	PER CENT RETAINED	PER CENT REWARDED
Applicants passing test	125	67	73	90
Applicants hired without passing test	62	33	27	10
TOTALS	187	100	100	100

Adapted from text and tables, Wallace, Thomas H., "Pre-Employment Tests and Post-Employment Performance," *Journal of Business,* 1955, **28,** 72–75.

EFFECTIVENESS WITH CLERICAL EMPLOYEES

Table 5-II gives some evidence for the effectiveness of tests in one situation. Four tests—Mechanical Comprehension, Personnel Classification, Minnesota Clerical, and a phonograph record stenographic test—were studied in connection with retention on the job and presence or absence of pay increases, either for merit or for promotion. Not certain that hiring cut-off scores were at an appropriate level, the company hired also the top one-third of applicants who did not reach the cut-off points. Those selected without reaching the cut-off score were less likely to be retained or to be rewarded.

HOW MANY TESTS?

There are hundreds of different psychological tests, but there are obviously fewer basic separate abilities and other personality traits. Determination of the basic personality traits is a fundamental psychological problem that is of considerable importance to industrial psychology. It is most apparent in vocational selection, but it also cuts across other personnel policies. In vocational selection, for example, there are thousands of separate occupations. One way of trying to develop precise selection tests would be to make up a separate test or series of tests for each of these thousands of occupations. This enormous job has not proved practical, and it is not necessary because there is considerable overlap in the ability requirements for various jobs. Workers in metal structures require some of the same abilities as workers in wooden structures. The technical problem is to find the least common denominator of personality traits, by factor analysis, which was introduced in Chapter 3.

Where tests are used for selection or placement, it has usually been found desirable to give several tests, called a "battery," rather than a single test. The validity for the battery is generally higher than that for a single test because the battery can measure more of the pertinent factors of a job. The goal in making up a battery of tests is to select tests which correlate as high as possible with the criterion and as low as possible with each other so that each test's contribution is unique to the greatest extent possible.

VALIDITY

The most important characteristic of a test is whether it measures what it is supposed to measure—whether it is valid. Another consideration, although of less interest to, and less studied by, industry, is reliability, the extent to which the test will give the testee approximately the same score or the same relative ranking on retaking the test under the same conditions. Reliability is consistency in results. Without reliability, dependence cannot be placed on a test, for a measure taken today would give quite different results if the subject had taken the test yesterday or should take it a week hence.

Coefficient

Tests customarily are spoken of as having a validity or reliability coefficient or both which is expressed by the coefficient of correlation, which was explained in Chapter 3. The criterion is some measure of performance on the job or of training success. A validity coefficient, at most, can be no higher than the reliability criterion to which the predictor is related. If the criterion were a perfect measure of job success and the test were perfectly correlated to the criterion, the job and test would be perfectly related. Generally the highest correlation achieved in test validity is about .60, and the lowest limit used for inclusion of a test is .25 to .30, depending on the uniqueness of the characteristic measured and the significance of the data as determined by the size of the sample.[11] A validity of .25 on 500 cases is more significant than one of .45 on 15 cases.

Reliability coefficients generally are .85 or higher when a test has been well prepared.

Precise prediction is desirable but not generally necessary. It is usually sufficient to be able to place a person within a broad range, say in the top third of applicants, rather than in the top 1 per cent. A test of moderate validity thus can distinguish between the highly eligible and the clearly ineligible, leaving an intermediate group of candidates in which the state of the labor market will dictate whether or not the candidate will be selected.

A TEST OF STENOGRAPHERS

In one administration of part of the Short Employment Test (SET) to seventy-four stenographers, the relationship between test scores and proficiency was investigated.[12] Chance—that is, if the test score had no relationship to job performance, if the validity were 0—would place one-third of the low-proficiency stenographers in each of the thirds into which test scores were divided. Chance results would similarly place one-third of the stenographers who were average in proficiency, and one-third of those highly proficient in each of the thirds into which test scores were divided. Actual results, as given in Table 5-III, show that by eliminating the lowest third on test scores the company would eliminate 53 per cent of the low-proficiency stenographers, but it would also

TABLE 5-III

Per Cent of Stenographers in Each Third on SET-Clerical Who Earned Various Proficiency Ratings

SET-CLERICAL TEST SCORE	PROFICIENCY RATING		
	LOW	AVERAGE	HIGH
Upper third	18	33	50
Middle third	29	36	28
Lowest third	53	31	22
TOTAL PER CENT	100	100	100
No. of Stenographers	17	39	18

"Better than Chance," *Test Service Bulletin* No. 45, New York: The Psychological Corporation, May, 1953, Table II, p. 3.

TABLE 5-IV

Expected Job Success from Test Score, Test Validity, and Percentage of Success for That Job

TEST SCORES BY		PERCENTAGE OF EMPLOYEES CONSIDERED SUCCESSFUL							
		80%				70%			
PERCEN-		VALIDITY OF TEST				VALIDITY OF TEST			
TILE	DECILE	$r=.30$	$r=.40$	$r=.50$	$r=.60$	$r=.30$	$r=.40$	$r=.50$	$r=.60$
90–99th	10	92%	95%	97%	99%	86%	91%	94%	97%
80–89th	9	89	91	94	97	81	85	89	92
....	....	....	....	....	....	....	....	....	....
1– 9th	1	63	56	49	40	50	43	35	27

Extracted from "Better than Chance," *Test Service Bulletin* No. 45, New York: The Psychological Corporation, May, 1953.

lose 22 per cent of its high-proficiency stenographers. This is a demonstration of what happens with a test of average validity, .38. If these data held true for new hires, there would be a question whether the loss of 53 per cent of low-proficiency stenographers would be outweighed by the loss of 22 per cent of high-proficiency stenographers.

Steps

In validating personnel tests these steps are employed:

1. Use job description as discussed in Chapter 2 to find the aptitudes that appear to be important in job success.
2. Obtain a measure of success on the job, as presented in Chapter 3.
3. Choose tests for trial on the basis of likely qualifications, as shown in Step 1.
4. Administer tests chosen to employees whose records of job success are available.
5. Determine those tests which actually distinguish between successful and unsuccessful employees. Try these tests on new employees without using the results in the hiring decision. Since experience on the job may have affected the scores of old employees, it is necessary to check the tests with new employees.
6. Follow up test results by comparing the job success of new employees with their test scores. The extent to which job success for new employees is predicted by test scores is a measure of validity.

Expectancy tables

To give greater meaning to test scores for the average businessman, tables have been developed to show the percentage that will be successful if only those applicants who attain certain minimum scores are hired. Tables have been developed which show the proportion expected to be satisfactory among applicants selected, based on percentage of present employees successful, the validity coefficient of a test, and the applicant's standing on a test.[13] Table 5-IV shows a part of these expectancies. Coefficient of correlation is designated by the symbol r. Where 8 out of 10 people succeed on a job and a test correlates .30 with the criterion of job success, 92 per cent of people scoring in the tenth decile would be successful. Similarly, where 7 out of 10 people succeed on a job and a test correlates .50 with the criterion of job success, 89 per cent of people scoring in the ninth decile and 94 per cent of those scoring in the tenth decile would be expected to be successful. Where the cutting score would be set would depend on the selection ratio, or the percentage of applicants who must be hired.

Graphs which serve a similar purpose may also be made. Figure 5-2 shows such a graph for a clerical test. If a test score of 23 were used for

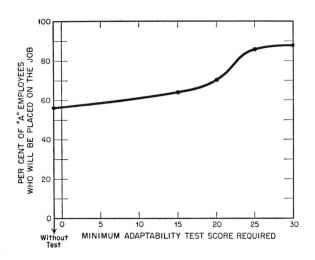

Figure 5-2. Employees Who Would Have Been Rated "A" with Different Test Scores.

(Tiffin, Joseph, and C. H. Lawshe, Jr., "The Adaptability Test: A Fifteen Minute Mental Alertness Test for Use in Personnel Allocation," *Journal of Applied Psychology*, 1943, **27**, 152–163.)

selection, at least 80 per cent of industrial clerical employees would be good. Without test selection less than 60 per cent of these employees were rated as good.[14]

Average validities

In a survey of research since 1919, Ghiselli computed averages from validities reported for aptitude tests in studies of many different jobs.[15] The mean validity correlations between aptitude test and proficiency was only .16. The mean validity correlation between aptitude test and training records was .27. There was a wide range of results depending on the study, the job, and the test. Proficiency and training criteria differed. One can select people to succeed in training who may not perform best on the job. Validities of .50 and more are shown in Tables 5-V and 5-VI where at least 100 cases had been studied. These tables show that occasionally some measure shows validity when there is little or no apparent connection between the test and the job, such as the correlation of Cancellation tests with proficiency ratings for Rubber Goods Workers. The explanation may be a general factor of intellectual ability. This explana-

TABLE 5-V

Average Validity Coefficients of .50 or More with Proficiency Criteria

(*N* = 100 or more)

r	JOB	TEST
.66	Bench Work, Assorted Materials	Mechanical principles
.56	Builders of Aircraft, Skilled Workers	Intelligence
.56	Welders and Flame Cutters, Skilled Workers	Spatial relations
.53	Statistical Clerks and Compilers	Arithmetic
.51	Mechanics and Repairmen, Semiskilled Workers	Intelligence
.51	Rubber Goods, Semiskilled Workers	Cancellation
.50	Retail Manager	Intelligence
.50	Inspecting and Testing	Intelligence

Selected from Ghiselli, Edwin E., "The Measurement of Occupational Aptitude," *University of California Publications in Psychology*, 1955, **8**, No. 2, 165–211.

TABLE 5-VI

Average Validity Coefficients of .50 or More with Training Criteria

(N = 100 or more)

r	JOB	TEST
.61	General Recording Work	Arithmetic
.59	Stenographers and Typists	Cancellation
.57	Manufacture of Radios and Phonographs, Semiskilled Workers	Finger dexterity
.54	Manufacture of Radios and Phonographs, Semiskilled Workers	Arm dexterity
.50	Manufacture of Radios and Phonographs, Semiskilled Workers	Hand dexterity
.50	Electricians, Skilled	Intelligence

Selected from Ghiselli, Edwin E., "The Measurement of Occupational Aptitude," *University of California Publications in Psychology,* 1955, **8,** No. 2, 168–198.

tion is strengthened by the prominence of intelligence tests for predicting proficiency criteria for both factory and office jobs.

OCCUPATIONAL ABILITY PATTERNS

Several attempts are being made to include in one integrated series of tests all the abilities which are necessary to job success. One example is the General Aptitude test battery of the United States Employment Service which measures ten aptitudes or abilities: intelligence, verbal, numerical, spatial, form perception, clerical perception, aiming, motor speed, finger dexterity, and manual dexterity.[16] There are fifteen tests, eleven of which are pencil-and-paper. All fifteen tests take just over two hours to administer. Norms are based on scores made by successful members of an occupational group as compared with the average scores of people in all occupations studied. Norms are further set in such a way that recommended critical scores would eliminate the lowest third of employees. General mechanical repairmen and men who do machining of metal have been found to have the same pattern of abilities. Employees in both of these job families, each of which includes a number of occupations, were found to be just average on intelligence, numerical ability, and spatial ability, and a little below average on finger dexterity. The job families of structural workers in heavy metal and wood and of plumbing require only three of the ten abilities and finger dexterity. Approximately 2000 occupations have been studied and classified in this way; they have been reduced to twenty job families, for which desirable ability profiles have been determined. The battery is used in placement of workers by matching up the individual profile with the requirements of the job.

For 134 clerical workers the tests from the General Aptitude test battery measuring intelligence, verbal, numerical, and clerical perception correlated .56 with the rank-order ratings of supervisors on quality and quantity of work and over-all proficiency. The correlation between average piece-rate earnings over a two-week period of ninety-one mounters of filaments for electric lamps correlated .45 with a combination of scores for form perception, aiming, and finger and manual dexterity.[17]

SELECTION

The uses of tests are varied, as shown in Table 5-VII, although essentially they are three: selection, promotion, and, to a considerably lesser extent, counseling. Only about one-third of the companies reporting in this study had a testing program.

Selection is the choosing of an applicant for employment. Placement, or assignment, is the fitting of the selected person into a job consistent with his traits and, ideally, into one which demands of him the use of his highest potential. Counseling consists in advising an employee or, preferably in most cases, in listening to his stating his problem and enabling him to find from his own thinking and talking a solution for that problem which is satisfactory to himself.

Employment or selection tests are used mainly to determine which workers can perform fastest or most accurately and would be likely to contribute most to the production of the plant if they were hired. Tests are used to select those persons who are most likely to stay on the job. Still another use is to avoid hiring trouble makers or psychoneurotics. This chapter and the next are concerned primarly with tests in relation to job performance. Tests for other uses will be referred to in other chapters.

Psychological testing varies from one short standardized test of mental ability taking about twenty minutes through a wide range of stand-

TABLE 5-VII

How Companies Use Tests

USES	FOR HOURLY WORKERS		FOR SALARIED WORKERS	
	PER CENT OF ALL FIRMS	PER CENT OF USING FIRMS	PER CENT OF ALL FIRMS	PER CENT OF USING FIRMS
Total companies using tests	31.8	100.0	43.1	100.0
At time of employment	23.7	74.4	39.3	91.2
When considering individual for promotion	21.7	68.3	22.4	51.9
In connection with employee counseling	8.9	28.0	10.4	24.1
When filling certain positions	.8	2.4	—	—
When selecting apprentice candidates	.6	1.8	—	—
In making transfers	.6	1.8	1.4	3.2
In placing trainees	.4	1.2	.2	.5
In training and reassignment	.4	1.2	.4	.9
In measuring results of training programs	.2	.6	—	—
In organizational planning	.2	.6	—	—
In analyzing absenteeism, accidents, etc.	.2	.6	—	—
In connection with research to evaluate tests	—	—	.2	.5

Adapted from National Industrial Conference Board, Studies in Personnel Policy No. 145, *Personnel Practices in Factory and Office* (5th ed.), New York: 1954, Table 12, p. 12, and Table 211, p. 69.

ardized and specially developed tests taking hours to administer. The aim is to reveal something about the individual's mental attributes, his preparation or potential for some particular job or jobs, and his personality and interests. Types of tests used, as revealed by one study, are

111

TABLE 5-VIII

Types and Use of Tests

TYPE OF TEST	PER CENT OF ALL COMPANIES REPORTING USE	PER CENT OF USING COMPANIES REPORTING USE
Stenographic or clerical	73	98
Mental (intelligence)	56	75
Mechanical aptitude	40	54
Personality or interest	40	53
Performance	33	45
Trade	30	40
Dexterity	28	38

Adapted from Spriegel, William R., and Alfred G. Dale, Personnel Study No. 8, *Personnel Practices in Industry,* Austin: University of Texas, 1954, pp. 20, 55.

shown in Table 5-VIII. These data are not from the same source as those of Table 5-VII and so will not agree as to percentage of companies using tests. The sample of companies in Table 5-VIII is less representative than that in Table 5-VII. The relative popularity of various types of tests is probably adequately shown in Table 5-VIII, in spite of the over-all figures being too high.

PLACEMENT

At the time of employment, selection and placement are often coordinate and inseparable parts of a single process. As a rule, a small company has only one or a few vacancies at any one time, and consequently it must consolidate selection and placement. The successful applicant will be selected for a specific place.

In large companies, where there are a number of employment possibilities, selection and placement may become distinct processes, perhaps even handled by different groups of people within the personnel department. The selection personnel may have only background interest in placement. Their main task may be to choose persons to whom limited offers of employment are to be made, who will undergo a program of training, and who, if successful in their training, will then receive a more enduring employment offer. The actual placement decision may be deferred until the new employee has nearly finished his training, when his position will depend on the personnel needs of the company at that particular time and on how he has met the required standards for the jobs which are open. The training period may even be of indefinite length, the training group serving as a pool of labor to be drawn upon as needed. Selection for an actual job, as a separate process from placement, may be made by the personnel department, but rarely does this department do more than make a tentative selection, the selection to be confirmed or denied by the operating department.

Psychological testing, then, ordinarily does not so much say "Hire this man" as it says "Here are men satisfactory for the job; take your pick." It curtails and at the same time eases the operating management's job by eliminating those who, by testing, are predicted to be the least favorable risks. The increase of work for the personnel department and the decrease in work for the operating department is well illustrated by an example from the military service.[18] During the war the Air Force, before screening by tests, put 397 men into training in order to be able to graduate 100 pilots. With testing and a cut-off in the medium ranges, only 202 had to be put into training, but it was necessary to test 553 to get the 202. As the cut-off was raised, it was necessary to test approximately 1000 men in order to get 156 from among whom the 100 could be graduated.

PROMOTION

Promotion is one of the most important placement problems, because it often involves advancement to a supervisory position. The first promotion from the ranks to supervision is critical, not only to the plant but also to the individual. A man's usefulness to his company may be destroyed if it becomes necessary later to release him from a supervisory position. The supervisor exerts an important influence on the men working with him, and thus on the welfare of the company itself.

As most management personnel are promoted from within, a continually expanding body of fact and opinion has been accumulated on the individual to aid in the more informed selection of management personnel. Something is known of the candidate's abilities and personality through his performance. Early test results may be available; additional tests may be administered. The exact nature of supervisory and executive success has not been sufficiently well identified to permit the development of valid tests.

The selection for the first position in supervision is almost as "blind" as that for the first position with the company, even when the choice is made from within the company. The qualities demanded of a foreman are different from those demanded of a rank-and-file worker, even if he is to supervise the same machines which he formerly operated. Indeed, it frequently happens that a man who is successful in a production job does not do well when he is promoted. Higher management, similarly, may demand other skills than those needed by a good foreman, so that the problem continues through all management levels.

As a rule, in the interest of company morale and loyalty, it is wise to promote from within rather than to go outside the organization to fill supervisory and executive positions, although this may not always be possible. One survey found that 25 per cent of the companies selected foremen only from the ranks, and there were only 9 per cent that selected less than 75 per cent of foremen from the ranks.[19] Table 5-VII suggests the importance of testing in promotion.

In its program of testing for promotion to supervisory positions, the Standard Oil Company of New Jersey, at its Baton Rouge Refinery, studied seven measures—Otis Test of Mental Ability, Bennett Test of Mechanical Comprehension, RBH Shop Arithmetic Test, Bernreuter Personality Inventory, Kuder Preference Record, RBH Supervisory Judgment Test, and RBH Individual Background Survey, a list of personal characteristics.[20] The Background Survey, the Supervisory Judgment Test, and four of the nine parts of the Kuder—mechanical, computational, scientific, and social service—were found useful, with an over-all correlation of .62 with a consensus of opinion rankings. Of 104 supervisors appointed through 1953 with the aid of the tests, 13 had been rated for three years, 77 per cent of whom rated above the average for all supervisors; 82 had been rated for their second year, with 80 per cent rated above average; and all for the first year, with 92 per cent rated above average.[21]

KINDS OF PERSONNEL TESTS

Personnel tests used in industry may be divided into six kinds: intelligence or mental ability, clerical ability, mechanical ability, personality, interest, and achievement. Intelligence or mental ability tests measure the ability to learn. Their purpose is to measure native intelligence, although it is generally not completely achieved since the test score typically is contaminated by education or other experience. There is a division of opinion about the relative contribution of heredity and childhood environment to intelligence test scores. There is agreement that when people reach adult age their ability to learn has become stable.

The nature-nurture controversy is therefore unimportant for the appraisal of adults, since their intelligence level has become set, whatever the source of intelligence.

Clerical ability

Clerical ability tests measure aptitude to do relatively simple paper work. They measure the speed and accuracy with which one can perceive differences in numbers and names. This is related to tasks of filing and checking accounts. Some clerical ability tests measure other factors which are also measured by intelligence tests, namely, verbal comprehension and mathematical reasoning. Whether both an intelligence test and a clerical ability test would be needed would therefore depend on the complexity of the latter and on the job under study.

Mechanical ability

Mechanical ability tests measure the ability to trouble-shoot and hence to repair faulty machines. They do not ordinarily measure manual dexterity, which is independent of mechanical ability, but incidentally can be measured by separate tests. The main ability factor measured is one of spatial relations. This is the ability to visualize the way parts of a machine could be put together or taken apart without actually performing the operations of assembly or disassembly.

Personality

Personality tests attempt to measure the nonintellectual traits. There is less evidence for the validity of personality tests in industry than for the other four types of tests. There is wide agreement that the nonintellectual aspects of personality are most important for failure at work and also important for the success of managers. It is doubtful that valid personality tests have been developed which can be administered by persons without thorough psychological training. The evidence is not convincing that even the most complex personality tests have been proved valid for solving industrial problems. Still it will be worth while to look at the evidence.

Interest

Interest tests measure one's interests, either in terms of their similarity to those of successful persons in each of a number of occupations or in *a priori* terms. In the latter type of test, interests are measured for clusters of work tasks, such as one's interests in computational activities. There is a similarity between some questions on interest tests and those on personality tests. The connection between interests and personality may be

115

profound. One theory of interests would trace their origin to personality. For some reason there has been much greater proof in industry of the usefulness of interest tests, especially Strong's Vocational Interest Test, than of personality tests.

Trade

An achievement test may be a test of specific performance; for example, a stenographer may have to transcribe dictation she has taken, or the experienced operator may be tested on the knowledge he should possess, as in the sets of questions prepared by the United States Employment Service for oral administration and answer by persons applying for job placement services. Impromptu and informal proficiency tests are undoubtedly one of the oldest aids to the employment process. To some extent the trial period in a job is essentially a prolonged proficiency test.

EFFECT OF FAKING

Results on many personality and interest inventories may be slanted by the discerning subject. The testee can imagine the desirable personality for the position for which he is applying and answer to fit his concept of the role. Most studies of faking have been made in the laboratory rather than in industry, the subjects imagining themselves in two different situations. In one such study a group of people who had not received previous course instruction on personality and interest inventories imagined themselves as applying first for sales work and subsequently for library work.[22] All but three "salesmen" scored above average on self-confidence, while "librarians" were almost as much below average as "salesmen" were above. The lowest 5 per cent in the "sales" scoring had more self-confidence than applicants at the fiftieth percentile of the "librarians."

An English study was able to compare groups in a work situation.[23] The inventory was given to some subjects as a step in the application process, and to others as a part of a research study immediately after they had been hired. A test for sociability showed no significant difference between the two groups, but on a test for emotional maladjustment the applicant group scored "markedly and consistently lower" than the hired group. Under research conditions 12 per cent of the subjects had scores at the "probably maladjusted" level, while only $1\frac{1}{2}$ per cent of the applicant group attained such scores. From this it appeared that "adjustment inventories and psychosomatic questionnaires are responded to differently when in a real life situation there is some incentive not to admit personality defects."

EFFECT OF PRACTICE

Practice in taking a personnel test usually raises one's score slightly. Practice in taking a mental-alertness test of the Life Office Management Association raised scores on an average of twelve points from 114 to 126. Where it is known that a person has previously taken such a test, the practice gain can be compensated for by raising the passing score for such persons.[24]

Scores on the Placing test of the Minnesota Rate of Manipulation test for manual aptitude improved with practice.[25] Nine subjects had three practice trials for ten days and every subject improved. All subjects at the end of the ten days were at the ninety-ninth percentile. On the first trial the slowest subject's score was at the sixty-fourth percentile.

The practice effect over relatively short periods of time was measured on scores on the Minnesota Vocational Test for Clerical Workers.[26] More than 90 per cent of the subjects on their third trial reached or exceeded the mean score attained on the first trial. Women averaged higher scores than men on all three trials. This test is also reported to have a normal practice effect of 7 to 12 per cent after three- to six-month intervals.

EFFECT OF TRAINING ON TEST SCORES

Although several studies have shown the effect of practice on personnel-test scores, there have been fewer studies of the effect on the scores of training in activities related to the test. The questions on one particular type of mechanical-aptitude test, Surface Development, looked so similar to the work done in mechanical drafting that Air Forces officials were suspicious that it would reflect only training and not aptitude. The extent to which Surface Development is influenced by training in mechanical drafting and blueprint reading has been studied in two different training situations. One hundred airplane mechanics who had had six weeks' training in mechanical courses, including forty hours of mechanical drafting and blueprint reading, were given the Surface Development Test. Their test scores were compared with a similar group of one hundred enlisted men, also selected as prospective airplane mechanics, who had not yet had this training.[27] The two groups were matched for ability on the basis of a mental-alertness test. The group trained in mechanical drafting had only a slightly higher score on the Surface Development Test, 0.5 point, which could well have been due to chance.

A second study showed that a greater amount of training in mechanical drafting would improve scores on the Surface Development Test appreciably. A class of Engineer enlisted men who took a nine-week drafting course which included four hundred hours of training in drafting was tested before and after on the Surface Development Test. Here the test scores increased by 21 points after training. This gain cannot be compared directly with the gain of 0.5 point in the airplane mechanics study because a longer test form was used with the Engineer group. Part of this difference of 21 points was due to practice in taking the test, for a control group which took no training in drafting showed a gain of 12 points when it took the test before and after a course in Water Purification in which there was no training similar to the abilities required by the Surface Development Test. After the 12 points due to practice on the test had been allowed for, 9 points remained which could be attributed to training in drafting. This amount is so significant that it could not be attributed to chance.[28]

From these two studies in combination it may be concluded that this test of mechanical aptitude is not impervious to the effect of training, but neither is it very sensitive to it. No doubt the effects of training would vary with the type of training and with the type of test. The influence of training and practice would have to be determined specifically for each general type of test and for each training and practice situation before the exact influences could be known. The above results, however, indicate the trends that might be expected.

Experience in clerical work of at least a year raises the scores on the Minnesota test for clerical workers by 8 points.[29] The mean score of the inexperienced group is approximately 120, that of the experienced group approximately 128. The difference between the experienced and inexperienced clerks is not due to intelligence or to age; it appears to be due only to experience. The difference is approximately the same for each of the two parts of the test, number checking and name checking.

SUMMARY

The selection of the right people for jobs can often increase productivity, decrease turnover, and bring other advantages. The importance of selection has naturally led to a great interest in personnel tests. Tests have frequently failed to bring the spectacular results that were expected of them, and consequently in many instances they have been violently rejected.

Personnel tests can be useful in many situations if handled carefully. There are so many possible pitfalls that this is the place for a professional and not an amateur. Any company which attempts to use personnel tests needs a psychologist to work with its personnel manager and line management.

A substantial amount of research that is time-consuming and expensive is still required in most instances for a company to find out whether tests are desirable and, if so, which ones should be used. Although expensive, the tests often more than repay the research costs if found valid.

To find out whether personnel tests will benefit a company requires that for each job under consideration there be a reliable criterion of success on the job. This is often not available, but it is an important by-product to develop, whether or not testing proves desirable.

It is necessary to have a job description, which will yield realistic hiring specifications so that trial tests can be selected from among the hundreds of tests on the market. In some instances it will be found desirable to construct new tests.

Before test results are used as the basis for hiring an employee, the test should be proved with a group of old employees and separately with a group of new hires. There is no advantage in using the test; in fact there is a loss, unless significant correlations are obtained in both instances with the criterion of success on the job. The loss is the rejection of qualified applicants on the basis of invalid test scores.

Detailed results of some successes and a few failures in the tryout of tests are given in the next chapter.

RECOMMENDED READINGS

Dorcus, Roy M., and Margaret Hubbard Jones, *Handbook of Employee Selection,* New York: McGraw-Hill Book Company, Inc., 1950. An extremely thorough presentation of all reports to date on the results of scientific selection attempts. Although all selection procedures are reported, the bulk of the evidence pertains to tests.

Jones, Margaret Hubbard, "The Adequacy of Employee Selection Reports," *Journal of Applied Psychology,* 1950, **34**, 219-224. A criticism of the adequacy of employee selection reports and a list of desirable standards to use in making such reports.

Lawshe, Charles H., Jr., *Principles of Personnel Testing,* New York: McGraw-Hill Book Company, Inc., 1948. A clear presentation of the steps necessary in adopting a testing program.

6

Personnel tests (concluded)

It was pointed out in the preceding chapter that personnel tests might be classified as tests of mental ability, mechanical ability, clerical ability, personality, and interest. This chapter will discuss tests under these headings and a few other tests that do not fall into these categories.

History

Mental ability was the first area of scientific study in the field of psychological testing. The Binet-Simon Scale, published in 1908, was the first mental-age scale of general intelligence. It was adapted in 1916 in English as the Stanford Revision of the Binet-Simon Scale, and was subsequently revised in 1937. The Stanford-Binet tests may be administered to only one person at a time and they have been used more for children than adults, and consequently have had little utility for industry. Group intelligence tests in industry were developed from the intelligence tests that were used first in schools and next in the Army.

Extensive research has been devoted to mental abilities and to tests of mental ability, in education, in the military services, and in industry. The greatest amount of data for adults from a single test are those on the Army General Classification Test (AGCT), a test of "general learning ability," administered during World War II to nearly ten million Army personnel. The test subsequently was made available for civilian use. The Army also used mental tests in World War I, primarily the Army Alpha. Tests of other components of the Armed Services are less well known. All have used tests of special abilities as well as of mental ability. Many types of questions are used to measure the several factors of which mental ability is comprised. Some of the most frequently used items are analogies, arithmetic reasoning, inference, nonverbal reasoning, problem solving, reading comprehension, and vocabulary meaning.

Correlations with job success

High scores on intelligence tests are associated with success in occupations which require an extensive background of academic study and in occupations dealing with intangibles and abstractions, such as accounting, medicine, engineering, and law. Occupations requiring little or no academic education, such as lumberjack, miner, common laborer, farmer, are often most successfully filled by persons who attain relatively low scores on tests of mental ability. This does not imply, of course, that all laborers, for instance, attain low scores; often high mental abilities are found in such groups. Circumstances or choice may have prevented an individual with high mental ability from continuing his education and from qualifying for an occupation requiring higher mental scores.

Intelligence test validity coefficients for predicting training success have averaged about .35 for clerical occupations and for apprentices in trades and crafts, and they have been substantial for service and protective workers, but of little value for persons engaged in manipulative and observational occupations.[1] The value of an intelligence test for predicting training success depends to some degree on the extent to which the training content requires reading and writing.

Intelligence tests have been of value in predicting production of general clerks, salesmen, electrical workmen, and inspectors. There are fairly good validities for foremen, assemblers, complex-machine operators, gross manual workers, processing workers, protective workers, and recording clerks. They have been of little value for selecting computing clerks or salesclerks, machine tenders, mechanical repairmen, packers and wrappers, service workers, structural workers, or vehicle operators.

SUPERVISORS

Intelligence has been found to be moderately important in a few supervisory jobs. An intelligence test, the Otis Quick Scoring Test of Mental Ability, correlated .42 with ratings among supervisors in several aviation plants.[2] With a group of cotton mill supervisors the coefficient of correlation was .37 between I.Q. on the Otis Self-Administering Examination and ratings (see Figure 6-1).[3] Ratings of 3 were the minimum for satisfactory supervisors. Though Figure 6-1 shows that no supervisor was unsatisfactory who had an I.Q. over 100, it would not be economic to cut off selection at 100, for nineteen satisfactory supervisors would be lost in order to eliminate eight unsatisfactory ones. Ninety would be a better cutting score, since by its use only five clearly satisfactory supervisors would be lost plus eight borderline ones in order to eliminate six who were unsatisfactory.

At the Procter and Gamble Company supervisory ratings correlated

.71 with a tailor-made test composed of intelligence, information, interest, and mechanical-aptitude questions.[4] A large part of the greater validity of this Procter and Gamble test was due to the care with which the questions were selected. An analysis was made of each of 820 questions considered. Finally only eighty-five questions were selected, and they were answered correctly by a higher percentage of good than poor supervisors. Figure 6-2 shows two good items and one poor item. Items B and C are "good" items because they were both answered correctly by more medium supervisors than low supervisors, and by more high than medium supervisors.

Summary

In some groups of clerks, salespeople and supervisors, employees who are rated high have slightly higher intelligence test scores than employees who are rated lower, but in other samples of clerks, salespeople,

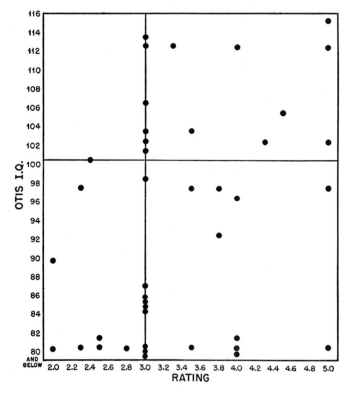

Figure 6-1. Otis I.Q.'s vs. Rating for 41 Supervisors.

(Harrell, T. W., "Testing the Abilities of Textile Workers," *State Engineering Experiment Station,* Bulletin 5, The Georgia School of Technology, 1940.)

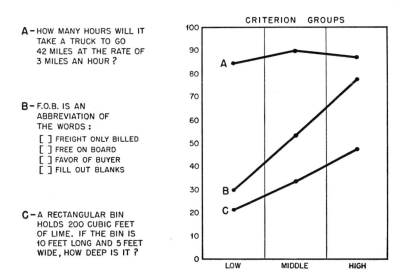

A – HOW MANY HOURS WILL IT TAKE A TRUCK TO GO 42 MILES AT THE RATE OF 3 MILES AN HOUR ?

B – F.O.B. IS AN ABBREVIATION OF THE WORDS :
[ ] FREIGHT ONLY BILLED
[ ] FREE ON BOARD
[ ] FAVOR OF BUYER
[ ] FILL OUT BLANKS

C – A RECTANGULAR BIN HOLDS 200 CUBIC FEET OF LIME. IF THE BIN IS 10 FEET LONG AND 5 FEET WIDE, HOW DEEP IS IT ?

Figure 6-2. Example of "Good" and "Worthless" Items.

(Uhrbrock, R. S., and M. W. Richardson, "Item Analysis: The Basis for Constructing a Test for Forecasting Supervisory Ability," *The Personnel Journal,* 1933, **12,** 141–154.)

and supervisors there is little if any difference in intelligence between employees rated high and low for work performance. There are two likely reasons for the differences in results. One clerical job may require more ability than another, even if it bears the same job title. In the second place, applicants for one job may vary widely in intelligence, so that the dullest are clearly incompetent, whereas in a second job all applicants may be of sufficient intelligence that it is not a significant variable. Where all applicants are able enough, the correlation with success will be insignificant. If some are able enough and others are not, the correlation will be higher. From these results it can be concluded that in some companies and some jobs intelligence tests are slightly useful as one piece of evidence for selection. Their usefulness should be proved for the particular job in each company before they are used.

MECHANICAL ABILITY

In this machine age, it is to be expected that a large part of the effort in personnel testing has been applied to aptitudes in connection with machines. Worker-machine relationships vary tremendously—from a simple operating job, to a skilled operation such as a lathe, and on to complicated repair work and trouble shooting. Tests in the mechanical ability area cover an extensive range—from those of a more or less theoretical nature, through performance tests of a practical nature, to those of routine performance with tests of dexterities. There are tests measuring, for instance, spatial relations, speed of perception, mechanical principles, mechanical comprehension, tool knowledge, trac-ing, tapping, finger and hand dexterity. Accompanying these in many mechanical ability tests are tests of such mental abilities as vocabulary, reasoning, and reading and mathematical comprehension. There is also a wide range of tests of skills in specific operations or with specific ma-chines, largely developed by individual companies for their own use, although some are standardized tests.

Tests of mechanical and clerical abilities are used primarily for rank-and-file positions. For supervisory and executive posts they are less applicable, first because, while a foreman or supervisor may need to have knowledge about the mechanical tools of his area of supervision, excellence in operating ability is less important than management skills, for which other measures are more appropriate, and secondly because supervisory jobs are usually filled by promotion. A great deal is already known, consequently, about the abilities and personal qualities of the candidate.

Studies of skilled mechanical workers have as a rule been in terms of correlations with training records rather than with objective measures of success on the job. Success in training for skilled mechanical work has correlated significantly with several tests, mainly those which measure spatial relations—such as the Minnesota Paper Form Board, O'Connor's Wiggly Block, and parts of the MacQuarrie Test for Mechanical Ability —although few studies confirm the validity of a particular test for a particular occupation among two populations. One exception has been the Surface Development Test, which predicted the training records of a course in mechanical drafting and blueprint reading taken by airplane mechanics, discussed in the preceding chapter.

The mechanical ability for skilled mechanical work is more in the head than in the hand. The central ability is space relations; there may be a perceptual speed factor and possibly a reasoning factor. In addition, tests of mechanical ability often have in them a factor of experience on mechanical work. A factor of manual dexterity has been located in tests which require routine quick movements. The results of tests for semi-skilled mechanical occupations are less positive than those for skilled mechanical occupations. Positive results have been reported that have been statistically significant, but the size of the validity coefficients has generally been below .40. The studies have frequently had small numbers of cases and relatively large numbers of tests, so that chance would produce in a single study at least one apparently valid test. There is practically a complete absence of a thorough report of the same test's being valid in two independent studies of the same occupational group. From these modest results and from the relatively low correlations between different tests of manual ability, it has been concluded that manual ability is often highly specific to the particular industrial job.

Training

In an extensive survey of aptitude and intelligence test results, tests of intelligence, arithmetic, spatial relations, speed of perception, and mechanical principles proved best in predicting training achievement in trades and crafts.[5] Intelligence tests were of little value for lower-level industrial occupations, though arithmetic and dexterity tests showed some good results in limited studies; spatial relations and speed of perception showed fair validities in the occupations on which data were available.

Job success

For predicting job proficiency in the higher mechanical skills the same kinds of tests are valid as for predicting training success, but validities for intellectual and spatial tests are lower and those for motor ability tests are a little higher. This makes sense in that reasoning tests are more valid for learning than for doing the job. For job performance on lower-level mechanical jobs, motor abilities showed low average validities, but mechanical principles had moderately high averages.

Tests of mechanical principles were moderately valid in predicting both training progress and proficiency for vehicle operators. Motor tests gave low average validities for clerical personnel; spatial tests were of little value for general and recording clerks but were the best type for computing clerks.

Supervisors

The results of several aptitude tests have been compared with supervisory success. Each of two tests of mechanical ability correlated significantly with the ratings of first-line supervisors in aviation plants.[6] Coefficients of correlation between ratings were .45 for the Bennett Test of Mechanical Comprehension, and .33 for the Minnesota Paper Form Board.

In a study of governmental supervisors the Gottschaldt Figures Test was one of four tests found to differentiate between those whose salaries were relatively high and those whose salaries were relatively low, age being constant.[7] Part of this test is shown in Figure 6-3. This test measures an ability to resist a pattern that is present and measures to a lesser extent a factor "concerned with the manipulation of two configurations simultaneously or in succession." It was also found to be one of several tests that differentiated between most promising and least promising administrators in training.

125

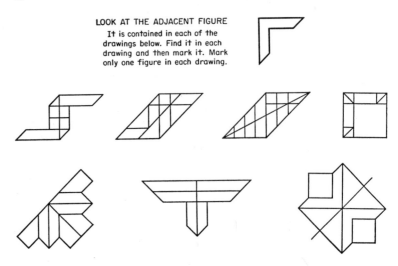

LOOK AT THE ADJACENT FIGURE
It is contained in each of the
drawings below. Find it in each
drawing and then mark it. Mark
only one figure in each drawing.

Figure 6-3. The Gottschaldt Figures Test, Part II.

(Thurstone, L. L., *A Factorial Study of Perception,* Chicago: University of Chicago Press, 1944.)

TABLE 6-I

Correlation between Test Scores and Efficiency on Job of Inspectors in an Aircraft Factory[a]

TEST	r
Mechanical Ability, MacQuarrie	.65
Mental Ability, Otis	.65
Practical Judgment, Cardall	.61
Minnesota Paper Form Board	.47
Industrial Training Classification	.42
Mechanical Comprehension, Bennett	.32
Mechanical Aptitude, O'Rourke	.24

[a] Efficiency on job is an average of two ratings.

Adapted from Sartain, A. Q., "The Use of Certain Standardized Tests in the Selection of Inspectors in an Aircraft Factory," *Journal of Consulting Psychology,* 1945, **9,** 234–235. Reprinted by permission of American Psychological Association.

Inspectors

Aircraft inspectors' ratings correlated .79 with a series of seven tests, including several of mechanical ability.[8] The tests and their agreement with the ratings are listed in Table 6-I. The mechanical ability tests in this study, all of which were paper and pencil tests, were those of MacQuarrie, Bennett, and O'Rourke, plus the Minnesota Paper Form Board. The other three tests are measures of intelligence. It would not be desirable to use all these tests for selecting inspectors, since there is a great deal of overlap in what they measure. It would be necessary to compute a multiple correlation between the best combination of tests and ratings in order to determine which tests should be used.

Operators

Ratings of machine-tool operators were correlated with five psychological tests.[9] The relationship between the scores on two of these tests,

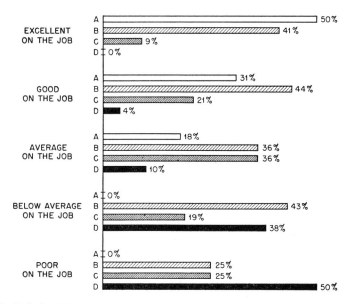

Figure 6-4. Relationship between Mechanical Comprehension and Hand-Tool Dexterity Test Scores and Job Proficiency Rating of Machine-Tool Operators. (Scores ranging from high to low are designated by letter from A to D. " 'A' represented the top 20 per cent or 81st to 100th percentile; 'B,' 61st to 80th percentile; 'C,' 31st to 60th percentile; and 'D' the bottom 30 per cent.")

(Bennett, George K., and Richard A. Fear, "Mechanical Comprehension and Dexterity," *The Personnel Journal*, 1943, **22**, 12–17.)

mechanical comprehension and hand-tool dexterity, and ratings on job proficiency is shown in Figure 6-4. These two tests had the highest correlation with proficiency ratings by supervisors, multiple $R = .67$. The other three tests, a nonverbal intelligence test, a miniature test for the engine lathe, and a hand-eye coordination test set up like a drill press, did not improve the prediction of success over using only the mechanical comprehension and hand-tool dexterity tests. Figure 6-4 shows that, of the excellent employees, 50 per cent had A test scores and none had D scores, whereas the scores of the employees who were poor on the job were precisely the opposite. "Only new applicants scoring 'A' or 'B' on the tests were hired . . ."

The Purdue Mechanical Adaptability Test, consisting of practical information items, has been shown to be related to the success of screw-machine operators and electrical apprentices.[10] The relationship between test scores and electrical apprentices' ratings by supervisors is shown in Figure 6-5.

A manual test, a modification of the Minnesota Rate of Manipulation Test, correlated .66 with ratings for sixty converting-machine operators in a paper mill.[11] This test is one in which round wooden blocks are moved from one location to another.

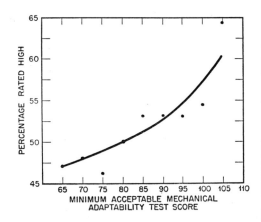

Figure 6-5. Graph Showing Percentage of Trade Apprentices in an Electrical Company Who Are Rated "High" When Successively Higher Critical Scores Are Employed.

(Lawshe, C. H., Jr., Irene A. Semanek, and Joseph Tiffin, "The Purdue Mechanical Adaptability Test," *Journal of Applied Psychology*, 1946, **30**, 442–453. By permission of the American Psychological Association.)

CLERICAL ABILITY

Successful tests for clerical occupations differ according to the nature of the clerical job, but some generalizations can be made about the more successful tests. Ratings and training-school records in skilled clerical work have correlated significantly with clerical aptitude tests similar in content to intelligence tests except for the omission of space relations. Much clerical work requires a perceptual factor that is measured by checking names and numbers. This factor is more important than reasoning ability for routine clerical workers.

Clerical ability tests include such measures as reading comprehension, cancellation, substitution and coding, spelling and grammar, alphabetizing, arithmetic, and verbal facility. Some tests endeavor to locate such abilities as concentration, mental alertness, accuracy, and dependability.[12] Though finger, hand, and arm movements are common in clerical occupations, tests of dexterity have shown low validity; the required dexterities are, no doubt, possessed by nearly all persons There are many tests, both standardized and company-developed, for specific jobs or machine operations, such as the achievement tests of speed and accuracy for typists.

Training

Average validities have shown that intellectual tests are superior to other types of tests in the prediction of trainability—arithmetic was the highest predictor of trainability for general and computing clerks, but cancellation was highest for recording clerks.[13] Number comparison also has been high for predicting a training criterion among clerks. Job proficiency has been best predicted on the basis of moderately good validities on intellectual tests, intelligence and arithmetic being highest for general clerks, immediate memory for recording clerks, and name comparison for computing clerks. Other types of intelligence tests frequently had validities close to these, for predicting both training success and proficiency.

Bank employees

Scores for a number of clerical tests administered to various groups of bank employees are shown in Table 6-II. Each of the different clerical jobs within a bank requires separate criteria of success against which to compare test scores. Comparison of these scores with those on mental ability tests for bank personnel show that, in these circumstances at least, the clerical tests are more useful measures.

129

TABLE 6-II

Correlation of Test Scores and Criteria for Bank Clerical Employees

GROUP AND CRITERION	MINNESOTA CLERICAL			GENERAL CLERICAL						SHORT EMPLOYMENT TEST			
	NUMBERS	NAMES	COMBINED	CLERICAL	NUMERICAL	VERBAL	TOTAL	ALPHA NUMBER SERIES	HAY NAME FINDING	V-1	N-1	CA-1	SRA—TOTAL
Distribution—transit and commercial bookkeeping departments: training grades							.32						.36
Tellers: training grades							.32						.25
Clerks and typists:													
speed in work	.29	.38	.38	.46	.32	.38	.48	.28	.37				
accuracy	.36	.39	.42	.42	.39	.34	.46	.25	.36				
ability to grasp new ideas	.30	.45	.43	.46	.43	.49	.56	.39	.39				
Experienced proof-machine operators: production record										.06	.24	.24	.38

Adapted from American Bankers Association, Customer and Personnel Relations Department, *Clerical Testing in Banks,* New York: American Bankers Association, 1952, pp. 45–51.

Machine operators

The use of tests in selecting machine bookkeepers has been studied over a period of years.[14] A thorough job analysis was made, and the criterion of performance was developed carefully to make it reliable. Selection tests raised production from 105 in 1937 to 117 in 1943.[15] The validity coefficient was .70 for a battery of three tests, completing Number Series, Name Finding, and Number Checking.

Training records of persons learning machine calculating gave a multiple correlation of .54 with three tests, Number-Dot Location, which used a keyboard similar in appearance to that on a calculating machine, Arithmetic Computations, and Number Comparisons.[16]

PERSONALITY

Personality can be defined as the sum total of a person's responses. The term "personality tests" has been used for measures of nonintellectual traits and not for abilities. These temperamental and other nonintellectual personality factors are important to success and failure on a job. There can be no question of that if one has had to work in a situation where clashes in personality existed among co-workers. Even a single violent disagreement over objectively trivial events has been the cause of the voluntary resignation of more than one good worker. Although most of such disagreements are due to misunderstandings which often can be avoided by successful training of supervisors in the principles and practices of human relations, personality is important. It is extremely important to pick supervisors whose personality will be sufficiently stable to meet the stresses to which management is subject. It is important to avoid putting potential trouble makers in jobs that will tax their capacity for self-control.

The interview and the application blank discussed in Chapter 4 have the appraisal of personality as their major purpose. The weighted application blank has led to extensive inventories of biographical data. These inventories are more similar to personality tests than they are to shorter, traditional application blanks.

The most common method of appraising personality is through casual observation, about which little research has been done. Observation has occasionally been systematized, however, through *peer ratings,* in which associates write on a prepared form their appraisals of the personality of, for example, a classmate, and through *controlled observation.* In controlled observation one person or a group is assigned a task. Personality is appraised by one or more observers who study and rate the reactions of the people being tested. The method of appraising personality believed best by clinical psychologists is the *projective test*, in which the subject is asked to describe what he perceives in a set of ambiguous pictures. This is thought to be valuable because the subject will let himself go and reveal his true personality more than with other methods. The most common method, because it is cheap and convenient, is the use of *inventories*, a pencil and paper test with predetermined responses, consisting of questions about one's behavior or feelings, or what one judges the feelings or behavior of others to be. Selected studies in which each of these methods has been used in a work situation will be described.

Projective tests

Unstructured, free association, or projective tests, provide a stimulus, which is often quite ambiguous; the subject is allowed to roam at will in making his response. The subject must contribute order and meaning from within himself; it is these projective reactions to the unstructured situation which give clues to the personality. This type, then, is more similar to the essay question in an examination, though the stimulus is usually not so definite as that in an examination.

It is not generally possible to reduce the results of unstructured personality tests to a mathematical or letter score. Evaluation is customarily made through a discussion of the qualities revealed by the subject and their applicability to the situation at hand. Interpretation is subjective, because it depends both on the meaning attributed to reactions and the exact nature and all the innuendos of the reactions as recalled from memory and as contained in the psychologist's notes. Detailed knowledge of the subject's background is a decided advantage in evaluating test results. These devices perhaps have potentiality, but it may be that most of them are too clinical to be of great present value to business. Furthermore, there has been no clear-cut proof of their value to industry, even in the hands of clinical psychologists. Also they are costly both in money and in time, as compared with pencil and paper tests.

It is difficult to evaluate the status of projective tests in industry. There have been a few dozen studies, mainly of the Rorschach Test, a series of ink blots, and, to a lesser extent, of the Thematic Apperception Test, a series of pictures which can be perceived and interpreted in different ways. That studies of projective tests are increasing in frequency indicates a growing interest in industrial applications. The design of these studies has been of two types. One type describes the characteristic personality of an occupational group, executives for example, as it differs from that of men in general. The second type of study design compares personality for effective and less effective members of an occupational group, mechanics for example.

Some of the studies of each type report positive findings; that is, the personality of one occupational group is different from the personality of men in general, and the personality of effective members of an occupational group is different from that of less effective members. Some of these studies are interesting and plausible to read, but there are objections from a rigorously scientific point of view which prevent the reporting of them in detail. Some of them present no statistical evidence but merely explain that the tests are of such a clinical nature that their results cannot be quantified. Other studies present statistically significant differences for some test items. There are, however, so many test items that chance alone would make it probable that some items would appear significantly different. A repeated study showing the same difference on a second group would make the results tremendously more convincing, but such a demonstration has not been found.

It must then be concluded that the validity of projective tests has not been demonstrated for industrial selection. They are still being studied.

Controlled observation

Personality has been appraised through controlled observation of small-group behavior. This has been done not only in the leaderless discussion groups mentioned in Chapter 4, but also in the observation of performance when a man is assigned a task to perform with a group. Such techniques were developed by the German and British armies and later modified by the United States Office of Strategic Services in selecting spies. In one instance a candidate was asked to construct a shack and was provided material and helpers. The helpers were stooges who had been instructed by the observers to sabotage the appointed leader. Observers were therefore prepared to notice how the leader reacted to the potentially frustrating situation.

An English coal company adapted these procedures to the selection of supervisors.[17] One of the tasks was a group discussion similar to the group interview mentioned in Chapter 4. In this discussion seven candidates acting as a board of directors were asked to work out the most profitable weekly coal allocation from a production schedule, a sales estimate, a list of transport changes, and two maps. Several observers were present to observe their performance. There were other situations in which the group was assigned tasks, the performance of each member was observed, and the end product was appraised.

133

The observation of personality at work in small groups is a fruitful field for study at the present time. It appears to be more valid than testing personality with pencil and paper tests. Whether it is worth the expense has not been proved, but until and unless some better method has been demonstrated, it does deserve much more tryout than it has had so far.

Peer ratings

The opinion of one's fellows has often been thought to be a good measure of personality, and perhaps the best, but in industry it has almost never been reported to have been used, although ratings of superiors are common. Opinion of one's fellows has been shown in a study of Marine Corps officers to be the best predictor of effectiveness in combat—better than ratings of leaders, school grades, written personality tests, intelligence, and mechanical-aptitude tests.[18]

Inventories

A survey has been made of 113 reports dealing with personality inventories in employee selection.[19] Average validities showed little correlation where personality would be expected to be important, as for general supervisors and foremen, and somewhat greater but only fair validity for occupations where personality factors would seem less important, as clerks, tradesmen, and craftsmen. Sales clerks and salesmen both showed the highest results with average correlations of only .36 between test scores and ratings of success on the job. There have been many proposals that personality tests should and could keep misfits out of industrial jobs, but there have been few demonstrations of what they have actually accomplished. The Guilford-Martin Personnel Inventory has been studied in relation to two troublesome groups of employees.[20] This inventory is scored for three traits that were found by analyses to make up separate factors of the symptoms of paranoia. Paranoia appears to be the central mental disease of industrial trouble makers. The three factors on which separate scores are obtained are:

Cooperativeness, as opposed to fault finding, or an overcriticalness of people and things.

Objectivity, as opposed to personal reference or a tendency to take everything personally and subjectively.

Agreeableness, as opposed to belligerence or a domineering attitude and overreadiness to fight.

Results are summarized in Table 6-III. There is a trend for employees rated unsatisfactory by their bosses to be unsatisfactory on the personality test, but the relation is far from perfect. Of twenty-two aircraft

TABLE 6-III

Company Ratings of Satisfactory and Unsatisfactory Workers Compared to Ratings on the Humm-Wadsworth Temperament Scale and the Guilford-Martin Personnel Inventory

	COMPANY RATING	
	UNSATISFACTORY	SATISFACTORY
Company A		
($N = 48$ Aircraft Parts Workers)[a]		
Humm-Wadsworth Rating		
Satisfactory	6	18
Unsatisfactory	16	8
Guilford-Martin Rating		
Satisfactory	7	19
Unsatisfactory	15	7
Rating on both H-W and G-M		
Satisfactory	2	16
Unsatisfactory	11	5
Company B ($N = 43$ Textile Workers)[b]		
Guilford-Martin Rating on cooperativeness		
Satisfactory	2	19
Unsatisfactory	11	11

[a] Adapted from Dorcus, Roy M., "A Brief Study of the Humm-Wadsworth Temperament Scale and the Guilford-Martin Personnel Inventory in an Industrial Situation," *Journal of Applied Psychology,* 1944, **28**, 302–307.

[b] Adapted from Martin, Howard G., "Locating the Troublemaker with the Guilford-Martin Personnel Inventory," *Journal of Applied Psychology,* 1944, **28**, 461–467. Reprinted by permission of American Psychological Association.

parts workers who were unsatisfactory, the Guilford-Martin test located fifteen but missed seven. This table also shows the result of the Humm-Wadsworth Temperament Scale on one group. For this group the middle cases are omitted, so the differentiation between groups as shown here is greater than it would be if the normal range were included. The two tests are about equally effective; the Humm-Wadsworth test, however, is more difficult to obtain and use because it is necessary to have approval from the author before using the test.

Scores on the Humm-Wadsworth Temperament Scale were compared with ratings of eighty-five salesmen.[21] These salesmen had been unanimously rated as either successful or unsuccessful by three supervisors; salesmen rated successful by one supervisor and unsuccessful by another were omitted from the study. Of the salesmen selected by the test at time of hiring as good prospects, 83 per cent were successful on the job as compared to 73 per cent of the total group of eighty-five

TABLE 6-IV

E. Q. Test Trait Score Means According to Hierarchy Level

	TOTAL GROUP	HIERARCHY LEVEL				
		I	II	III	IV	V
Objectivity	4.4	4.3	4.2	4.2	4.6	4.5
Social Dominance	6.7	7.2	7.5	6.7	6.4	6.1
Extroversion	3.9	3.7	3.9	4.0	4.0	3.8
Drive	5.9	5.6	5.8	6.0	6.2	6.0
Detail	4.3	3.2	3.9	4.4	4.7	4.9
Emotionality	4.0	3.0	3.7	3.7	4.3	4.9
Adjustment (poor)	3.6	2.8	3.2	3.7	3.8	4.4

Levels:
   I. President, vice-president, treasurer, general manager, general sales manager, executive engineer.
   II. Works or plant manager, sales manager, chief engineer, chief industrial engineer, controller, industrial relations director, purchasing director.
   III. Production superintendents, industrial salesmen, sales engineers, department or section heads in accounting, industrial engineering, design engineering, inside sales, purchasing and personnel.
   IV. Production foremen, accountants, design and process engineers, time study and production control men, sales correspondents, junior industrial salesmen, personnel men.
   V. Clerks and factory workers.

Adapted from Meyer, Henry D., and Glenn L. Pressel, "Personality Test Scores in the Management Hierarchy," *Journal of Applied Psychology,* 1954, **38,** 73–80; Table 1, p. 75.

salesmen who were successful. On individual components of the test, no significant difference appeared between successful and unsuccessful salesmen. Perhaps the over-all profile has a meaning separate from the individual trait scores considered separately. This point needs further study.

The Employee Questionnaire, a brief industrial personality test, showed valid trends in distinguishing among five levels in a hierarchy of jobs from factory worker to top executive (457 subjects) for the qualities poor adjustment, emotionality, detail, and social dominance, but not for extroversion, drive, and objectivity, as shown in Table 6-IV.[22] Social dominance score increased with higher rank of job, while the scores for poor adjustment, emotionality, and detail decreased the higher the job level.

A battery of two standard ability tests, three new tests, and an interest and background inventory was administered to supervisors, both in offices and in production, of an electric power company.[23] Scores were compared with a supervisory performance rating. The best results were obtained from one of the new tests which measured social attitudes. It gave correlations ranging from .22 to .49 with supervisory performance of various groups of supervisors. From the fact that a test to measure knowledge of leadership skills was unsuccessful but scores on a measure of social attitude did correlate significantly, it was concluded that "perhaps leadership training should concentrate on changing attitudes, rather than on attempting to change performance by teaching skills."

EMPATHY

A test requiring the subject to put himself in the place of various groups of people is called the Empathy Test. The subject is required to rank various types of music "in order of their probable popularity among the non-office workers of the United States"; well-known periodicals according to his estimate of their circulation; and "commonly annoying experiences according to their specific annoyance to the general population." The test correlated .44 for sales records and .71 for ranking by the sales managers among salesmen of two companies.[24] The groups were so small, however, totaling thirty-two, that results may be taken only as suggestive.

FORCED CHOICE

The forced-choice type of question, which was introduced in Chapter 3 as a type of merit rating, has been used in personality tests. The subject is provided with an item made up of two pairs, or possibly a single pair of descriptive adjectives, behavior types, or statements, so

137

assembled that each pair describes qualities of equal social desirability. The two items of each pair have the same preference value but different discrimination values. Each statement of a pair would be preferred equally, but there would be a difference between the statements that would discriminate on personality. To the subject there is no clear correct answer; he must select the statement which best or least fits his personality. The advantage of this type of question is that it eliminates or reduces faking. The device has not been in use for enough time for extensive study, but validities of .32 to .55 have been reported for various groups of Army officers.[25] The Jurgensen Classification Test, one of the forced-choice type, showed some validity with a small sample of thirty-three bake shop managers, .39 with a composite criterion, but failed to distinguish between 176 good and poor supervisors in forty-five plants.[26]

Summary

A variety of personality tests have been tried with industrial groups. Inventories are the most frequently used of the various devices. Projective tests, such as the Rorschach, are the least susceptible to faking, with the possible exception of the forced-choice type of inventory. Some positive results have been obtained for each type of personality test, and some negative results. Results have been obtained which show more desirable scores for supervisors and less desirable scores for trouble makers. The results are not sufficiently positive to warrant the use of a personality test within a company or for a job until it has been validated in that company or for that job situation.

INTEREST

Interest tests are based on the fact that successful men in an occupation have interest patterns that are significantly different from those of men in general. These tests are also based on the assumption that, the greater the similarity of a subject's interest patterns to those of men already performing competently within the field, the greater are his chances for satisfaction in that occupation. By establishing the interest patterns of men in an occupation in contrast to the patterns of the population of men in general, scales are provided against which tests of other men may be compared. Interest tests are meant only to ascertain the relationship of the subject's test results to interests exhibited by successful members of an occupational group; they are not expected to differentiate within a group between the most successful and the least successful members. The tests are most useful in that they show what occupations ought not to be attempted because of lack of similarity of interests, rather than in positively pointing the way to an occupation.

A high degree of similarity of interest, of course, is not a guarantee of success in the occupation; there is considerably more to success than interest. There is ability as well as personality, and these are not measured by interest tests.

It would appear to be almost axiomatic that vocational interest and job satisfaction are closely allied, perhaps even two phases of the same thing. A group of people who wanted clinical advice, mainly persons in the three highest occupational classes—professional, semiprofessional, and managerial, but including also some persons in clerical, skilled trades, and retail business—was studied to find how closely vocational interest and job satisfaction were related.[27] Clinical diagnoses of occupational dissatisfaction were made; vocational interests were measured by test scores. "Most adult males," it was found, "who complain of occupational dissatisfaction show no primary pattern of interest in the group of occupations which embraces their present occupation. Sixty-two of the 76 men fall into this category."

Correlations between interest and aptitude have been negligible or positive, but never high. Scores on the Kuder Preference Record were correlated with the Minnesota Clerical Test for 231 volunteer, white, female clerical workers in the offices of a large national firm as a measure of interrelation of interest and aptitude.[28] In other studies also "consistent findings of slight or insignificant relationship between vocational interest and clerical aptitude are generally confirmed by the few studies on other general aptitudes as well as general intelligence." Of 108 correlations three had only minimum significance and only five were a little better. There was only one significant correlation on a "logically appropriate key," that of $-.37$ between clerical interest and name checking for stenographers.

Interest test scales have been developed with one of two general ideas in mind: first, calculation of interest patterns for specific occupations or professions, as Strong has done for such occupations as certified public accountant, farmer, doctor, office worker, production manager, printer; and, secondly, division of items and computation of scales for what are assumed to be factors of interest, by Kuder, with such areas as mechanical, literary, musical, social service, masculinity-femininity.

The types of interest measures are similar to those of structured personality measures. A frequently used type of question involves an activity or an occupation which one marks Like or Indifferent or Dislike, or Yes or No or ?.

Interest tests are, in general, most useful in vocational guidance, but they are used in some company employment offices. For a labor market where there are many applications for any available position, for rather specialized positions in which extraordinary care in selection is advisable, or for very large companies with a variety of jobs and elaborate personnel procedures, it is possible that selection may be approached from much the same standpoint as vocational guidance. Interest tests have been most typically used with professional groups and only rarely with the occupational groups which make up the bulk of industrial employees. There is increasing recognition of the need for placement and guidance in industry as a part of the selection process.

Strong Vocational Interest Test

The Strong Vocational Interest Blank for Men was published in 1927 and revised in 1938. The revised test consists of 400 items in such areas as occupations, school subjects, amusements, activities, peculiarities of people, and personal abilities and characteristics. The questions are answered largely on some variation of "Like, Indifferent, Dislike." At the present time scoring scales are available for forty-four occupations and for such nonoccupational interests as masculinity-femininity, occupational level, and interest maturity. Although the measure was intended for counseling and guidance purposes, it has been widely used for industrial selection and placement as well.

A follow-up study was made of college graduates who took the Strong Vocational Interest Test in college and again an average of eighteen years later. There were 663 who were engaged in occupations for which there are interest scales.

Expectancy ratios show that the chances are 78 to 22 that a student with an A rating in an occupation will enter that occupation, and, conversely, and just as important in vocational counseling, that the chances are 83 to 17 that a student with C rating will not enter that occupation.[29]

Continuous employment for about eighteen years in an occupation is accompanied by a slight increase in test score. A change in employment is accompanied by a change in interest scores. When there is an occupational change, interest scores decline after an occupation is left, but increase on retest for the new occupation. Men who change occupations do not have as high mean scores, either before or after the change, as do men who do not change occupations.

Although the test is not intended to be a predictor of success, a spectacular instance where it did predict performance was with life insurance agents.[30] The men who scored high on the Life Insurance Salesman scale sold more insurance and had less turnover than those who scored low. Results are shown in Table 6-V. One man who was

TABLE 6-V

Scores on Strong's Vocational Interest Test vs. Production of Insurance Agents

		REMAINING 1 YR.			REMAINING 2 YRS.		
SCORE ON STRONG INTEREST TEST	NUMBER CON- TRACTED	NO.	PER CENT	MEDIAN 1ST YR. PRO- DUCTION OF THOSE RE- MAINING AT LEAST 1 YR.	NO.	PER CENT	MEDIAN 2ND YEAR PRO- DUCTION OF THOSE RE- MAINING AT LEAST 2 YRS.
A	228	152	66.5	155,414	97	42.5	206,680
B+	72	42	59.1	112,839	23	32.4	144,446
B, B−, C	76	26	34.2	73,814	12	15.8	133,039

Bills, Marion A., "A Tool for Selection That Has Stood the Test of Time," in Thurstone, L. L. (ed.), *Applications of Psychology,* New York: Harper & Brothers, 1952, Table II, p. 133.

hired with an A score would sell more in the second year than four men hired with B, B−, and C scores. These results were independent of experience in selling insurance, education, and age. The letter scores have the following meaning:

The rating A means that the individual has the interests of persons successfully engaged in that occupation; the rating C means that the person does not have such interests; and the ratings B+, B, and B−, mean that the person probably has those interests but we cannot be so sure of that fact as in the case of A ratings.[31]

Summary

Men in various business and professional groups have distinctive interest patterns. Interests become crystallized at about 18 or 20 years of age and remain essentially similar for at least twenty years. It is desirable to consider the interests of candidates in selection and in placement. Interests are often different from abilities.

OTHER TESTS

There are many tests which do not fit into the classification system of mental, clerical, and mechanical abilities, personality and interest tests. Some jobs require outstanding vision.

141

Visual demands appear to be highly specific to the nature of work; it is necessary, consequently, to set standards separately on each job where vision is important. Superior near-visual acuity was the important visual characteristic of satisfactory radio-tube assemblers, and good acuity for distance vision was a handicap to the success of loopers in a hosiery plant.[32] The most successful milling-machine operators were those whose right eyes slanted upward, because such an adjustment was necessary, presumably, to operate the machine successfully.

The coefficient of validity was .75 between incidence of units which inspectors of rayon yarn cones should not have set aside for foreman's decision and three visual tests.[33] Three criteria—defective units, hourly production, and units set aside for foreman's decision—were determined even more successfully by a combination of visual tests, the combination differing in each case to obtain the best correlation.

Among tests in special areas are the Sales Aptitude Index for prospective life insurance salesmen, which includes items on personal history, interests and attitudes, and personal characteristics, and How Supervise? The latter is intended to serve as an aptitude test for supervisors, and it is essentially a test in human relations.[34]

How Supervise?

In developing the How Supervise? test the procedure was to have first-line supervisors rated by their bosses. It was expected that these ratings would be the basis for dividing the supervisors into two groups, the best and the worst. Then the items on the test that differentiated between these two groups would be a measure of supervisory skill in human relations. This procedure was abandoned because the bosses did not agree about who was a good and who a poor supervisor, the reliability of bosses' ratings being only .62 for four independent ratings. After the idea of bosses' ratings had been scrapped as the main criterion of the acceptability of a question, the test author turned to personnel experts. A group of writers on industrial relations and industrial personnel officers were asked to give the correct answer to each question. Personnel experts agreed on the best answer to the items with a reliability coefficient of .91. In some instances the items on which there was a significant difference between the answers of supervisors that were rated "good" and those rated "poor" by management bore out the hypothesis that good supervisors believe in smooth human relations. This is true in that good supervisors rejected the statement that "About half of the workers in our plant are just naturally stubborn and uncooperative." The supervisors who were rated poor by management were more likely to consider "half the workers stubborn and uncooperative." In a number of instances, however, the answers were not what the test author seemed to expect, for the supervisors certified by management as good gave answers demonstrating poor human relations, while poor supervisors answered in terms of good human relations. For example, good supervisors stated that "dissatisfied but capable workers" should not be transferred to other jobs, but supervisors who were rated poor by management believed that such workers should be transferred. Human relations appears to be only partly accepted by supervision.

There are several ways of explaining this failure of first-line supervision to be favorable toward human relations and mental hygiene. One is that training has not as yet been effective. The other alternative is favored by the investigator, namely, that the supervisors' opinions reflect the views of their bosses.

For three small groups of foremen in metal fabricating plants, How Supervise? gave total validities, when compared with supervisor ratings, of .27.[35] How Supervise? may measure supervisory knowledge for better-educated supervisors (twelfth grade and up), but, for the less well-educated, scores appear to measure intelligence or reading ability more than knowledge of supervision.[36] The test was found of little value in connection with various measures of supervisory ability for life insurance managers, but again seemed related to "educational achievement."[37]

SUMMARY

Personnel tests have been shown to be important in nearly all phases of industrial personnel work in which it is desirable to pick out certain men from the general group. Selection and placement can be improved by the use of carefully chosen tests, provided that there is a considerable range of talent available for testing and that the jobs are such that they cannot be successfully performed by all applicants. A test that is too easy or one that is too difficult or a group in which the abilities are too nearly alike throws the applicants all into one tight group; the narrow range of their test scores does not permit discrimination among the subjects. Selection aided by adequate psychological testing measures can choose better the men best qualified for the job, the men who probably will remain with the job, and the men most suitable for training or promotion.

It should not be inferred that testing is infallible. Testing results are in terms of probabilities. The selected men probably will meet the expressed needs for which they were chosen. But some men selected will be unsuccessful, and some men eliminated by the testing would have been successful if they had been selected. Prediction fails because a test

143

does not correlate perfectly with a criterion and the criterion with the job, but also because prediction or selection is couched in terms of normal expectancy, and the human element introduces a possibility of departure from normal expectation. As with insurance, where it can be predicted that so many people of age 60 will die within the year but it cannot be said exactly who among the 60-year-olds will die, testing can predict that 90 per cent of men with test scores of 120, to select an arbitrary situation, will be successful, but it cannot select the 90 per cent, or the 10 per cent, by name.

One or more of the six major types of psychological tests is often able to differentiate among individuals for industrial purposes, but the same test frequently is unsatisfactory in a second group which on the surface appears to be substantially the same as the earlier, successful group. Not all six of the types of tests are equally valid in general and certainly not in particular, nor have test development and testing been carried far enough to furnish a measure adequate for every need and for every situation where discrimination is necessary.

Achievement tests have been found useful for selecting competent stenographers and persons to fill other clerical occupations. Knowledge tests have proved useful for many skilled trades.

Two types of tests, the clerical and the mechanical ability tests, have obvious surface validity for industry, and this surface validity has been substantiated in many instances, but the tests are by no means valid for all clerical or mechanical jobs. Mechanical and clerical abilities are to some extent separate from mental abilities, but to some extent they overlap. Mental ability, of course, is involved in a widely varying degree in all occupations. The academic requirements of the professions and of many other occupations serve as a refining element for those fields, and it is thus unusual to find below-average mental abilities in such professions and occupations. Other than this selection by education, there is little limit on the levels in mental abilities one may find in almost any occupation, although there may be a mode at some narrow range. Occupations with a low degree of challenge and a high degree of routine generally lack appeal for groups of superior intelligence; people of limited mental ability may do quite well in such jobs, but some people may be forced into these jobs because lack of education, rather than low mental ability, denies them other opportunities.

There are many personality tests on the market, but their usefulness for industry is still problematical. They are the least accepted of the major types of psychological tests.

Tests of mental ability are widely used for all types of occupational groups. Tests of clerical and mechanical abilities are somewhat more restricted to the lower-level jobs of factory and office. Tests of clerical ability probably approach more universal use for their appropriate type of job than any of the other available types of tests. The measures of interest and personality are used for sales as well as for supervisory (especially those ranks above the foreman level) and executive personnel. In many instances two or more types of tests are used in order to obtain a battery which will test key factors adequately and which will contribute to the highest effectiveness in prediction or selection.

There are no reports of valid measures for selecting executive and management personnel above the level of first-line supervisors, although several long-range studies are now in progress to try to determine how to select executives. The small number of executives whose results are comparable makes it an extremely difficult research problem to determine scientifically just what qualifications are critical. Some companies believe that psychological tests of intelligence, interest, and personality do give useful results in the selection of executives, but the proof of such measures for this problem has not been demonstrated.

RECOMMENDED READINGS

Buros, Oscar K. (ed.), *The Fourth Mental Measurements Yearbook,* Highland Park, N. J.: The Gryphon Press, 1953. Contains extremely critical reviews of tests. Along with the previous editions, this is an encyclopedic account of the vast literature on the validity of personnel tests.

Strong, Edward K., Jr., *Vocational Interests 18 Years after College,* Minneapolis: University of Minnesota Press, 1955. A follow-up on the placement and interests of men who took the Vocational Interest Test while in college.

Whyte, William H., *The Organization Man,* Part IV, "The Testing of Organization Man," and Appendix, "How To Cheat on Personality Tests," Garden City, N. Y.: Doubleday & Company, Inc., 1957. An adversely critical look at the use of personality tests in business.

7

Training

The training of employees to make new products and provide new services and to make old products and provide old services more cheaply has no doubt contributed to the progress of the United States in peace and war. Much of the training in industry is more progressive than that of our public school system. Industrial training has smaller classes, more adequate training aids, carefully developed lesson plans, and close supervision.

Industrial training is given all ranks of employees. Giving formal training to executives is a fairly recent development, and it is still much more controversial than the training of rank-and-file employees. Consequently, more attention will be given to the training of executives and supervisors than to the training of other employees here.

The value of the training program depends to a large extent on the selection of the trainees and the grading of the results of their training. This is particularly apparent with management trainees. Management wants to select the young men who will learn best to become managers. Selection of the most apt pupils makes the job of training easier. If trainees are given ratings, raises, or promotions on the basis of actual performance in training, they will be motivated to learn and the training will be effective. If trainees are not graded fairly in terms of their performance, they will not be motivated and training will be ineffective.

Steps in learning

Four steps are essential for training or learning to occur. These are: (1) a stimulus; (2) a response; (3) a motivation or drive; and (4) a reward or incentive.

There must be present a stimulus that is clear to the learner. The industrial interest in communications is largely a recognition of the fact that the stimulus or message has to be clear for communication to occur. Unless a reader understands the message on the paper, he cannot be

146

expected to be influenced in the direction that the communicator intends. Although training stimuli are usually words, whether spoken or written, there are other kinds of stimuli as well. There may be a machine, or a picture, or a demonstration by a person. In any event, it is necessary to have a stimulus known and understood by the learner before training can be effective.

The response means the act that the training is intended to teach, whether it is saying a string of words, as in the Pledge of Allegiance to the Flag, or operating a telegraph key, as in learning to transmit messages by the Morse code. The learner has to be able to perform the act. Furthermore, he needs to be allowed and encouraged to practice the performance of the response; in short, he needs to practice.

There must be motivation or drive before there can be learning. Motivation includes interest and the attitude of wanting to learn. If a person does not want to learn, he will not learn even though he understands clearly what is being taught and has perfect capacity to respond in the way that would show the learning. This means that the trainer or the training company needs to select trainees on the basis of motivation and needs to have policies and practices that will encourage the continuation and growth of motivation. This includes the leadership "climate" of the organization discussed in Chapter 15.

The training organization should be concerned not only that motivation, rather than frustration, is present, as discussed in Chapter 10, but should also determine the specific motivation of the learner. In other words, what does the employee want that the company can give him? Some people may want promotion or more pay; others may want only to do a better job at present, or may want recognition for performing well.

Reward or incentive is what will satisfy a motive. Praise is the incentive that will satisfy the motive of social approval. For training to be effective, the learner must be rewarded, or at least have faith that he will be rewarded in the foreseeable future. When a trainee is not rewarded and loses confidence that he will be given a reward, he will stop learning and may even unlearn some of the skill that he already knows.

Training to be effective by having the learner learn must include all of these four steps, clear stimulus, known response, motivation of the learner, and a reward that the learner wants. Industry is perfectly aware of the first two, stimulus and response. There has been less attention to the actual motivation of the learner and to the giving of an adequate reward, or making it clear that a wanted reward will be forthcoming. Part of the difficulty with training has been a rebellion on the part of trainees to the regimentation of an autocratic management. In the terms used here, the trainee has not wanted to learn because he has not seen that the reward or hope of reward was adequate for him.

Company practice

The majority of companies give formal on-the-job training for new employees, one survey showing 87 per cent of companies in the United States in 1953 giving this training.[1] Training for foremen has been increasing to the extent that, in 1953, 72 per cent of United States companies reported classes for foremen. The training of higher executives has attracted a great deal of attention, and there is a trend toward the provision of systematic training, within or without the company, by more companies, but still only a minority of companies do this. A substantial survey of companies with 250 or more employees concluded that about 13 per cent of the companies had a management development plan.[2]

Who should be the trainer?

The trainer should be the immediate supervisor when he is qualified. A subordinate can be expected to put more importance on training if it is carried out by the supervisor. There are occasions when the supervisor is not qualified and when someone else has to act as trainer—either someone from a training department, or someone from outside the company. The role of the training department ideally should be that of adviser to line supervisors.

Basis

Industrial training is based mainly on judgment rather than on scientific facts. Three important issues that need to be considered with respect to any training program are: (1) the needs for training, which should set clear objectives; (2) the method or methods to be used; and (3) an evaluation of the results of training.[3] These three issues will be discussed in turn.

NEEDS

Training should be based on the company's need for it. This fundamental has occasionally been obscured by training departments which conduct training for the sake of training rather than to satisfy a need. There is usually a feeling that training is necessary, but the need is established most frequently by what the "boss wants" rather than by any more exact demonstration. It is possible that measurements of production, or accidents, or other objective events would show a need which training might fulfill. Another approach is to ask employees whether they need this or that training.

Human relations

The primary training need of supervisors is in "human relations," as reported by a survey of rank-and-file employees and by a tabulation of the content of management training courses.[4] Other evidence also indicates that human relations is believed to be the primary training need of supervisors and managers. Exactly what is meant by "human relations" in these surveys is not clear. One goal is to reduce misunderstandings between employees and supervisors. This carries with it several subgoals of understanding people better through understanding individual differences, understanding the way attitudes are formed and their influence on thought and behavior, understanding motivation and frustration. These understandings would result in an over-all increase in tolerance and consideration, in sensitivity, empathy, or the knowledge of how the other person feels.

The need of executives, or of managers at all levels, to have a better understanding of people so that they can deal more successfully with them is widely accepted, although the formulation of the need in terms that can be operationally useful is much less well accepted. Much of management training is based, either explicitly or implicitly, on the assumed need of changing subordinates. The management trainee tries to manipulate his subordinates through human relations skills. This concept of needs is probably incorrect and doomed to failure. A much more defensible concept of needs is that it is primarily the manager who has to change if he is to profit in the area of human relations. By a greater awareness of people and their characteristics he can be more considerate in dealing with them, and the work group will become more effective.

Production

Increase in production calls for training, whether in a factory, to turn out more products, or in a sales organization, to make more sales. This is another way of saying that training is needed to further the main goal of the company, whatever that goal is.

Waste

Reduction of waste requires training in some companies. This means that the quality of production must meet a certain level.

Upgrading

The qualification of employees for promotion is often an important need. The shortage of well-qualified managers due to the rapid expansion of business and the decrease in business management experience during the depression and during World War II has resulted in a recent emphasis on management development courses.

Satisfaction

In recent years satisfaction of employees has been highlighted as a need that can be satisfied in part by some training. It is particularly prominent in induction training. When first employed, the worker is likely to feel lost and anxious unless training makes him feel at home.

Safety

The need for safety is often prominent in training. This subject is discussed at length in Chapter 9.

Versatility

The goal of making employees versatile by being able to perform successfully in more than one job represents another need for training. In this way there will be less turnover when production changes occur, and less interruption when there are absences. Such versatility can be expected to lead to greater interest and to less boredom on highly specialized jobs.

Free enterprise

The need to have employees understand the free enterprise system so that they will not accept communism and will be more understanding of American business management has been felt by many companies. It is questionable that employee see this as a need as frequently as management does.

Culture

Some industrial training or education programs train for the purpose of instilling culture. In the International Harvester Company, for example, there has been an "off-hour" program which the company sponsored during employees' leisure time. The company encourages and supports courses in high schools and colleges. The selection and content of the courses are determined by the interests of the employees and not by the company. This company believes that it is beneficial to employee morale to encourage study in off hours, whether the subject is as remote from building trucks as music appreciation or folk dancing. Not all companies agree that this is a desirable expense. Which is the majority opinion is not known.

Summary

From this variety of training needs it can be seen that the needs vary from one industry to another, even from one company to another, and that within a company the needs vary from time to time. This means that each company should determine its training needs before beginning a training program. The needs, if they exist, will be the basis for setting objectives. Unless there are clear objectives, there will be no way of finding out whether training has been successful.

TRAINING METHODS

The ultimate problem of training methods is to determine which method is superior for each need and each situation. The problem is almost never solved. The results of training, as will be seen later, are almost never demonstrated for a single method, let alone by a comparison of two or more methods. Consequently a discussion of methods consists more of a list of some of them, and opinions about them, than demonstrated facts about their efficiency.

Unsystematic on-the-job training is probably the most frequently used method in American industry, although a number of systematic procedures are fairly widely practiced. For management training the conference method is by far the most popular. Role playing is often used in sales training and is coming to be used more in management training. Management training has come to be recognized as probably the most important industrial training task in America. It is an important phase of executive development which, *Fortune* has declared, is the most important management problem of today. Aside from training, the other key steps in executive development are the selection of potential executives and their evaluation, in order to improve the functioning of the organization; this is closely connected to the training step. These three steps, selection, training, and evaluation, are all psychological steps, regardless of the complexity or the simplicity with which they are performed. The way they are carried out in American industry depends a great deal on the findings of psychological research, but a considerable amount of research remains to be done on each for the proof, or possibly the determination, of the best methods.

Management training on the job is often of a coaching nature. Some companies favor a rotation system whereby a manager or a prospective manager can get a greater variety of assignments than he normally could by ordinary job changes. Formal training is becoming increasingly popular for managers, either as conducted within the company or in special university programs, of which there are now several dozens.

Systematic vs. unsystematic training

Three companies have reported that systematic training proved more effective than unsystematic.[5] The systematic training in each instance

HOW TO GET READY TO INSTRUCT

HAVE A TIMETABLE—
how much skill you expect him to have, by what date.

BREAK DOWN THE JOB—
list important steps.

pick out the key points. (Safety is always a key point.)

HAVE EVERYTHING READY—
the right equipment, materials, and supplies.

HAVE THE WORK PLACE PROPERLY ARRANGED—
just as the worker will be expected to keep it.

HOW TO INSTRUCT

Step 1—PREPARE THE WORKER

Put him at ease.

State the job and find out what he already knows about it.

Get him interested in learning the job.

Place in correct position.

Step 2—PRESENT THE OPERATION

Tell, show, and illustrate one **Important Step** at a time.

Stress each **Key Point.**

Instruct clearly, completely, and patiently, but no more than he can master.

Step 3—TRY OUT PERFORMANCE

Have him do the job—correct errors.

Have him explain each **Key Point** to you as he does the job again.

Make sure he understands.

Continue until **You** know **He** knows.

Step 4—FOLLOW UP

Put him on his own. Designate to whom he goes for help.

Check frequently. Encourage questions.

Taper off extra coaching and close follow-up.

If the Worker Hasn't Learned, the Instructor Hasn't Taught.

Figure 7-1. Outline of Job Instruction Course.

("Training Within Industry Report," *War Manpower Commission Bureau of Training,* Washington: U.S. Government Printing Office, 1945, pp. 33–34.)

152

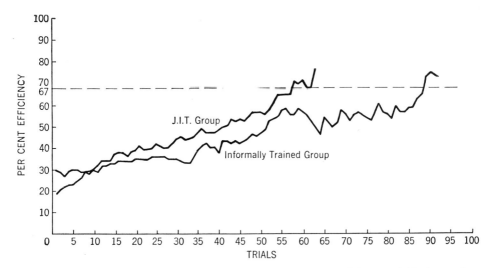

Figure 7-2. Efficiency of a Job Instruction Trained Group of Typists and an Informally Trained Group of Typists.

(Mahler, Walter R., and Willys H. Monroe, *How Industry Determines the Need for and Effectiveness of Training*. A contract research report to Personnel Research Section, Adjutant General's Office, New York: The Psychological Corporation, 1952, p. 76.)

was done in a vestibule school; that is, the training group was separated from employees already on the job. The job instruction practices of the Training Within Industry program developed during World War II were specifically followed in the first two of the three examples. These job instruction practices are shown in Figure 7-1.

Systematic training in a chemical company proved more effective in teaching employees to weigh one grain of streptomycin under sterile conditions and to fill capsules. The employees required less time to reach standard performance. Turnover was cut greatly.

The second demonstration of the effectiveness of systematic training studied typists in the Atlantic Refining Company. The superiority of the systematically trained group is shown in Figure 7-2. There were only four typists in the group that was systematically trained. As shown in Figure 7-2, this group reached the desired level of proficiency in 65 per cent of the time required by the group that was trained unsystematically. The extra trials to reach the desired level required three months longer training for the unsystematically trained group. The intelligence and typing ability of the two groups was checked, and they do not explain the superiority of the four typists who were systematically trained.

153

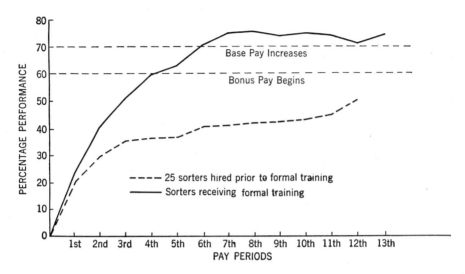

Figure 7-3. Effect of Training on Efficiency in Sorting Cork.

(Mahler, Walter R., and Willys H. Monroe, *How Industry Determines the Need for and Effectiveness of Training*. A contract research report to Personnel Research Section, Adjutant General's Office, New York: The Psychological Corporation, 1952, p. 77.)

A third study showed that formal training was superior in teaching people to sort cork on the basis of different grades. These results are shown in Figure 7-3. After fourteen weeks of training, the seventh pay period, the formally trained group had a performance rating of 78 per cent as contrasted to only 41 per cent for the sorters who had not been formally trained. At the end of twelve pay periods the formally trained group was still far superior.

Individualized training

The Procter and Gamble Company has been giving foremen individualized training in a way that sounds interesting.[6] Foremen are taught on the job to do one step at a time. The responsibility for deciding how long to spend on each phase of the job is left with the trainee foreman. An introduction to this program is shown in Figure 7-4, and an outline of the foreman's responsibilities is shown in Figure 7-5. Typical assignments for one area of responsibility are shown in Figure 7-6. The trainee foreman is asked to keep notes in a Job Control Book, which serves as a reference for him in scheduling production and in his other areas of responsibility. Although no results have been reported as yet of the effectiveness of this individualized training, it has several features

154

P & G Factory   October 11, 1955

FOREMANSHIP TRAINING PROGRAM

WALTER JOHNSON

Making Ivory Bar

I. Introduction

The objective of this program is to give you an opportunity to become a member of Procter & Gamble management by learning how to supervise the Ivory department. Each assignment is designed to bring out certain information or to develop a skill that you will need in managing the department.

The foreman of a department is responsible for the details of running his department. As a foreman trainee, you are responsible for getting the detailed information from each assignment. You must be sure that you cover each phase of the program from the standpoint of what you need to know to operate the department rather than what the operator or staff man with whom you are training needs to know to handle his job. When you have obtained enough information about each responsibility, you should actually perform it. The training period is an opportunity to practice performance on each of the foreman's responsibilities before you assume them.

You will be checked on each phase of training by your supervisor or one of the staff supervisors, or both, to be sure you have obtained the necessary information and know how to use it in your future job.

The effective foreman must budget his time to be sure that he covers all of his responsibilities and is not sidetracked by the pressure of current problems. To give you experience in allocating your time, it will be your responsibility to make your own appointments with the individuals from whom you will be getting information. As in the operation of a department, the supervisor provides the opportunity and the guidance. The execution is the responsibility of the foreman.

Figure 7-4. Introduction to a Training Program.

(Rood, Joseph E., "How Foremen Trainees Learn by Doing," *Personnel,* 1956, **32,** 409–422. By permission of the American Management Association, Inc.)

155

IV. RESPONSIBILITIES WHICH MUST BE PERFORMED

There are certain administrative duties which a foreman must perform in order to supervise his department. Some of these he does personally; the majority of them are delegated but must be followed up.

So that you will be qualified to handle all of these responsibilities, you should actually perform each one during the course of your training. When you take over each item of the foreman's planning, control, or paper work, you should continue this function so that when you take over the department there will be a smooth transition.

In addition to your problem assignments, there is certain material you will need that is purely information rather than development of skill. This type of information is covered in Pre-foremanship Meetings and discussions with the Superintendent.

Following are the foreman's responsibilities covered in your program which you will be expected to learn:

1. Operating details.
2. Scheduling.
3. Assigning work.
4. Arranging repairs and equipment maintenance.
5. Checking quality on a routine basis.
6. Maintaining department appearance.
7. Controlling costs.
8. Training employees.
9. Promoting the safety and health of employees.
10. Applying the contract and rules and regulations to Department operations.
11. Supervising people.

A section of the training program is devoted to each of these responsibilities. Before starting the training assignments in each section, you should contact your supervisor and have him go over the section with you.

In several assignments, we say "take over the foreman's responsibility." This is a step-wise process in which, after you have enough information, you sit in with the foreman while he is doing the job. After you have seen him do it, you then do it yourself under his observation. Qualification means doing the job on your own and being able to explain to the supervisor the reasons why it is done just that way.

Figure 7-5. Explanatory Outline of Foreman's Responsibilities.

(Rood, Joseph E., "How Foremen Trainees Learn by Doing," *Personnel*, 1956, **32**, 409–422. By permission of the American Management Association, Inc.)

SCHEDULING

A. Training assignments:
1. List in your Job Control Book the Average Schedule, Quarterly Schedule, Monthly Schedule, and Long Range Schedule for the department.
2. Analyze monthly schedule and calculate number of freezer line days and packing line days necessary on each bar size. Coordinate capacities of freezers and packing machines.
   (a) Capacity of each freezer line and each packing line.
   (b) Amount of freezer run necessary for one line day of packing for each size.
3. Order soap, other raw materials, and packing supplies for delivery based on inventories, estimated usages, and time necessary for delivery.
   (a) Procedure for placing each kind of order.
   (b) Procedure for taking inventory.
   (c) Minimum safe inventory to avoid shutdown.
   (d) Maximum allowable storage.
4. Make out production records and reports as required.
   (a) What records and reports are required.
   (b) The purpose of each and the proper distribution.
   (c) The frequency necessary and the importance of being on time.
5. Etc.

B. Sources of information:
1. Operating experience.
2. Kettle House or Hydrolyzer Foreman.
3. Cost Department.
4. Factory office.

C. The Bar Soap Supervisor will be responsible for final qualification on scheduling.

Figure 7-6. Assignments for One Area of Responsibility.

(Rood, Joseph E., "How Foremen Trainees Learn by Doing," *Personnel*, 1956, **32**, 409–422. By permission of the American Management Association, Inc.)

to commend it. Each person is learning at his own rate. If he needs longer on one area than on another, he can spend the extra time. The trainee is active. He is practicing what he has to do on the job. The training is clearly practical in that he is learning to do what he will have to do on the job.

Conference vs. lecture

The conference is widely preferred over the lecture in management training because people participate more in a discussion. One study has been reported in which the conference was compared to the lecture method.[7] Two groups of foremen were taught economics, one through the use of conferences, the other by lectures. Objective tests were given at the beginning and end of each course. There was no significant difference between the gains of the two groups. There is no evidence here that the conference method results in more learning than the lecture method. The advantage of the conference appears to be in its acceptability rather than in its efficiency.

Case discussion

The discussion of actual business situations is very popular as a method of management training. The case for discussion should be an actual case which presents or has presented some problem to be solved. Managers or potential managers almost always have different points of view in discussing a case. Such differences arouse interest by providing what is often a heated discussion. This keeps the trainees more alert than most lectures do. The differences that are expressed bring people to recognize that there is more than one point of view in perceiving a human situation. This in turn leads to a recognition of the necessity for more care in reaching decisions about people. It also makes people more tolerant through the knowledge that there are varying attitudes that are equally defensible. The case method makes people critical of generalizations about human relations principles and more inclined to emphasis on a situational approach to problems.

Role playing

Role playing is particularly advantageous in teaching human relations and sales procedures. It forces a person to put himself in the place of another and therefore makes him feel what it is like to be in another's shoes. Role playing requires a lot of time, and, at first, trainees may be embarrassed and may make fun of what they are doing. It can be very effective as a supervisory practice when a qualified trainer is available. There are no statistical results as to its effectiveness for human relations or sales, but one successful use has been reported.[8] Supervisors in the United Parcel Service were able to reduce the percentage of undeliverable packages through the use of role playing. The plays were acted among the supervisors, who practiced persuading drivers to use methods, with which the drivers were already familiar, to avoid making another trip for a delivery.

Role playing goes a step nearer reality than the case method does. In the case method a decision will be reached that a manager should talk to a subordinate and find out why he did a job in a certain way. Role playing requires that the manager actually try to carry out the assignment. It shows that it is generally easier to say what to do than it is to do it. Typically, a role play will have different instructions for each player, so that there is some lack of complete understanding just as there generally is in real life when a human relations problem is present.

Role playing involves feelings more than does any other training method. It therefore has the best chance of changing attitudes, which is one of the main objectives of management training—to create attitudes in managers which will make them aware of the feelings of others.

RESULTS

The results of training are not usually demonstrated, perhaps because they are considered too obvious to justify the research effort. There have, however, been a number of measurements which prove that training of one kind or another gets better results. A few of these which show improvements in production as a result of training methods have been referred to already. Other studies have shown that the effects of training can be measured, that early progress can be considered a reasonably accurate prediction of later progress, that waste can be reduced through training, and, in one instance, that sales training proved worth while. There has been increasing interest in attempting to measure the value of management training. The evidence has not been reassuring. It has been shown that managers can learn to read better, that they like training, and that their attitudes as measured in questionnaires are changed in the direction intended. The only two thorough studies of the influence of management training on behavior did not give positive results. In one of these studies, one group of managers improved and the other became worse. In the second study, managers improved immediately after training, but six months later were worse off than before the training began. These studies that attempt to measure the results of human relations training will be presented in Chapter 15 in more detail.

Performance during training

When performance has been measured during the training period, early progress has been shown to be predictive of the final level of training and on-the-job performance. This has been reported for only four groups of employees; three groups were in the textile industry, and the fourth was composed of billing-machine operators.[9] In general, employees who are quick to learn at first reach higher levels of learning and reach higher levels of eventual production than do those who are slower to learn. Prediction from training records is more accurate for some groups than for others. Prediction from training records is, in general, more accurate than prediction from aptitude tests.

The difference in production between fast and slow learners in a textile job is shown in Figure 7-7. The job consisted in preparing spools for rug looms. The nine fast learners reached the company's standard of production after an average of 8.4 months of training as contrasted with 12.7 months for the 12 slowest learners. As shown in Figure 7-7, the fast learners had better records in the first week of training and in every week thereafter. These differences were stable enough to be used with new learners. If a learner showed up as slow in the early weeks of training, he could be removed from this job because of the likelihood that he would not be efficient on it.

The solid line in Figure 7-7 shows an Index of Predictive Efficiency.

The supervisor by knowing how the employee performed during the first week of training could predict whether or not he would be fast or slow in reaching average production in a manner which would be more accurate by twenty per cent than would a chance prediction. At the end of two weeks on the job, knowledge of an employee's production would increase the accuracy of the supervisor's prediction forty-four per cent. At the end of six weeks of training his accuracy would increase sixty-three per cent if he knew how the employee had produced during training. The supervisor would not increase his accuracy of prediction from knowledge of how the worker produced during the remaining two weeks of the first eight weeks on the job.

This Index of Predictive Efficiency enables the supervisor to decide whether to retain or dismiss a worker in terms of the current labor situation. If the labor market is tight, the worker could be retained for six weeks before deciding whether to release him. However, if the market is loose, the decision could be made at an earlier period. A second factor which must be considered is the cost of the training. If workers are scarce and training relatively inexpensive, one can keep trainees until failure is nearly certain; if the labor market is loose and training costly, it is uneconomical to continue training workers with lower probability of success.[10]

Waste

Waste has been reduced by training in the cotton textile industry in several instances that have been reported. The effect of training has also been shown to last over a considerable period of time. For example, the

Fieldcrest Mills found that training was still effective two years after the training had occurred.[11] These results are shown in Table 7-I. The ratio was 2.50 before training, and it dropped to .94 after training. In the twenty-week period ending 103 weeks after training, the waste ratio was substantially the same as just after training, 1.01. In the following twenty weeks there was a sharp drop to .71, or the lowest waste of all. The training in waste reduction of employees in the mill other than those under study was offered as the explanation of this drop. It was thought that the training "spilled over" to the operators who were not now receiving formal training. At this point refresher training was given, and it resulted in still further reduction in waste to the low ratio of .52.

This study demonstrates, as have several other studies, that waste can be reduced and that the reductions persist for a substantial period of time. It is unique in showing that refresher training can be effective in bringing even better records.

Sales

An impressive study of the effectiveness of training on life insurance agents has been made.[12] The life insurance industry universally gives sales training, but before the Purdue Study was made there had been

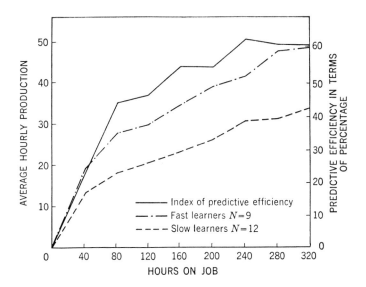

Figure 7-7. Production of Fast and Slow Textile Learners and Predictive Efficiency.

(McGehee, William, "Cutting Training Waste," *Personnel Psychology,* 1948, **1,** 331–340.)

TABLE 7-I

Means and Standard Deviations of Waste Ratios
for Specified Periods

PERIOD AND PERIOD NUMBERS	MEAN	STANDARD DEVIATION	NUMBER OF WEEKS
1. Pretraining	2.50	.42	10
Initial Training and Follow-up			
2. Training	1.50	.45	3
3. Reinforcement	.87	.06	12
4. Post training	.94	.16	14
2-4. Total 29 weeks	.96	.24	29
Present Follow-up			
5. 1st 20 weeks	1.05	.17	20
6. 2nd 20 weeks	1.03	.15	20
7. 3rd 20 weeks	1.01	.19	20
8. 4th 20 weeks	.71	.31	20
5-7. Total 60 weeks	1.03	.17	60
5-8. Total 80 weeks	.95	.28	80
9. Final 26 weeks	.52	.07	26

McGehee, William, and Dwight H. Livingstone, "Persistence of the Effects of Training Employees To Reduce Waste," *Personnel Psychology,* 1954, **7,** 33–39.

some question whether training helped or whether salesmen were born rather than made. There was evidence that with experience salesmen sold less rather than more insurance. The peak of performance was reached in the second three months on the job. Sales for one large group of agents amounted to $143,300 during their first year and to $135,100 in their second year.

It was not possible for the authors of the Purdue Study to compare training with no training because no insurance company was willing to skip training, even though it had not been proved to be effective. The design of the study was to compare an unusual training program with the customary company training. The experimental training was a year's course at Purdue University conducted by the Institute of Life Insurance Marketing. This training differed from company training in "requiring: attendance at college classes, a considerable time away from the field, field work under the supervision of a special faculty, and continuous training and supervision over a one-year period."

Two hundred and forty-one agents attended the Purdue course. They were matched with a control group who did not have this training. It was recognized that the Purdue-trained group was unusual in that its members were above average in ability and motivation, since their companies paid part of their expenses during this unproductive year. Consequently, it was seen that the control group consisting of agents not attending the course would have to be similarly unusual. Members of this control group had to survive on the job for the twelve months of the Purdue Training period to make training comparisons possible. Each one of the Purdue-trained men was matched on five variables with a member of the control group. Where matching was not possible, the edge was given to the control member of the pair. The variables on which matching occurred were: (1) length of experience in selling insurance before the beginning of the Purdue study; (2) marital status; (3) production, or amount of sales before the Purdue training; (4) Aptitude Index; (5) age.

An actual example of the way the control group was matched with the experimental was as follows:

Agent X entered Purdue after six months of experience . . . His production level was $12,500 per month. He is married, 28 years of age, and obtained a B rating on the Aptitude Index. Since at the time of graduation, Agent X had survived in the business for 18 months, the [control] group . . . with this minimum 18-month survival was taken as the source of the match. Within this group, the married men were examined to find those whose production level for the first six months was approximately $12,500 per month. Among these, a search was made for men whose age was near 28 years and whose Aptitude Index rating was A or B. The end result is . . . [control] Man X . . . a survivor for at least 18 months with a production level of $12,600 per month during the first six months, . . . married, aged 29, with an A rating on the Aptitude Index.

The same matching procedure was repeated for each of the 241 pairs.

The salesmen trained at Purdue stayed on the job longer, had better production records, and were rated as more successful. Exactly half of the control group quit or were fired during the study, as compared with only one-third of the Purdue-trained men. The study lasted for several classes and cut off so that the average Purdue-trained man had been on the job twenty-three months after training. The Purdue graduates sold 53 per cent more insurance than the control group, although before training their production was the same. Of 230 pairs on whom production figures could be obtained, the Purdue men sold $59,666,000 and the control men sold $38,960,000 over an average time of twenty-three months. The increased production was enough to make up completely for the three months during training when the Purdue men were not selling. The effect on sales would make it appear that the Purdue-trained men will sell $39,600 more each year because of their training. If "success" is defined as monthly sales of $15,000 plus surviving during the period of the study, the Purdue group had 41 per cent who were successful and the control group only 22 per cent.

The training had its main effect on low-producing men, which is what a company would want. As was shown earlier for other jobs, success is usually predicted fairly well from early progress in training. This is generally true of life insurance agents, and it was true of the control group. It was not true of the Purdue-trained group. The training had enough effect on low producers to upset completely the relationship between early poor records and later success after training.

Managers

The results of management training are difficult to measure for several reasons. There are often insufficient numbers of managers at the same stage of training so that they form a sufficiently large population for a comparison of their performance to be statistically meaningful. More basic is the fact that there is almost never, if ever, a yardstick of management success that can be applied to the evaluation of the effectiveness of management training.

Most, but not all, companies are convinced on the basis of experience that management training does produce worth-while results. The other extreme point of view is that managers are born, or at least that their personalities are determined by the time they are employed, and are not made. At this stage of our knowledge, or ignorance, it is safer to conclude that the characteristic of management success is a combination of training and the personality that the manager brings to the job. While there are no exact measures of the relative contributions, it seems likely that training in the formal sense contributes less than the personality, including all abilities, that the manager brings to the job. Still, training is of sufficient importance that it should be pursued, and the needs, the best methods, and the ways of evaluating it should be found.

It has not been proved that management training changes managers' actions on the job in a desirable way. There are numerous demonstrations that managers say that they like the training that they have received, and there are a somewhat smaller, though still considerable, number that show that managers' attitudes are changed by training in a direction that is desired. A few instances have shown that managers have in fact learned certain content that was contained in a course. These are interesting but not so crucial as what the manager actually does rather than how he feels, or what he says he would do. Studies of leadership behavior will be described in Chapter 15.

SUMMARY

When management offers training, it needs to consider the motivation of the trainee and whether or not the reward offered for learning will satisfy the motivation.

When training is being considered, it is necessary to be critical as to whether or not there is a real need, and, if so, just what it is. If it is decided to give training, the method or methods to be used have to be decided upon. Attention should be given to evaluating the results of training.

Training has been shown to be effective in raising production in manufacturing and in sales, in decreasing waste, and in other objectives desired.

Management training has become a prominent part of executive development in American industry. The primary need underlying such training is the need to understand people. Methods for pursuing this objective have mainly been the conference, case discussion, and role playing. Results of management training have rarely been rigorously measured. Some disquieting results along this line will be presented in Chapter 15.

RECOMMENDED READINGS

McGehee, William, and Dwight H. Livingstone, "Persistence of the Effects of Training Employees To Reduce Waste," *Personnel Psychology*, 1954, **7**, 33-39. Measurement of the effects of a training program extending over several years.

Rood, Joseph E., "How Foremen Trainees Learn by Doing: A Company Program," *Personnel*, 1956, **32**, 409-422. A very thorough training program in the Procter and Gamble Company.

Wallace, S. Rains, Jr., and Constance M. Twichell, "The Purdue Study," *Manager's Magazine*, 1953, **28**, 7 ff. An objective study with a control group which shows impressive results of training.

8

Human engineering

Some of the psychological aspects of work and fatigue have been discovered and been well understood, others have been discovered but not
applied widely, and perhaps others remain to be discovered. The term
"human engineering" probably fits these various aspects better than any
other single term. Human engineering is the study of people at work and
of work methods; it includes a study of equipment design, pacing of work,
hours of work, and environmental conditions of work; its purpose is to
improve productivity and job satisfaction.

Economic aspects

The main objective of motion and time study and other changes in work
methods has been to increase production and therefore profits. This
objective has been reached in many instances. Among the many demonstrations was the spectacular example of loading pig iron; through a
study of this operation, production was raised and fatigue reduced. Procedures at the Bethlehem Steel Company installed by Taylor, the origi-
nator of scientific management, increased the amount of pig iron loaded
from 12.5 tons to 47 to 48 tons per man-day.[1] The company saved at the
rate of $75,000 to $80,000 per year by reducing the average cost of
handling from 7 cents to 3 cents per ton. Wages were also increased
substantially, from $1.15 to $1.88 per day, but naturally fewer men were
needed because of the great increase in productivity.

Providing good working conditions is often thought to increase production. This is frequently justified on the grounds that it leads to improved morale, which in turn is believed by many businessmen to cause
higher productivity and profits.

Objections by labor

There have been many objections by labor to the practices of scientific
management, although there have been instances of cooperation from

labor unions, such as those in the automotive and garment industries. Both organized and unorganized labor have opposed the changes of scientific management and, although they mention physiological fatigue as a reason, probably feelings are a more important reason.

Labor's opinion of efficiency experts has been generally low. Most efficiency experts, especially in recent years, have sincerely applied motion and time study principles. When these sincere men have failed to obtain acceptance, it has probably been because of a failure on their part to be sensitive to the human relations problems which are inevitably present in changes, as well as because of weaknesses in the techniques of motion and time study. Another difficulty in the past has been that, in many instances, the details of motion and time study have been kept secret from employees. Such secrecy was used, and is still used in some companies, in an effort to prevent employees from defeating the efficiency objective of the system by learning about it in detail. It is accepted that employees should be persuaded, but the more fundamental point that they should have a share in developing the new idea if they are really to accept it is rarely put into practice.

Motion and time study have at times led to rates of pay getting out of line, and this has resulted consequently in employee dissatisfaction. In order to secure employee cooperation, motion and time analysts have promised that employees whose jobs were being analyzed would have a raise in pay proportionate to resulting gains in output. This has sometimes brought the pay of these jobs out of line with those in the plant or in the community. Labor should share in these gains, but the sharing should probably not be limited to those workers whose jobs were studied. Perhaps the whole plant should benefit from increased productivity, since, in the long run, it is the group attitudes of employees which will make future changes easy or hard.

Perhaps labor unions object to time study because employee actions are thereby analyzed as if the worker were a machine. Aside from that, there have been four objections to the accuracy of time study: (1) mechanical errors such as variations in working conditions and in the quality of tools and raw material; (2) errors in allowances for fatigue; (3) psychological sources of variation such as individual differences and motivation; and (4) sociological sources of variation such as the work group's notion of a fair day's work.[2]

Psychological aspects

Psychological contributions to human engineering are of three types: (1) principles and practice of human relations to obtain cooperation in changes; (2) research on methods to ensure that adequate experimental and statistical controls have been used to make findings accurate; and (3) recognition of psychological characteristics of workers, that is, human capabilities such as limits of perceptual speed and tendency to boredom under certain conditions.

Time study has often had psychological and social sources of error in its application because of insufficient stress on individual differences, reaction to boredom, and motivation. The use of time study, as well as of motion study, generally implies that there is one best way of work. Differences between individuals make it unlikely that there is one best way of work, as indicated in the discussion of motion study below. Even if there were one best way of work under ordinary conditions for the worker, he might, when bored, find it more comfortable to do the job in a different way and would thereby differ from the rate of output clocked by the time study man.

Motivation is perhaps most important in explaining why employees do not respond to time study as the engineers expect them to do. Chapter 10 presents some of the basic problems of motivation. It is assumed, when time study is used to set incentive pay plans, that workers will be motivated to produce all that they can when they are promised extra pay for extra production. The fact that it often does not work out that way has been a source of surprise to management.

The emphasis on time study as the basis for piece-rate pay plans overlooks the full meaning of employee morale. It oversimplifies it by assuming that more money on the job is the only incentive. Certainly, under many conditions money is a powerful incentive. There are, however, other powerful incentives in the work situation that must be recognized before the effectiveness of the promise of more money can be determined. The influence of the work group on employee morale is at times a more powerful force. Just how this works in defeating time study expectations will be detailed later in the discussion of restriction of output.

The lack of acceptance to the introduction of improved work methods would be largely avoided if workers were afforded greater participation in the origin of these improvements. Management has not shown general agreement with the idea of worker participation, but it would be well advised to obtain employee participation in the planning of work method improvements. The advantage of worker participation is that people are much more willing to do what they have had a hand in or what they accept willingly than what is forced upon them, however logical the procedure. The Federal Steel Company made a net saving a year of $166,200 by securing worker participation in improving work methods, which in this instance had been planned by a CIO Steelworkers Union research committee.[3] Some managements would be afraid to allow participation by the union on production matters, but would not have the same fear in dealing with employee groups directly rather than through union representatives.

Morale of employees needs to be recognized as a factor in the introduction of new methods. Generally there is resistance to change unless people have had a part in originating the change. Such participation is rare at the rank-and-file level in American industry. It is important to recognize the attitudes of employees toward the new method, toward their job as modified by the new method, and toward their company and immediate supervisor for promoting a change in methods. One should expect management and employees to have different points of view regarding a new method. The weight of the work group in the formulation of attitudes about a change should be appreciated.

Plans for increasing production by improving working conditions, shortening hours of work, and introducing rest pauses have been made mainly by engineers, although these developments involve psychological problems, such as the determination of true cause and effect under sufficiently controlled conditions. The separation of the influence of fatigue from monotony at work has still in many instances remained obscure. Determining whether an increase in production is actually due to a specific change in conditions or to a favorable attitude of appreciation poses a fundamental problem requiring more rigorous experimental controls than have customarily been used.

JOB METHODS

Job methods have been made more efficient through the design of more automatic machines and through an analysis of motions. Motion study can be a very complex procedure, as will be shown below, or it can be a relatively simple process. A relatively simple approach was the basis for one of the courses of the Training Within Industry program of World War II, which included the elements of motion study. The outline of this course, which was given to supervisors, is shown in Figure 8-1.

Equipment design

From the standpoint of human engineering, equipment design attempts to make the best working fit between man and machine. This field takes into account more areas of knowledge than does the usual motion and

Step I—BREAK DOWN the job
    1. List *all* details of the job *exactly* as done by the *Present Method.*
    2. Be sure details include all:
        —Material Handling.
        —Machine Work.
        —Hand Work.

Step II—QUESTION every detail
    1. Use these types of questions:
        WHY is it necessary?
        WHAT is its purpose?
        WHERE should it be done?
        WHEN should it be done?
        WHO is best qualified to do it?
        HOW is the "best way" to do it?
    2. Also question the:
        Materials, Machines, Equipment, Tools, Product Design, Layout, Workplace, Safety, Housekeeping.

Step III—DEVELOP the new method.
    1. ELIMINATE *unnecessary* details.
    2. COMBINE details when practical.
    3. REARRANGE for better sequence.
    4. SIMPLIFY all necessary details:
        —Make the work *easier* and *safer.*
        —*Pre-position* materials, tools and equipment at the best places in the *proper work area.*
        —Use *gravity-feed* hoppers and *drop-delivery* chutes.
        —Let *both* hands do *useful* work.
        —Use *jigs* and *fixtures* instead of hands for holding work.
    5. *Work out* your idea *with* others.
    6. Write up your proposed new method.

Step IV—APPLY the new method.
    1. *Sell* your proposal to the *boss.*
    2. *Sell* the new method to the *operators.*
    3. Get final approval of all concerned on *Safety, Quality, Quantity, Cost.*
    4. Put the new method to work. Use it until a *better* way is developed.
    5. Give *credit* where credit is due.

Figure 8-1. Job Methods Outline.

("Training Within Industry Report," *War Manpower Commission Bureau of Training,* Washington: U.S. Government Printing Office, 1945, pp. 37–38.)

time study analysis. Motion and time study usually attempts to adapt the man to the machine, whereas human engineering places more emphasis on changing the machine if necessary. One book, *Human Factors in Engineering Design,* includes discussions of sight, visual displays, hearing, speech, human movements, controls, fatigue, and working conditions as well as motion and time study.[4] Some of the problems of design touching on human responses merge from psychology into physiology, such as the regulation of oxygen, temperature, ventilation, humidity, noise, vibration, acceleration, and motion. Concern with human capacities and limitations should be a fundamental part of the design of equipment, whereas motion and time study devises the best methods for working with the completed machines and considers only minor changes in equipment.

The design of any tool or piece of equipment should be based on the capabilities of prospective operators. For instance, sledge hammers are always built light enough to be within the lifting capabilities of a very strong man. The need for considering the human limitations of reach and for considering ease of motions in the design of machines had been recognized as early as the 1920's, but the problems of World War II brought the matter of equipment design in terms of human capacities to a more prominent focus. Greater awareness of the potentials of human engineering and greater need because of more complicated equipment combine to increase the civilian need for human engineering development.

AUTOMATION

The trend toward more complicated and automatic machinery is increasing productivity and lessening the physical aspect of work, but it is also making design and repair tasks harder and more numerous. Machines are becoming substitutes for people on the more routine jobs, but people must design, build, and maintain the machines. More automatic equipment increases the ratio of maintenance personnel to operators. In one factory this ratio changed from 1 to 5 to 3 to 5, and it is expected to go to 1 to 1 in the near future.[5] The over-all effect will be the upgrading of jobs as more people must learn to repair equipment and fewer people will work as semiskilled operators.

ARMED FORCES

In the Army Air Force, psychological factors of equipment design have shown their practical nature in several types of problems.[6] Designs have been improved for air navigation scales and for instrument dials because accuracy in reading them was found to depend on the scale

PROBLEM: (from Miles, W. R. Red goggles for producing dark adaptation. *Federation Proceedings*, 1943, **2,** 109–115)

It is well-known that the ability of the eyes to see in low levels of illumination is a function of the amount of time that they take to adjust or adapt to this low level. In complete darkness, the process is reasonably complete in 30–45 min. . . . For efficient seeing at night, maximal sensitivity is desirable, but exposure of the eyes to light quickly wipes out the advantages of adaptation in the dark. The practical problem, then, is how to protect dark adaptation so that personnel may engage in normal activities in lighted surroundings and still be maximally sensitive for seeing in the dark. It is inefficient and tiresome to require lookouts, for example, to sit in complete darkness for 30–45 min. before going on duty.

Pertinent Handbook Data:

1. Dark adaptation. . . . Increase of sensitivity of 15,000X occurs with complete dark adaptation over the completely light-adapted eye.

2. Effect of wavelength of stimulus on brightness . . . shows that the stimulating effectiveness of light is a function of its wavelength . . . two different processes are present in the eye for seeing at high and low levels of illumination and the wavelength characteristics of the two systems differ.

Solution:

Use of dark adaptation goggles with red filters which pass no visible radiation shorter than 620–640 mμ. While wearing these goggles, personnel may read or carry out duties in moderately high illumination using the daylight vision system and still be able to see efficiently in relative darkness using the night vision system when they remove the goggles.

Figure 8-2. Sample Human Engineering Problem.

(Institute of Applied Experimental Psychology, Tufts College, *Handbook of Human Engineering Data,* 2nd ed., Medford, Mass., Tufts College, 1952, Part I, Chapter I, Section I, Table 1–1.)

divisions and on the size and number of numerical markings. Designs of aircraft controls have been improved through findings that show the direction and plane of movements that are most accurate. Psychologists selected the interphone equipment for military aircraft during World War II that would permit speech to be heard most clearly.[7]

Much of the present knowledge about people that would be useful in solving human engineering problems has been gathered together in *Handbook of Human Engineering Data,* prepared for the U. S. Navy by the Tufts College Institute of Applied Experimental Psychology.[8] This handbook contains extensive information about the capabilities of people in the areas of vision, audition, skin sensitivity and muscle sense, motor performance, physiological conditions as determinants of efficiency, intelligence, and learning. Figure 8-2 illustrates the solution of a human engineering problem through the use of the handbook. It shows how immediate dark adaptation can be achieved by a pilot's wearing red goggles rather than having his eyes closed or staying in the dark for 30 minutes or more. The supporting data, which document the advantage of the new system over the old, are referred to in the figure.

INDUSTRY

Human engineering as such has not been extensively used in the design of civilian equipment. In 1954 full-time human engineering specialists were employed by only about a dozen American firms.[9] Consulting work in human engineering is being done by a few civilian firms.

Some idea of human engineering work for equipment design can be gathered from a few of the problems faced by one aircraft factory.[10]

What is a comfortable finger pressure for knobs?
How much force should be required for a wheel control?
What is the volume occupied by a man?
What are the angles of vision from a prone position?
How far away can a pilot see another airplane?
What is the weight of the human head and brain?
What should be the height of a "no smoking" sign?
What are the effects of drugs on the human body in flight?
How much work-space is required for a bartender in a cocktail lounge?

The Bell Telephone Company felt that it was able to reduce the weight of telephone handsets and wanted to know if it would be desirable to do so.[11] In reply to an informal survey, 80 per cent of customers said that the present weight was just fine. The Bell Telephone Laboratory did not rely on what people thought they would prefer, but built and installed a number of lighter-weight handsets. After using the lightweight handsets for a while, 100 per cent came to prefer them over the standard-weight handsets. Armchair thinking on man-machine relationships might have resulted in the conclusion that the current handset weight was better, whereas the operational test of the two types showed that the lighter weight was more desirable.

In designing civilian aircraft the desirability of considering human capacities, not only of operators but also of passengers, has been considered at length.[12] The primary goal of these considerations is safety for the features that affect the crew, and comfort for those that affect the passengers. The evidence accumulated so far about the advantages of this or that feature of equipment design is of the laboratory rather than the operational variety. It is possible to show, for example, that a certain dial arrangement or a certain type of control results in fewer errors, or increased speed, or increased accuracy in performance in a laboratory situation.

A new cab has been designed with human engineering objectives for a dragline, a piece of mining equipment that digs ore and costs over a million dollars.[13] The changes in the new cab with respect to the old cab were many, but they were essentially of three kinds: (1) the working environment, including better lighting, more comfortable seating; (2) visibility of the area from which the ore is dug; (3) information about conditions of the equipment and controls for regulating the equipment. The new design was compared with the old one over a two-week interval; it was 10 per cent faster even though no allowance was made for training the operator on the new equipment.

There have been a number of design decisions in industry to fit in with human capacities, although as a rule the design of industrial machinery has not considered the operator carefully. No concrete results have been reported for the most part in situations in which human factors have been given due consideration. In one case, however, the substitution of a smaller screw driver in the assembly of electrical equipment resulted in an increase in output of between 15 and 25 per cent.[14]

Human engineering should be able to increase the usefulness of many civilian machines and tools. There seems to be room for improvement in controls, indicators, and work-space arrangement on the basis of what has already been learned in the human engineering of military equipment.

Motion study

Motions were first classified into their elements by Gilbreth, who called them *therbligs* (after his name spelled backward, with one transposi-

PHYSICAL ELEMENTS

Transport Empty
Grasp
Transport Loaded
Release
Change Direction
Hold
Assemble
Disassemble
Use

SEMI-MENTAL ELEMENTS

Search
Find
Select
Pre-Position
Position

MENTAL ELEMENTS

Plan
Inspect
Memory

DELAY ELEMENTS

Avoidable Delay
Unavoidable Delay
Balance Delay
Rest for Fatigue

Figure 8-3. Classification of Motion Elements.

(Adapted from Kosma, Andrew R., *The ABC's of Motion Economy,* Newark, N. J.: Institute of Motion Analysis and Human Relations, 1943, pp. 70–71.)

tion). All manual work could be analyzed into these elements and consequently studied and rearranged as desired. The elements of motion are shown in Figure 8-3. These elements of motion can be used to break down any job and to show the details of materials handling and handwork, as called for by Step I of the Job Methods program (Figure 8-1). The elements can then be questioned as indicated in Step II, and the terminology of the motion elements can be used in Step III to develop an improved method.

The therbligs are not independent of each other. The time it takes to make a motion depends on the pattern of which it is a part. In a task which required the turning of three different types of selector switches exactly 30 degrees, the times for the therbligs which occurred before and after turning the switches varied significantly. The time for *transport empty* plus *grasp* was much shorter when the selector switch knob would turn 30 degrees and no further than when it would turn freely with no stops.[15]

Another experiment showed that an increase in the difficulty of *select* increased the times for surrounding therbligs.[16] In an assembly operation when the subjects were required to *position* washers with a marked side always up rather than with either side up, their times increased for the four other therbligs. If therbligs were independent of each other, the only increase would have been in the *selection* time and in one of the other four (to turn over some of the washers). It was also found that an increase in the distance from the washer supply to the assembly area changed only the *transport* times and not the times for the other therbligs. This experiment and the one before it showed increases in the time for surrounding therbligs when the amount of discrimination required in one therblig increased. The second experiment also showed that a change in transportation distance did not change times for surrounding therbligs. The effect of a change of one therblig on other therbligs in the same cycle depends on the nature of the change and may or may not cause a change in performance times.

PRINCIPLES

The psychological principles of motions in work have been formulated as follows.[17]

1. Successive movements should be so related that one movement passes easily into that which follows, each ending in a position favorable for the beginning of the next movement.
2. The order of movements should be so arranged that little direct attention is needed for passage from one to another. In other words, they are so arranged that the mind can attend to the final aim or end of the operation instead of being distracted by the work of initiating successively the several movements which are involved in a task.
3. The sequence of movements is to be so framed that an easy rhythm can be established in the automatic performance of the various elements of the operation.
4. From the principles which have been stated follows the corollary that a continuous movement is preferable to angular movements involving sudden changes in the direction of movement.
5. The number of movements should be reduced as far as possible within the scope of limitations suggested above. In general, reducing the number of movements will facilitate a rhythmic method of working and automatization as a means of reducing the volitional direction of work.
6. Simultaneous use of both hands should be encouraged.
7. When a forceable stroke is required, the direction of movement and place-

176

Figure 8–4. Slides. Arrangement of the work place when both the terminal points and paths of the motions were fixed. Only one arrangement is shown— the motion path of the operator's hands makes an angle of 60 degrees with the plane of the front of the operator's body.

(Barnes, Ralph M., and Marvin E. Mundel, "A Study of Simultaneous Symmetrical Hand Motions," *University of Iowa Studies in Engineering*, Bulletin 17, 1939. Reproduced by permission from *Motion and Time Study*, 3rd ed., by R. M. Barnes, New York: John Wiley & Sons, Inc., 1949.)

1. Long Forehand Sweep

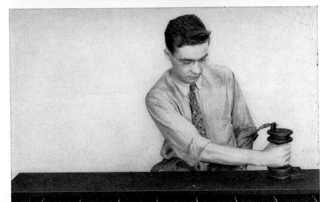

2. Long Backhand Sweep

3. Short Forehand Sweep

Figure 8–5. Starting Positions for Test Motions

4. Short Backhand Sweep

5. Forward Thrust

6. Pull

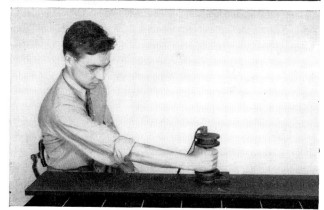

(Koepke, Charles A., and Lee S. Whitson, "Summary of a Series of Experiments To Determine the Power and Velocity of Motions Occurring in Manual Work," *Journal of Applied Psychology*, 1941, **25**, 251–264.)

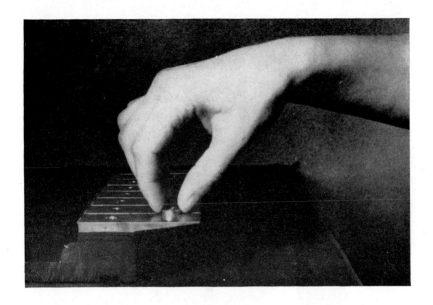

Figure 8–6. Examples of Grasp. Top: *Pinch or pressure grasp being used to pick up a brass washer ⅛ in. thick.* Bottom: *Hook or lip grasp being used to pick up a brass washer ⅛ in. thick.*

(Barnes, Ralph M., and Marvin E. Mundel, "A Study of Hand Motions Used in Small Assembly Work," *University of Iowa Studies in Engineering,* Bulletin 16, 1939.)

ment of material should be so arranged that, as far as practicable, the stroke is delivered when it has reached its greatest momentum.

ONE BEST WAY OF WORK

Efficiency experts have stressed that the purpose of motion study is to find the one best way of work for each job and to train every employee so that he performs in that one best way. This "one best way" may be the result of the logical analysis of the most efficient way, or it may be a synthesis of the work methods of several of the fastest and best workers. Psychologists have raised the objection that, because of individual differences, the best way of work for one worker is not necessarily the best for others. This objection has come to be recognized by some efficiency experts. Employees should be taught a good way to work, but they should be allowed to express their individual initiative after that. Motion economy should not prevent employees from having some motions that look inefficient but contribute to the rhythm of work.

Evidence against one best way of work in one situation is shown in a motion study wherein the subjects pushed slides back and forth.[18] The experimental setup when both the terminal points and the path of motion are fixed is shown in Figure 8-4. The average results showed that motions were fastest when there was a 60-degree angle between the plane of the operator's body and the motions of the hands. This is the arrangement shown in Figure 8-4. The fastest workers, however, worked fastest when the angle was 0, or when the hands were moving in opposite directions parallel to the body. Thus, if the best way for the fastest workers were imposed upon the majority, they would be prevented, by their individual differences, from working at their highest speed.

LABORATORY STUDIES

Refinements in connection with the use of the smaller muscles is called intensive motion study. The Motion and Time Study Laboratory

Figure 8-7. Average Total Cycle Time for Two Grasps with Varying Washer Thicknesses.

(Barnes, Ralph M., and Marvin E. Mundel, "A Study of Hand Motions Used in Small Assembly Work," *University of Iowa Studies in Engineering,* Bulletin 16, 1939, p. 16.)

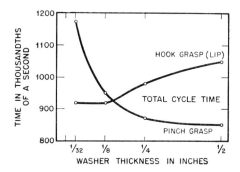

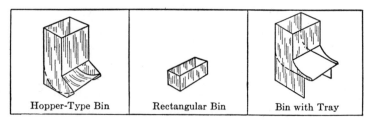

| Hopper-Type Bin | Rectangular Bin | Bin with Tray |

Figure 8-8. Types of Bins.

(Barnes, Ralph M., and Marvin E. Mundel, "A Study of Hand Motions Used in Small Assembly Work," *University of Iowa Studies in Engineering,* Bulletin 16, 1939, p. 28.)

at the University of Iowa has completed several studies which show findings on intensive motion study that can be applied in industry. One study compared two methods of grasping washers.[19] The two methods of grasping, pinch and hook, are shown in Figure 8-6. These two methods were compared with respect to grasping four washers of varying thicknesses. The hook grasp is faster for the thinner washers, the pinch grasp is faster for the thicker washers, as shown in Figure 8-7.

A bin with an attached tray was proved the most efficient equipment for operators who were picking up nuts and screws.[20] Three types of bins were compared, as pictured in Figure 8-8. The bin with the tray was the best arrangement for speed. Motions were 21 per cent faster with this arrangement than for the second-fastest arrangement for picking up nuts, and similarly 10 per cent faster for picking up screws.

Another laboratory experiment has to do with hand motions.[21] The purpose of this experiment was to determine which motions of the hands resulted in the greatest power and velocity. Six motions were compared: "(1) long forehand sweep; (2) long backhand sweep; (3) short forehand sweep; (4) short backhand sweep; (5) forward thrust; (6) pull." The starting positions for these motions are shown in Figure 8-5. "A straight pulling motion from a position in front of the body was found to give the greatest power . . ." The Procter and Gamble Company has used the result in arranging the work of soap packers and other manual workers.

TRAINING IN MOTIONS

The importance of training in correct motions is shown spectacularly in a study of two girls learning to polish forks.[22] One day's training in the correct motions of polishing reduced the time per fork from 75 to 30 seconds. Similarly, twelve experienced workers were trained through the use of an instruction card to take the desirable number of strokes in roughing spoons. It had been noticed that the workers varied a great deal one from another in number of strokes, time, and metal removed, and that the workers did not know how many strokes they were taking. Time to rough three dozen spoons was reduced from 126 to 89 minutes by this training.

POSTURE

The effectiveness of more comfortable posture was shown when 18.1 units of spoons and forks were polished per hour by sitting workers, in comparison with the 16.3 units polished when workers were standing. Since there was no control group, this result might be questioned. Was the improvement due to the seat, or due to improved attitudes when the worker was shown that she was of some importance?

TIME STUDY

Time study attempts to determine a standard day's work by finding the amount of time needed for workers to perform factory operations. The purposes of time study are to provide production data and to provide incentives for employees. Only the incentive purpose is considered here. Time study is carried out by studying one or a few workers and carefully measuring with a stop watch how long it takes to perform each operation on the job. It is desirable to do a motion study first, so that during the time study workers are using only those motions that are necessary and most desirable in pattern. Otherwise, if time study is done without motion study and pay rates are set on the basis of the time study, workers may find a better method of work and be paid much more than management had planned. It is regarded as too expensive to measure the time of a large group of workers; thus measurements made on one or a few workers are applied to the group by estimates of how these workers compare with average workers. These estimates or compensations are called "leveling" and are the source of much controversy, as labor unions insist that standards should be set on only the average worker. After times have been measured for the various operations of a job, allowances are made for fatigue and for visits to the washroom.

Time study has been widely adopted in the United States and other industrialized countries, but there has been great hostility to it. In spite of many union-management disagreements, there are several examples of union-management cooperation. An early example was the International Ladies Garment Workers' Union and the Dress Manufacturers' Association.[23] The union and the association formed a "board of control" which passed on changes growing out of a laboratory shop.

179

Leveling judgments

How accurately a time study engineer can adjust his measurements of one worker to the speed of a group of workers involves his judgment as to the skill and effort of the employees being timed. These leveling adjustments are made when the worker being timed is believed to be either above or below average in skill or effort. The leveling method assumes that, because these adjustments are made, the pay rates will be fair no matter what the skill and effort of the worker on whom the rate is set. The leveling method, although it is only one method of correcting, is a popular one. Unions, on the other hand, object to the use of an above-average employee in setting rates, which they insist, should be set on average employees.

If time study principles and applications were perfect, (1) all time study engineers would arrive at the same time for a job regardless of which worker each of them studied, and (2) this agreed-upon final time would entail a normal amount of effort which would be the same amount of effort for all kinds of jobs studied, and (3) the time standards would result in average earnings for each job studied at equitable pay levels determined in advance.[24] In other words, if it was decided in advance that machinists should be paid more than grinders, the earnings would average out that way, and there would be none of the upsets that occasionally occur. Published research work has shed light on only the first of these conditions, the consistency of time study engineers studying the same job. Here there are three measures of consistency. There is consistency of a time-study engineer with himself, with another engineer observing the same worker, and with another engineer viewing a different worker working at the same job.

RESULTS

There have been several studies of more than one engineer observing the same employee. Twenty-four time-study practitioners were divided into pairs which studied the performance of one operator at a time. All the time study men used the same division into elemental motions and had an unlimited length of time for each study. It was found that the average deviation of each time study expert from the average of the whole group was 21 per cent,[25] the average deviation for men from the same organization was 9 per cent, an indication that training and similar procedures reduce differences. In fact, Barnes found that, when five time study men had been thoroughly trained, their computations of time for a job varied only ±5 per cent from the average.[26]

Another study used the ratings of two professors on the industrial engineering staff at Purdue, two practitioners from a large firm, and two advanced students who had had several years experience in time study work in industry. These men viewed one worker at one job at one speed. They judged the extent to which this worker differed from a normal pace that was determined in a preliminary session. Their average errors from correct judgments of a normal pace were 14.5 per cent.[27] This study also found that raters overrate slow workers and underrate fast workers. With 100 as normal, the highest rater's ratings for four jobs averaged 28 points above the ratings of the lowest. The worker on piece rates could be very lucky or unlucky, depending on which of those two raters set the rates for his job.

Another study confirms the finding that raters overrate slow workers and underrate fast workers.[28] Motion pictures were taken of operators folding sheets of gauze. This operation was selected because it is highly repetitive and consequently easy to study. The operators were all experienced. Three engineers served as observers to make ratings of effort and skill. These ratings were combined into one leveling factor for each operator. One frame of the motion picture was equivalent to 1/16 second. Four or five work cycles were photographed for each operator, and the number of frames taken per cycle was the average number of frames per cycle of work, that is, to fold one piece. The mean number of actual frames taken for all the operators was 99. According to the leveling assumption, when the leveling factor is multiplied by the actual number of frames taken for each operator, the result should be 99. This was not the result in some instances. The time study engineers overestimated considerably the speed of some operators and underestimated the speed of others. This was demonstrated in the variations from the correct result of 99, in that judgments varied all the way from 59 to 124. For the fastest operators the rate set would be too "tight"; that is, workers would have to work faster than the average to reach the standard set. And, conversely, were the rate set from the slower operators, it would be too "loose"; that is, workers would not have to work as fast as the average to reach the standard set. As the unions have advocated, only when rates are set from average operators does the leveling procedure work out equitably. But, if rates were set from average operators, there would be no need for leveling. To generalize, the corrections of the leveling procedure are not sufficient.

Standard data

In the opinion of Barnes, mechanical errors of measurement in time study have been reduced by the use of standard data.[29] Standard data are the results of previous studies of the time it takes to make frequently used motions of feet and hands. It is recognized that such standards apply only to the object or general operation in question, as, for example, it might take a different time to pick up a pencil and to pick up a button. Furthermore, it is recognized that the time for a motion varies with the location of that motion within the cycle of motions. Standard data should be checked within the cycle of motions, and within the organization where they are used.

The reliability of using standard data was tested in a study of four operations. Six time study men representing six companies appraised moving pictures of these four operations. Each man used his own system of standard data. The variations from the group averages ranged from +23 per cent to −12 per cent. The two companies with the most accurate reliability varied from the group averages only +2 per cent and −8 per cent. This suggests that the reliability of using standard data is just about as accurate as time study by stop watch. Whether the standard data are more valid in measuring the true time for these operations is not known.

Errors in time study are greater than would be suggested by the apparent objectivity of stop watch readings. No matter whether standard data or the time study expert's adjusted time is used, there is always a judgment of normal pace. Time study men working in the same plant are more consistent with each other than with time study men in general. This does not eliminate errors because time study men have to judge a worker as either high or low or average in speed. Differences can be reduced considerably by training.

Restriction of output

Worker reaction to time study connected with wage-incentive systems has often been a restriction of output. The extent of restriction is not known exactly, but a survey made shortly after World War II reported that 55 per cent of business executives stated that output had decreased as compared with prewar performance and 27 per cent stated that "production limits" had been set by labor unions.[30]

Restriction of output exists extensively in unorganized plants as well as in those which are unionized, and in boom times as well as depression.[31] In fact, it was among unorganized workers that the most extensive study of restriction was made. Another student estimated that restriction of output cut 25 per cent from production.[32] Restriction of output is of interest psychologically, not primarily because of the economic loss but as a symptom of lack of motivation.

Mathewson studied restriction among unorganized workers by direct observation and interview.[33] Two hundred twenty-three cases of restriction in a variety of plants in several sections of the United States were found and recorded in detail. Mathewson made his observations of restriction by working in industry as a laborer and at other times as a skilled worker. He was also assisted by six workers who reported to him the details of cases of restriction in their group.

Mathewson found that restriction, although not universal, was widespread. The majority of executives in the plants where restriction was widespread were either ignorant that it existed at that time or considered that its existence was negligible in extent. The remainder of the executives were evenly divided among those who knew nothing of any important problem of restriction and those who believed that restriction was unavoidable.

Restriction is caused by a work group's deciding what is a fair day's work and then making members of the group conform to a pace that will meet the standard set by the group. In a number of instances the first-line supervisor tells a worker not to produce so much. The supervisor restricts output so that his men will not run out of work, for they will then appear idle and either draw the wrath of higher supervision or be laid off. The first-line supervisor prefers not to have his men laid off because he does not like to see them suffer hardship, nor does he like to have to break in new men when business picks up again.

Mathewson found that pay system was a major source of restriction. The worker was told that under a piece-rate pay plan he could make as much money as his production would warrant. In the long run it did not turn out that way. Rates were often cut after workers were found to be making too much money as a result of increasing their production. Workers came to believe that they could make only a given amount on a particular job. This amount had to be consistent with the general wage pattern. If a machine operator made more money than a skilled mechanic, there was dissatisfaction among skilled mechanics and others. The logic of time study was that, for a job of given skill, effort being constant, a worker would make the same amount of money as for another job of the same skill. But it did not work out that way. Time study had not become that accurate a science. Fear of layoff was also important as a reason for restriction. Workers believed that if they did all the work in sight they would be laid off.

These studies in industry have found that social approval, or the attitudes of the group, was a most powerful motive. Management still seems shocked and surprised that serious restriction of output appears, that workers are not motivated primarily by the pay check. Determination of group attitudes would give management a better ground for understanding the worker.

Another study of restriction has shown how it operated.[34] In three plants there were only 14 "rate busters" out of approximately 350 workers. In these plants the attitude of the group was clearly the reason for setting the standards for a day's work. Workers were indoctrinated by management on how much they could make by working hard, but almost all of them went along with the work group. The incentive system was liked by these workers, but not for the reasons that management thought it should be. The workers approved it because it allowed them to have a great deal of free time. They could reach the standard in much less than the total working day. The system was not looked upon by the workers as giving them an opportunity to make more money.

There was great pressure from the group on nonconformists. If a new worker did not agree to conform to the group's standard of production, he would have a hard job exceeding that standard, because the group had secret tricks. These consisted of special devices and methods to make the work easier, and also of knowledge of inspection standards. Another group pressure on nonconformists, after they had reached production standards, was ostracism, shown in the following conversation.

ED: That guy [pointing to an operator] is the greatest rate buster in the shop.

MIKE: That's no lie. He's ruined every job on that machine. They've cut him down to the point where he has to do twice the work for half the pay. A few more like him would ruin this shop. [The observer learned later from the timekeeper that this rate buster had a very high "take-home."]

ED: It's guys like that that spoil the shop for the rest of us. Somebody ought to take a piece of babbit and pound some sense into his thick skull. That's the only kind of treatment a guy like that understands.

MIKE: We're handling him the best way as it is. The only way to handle those ———————— is not have a thing to do with them. That guy hasn't got a friend in the place and he knows it. You can bet your life he thinks about that every time he comes to work.

Four characteristics differentiated the conformers from the rate busters in one plant, although the latter group was not large enough to make the results certain. The conformers, who restrict output, were more likely to have a city background, were more likely to have ancestors that have been in the United States for a relatively short time, were more "prounion" and "pro–New Deal" (Figure 8-9). Machine workers were not motivated by pay incentives as management expected them to be. The reason, according to these investigators, is that restriction and con-

50 CONFORMERS		14 NONCONFORMERS	
Rural	Urban	Urban	Rural
Mixed American	Ethnic	Ethnic	Mixed American
Not known / Pro-AFL	Prounion / Pro-CIO	Prounion	Antiunion
Not known	Pro-New Deal	Pro-New Deal	Anti-New Deal / Not known

Anti-New Deal

Figure 8-9. Differences in Personal Data between Employees Who Do and Do Not Conform to Group Standards of Output, by Percentages.

(Collins, Orvis, Melville Dalton, and Donald Roy, "Restrictions of Output and Social Cleavage in Industry," *Applied Anthropology*, 1946, **5**, No. 3, 1–14.)

formity to group standards are symptoms of aggression toward the "office" and toward management controls.

The Western Electric Company found that group attitudes may go either against the objectives of management, as in their Bank Wiring study, or strengthen the objectives of management, as they did among relay assemblers.[35] The management, and particularly the industrial engineers, at Western Electric had assumed that, if, for example, a wireman was paid $5 for every bank that he wired, he would wire as many banks as possible and thereby make as much money as possible. When the task is one that depends on the efforts of the group, the industrial engineer makes the same assumption and extends that assumption—that the group will exert pressure on each individual to put out as much work as possible so that each member will make the maximum amount of money. This sounds plausible, but it often does not work out that way. Many pay-incentive plans fail completely to act as effective motivation. Frequently the work group has built up attitudes against working as fast as possible. The group considers a certain amount of work a proper day's work. The motive of the social group is stronger than is the pay incentive.

Bank wiremen at Western Electric restricted their output generally and significantly. The bank-wiring group studies were based on nine wiremen, three solderers, and two inspectors, who were studied in an observation room apart from the regular department. A wage-incentive system was in effect which provided for group piecework. The more units completed, the more money each employee would receive. The employ-

185

ees' concept of a day's work was two equipments per day, which was below the standard set by management for paying a bonus. It was not known how this standard originated. When the standard was reached, employees stopped work in the observation room as well as in the regular department. Group pressure was exerted on fellow employees not to exceed the group standard and to maintain output at a regular rate. On occasions when output actually exceeded the group standard, the additional output would not be reported but would be held back and reported later. Output was greater for each wireman during the morning than during the afternoon. The greatest differences occurred between morning and afternoon output for the fastest wiremen, the two fastest of whom produced more than 60 per cent more during the morning than in the afternoon. These differences were due not to fatigue but to the group pressure to maintain uniform output.

Group attitudes were prevalent in regulating other conduct besides production of the bank-wiring group. These group attitudes regulated the workers' reactions to all outsiders and particularly to supervisors. Workers did not confide in supervisors, who were looked upon as outsiders. The group attitudes decreed that workers would have to do a certain amount of work but that they should not do too much, even though a group bonus plan was in effect that would have resulted in additional pay for more work. The workers could have done much more than they did without physiological damage.

All wiremen were restricting output. The explanation offered by the investigators was the effort of the group to resist change. They rejected the hypothesis that it was done because of any hostility to management, or to safeguard work or stave off unemployment. In this connection it is interesting to contrast the view of Gardner, who had been employed by the Western Electric Company.[36]

His views as to restriction in general are not at all consistent with those expressed by Roethlisberger and Dickson about restriction among the wiremen. Briefly, Gardner has a simpler view, that the major cause of restriction is the workers' lack of confidence in management. Regardless of the explanation, the fact is clear that restriction is widespread.

Social sources of error in the application of time study are closely related to those of motivation discussed above. Rate of work is often dependent on the approval of the group rather than individual motivation. Consequently a system of time study that does not give full attention to group attitudes will not be completely successful. It has been suggested that a social group such as a work group tries to maintain its equilibrium by continuing to work at its accustomed rate.

Effect

The Hawthorne study at the Western Electric Company had the effect of reducing the importance of fatigue as an industrial problem by showing the greater importance of human relations in that situation. This shift of emphasis from problems of human engineering to those of human relations was especially timely when it was first made in the 1930's, and it still deserves priority in United States industry. But the pendulum swung too far in dismissing fatigue completely.

Relay Assembly study

The fatigue studies at Hawthorne were made on the job of relay assembly, which is very light work. Conclusions therefore do not apply to heavier work.

Changes in output were used as an index of fatigue. This is legitimate if, but only if, motivation is at a maximum. Motivation was changing throughout the study; the employees showed more favorable attitudes. When motivation is low, effects of fatigue become easily apparent in reduced output, but, when motivation is high, the effect of fatigue can be delayed until physiological exhaustion occurs.

One of the early Hawthorne studies concerned conditions of work. The relation between intensity of illumination and output was studied. Employees reacted not to the actual illumination but to what they thought the illumination was. This was shown when production increased after an electric light bulb was changed. The actual brightness was the same, but the employees thought the light was brighter. The illumination study at Western Electric was disappointing to the investigators because they had failed to keep constant the variable of employee suggestibility. Consequently an attempt was made to set up an experimental situation in which this variable would be held constant.

The next attempt in the Hawthorne studies was to investigate fatigue and output as they were influenced by hours of work, rest pauses, and other factors. The attempt was made in a study of relay assemblers at the Hawthorne plant. This study is important for two reasons.[37] It is not only one of the few industrial studies to show a definite relation between morale and production, but it also changed the direction of industrial research to an emphasis on group attitudes. As the pioneer study in human relations, it has led to other studies within the plant and outside that have emphasized personal relations. For these reasons the study will be reported in detail. It is referred to in several chapters because it does touch on several topics. It demonstrates the importance of attitudes, so that it might seem to belong in Chapter 11. The reason for not including it there is that the material in that chapter has to do with studies using questionnaire and interview. Interviews are used in the Relay Assembly study, but the interview is not the distinctive feature. The distinctive feature is that direct observations were made of what people did in an industrial situation for a period of several years. The study began as an investigation of the effects of rest pauses and hours of work and consequently is related to fatigue. It cuts across motivation. The Relay Assembly study is an important investigation which crosses several chapter lines.

The purpose of the Relay Assembly study was to investigate the influence on production of hours of work and rest pauses and to learn something of human reactions within industry. The choice of relay assembly for study was made because production was determined entirely by the individual operator and was easily measured. Telephone relays were assembled at the rate of approximately one per minute and consequently afforded a convenient measure of production.

The method of study was to select five experienced assemblers, put them into a special test room, and change the experimental conditions of hours, rest pauses, and lunches. Five girls were selected for study who had been assembling relays so long that their production was no longer improving with practice. These five girls were asked whether they would be willing to take part in such a study and they agreed to do so. Before they were put into the Relay Assembly test room, production records were kept as a basis of comparison.

The system for pay in the regular department where the girls had been working was group piecework. There were approximately one hundred employees in their department, all of whom were paid in proportion to the output of the entire department. A minimum amount of money was guaranteed each assembler, no matter how few relays she put together, or how few were assembled by the entire department. The pay of an assembler was this minimum amount plus a fraction of money allowed for whatever surplus work was done above a quota.

Before going into the test room, the girls were told the purpose of the investigation, and during the study their suggestions were solicited and each proposed change was discussed with them. Occasionally a proposed change disliked by the assemblers was rejected. These discussions occurred with the plant superintendent—a mighty person whose social distance from assemblers was great because ordinarily there were so many intervening layers of supervision that no assembler would have an opportunity to talk with him.

188

The girls worked in the test room for approximately five years until the depression of the thirties caused their layoff on account of seniority rules. During that time a number of conditions of work were changed in order to study their possible effect on output. These periods varied in length but typically lasted for several weeks. During some periods hours of work were shortened, then returned to the original amount, rest pauses were introduced, then taken away, and in some periods free lunches were provided by the company.

During the first period in the Relay Assembly test room no change was intentionally made by the investigators other than to move the girls from their regular shop department. The second period introduced a change in the procedure. Instead of being paid according to the production of the larger group in the regular department, the girls were paid according to the output of the five assemblers in the test room. This change could be expected to have an important effect on production. In an independent study such a change alone accounted for approximately half of the entire 30 per cent increase in production that occurred in the original Relay Assembly group.

Elaborate records were kept. Production records in half-hour intervals were made. An observer in the test room recorded all conversation and other circumstances. Records of periodic interviews with each assembler were kept. Thorough physical examinations were made from time to time, including an account of amount of sleep and other activities off the job.

The girls were told to work at whatever rate was comfortable to them. They were told not to hurry or to try to work as fast as they could except during occasional brief speed trials. On the other hand, it was not very long until the girls had decided that the purpose of the study was to see how fast they could go, but in this decision they were not intentionally assisted by the persons conducting the study.

The assembly of relays was speeded up, and it continued to rise in speed for almost two years. This rate of production was approximately 30 per cent higher at the peak than in the beginning. This high rate was maintained until toward the close of the study. The study had to be stopped because the girls lost their jobs because of the depression and seniority rules. The slowing down toward the end of the study is interpreted by the investigators as due to the assemblers' being affected by fear of losing their jobs. In support of this, one of the assemblers is quoted as explaining the drop by saying, "We lost our pride."

An alternative explanation for the final drop in output is possible. The girls were stimulated by taking part in an interesting study that

189

seemed important. After several years of being the center of attention from high company officials and from distinguished visitors, this attention ended. Perhaps the nature of the job was such that, regardless of the depression, the girls would have lost interest. Perhaps their high output was due in part to their increased interest, which was a result of their temporary importance.

The correlations calculated between production records and the experimental variables were zero, indicating that there was no relationship between output and hours of work, rest pauses, lunches, amount of sleep, physiological condition, and aptitude measurements. On the other hand, the attitude of the group was improving constantly at the time production was increasing, and this attitude deteriorated when production fell off.

The main change in attitude was that the girls began to like their work better. They lost a feeling of anxiety that was said to be typical in the regular shop department. They were no longer afraid of their boss, and, as a matter of fact, one of them said that they no longer had a boss. She thought this because of the informal relations that had developed, even though their activities were actually supervised more closely than they had been in the regular department.

The relay assemblers became a social group. Friendly conversation became the rule in the test room, and it included everyone except the oldest girl. At first conversation was forbidden as it was in the regular department, since it was believed to interfere with efficiency. But, soon after the study was under way, it was decided to allow talking. Group activity extended beyond the plant to double dates, and to vacations together for the girls.

The development of effective informal leadership might also have been important in the rising production. There was group pressure to produce more during the time that production was rising. This pressure was applied mainly by one girl—not one of the original five—who soon after her entrance to the group became the accepted leader.

The influence of the working group has been shown in the Relay Assembly study by correlating output for each pair of assemblers.[38] On this job of assembling relays, which required only the physical efforts of a single operator and not necessarily the cooperation of the group, there were definite relationships in output that could be traced to personal relationships. Between members of one pair of operators who were good friends, there was at times an identity in amount of relays assembled as well as a close relation in fluctuations.[39] This high relationship lasted for several months, but it declined sharply in succeeding months. The one girl of the five who did not become a member of the social group and who was antagonized by the informal leader showed at times a definite negative correlation in number of relays assembled. Personal relationships are thus seen to be reflected definitely in speed of output.

In the Relay Assembly study the activity of the girls became directed toward the goal of higher production. Their egos became involved in this activity to the extent that they were genuinely participating. Although management did not give this goal intentionally, it shaped the goal of higher production by praising the girls when their production increased, or at least by expressing great interest at such times.

The rise in production and the growth of favorable attitudes have been attributed to the concept of participation, and at different times to successful supervision and the development of team spirit as well. All three explanations may be valid in part.

The Relay Assembly study is interesting not only for its positive suggestions but also for its negative ones. It showed that in this situation a number of supposedly important factors were really of no demonstrable importance, presumably because their effectiveness was blotted out by the more powerful effect of attitude and morale. These supposedly important factors are fatigue, rest pauses, hours of work, aptitude, and monotony. Granted that in some situations such factors will be important, still the findings here ring true for this particular situation. These findings are supported by a number of case studies which show that, when morale is high, nothing else matters as long as work is organized properly.

THE NATURE OF FATIGUE

Definitions

Fatigue has been described as a sort of "negative appetite for activity."[40] As defined in this chapter, fatigue, or activity decrement, means a reduced capacity for further work as a consequence of previous activity where a person was trying almost as hard as he could. Thus it includes both mental and physical reactions as well as the phenomenon of boredom and monotony.

Confusion often exists in differentiating the terms monotony, boredom, and fatigue. Monotony is a state of mind caused by performing repetitive tasks. It implies no emotional dislike. Boredom, or lack of interest, is characterized by depression and a desire for a change of activity. It is tinged with emotional distaste and is accompanied by a corresponding attitudinal outlook. Thus boredom is more heavily affected by such factors as personality, attitude, and interest patterns than is monotony. On the other hand, boredom can be differentiated from fatigue because it is a desire for a change in activity rather than for a rest or relief from work altogether.

The study and control of fatigue is difficult because it has three aspects. It has been defined in terms of one of these, namely, decline in quantity of work for a given level of effort. A second aspect is a feeling of tiredness, which is not necessarily accompanied by reduced capacity to work. The third aspect is physiological change. The most prominent physiological change is the accumulation of lactic acid in the blood caused by the breaking down of glycogen, or sugar, in the blood. Other physiological changes are believed to be present in the junction of the nerve and muscle cells, and under certain conditions changes in the capacity of the nerve fiber to conduct, and possibly changes in the brain. The physiological changes do not necessarily accompany changes in production or in feelings. Neither the physiological changes nor feeling changes are as convenient to measure as are the changes in production.

These three measures of activity decrement, the result of prolonged work, do not necessarily operate concurrently as to time or intensity. One can be exhibited without the other two; or two can operate without the other one; or all three can operate together. However, any general definition of fatigue must include all three.[41] Physiological changes occur almost as soon as work begins, and yet they are not necessarily highly correlated with the other two decrements either in quantity or in time. There is a tendency for the feeling decrement to appear sooner than the so-called work decrement.[42] Mention has been made earlier of the fact that the worker's particular level of motivation has a direct bearing on his productivity and feelings. In order to measure the effects of fatigue on production, it is necessary to control such variables as the nature, difficulty, and method of work, and incentives. For instance, improvement in illumination and rest pauses usually raise output. Some uncertainty exists, however, as to whether these improvements result from alleviated fatigue or result in improved motivation and a greater desire to work.

Connection with pay plans

Usually only plants having some type of wage-incentive plan have accurate records of production, and hence it is mainly under this system of wage payment that plant studies of fatigue are available. Although not the only measure, production records are the most common measure of industrial fatigue. Plants with wage incentives are preferable for fatigue study not only because of the presence of more accurate measures of output, but also because motivation is likely to be higher.

Work curves

A graph showing the level of performance against time spent at work is called a work curve. Since practices to alleviate fatigue depend to a large measure on the nature of the work curve, its discovery and use are important. No difficulty exists in obtaining such a curve where work is uniform and successive in terms of units produced. However, where work changes are frequent, in ordinary varied office work, work curves are most frequently obtained by the use of laboratory task tests. The results of these tests are then plotted and used as an index of fatigue for such jobs. Serious questions of the transferability of fatigue from the particular job to the test results have been raised. Motivation might be higher in the laboratory tests than on the job. The degree of transfer depends on the similarity of the task, environment, attitudes, and neuromuscular processes.[43]

Work curves can be typed according to the nature of the task involved, namely, simple muscular, complex muscular, and mental. A work curve is a composite showing the effects of fatigue and other variables over a period of time.

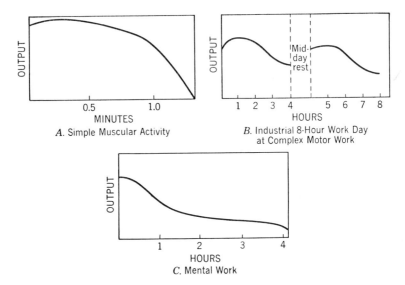

Figure 8-10. Types of Work Curves.

(Katzell, Raymond A., "Fatigue and Its Alleviation," in Fryer, Douglas H., and Edwin R. Henry (eds.), *Handbook of Applied Psychology*, New York: Rinehart & Co., Inc., 1950, I, 74–84.)

193

SIMPLE MUSCULAR WORK

The *first work curve,* Figure 8-10, is a simple muscular activity curve. It is derived by recording the units of output of a group of muscles against the force of some weight or spring. It can be seen from the drawing that the curve for simple muscular tasks shows a short warm-up period followed by a high level of performance. A gradual tapering off then appears. Subsequently a sudden drop occurs to a point of complete exhaustion. Such work curves have a general resemblance to motor curves, but they involve simpler coordination and fewer muscles. One can generally conclude from a study of such curves that, the more complex and rapid the task, the faster fatigue sets in. Moderate tasks permit a greater total amount of work before complete exhaustion occurs than do heavier tasks. Since each person has his own work curve, it appears possible to match the worker to jobs whose energy requirements more nearly approximate his own. Discovery of a person's work curve allows the scheduling of activities and rest pauses that fit his peculiarities.

COMPLEX MUSCULAR WORK

The *second curve* depicts the amount of work done per unit of time in a typical industrial situation at a complex muscular task. This job is assumed to be motor in nature and not monotonous. As interpreted, the initial upward slope of the curve indicates a warm-up period. This is followed by a gradual rise in production until midmorning, when a drop occurs. The afternoon curve, taken after the midday rest, is similar in appearance to the morning curve but it does not rise to as high a production peak and it falls more rapidly near the end of the day.

MENTAL WORK

The *third graph* shows a typical mental work curve. As in muscular work, mental work decrement occurs in quantity, speed, and accuracy of output. Again large individual differences and the nature of the work tend to determine the timing and extent of such declines. The work decrement in mental tasks requiring continuous attention has been attributed to interferences known as "blocks."[44] These intervals become longer and more frequent as the time spent at work progresses. These lapses in performance are sources of mistakes. In office or industrial work-places such blocks may cause accidents. Two experiments conducted to determine results of intense mental work suggest that a great deal of such work decline is really due to loss of interest and incentive and not exhaustion per se.[45] Blocking acts as a natural way of providing rest. Mental work that is varied can consequently go on with few interruptions, but work requiring constant attention will produce many blocks and consequently a sharp drop in output with the passage of time. As shown, the mental fatigue curve generally has no warm-up period or early spurt, but it shows a gradual but steady downward slope with some emphasis on deceleration at the later stages.

FATIGUE REDUCTION

The proper application of scheduled hours and rest pauses can go a long way in reducing the incidence of fatigue. Excessively long work days increase not only fatigue but also susceptibility to sickness, accidents, and absenteeism. Some of the studies to be cited point to the fact that reducing hours of work yields higher hourly production. Concurrently with hourly schedules, the distribution of rest pauses as to length, time, and frequency also influences production. Most of these procedures raise efficiency because of their effect on monotony, motivation, and attitudes, as well as fatigue.

Hours of work

The effect of hours of work on output is complicated because of changes in motivation that may be due to possible changes in pay. Output in relation to hours of work has been studied with respect to the length of the work week and the workday, and also in terms of the number of days worked per week. Results would be expected to vary depending upon whether the work is heavy and whether done by men or women. In general, the highest productivity per hour has come with a short work week and with the worker setting the pace.

WORK WEEK

Exactly how short the work week should be for greatest productivity per hour is not very clear. One study tried to relate total production and output per hour to work weeks of 36, 40, 44, and 48 hours.[46] This study showed that, although the 48-hour week produced the largest weekly output, it resulted in the lowest hourly output. The 40-hour week, on the other hand, showed the highest hourly output, though not the greatest total weekly production. The 36-hour week yielded less output per hour than the 40- and 44-hour weeks, but higher hourly production than the 48-hour week. This relatively poor showing for the 36-hour week may be due to the need of a warm-up period, to practice loss, or to poorer attitudes.

195

The optimum work week, according to this study, is the 40-hour week. This conclusion is supported by a most comprehensive study of production in relation to hours of work which was made during and after World War II in American plants.[47] Of the 800 plants surveyed, the results from only thirty-four plants were used because they were the only ones with adequate production records. Since there was no control group, it makes it difficult to be certain that the effect is due entirely to hours of work, on which the investigators were concentrating their attention. "As a general rule, the best records of output were found in plants that used wage incentives." This limitation has some advantage because it restricts the range of variables and presumably works in the direction of reducing differences in motivation. This study showed the 40-hour week to be more efficient in terms of productivity per hour, and also in terms of over-all cost, if the worker rather than the machine sets the pace. From management's point of view, not having to pay overtime wages is one reason for this superiority of the 40-hour week. Thus, in scheduling work, the effect of total hours on hourly production and the total aggregate output should be taken into consideration. Generally, when the machine sets the pace, longer work days are more efficient because the time of getting ready and of cleaning up are spread over a longer period of operation.

When workers included in this study were not operating on a wage-incentive plan, lengthening the work week made little difference in production. For instance, at 58 hours a week, workers paid on an hourly basis were producing about as much per hour as they had when working 40 hours a week. This would suggest that they were not so highly motivated on the 40-hour week as were the workers who were on wage incentive. Evidently the workers on hourly pay had not tired themselves out in 40 hours and so had a reserve of energy to work at the same rate of output during the 18 additional hours.

In general, when hours were increased in United States industry during World War II, production increased, but not in proportion to the increase in hours. In exceptional cases the work week was as long as 60 hours. Had sufficient workers been available, greater national production could have been obtained with a work week of 44 or 45 hours.

NUMBER OF DAYS PER WEEK

Results are somewhat contradictory when the efficiency found in a 6-day work week is compared with that of a 5-day week.[48] At the beginning of World War II a number of plants changed from a 5- to a 6-day week; and at the end of the war the change was in the reverse direction. The contradiction is that production per hour did not materially change in going from 5 to 6 days, but in shifting from 6 to 5 days it did improve materially. An explanation for the fact that hourly production did not fall off when the sixth day was added is that the wage incentive, in these instances usually one and a half times the base rate, was attractive enough to hold output up. When returning to the 5-day week, employees might have produced more per hour in order to make up for pay loss in their diminished hours of work.

WORKDAY

Studies of the length of the workday in relation to output are similar to those of the work week in showing maximum productivity with a moderate work time. The earliest study of the relation between hours of workday and production is one made by Robert Owen in 1816. He found that in his cotton mills as much work was done in a 10.5-hour day as in a 16-hour day.[49]

During the depression of the 1930's one plant changed from three 8-hour shifts to four 6-hour shifts 6 days a week.[50] In spite of two increases in pay of 12.5 per cent, the six-hour shifts were more economical to management because of increased production.

A comparison was made by the U. S. Public Health Service between two plants, one of which had an 8-hour day and the other a 10-hour day.[51] The work curve varied with the type of work; there was little variation in output in machine-paced work, but there was much variation in heavy muscular work. The conclusion was reached that in general the 8-hour day is preferable to the 10-hour day.

In the only modern study of the effect of hours per day on production, it was found that during a 5-day work week output dropped 4 per cent per hour when the workday was lengthened from 8 to 10 hours.[52] This was the finding in two groups which were both making gear couplings. The work was moderately heavy, and to a large extent it was paced by machine. For women in eleven groups, lengthening the workday from 8 to 9½ hours caused a decrease in hourly efficiency of about 5 per cent.

ABSENTEEISM

In several studies hours of work and consequent fatigue have been found to increase absenteeism, although, no doubt, hours of work in this case acted as more than the cause of fatigue. A worker might want to shop. During World War II absenteeism among women workers ran so high for a work week of over 48 hours that such long weeks were discontinued.[53] Another reason for absenteeism was that workers were making so much money they did not need to stay on the job full time. The addition of a sixth workday for men doing moderately heavy work caused a great increase in absenteeism on that day, as shown in Figure 8-11. In another study it was found that, when at the beginning of World War II the work week was changed from 5 to 6 days, there was a decided increase in absenteeism for women. This change, however, did not alter the absenteeism rate materially for men.

Fatigue tests

Hours of work have been studied with reference to performance on physiological and psychological tests, which give conclusive evidence of behavior differences due to hours of work.[54] The purpose of the study was to find what psychological and physiological evidences of fatigue resulting from driving a truck could be measured. Results are shown in Figures 8-12 and 8-13. No single test could be found that would correlate perfectly with hours spent in driving since last major sleep, but a combination of measures showed significant results. In the same study of

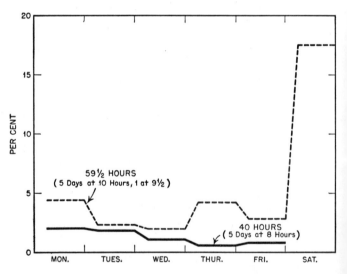

Figure 8-11. Daily Pattern of Absenteeism for Five- and Six-Day Weeks; Men at Moderately Heavy Work.

(Kossoris, Max D., "Hours of Work and Output: A Study of the Effects of Long Working Hours on Efficiency, Absenteeism, Industrial Injuries and Output," *Monthly Labor Review*, 1947, **65**, 5–14.)

DRIVERS WORSE THAN NONDRIVERS		NO CHANGES WITH DRIVING	DRIVERS SLIGHTLY STRONGER THAN NONDRIVERS
CONSISTENT CHANGE IN FUNCTION WITH HOURS OF DRIVING	LESS CONSISTENT CHANGE IN FUNCTION WITH HOURS OF DRIVING		
Speed of Tapping	Glare Resistance	Blood Potassium	Strength of Grip
Reaction-Coordination	Eye Movement	Blood Total Base	
Body Sway	Aiming	Urine pH	
Steadiness	Steering Efficiency	Differential White Cell Count	
Vigilance	Heart Rate	Spatial Perception	
Simple Reaction Time	White Cell Count		
Flicker	Diastolic Blood Pressure		
	Brake Reaction Time		
0 .2 .4 .6 .8 COEFFICIENT OF COMPARISON	0 .2 .4 .6 .8 COEFFICIENT OF COMPARISON		

Figure 8-12. Functions Tested Classified by Consistency of Changes Found with Hours of Driving. The lengths of the bars indicate the relative difference between the mean scores of the men who had driven and those who had not driven since major sleep.

(United States Public Health Service, "Fatigue and Hours of Service of Interstate Truck Drivers," *Public Health Bulletin No. 265,* Washington: U.S. Government Printing Office, 1941, p. 83.)

truck drivers, tests differentiated between rested persons and those who had been driving for some time. These tests were able to differentiate only between groups of truck drivers, and not between individual drivers.

The psychological tests which were most valid for determining fatigue were speed of tapping, reaction-coordination, body sway, steadiness of hand, simple reaction time, and flicker. In the flicker test a disk, partly white and partly black, was rotated. At a certain speed it is seen as solid gray. At lower speeds it flickers. Fatigued men saw it flicker more. These are tests that discriminate between groups of rested persons and those who have been driving a truck for several hours; they also discriminate among groups of drivers with varying numbers of hours of work.

Individual differences were found to be prominent among the fatigue tests for truck drivers. Individual differences work in two ways here: (1) some drivers are much better on the tests than others at the start of a workday; (2) some drivers change much less than others from the rested to the tired condition on the tested functions.

199

Rest pauses

Rest pauses have brought about increases in production of 8 to 20 per cent.[55] There is, however, considerable uncertainty about the extent to which the rest pause improves motivation and the extent to which it contributes to the alleviation of fatigue, since these two elements interact in their effect on performance and are hard to distinguish. Rest pauses were allowed American male hourly workers in 56 per cent of the companies reporting in 1954.[56] If authorized rest pauses are not allowed, unauthorized rests will be taken by workers to suit their own convenience.[57] Rest pauses are probably desirable in every type of work, although in the Relay Assembly group at Hawthorne the advantage was not apparent. In that study the more powerful effect of the group attitude outweighed the effect of rest. This does not mean, however, that for the same type of work under other conditions rest pauses would not result in a gain in production. In heavy muscular work, for instance,

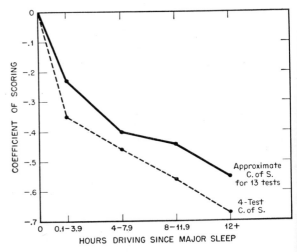

Figure 8-13. Results of Fatigue Tests. Solid Line: *average of the mean coefficients of comparison for 13 tests: heart rate, diastolic blood pressure, leucocyte count, flicker, aiming, saccadic interval, ataxiameter, glare test, vigilance test, tapping, steadiness, reaction-coordination, and simple reaction time.* Broken Line: *mean of the 4-test coefficient of scoring consisting of tapping, steadiness, reaction-coordination, and simple reaction time. The means in both cases are for men who had driven 0, 0.1–3.9, 4–7.9, 8–11.9, and 12 or more hours since major sleep.*

(United States Public Health Service, "Fatigue and Hours of Service of Interstate Truck Drivers," *Public Health Bulletin No. 265,* Washington: U.S. Government Printing Office, 1941, p. 80.)

pauses are particularly desirable and should be frequent. Recovery from fatigue is quite rapid at the start of a rest period, but then recovery is slower and extends over a rather long period of time before normalcy is reached.[58] The same study also pointed out that rest following work must be sufficient to permit complete recovery, for otherwise the remaining fatigue will require relatively longer pauses in subsequent periods. In general, rest pauses provide for recovery as well as resistance to future fatigue.

For most types of work, scheduled rest periods seem to be preferred over unscheduled ones. Employees, when left to their own ways, usually do not distribute work and rest efficiently. The scheduled rest, although it officially decreases total working time, reduces fatigue, sets a short-term goal for workers, and gives management control over the work-rest distribution.

COFFEE BREAK

There have been many complaints from management that the coffee break lasts too long. Before prescribing what to do about employees who take longer coffee breaks than management wants them to, one has to know why they do so. The reason will no doubt differ from one situation to another, but often it will be lack of interest in the job. Management has more often tackled, though not always solved, the immediate problem by administering or policing the coffee breaks instead of concerning itself more with the underlying problem of positive motivation toward work.

One top executive believes that "breaks" are essential in order to reduce office fatigue, and, if properly administered, will lessen immediate strain that comes from prolonged and monotonous physical and mental work.[59] This executive believes that the coffee break developed during a period of manpower shortage as well as a period of declining discipline. The result was stretched-out "breaks" of 30 minutes or more. Consequently the coffee break is held in ill repute by management today. This man's formula would be to introduce a break between 1 and $1\frac{1}{2}$ hours after starting time which would last for 10 or 15 minutes. Proper facilities must be available so that employees can be served within that time limit.

Coffee breaks were introduced mainly during and after World War II, and it is reported that on the whole they bring desirable effects. A survey of 1160 firms having coffee breaks found that 80 per cent of the companies had started coffee breaks since 1941, and 38 per cent after 1946.[60] It appears that the war period was responsible for the institution of the coffee break. Nearly half of the firms mentioned coffee breaks as an inducement when recruiting workers. The favorable effects

201

of coffee breaks were reported as: reduction in worker fatigue, by 82 per cent of the companies; improvement in morale, by 75 per cent; increased productivity, by 65 per cent; lower accident rate, by 32 per cent; and lower employee turnover, by 21 per cent. These management opinions are interesting for their enthusiastic confidence in the effectiveness of coffee breaks, but they should be accepted only as informed opinions and not demonstrated facts.

LOCATION OF REST PAUSES

The best answer to the question of proper scheduling of rest pauses can be obtained from a study of output records. Rest is most beneficial to output if scheduled just prior to the first drop in production. A rest break should be put there. One should then accumulate new data and schedule another rest period just prior to the next drop in production. It is desirable to give employees a chance to share in the decision as to when they are to take rest pauses and what they are to do during the pause. If it is necessary for management to make a final decision about trying rest periods, when workers do not wish to have them, the rest periods should be put on a trial basis with the understanding that the rest will be discontinued if it does not work out satisfactorily.

At the very best, distribution and length of rest periods is in part a trial-and-error process. No single schedule for any place of business exists, nor is there any static schedule for all kinds of work. In general, the duration of the rest period should be anywhere from 5 to 20 minutes, with heavier work requiring the upper limit. Management should schedule the pause to allow the completion of integral work sequences. Pauses should be more frequent near the end of the day. The longer the working span, the longer and more frequent should be the rest periods. Whether every one should take the rest at the same time is a moot question; but the answer is probably yes. However, the nature of the operation may dictate this decision. Some operations or services require continual "manning"; others may allow for mass breaks.

ENVIRONMENTAL CONDITIONS AFFECTING FATIGUE

Several environmental conditions, noise, improper light, and extreme heat, have all been shown to increase fatigue. Vast changes have occurred in all these areas in recent years. Many reports have described improvements in these conditions as contributing to fatigue alleviation, as shown by increased production, higher morale, lower accident rate, and less absenteeism.

Noise

Noise, or unwanted sound, probably increases fatigue, and under some industrial conditions noise causes deafness. It is commonly believed that workers produce a great deal more under conditions of quiet. The available evidence suggests that noise has an effect, but only a slight one, on production. One study of the reduction of noise concluded that it is an investment which under ordinary conditions will increase productivity by 10 to 15 per cent.[61] Noise will continue to be loud in much manufacturing industry even after all known methods are used to reduce it.

The effect of noise depends on the kind of noise and the kind of work. Mental work is affected more than manual work by noise.[62] The effect of noise is greater when it is irregular and also when it is interesting. Loudness being the same, noises that have a higher pitch are more annoying than those of lower pitch.[63] Sounds of either very high or very low tone qualities are more irritating than those in the middle zone. Thus a person may tolerate a sound of a certain intensity provided it falls into his middle zone of hearing, whereas he may be annoyed by a sound of equal intensity that has a high pitch or a very high or very low tone quality. Interrupted noises are generally more annoying than steady ones.[64] Sounds of longer duration usually have more of an adverse effect on efficiency than short-term exposures.

Noise requires more energy even when performance is not lowered, but the effect on both energy and performance varies as people become at least partly used to the noise. In a study of mental arithmetic, metabolism was much higher during the first noisy period, but sank rapidly with adjustment.[65] Noise also causes muscle tension. In a study of subjects pressing on keys, greater effort was exerted during noisy periods. There was greater pressure, and also the subjects articulated words more, no doubt to offset the distraction of the noise.[66] Noise caused muscle tension at first in subjects who were resting, but after five days of exposure to noise the muscle tension practically disappeared.[67]

The effect of noise on hearing has been proved more clearly than its effect on fatigue. Persons in occupations that are exposed to loud noises for a long time, such as boilermakers and airplane pilots, often suffer permanent deafness.[68]

More needs to be done to control noise in industry. It is unpleasant, it lowers production through causing fatigue, and under extreme conditions it causes deafness.

Lighting and color

There have been substantial changes in lighting and color in the American factory in an attempt to reduce fatigue. Proper light requires the right amount and kind for the job, an even distribution of light, and a minimum of glare. Brightness of light is measured in units of the foot-candle, which is the amount of light that can just be seen from a source one foot away. "Engineers nowadays say 50 foot-candles is a desirable lighting level in most manufacturing plants, or about three times above the lighting standard for factories two decades ago. Where fine work is required, recommended lighting may jump to 100 foot-candles or more."[69]

The entire work area should be uniformly illuminated. Areas outside the immediate focus of observation, wall surfaces for example, if un-evenly illuminated cause continual adjustment changes and consequently higher visual fatigue. Since the pupil of the eye must adjust itself when focusing on a bright spot and then on a dark spot, expansion and con-traction of the pupil sets up an increased strain and fatigue in the worker.[70]

Indirect lighting is the best method of producing uniformity. Eye muscles tend to pull toward areas of high illumination. Where the high point of light is not in the work area, a tug-of-war exists between the muscles that are concentrated on the work area and those that veer to the higher illumination.[71]

The human eye adjusts so readily to changes in illumination that the effects of poor lighting are usually not immediately observable to the untrained eye. Errors in judgment are often found when people's reports on brightness are checked against readings on light meters. In planning plant and office illumination, light meters should be used.

Poor illumination causes fatigue and irritability, and is a source of errors and industrial accidents. Money spent to correct improper light-ing will be more than repaid in higher output per worker, lower produc-tion costs, and a generally happier, healthier, and, probably, safer work force.[72]

The color of surrounding objects and surfaces is related to lighting. The use of white or light pastels improves illumination by reflecting a high percentage of light, while deeper tones have a considerably lower reflective value. The occurrence of glare should, however, be avoided. Although some reports point to happy combinations of color for all surfaces and equipment as increasing efficiency, again the problem of isolating other variables arises. Several studies made on the use of colored light show that people prefer the light of daylight color. The use of this so-called white light is said to assist materially in visual efficiency. Allis-Chalmers Manufacturing Company reported that a combination of in-creased lighting and interior repainting cut accident frequency about 50 per cent in a Milwaukee plant. To achieve this result foot-candles of its high ceiling lights were quadrupled, and the plant interior was re-painted—the ceiling a light blue, side walls light green, and traveling cranes yellow.[73]

Heat

Temperature levels commonly encountered in temperate zone working environments can affect worker productivity, comfort, and health. The effect of temperature on productivity becomes more pronounced as the physical effort required to perform the job increases, and it is extremely dependent on the degree of humidity accompanying the temperature level.

Studies made on a group of men copying Morse code signals, a job requiring little physical exertion but continuous mental application, showed a sharp increase in the number of errors per hour when the working environment temperature rose above 92 degrees Fahrenheit as shown in Figure 8-14.[74] Prolonged discomfort from heat will no doubt affect efficiency.

The effect of temperature on worker productivity was encountered at much lower temperature levels in physical work.[75] In these studies a

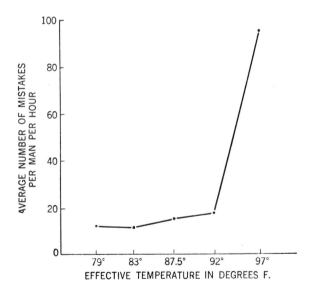

Figure 8-14. Errors of Wireless Operators at Different Temperatures.

(Mackworth, N. H., "Effects of Heat on Wireless Telegraphy Operators Hearing and Recording Morse Messages," *British Journal of Industrial Medicine,* 1946, **3**, 145.)

group of subjects repeatedly lifted a five-pound dumbbell and did other physical tasks. Output decreased 15 per cent when the temperature increased from 68 to 75 degrees.

Degree of humidity affected both the speed of work and the length of voluntary rest pauses of miners.[76] In comfortable air, miners rested 7 minutes per hour, but in air that was too humid they rested 22 minutes. It also took longer to fill a container with coal under the more humid condition. The combination of differences in time rested and differences in speed of work totaled to make over-all production 41 per cent less under more humid conditions.

The highest output in weaving was found with temperatures at 72.5 degrees to 75 degrees with relative humidity of 75 to 80 per cent.[77] In addition, atmospheric conditions affect weaving by causing more breaks in the yarn at low humidity, and consequently the operator's comfort is secondary to the product in this process.

Low temperatures can also affect productivity. Ability to make precise movements with the hands and fingers decreases markedly at below 50 degrees. In studies of munitions workers, accident frequency was at a distinct minimum at 67.5 degrees.[78] Reduction in the temperature level to 52.5 degrees caused an increase of 35 per cent in the accident rate. Similar effects were noted when the temperature was raised above 67.5 degrees. (See Figure 9-4 on p. 218.)

One additional source of worker discomfort should be mentioned, that of temperature gradients or differences. Discomfort has been reported where sizable temperature differences existed within a room, that is, cool air at floor level and warmer air at head level. Furthermore, where sizable temperature differences existed within a building and the nature of the work required worker movement from area to area, discomfort was noted.

Individual differences make it impossible to set exact temperature and humidity limits within which all workers will be satisfied. One study made by the American Society of Heating and Ventilating Engineers shows the temperature and humidity ranges preferred by people doing light work in the United States.[79] Fifty per cent of the subjects found temperatures of 63 to 71 degrees most comfortable in winter, and temperatures of 66 to 75 degrees most desirable in summer. Relative humidity between 30 to 70 per cent was preferred by half the subjects.

In light of these studies the installation of air-conditioning equipment might well be a practical investment and not a luxury item. Where more severe conditions of temperature and humidity are encountered under industrial conditions, several things may be done. Adequate ventilation, insulation, protective clothing and techniques of operation which remove the worker from the source of heat or cold—all are helpful. Rest pauses at frequent intervals under normal conditions of temperature and humidity and of sufficient length to permit full recovery will help.

Interesting results were obtained in studies to determine if incentives, which included coaxing, pleading for output, and praise for greater output, could offset inefficiencies created by high temperature levels.[80] As would be expected under high incentive, over-all production was greater; however, efficiency decreased with high temperature levels under conditions of high incentive by the same amount as under conditions of no incentive. While incentive increased production, it did not offset the effects of temperature.

It appears that selection of a proper operating temperature and humidity can only be made by considering many factors, such as worker comfort, worker productivity, accident rates, conditions required for the process or operation, and the economic feasibility of improvements to reduce extreme conditions. While the temperature and humidity selected will probably not be the optimum one for all conditions, it should reflect a practical and proper balance between the various factors involved.

SUMMARY

The results of time study on industrial efficiency are not known exactly. It is probable that time study accompanied by incentive-pay plans increases production. The amount of increase, however, is probably considerably less than the maximum possible because of labor's distrust of time study methods.

A major reason for this distrust is based on the choice of employees to be used for rate setting. Labor maintains that rates should be set only when average employees are studied. Industrial engineers claim that they can set fair rates with any employee by making suitable adjustments. The results that bear on the point demonstrate that these adjustments are seriously in error.

Motion study has produced spectacular improvements in some jobs. It should precede time study; otherwise workers may find a better method of work and be paid more than management had planned.

One controversial question concerning motion study is whether there is one best way of work that applies to every employee. Efficiency engineers have tried to find and apply a "best way" for each job. Psychologists doubt that there is a "best way," and the evidence for one job has shown that different people perform best with different methods.

207

Improvements in work methods, which are necessary if an industry is to be successful, should take human relations into account. Employees do not wish to change methods, and they resist doing so unless the group which has to make the change initiates the change itself, or has been persuaded that it is the thing to do. When changes are forced on unwilling employees, there is often an undercover battle between employees and management, which management, represented by efficiency engineers, often loses.

Management should encourage working groups to improve their own work methods. This would not mean the abolition of efficiency engineers, but would mean that efficiency engineers would work more closely with rank-and-file employees and with first-line supervisors.

Attitudes of employees toward motion study, time study, and the improvement of machinery with regard to human capacities should be systematically explored and should be considered in decisions concerning these points.

Employees have a great many ways of improving work methods which will be available to management only through successful personal relations based on mutual confidence.

Human engineering has been used extensively in the design of military weapons systems. The principles and methods have been used in a few civilian instances. Many additional improvements are possible with machines and tools.

Fatigue, a subtle process, with its three components of feelings, physiological energy store, and capacity to work, is important in American industry.

The best distribution of rest periods varies widely according to the type of work, the length of the work week or workday, and the age and sex of the worker. Scheduled pauses at intervals just prior to efficiency declines, as indicated by work curves, offer the best solution.

Production does not increase in direct proportion to increases in length of the work week. A 7-day week will yield less production than a 6-day week. A work week in excess of 40 or 50 hours will result in less production per hour, the specific results depending on the type of work and the play plan. In deciding upon a most efficient work schedule, it is advisable to distinguish between its effect on hourly production and its effect on weekly production.

Environmental conditions of noise, poor light, and extreme heat cause fatigue. People show adaptability to varying conditions of noise, light, temperature, and humidity, but, for maximum production, higher morale, and fewer accidents, management must be constantly alert to provide and maintain favorable environmental conditions.

RECOMMENDED READINGS

Chapanis, Alphonse, Wendell R. Garner, and Clifford T. Morgan, *Applied Experimental Psychology,* New York: John Wiley & Sons, Inc., 1949. Includes a thorough account of the human factors in equipment design.

Warren, Neil D., "Automation, Human Engineering and Psychology," *The American Psychologist,* 1956, **11**, 531-536. Presents current questions on automation and a history of psychological studies bearing on the topic.

Katzell, Raymond A., "Fatigue and Its Alleviation," in Fryer, Douglas H., and Edwin R. Henry (eds.), *Handbook of Applied Psychology,* Vol. I, New York: Rinehart & Company, Inc., 1950, pp. 74-83. A thorough, readable account of different kinds of fatigue and how they can be prevented and cured.

Roethlisberger, F. J., and William J. Dickson, *Management and the Worker,* Cambridge, Mass.: Harvard University Press, 1939. This is a classic, reporting the study which began as a fatigue study and ended as the landmark for recognition of the importance of human relations in industry.

9

Accident prevention

INTRODUCTION

Accident prevention can be a sound financial investment for both employees and employers. Though there are no available figures on the costs of accident prevention, the amount spent for such purposes is tremendously high. The National Safety Council reported in 1954 that industrial work accidents cost $3.2 billion, with an average cost to industry of $50 per worker. These figures indicate that industrial accidents are a tremendous financial problem.

Accidents are not only expensive, but they also lower the morale of the workers and in addition result in lower production rates. As a group, companies with excellent safety records probably have more satisfied workers than the companies with high accident severity and frequency. There is an interaction here. Just as accidents lower morale, poor morale appears to be a cause of accidents.

Simply stating the size and importance of the problem of the accident-in-industry does not give all the reasons for taking action to reduce it. There would be little basis for action if accidents happened purely by chance; there is a very real cause behind each entry into the fatality column and each injury. Experts believe that 98 per cent of these causes may be controlled or eliminated. We are beginning to make corrective strides in the field of industrial safety.

SCOPE

The psychological study of accident prevention requires a consideration of the human element in the occurrence of accidents. Causation of accidents, like any problem of causation, is a complex matter. Among 95,000 work accidents in Pennsylvania in 1952, an unsafe act was identified in 94.9 per cent of the accidents, and an unsafe mechanical or physical condition in 94.5 per cent. As these figures show, there were both an unsafe act and an unsafe condition in most of these accidents.[1]

Human errors are an important cause of accidents. In spite of this fact the safety engineer who is responsible for accident prevention in industry is often not a student of human behavior. Usually his background is basically engineering. The lack of qualified psychologists in the industrial safety field may stem from a lack of understanding of the need for such a specialist.

Although mechanical failures are not the primary consideration of psychology, the failure of a mechanical safeguard often touches upon human problems in addition to the engineering ones. For example, at one of the country's large printing establishments, the R. R. Donnelly and Sons Company, there was a job in which a big knife cut through stacks of paper. A safety device was installed to prevent the operator from cutting himself. This device was such that, to lower the knife, the operator had to release two switches, one on either side of him, simultaneously. In this way it was expected that the operator's hands and arms would of necessity be out of the way of the dangerous knife. One operator decided that he could press one of the switches with his knee. His free hand being in the way when the knife descended, he had a serious accident. This accident shows the difficulty of making any safety device foolproof, or at any rate idiot-proof. In addition to a device, no matter how plausible, it is necessary to consider the human element, and to teach the employees the meaning of the device.

The two most important aspects of the human element in accident prevention are equipment design and training. A third aspect which is of some importance, but is less important than it was recently thought to be, is that of individual differences. As a rule, the few psychologists employed by American industry in accident prevention are employed in the study of individual differences with relation to accidents. Though seldom recognized, there are quite technical psychological problems in the area of safety training. These problems are often in the form of the evaluation of different training approaches. What is the effectiveness of employee training in safety? How well do employees know and carry out safety regulations? What are their objections to safety glasses, safety shoes, or to wearing hair nets? How can machinery or processes be changed to take attitudes into account? How effective are safety contests and propaganda posters for safety? Just how much are employees "sold" on the real importance of safety? These are some of the training problems which deserve as much technical finesse as possible in reducing accidents. The big difficulty of methods here, as in all safety research, is that there are not enough accidents. There are not enough, that is, to provide a reliable criterion so that a safety campaign can be evaluated. Did it really have lasting effect? Was the greater expense of the confer-

211

ence method of teaching employees safety rules justified, or should the method of distributing booklets have been used?

ACCIDENT PRONENESS

Accident proneness is the continuing tendency of a person to have accidents as a result of his stable and persisting characteristics. For example, two individuals operating the same piece of machinery under identical circumstances have the same situational probability of having an accident. However, one may be inherently a poor operator in the area of coordination. Because of this lack of proficiency, he will have a greater probability of having an accident in circumstances requiring coordination. He is called an accident-prone operator.[2] Many studies in the field of industrial accident proneness have attempted to identify accident-prone individuals.

Unfortunately, the early evidence of "accident proneness," which was widely publicized, was misunderstood. A great deal of publicity came from the fact that a small percentage of workers were responsible

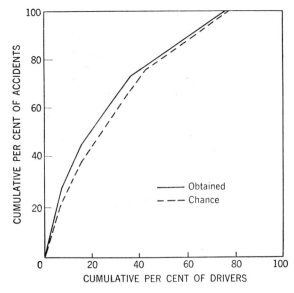

Figure 9-1. Relationship between Cumulative Percentage of Taxi Drivers and of Accidents.

(Mintz, Alexander, and Milton L. Blum, "A Re-examination of the Accident Proneness Concept," *Journal of Applied Psychology,* 1949, **33**, 195–211.)

for a rather large proportion of accidents. One study which was published as strong evidence for the importance of accident proneness concerned taxi drivers.[3] A simple chance distribution would explain the results almost as well, as shown in Figure 9-1. This figure shows that 74.8 per cent of the drivers had all the accidents, but on the basis of chance alone it would have been predicted that 76.5 per cent of the drivers would have had all the accidents. It is unjustified to argue that, because half of the drivers had 82.8 per cent of the accidents, those drivers are accident prone. With only chance operating, it would have been predicted that half of the drivers with the greatest number of accidents would have had 81.7 per cent of the accidents. While the obtained distribution and the chance distribution in Figure 9-1 look almost identical, they are significantly different. An element other than chance is operating, but chance alone could explain the bulk of the results. This is true of all other industrial accident data: chance alone could explain most of the accidents—60 to 80 per cent of the variance in accident occurrence—and only 20 to 40 per cent of the variance is accounted for by unequal liability. Unequal liability means the difference in situation of the employees, which could include difference in hazard plus accident proneness, if any.

Equal liability

In the majority of industrial studies that have been made, the evidence is clear that accidents do not happen to persons on the basis of equal liability. Some have more than their share of the accidents. According to one explanation the occurrence of one accident will predispose one to others. Such has been shown to apply to the accidents caused by airplane pilot failure. The second explanation is that because of their psychological make-up some people are more susceptible to accidents than others.

Biased distribution and unequal distribution

In the first study of the distribution of accidents among industrial employees, ten groups of women were selected for study where the risks within each group seemed approximately equal.[4] The size of the groups varied between 100 and 750. In two groups the distribution of accidents was the same as would have been expected on the basis of chance, but these were groups where equal risks were not so clearly present. There are two explanations for the other eight groups: biased distribution and unequal distribution. Biased distribution means that having one accident makes an employee more likely to have another. Unequal distribution

213

TABLE 9-1

Mean Number of Accidents per Month

(Period October, 1917–January, 1918)

MONTH	61 WOMEN HAVING NO ACCIDENTS IN JANUARY	55 WOMEN HAVING ACCIDENTS IN JANUARY	DIFFERENCE AND PROBABLE ERROR	
October	.43	.91	.48	.11
November	.16	.93	.77	.11
December	.12	.64	.52	.09
January	—	1.67	—	—

Greenwood, Major, and Hilda M. Woods, *A Report on the Incidence of Industrial Accidents upon Individuals with Special Reference to Multiple Accidents,* Industrial Fatigue Research Board, No. 4, London: His Majesty's Stationery Office, 1919, Table XII, p. 16.

means that, upon entrance to a job, one employee is more likely to have accidents than another. The explanation for this unequal distribution could be personality. In comparing the theories of these two distributions to each of the ten groups, the biased distribution fails to apply in five groups, the unequal distribution in two groups. Further comparisons show the unequal distribution to be the more generally applicable explanation. Three groups were studied, each group being separated into subgroups of those who did and did not have accidents in a particular month. Then a comparison was made with the accidents in other months. Table 9-I shows one such comparison. The group of women who had accidents in January had had significantly more accidents in each of the three preceding months. In the other two groups similarly studied, the trends were the same.

Under the theory of biased distribution, there is no reason to hold that an accident-free month would make one freer from accidents in the past. The biased distribution would hold only that the presence of an accident in one month would make one more likely to have an accident in the future. The unequal-distribution theory would hold that freedom from accidents would make it more likely that one would be free from accidents either in the past or in the future.

A further check was made on the applicability of the biased-distribution hypothesis. In a study of four groups, accidents were correlated for the entire group for two successive periods of three months. Under either the biased or the unequal distribution a positive correlation would result. The median correlation between accident rates for employees for one three-month period and the other three-month period is .61. If cases are omitted where the person had no accidents in the first three-month period, the correlation should increase under the hypothesis of biased distribution. It would remain the same under the unequal-distribution hypothesis. When such cases were omitted, the correlations did not increase; this result substantiates unequal distribution.

Chance

If the number of persons who have accidents is known, it is possible to predict the number of accidents that would occur among a group of workers according to chance from the shape of the curve of a chance distribution. If the actual average of accidents exceeds this chance figure, then either there are accident-prone persons in the group or there are unusually dangerous situations present, more dangerous to some employees than to others.

Kind of accidents

There is some evidence that proneness for one kind of accident is associated with a tendency to proneness for a different kind of accident, but this tendency is slight. It is so slight that only a small minority of industrial accidents can be attributed to such a general factor. Among trolley car motormen and motor coach operators, there was only a small correlation between collision and noncollison accidents, although the correlation was positive.[5] When drivers for a utility company who had had a high accident score were transferred to less dangerous work, they were found to have more personal injuries than the average worker.[6] A person who has accidents at home is a little more likely to have them at work, and vice versa.[7] Another example of the generality of accidents concerns a group of hospital patients who had fractures.[8] The majority of these persons had had at least three previous accidents; in a control group— of cases with heart trouble—the majority had had not more than one accident.

CAUSES OF ACCIDENTS

Industrial differences

The United States Bureau of Labor Statistics and the National Safety Council ranked forty major industries for both frequency (disabling work injuries per million man-hours exposure) and severity (days lost

215

per 1000 man-hours worked) of accidents. The most dangerous industries in 1954 were lumber, coal mining, marine transportation, other
mining, quarry, and construction. The safest included communications,
electrical equipment, and tobacco. It is noteworthy that the cement
industry had a frequency rate of 3.38, well below the all-industry average
of 7.22, but was above the industry average in severity rate, while the
converse was true of the printing and publishing trade. The number of
injuries in the steel industry is below the all-industry average, but above
it in the amount of time lost resulting from those fewer injuries.[9]

Environmental conditions of work

HEATING

In a boot and shoe factory a relationship was found between temperature and accidents. The accident rate was lowest between 55 and 59
degrees Fahrenheit, and highest over 69 degrees. Between 59 and 69
degrees the accident rate was moderate.[10]

An unusually thorough study of the effect of temperature on accidents was made over a period of four years among slightly more than
10,000 coal miners.[11] Figure 9-2 shows the relationship between temperature and accidents of varying severity. The most striking fact is that,
although all accidents increase somewhat with higher temperature, the
rise is appreciable only in the number of the slight accidents which
require the workers to be absent less than ten days. The interpretation
has been offered that this is due to the miner's decision. When conditions
are hot and unpleasant, he may decide to take off a few days with an

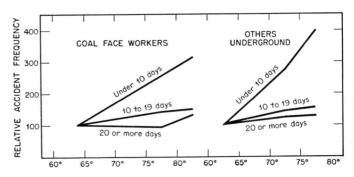

Figure 9-2. Accident Disability in Relation to Temperature.

(Vernon, H. M., *Accidents and Their Prevention,* Cambridge, England: The
University Press, 1936, p. 80.)

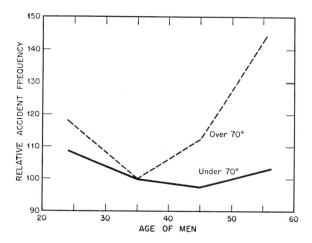

Figure 9-3. Relative Accident Frequency of Coal Face Workers in Relation to Age and Temperature.

(Vernon, H. M., and T. Bedford, *The Absenteeism of Miners in Relation to Short Time and Other Conditions*, Industrial Health Research Board, No. 62, London: His Majesty's Stationery Office, 1931.)

injury that otherwise might be so slight as not to be classified as an accident.

The only accident data that are not open to question are fatalities. Ordinarily there are too few of these to provide reliable data. However, in one study of a mile-deep Peruvian gold mine there were enough deaths to give significant results. There had been twenty deaths in a sixteen-month period in this gold mine, but, after the introduction of a cooling system which lowered the temperature from 89 to 80 degrees, there were only six fatal accidents in a comparable sixteen-month period.[12]

The relationship of temperature to accidents in coal mines is neatly shown in Figure 9-3, where age is also an important variable. High temperatures, over 70 degrees, was a much more serious cause of accidents in older men than in younger miners.

In munitions factories temperature has been shown to have an effect on the accident rate for both men and women, but the effect of high temperature is very different in the case of men, presumably because of the nature of their work and because of sex differences. The results are shown in Figure 9-4. The men were doing harder work, and consequently could be expected to be fatigued more and influenced more at the higher temperatures.

217

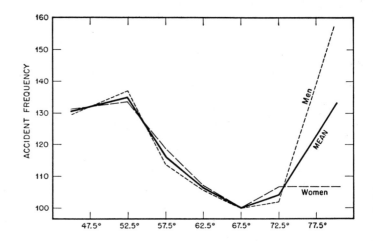

Figure 9-4. Accident Frequency in Relation to Temperature.

(Osborne, Ethel E., and H. M. Vernon, *The Influence of Temperature and Other Conditions on the Frequency of Industrial Accidents, from Two Contributions to the Study of Accident Causation,* Industrial Fatigue Research Board, No. 19, London: His Majesty's Stationery Office, 1922.)

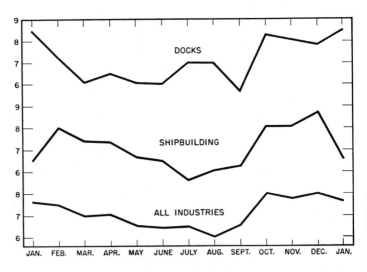

Figure 9-5. Seasonal Variations in Accidents Due to Persons Falling.

(Vernon, H. M., *Accidents and Their Prevention,* Cambridge, England: The University Press, 1936, p. 86.)

218

Accidents in industry have been shown to be due in some instances to insufficient light. Fatal accidents in 80,000 American factories were more frequent in the winter months, the maximum occurring in January.[13] But December, not January, is the darkest month. Since January is the coldest month, perhaps cold as well as light has something to do with monthly accident rates.

The influence of artificial illumination on accident rates varies from one industry to another. Lack of light is responsible for three types of accidents: contact with machinery, 27 per cent; object dropping on a person, 15 per cent; and "persons falling," 12 per cent. The accidents due to falls are most affected by artificial light. This is shown in Figure 9-5. Accidents due to falling are more numerous in the darker months.

Another type of accident clearly influenced by insufficient light is eye injury resulting from something getting in the eye. Such accidents occur, no doubt, because workers bring objects dangerously close when they have difficulty in seeing.

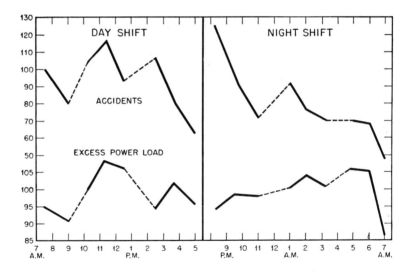

Figure 9-6. Accidents in Relation to Output.

(Osborne, Ethel E., and H. M. Vernon, *The Influence of Temperature and Other Conditions on the Frequency of Industrial Accidents, from Two Contributions to the Study of Accident Causation,* Industrial Fatigue Research Board, No. 19, London: His Majesty's Stationery Office, 1922.)

219

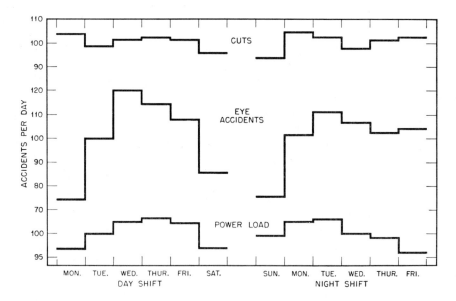

Figure 9-7. Diurnal Variations of Accidents and Output.

(Vernon, H. M., *Industrial Fatigue and Efficiency,* London: George Routledge and Sons, Ltd., 1921, p. 198.)

SPEED OF WORK

In three extensive surveys speed of work has been shown to be related to accident frequency during the daytime, although such a relationship did not obtain on the night shift.[14] Variations in accidents compared to output in shell manufacture are shown in Figure 9-6. During the day shift there is a similarity in the shapes of the curves for accidents and for output. Excess power load is a measure of output, since it shows what work was done over the minimum of the machines' running without any work being done. Although the two curves are similar during the day shift, they are by no means identical. This lack of identity is probably due to the fact that changes in output near the maximum output are more conducive to accidents than changes at a lower output level. For speed of work to cause accidents, the worker would have to be working above a safe range of speed.

The exact reason why there is no such similarity between accident and output curves during the night shift is not known, but a possible explanation is that on this shift workers ordinarily have been up for several hours before going to work, whereas they have been awake a much shorter time before beginning work on the day shift. For this reason output curves of these workers may vary. For some reason not clearly known, the frame of mind of the night-shift worker is such that accidents occur more toward the first part of the shift. It has been suggested that workers are more likely to be under the influence of alcohol, although there is no evidence of this influence on these accidents.

Accidents to the eyes correspond roughly with output, as measured by power consumption, in a fuse factory, although cuts give no such correspondence; see Figure 9-7.

Age and experience

The relationship of experience to accidents is strikingly shown in Figure 9-8. Approximately 50 per cent of the employees had accidents in their first six months of employment, 23 per cent in the next six months, and only 3 per cent had accidents after they had two and a half years of experience.

The injury frequency for newly employed workers is appreciably higher during the first few months on the job than it is in succeeding months and years. The frequency of accidents among street car motormen and motor coach operators continued to decrease sharply until these employees had been at work for six or seven months. In a large

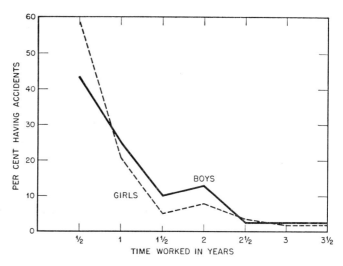

Figure 9-8. Relationship of Accidents Incurred by Young Persons to Years of Experience.

(Vernon, H. M., "Prevention of Accidents," *British Journal of Industrial Medicine,* 1945, **2,** 3.)

metals plant the frequency for two groups of workers was between 5 and 6 per 1000 man-hours during the first month. By the third month this had dropped to between 4 and 5 per 1000 man-hours, and at the end of six months the rate had declined to about 3.6.[15] The principal point determined by both of these studies was that workers have a greater accident frequency rate in the first few months on the job than during later periods.

Each of these two studies suggested the need for more efficient training—training of longer duration which would be concentrated on safe habits often omitted from training programs. In the large metals plant two groups were established. In the group that had formal training in job procedure and safety, the injury rate dropped faster and stabilized sooner than in the group in which no training was given. The trained group reached 3.8 (see Figure 9-9) in the third month, a rate that was not approximated by the untrained group until the seventh month.

In general, accident rates decrease steadily with age. The rate of accidents compared with age is illustrated in Table 9-II for both men

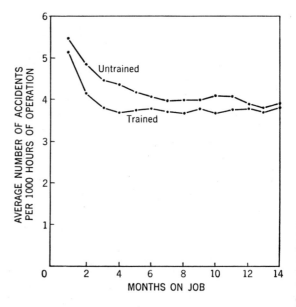

Figure 9-9. Accident Rate of Trained and Untrained Workers. The trained workers had formal training in correct job procedure and safety methods; the untrained workers did not.

(Adapted from Van Zelst, R. H., "The Effect of Age and Experience upon Accident Rate," *Journal of Applied Psychology,* 1954, **38,** 313–317.)

TABLE 9-II

Accident Rate by Age

AGE GROUP	MALE RATE PER HUNDRED	FEMALE RATE PER HUNDRED
17–21	172	41
21–28	75	36
28–35	65	17
35–45	50	26
45–60	42	37
60+	35	0

Mann, J., "Analysis of 1009 Consecutive Accidents at One Ordnance Depot," *Industrial Medicine*, 1944, **13,** 368–374.

and women in an ordnance depot. Accidents decrease steadily with age for men, but there is no clear correlation between accidents and age for women. The decrease with age, which is commonly found, is complicated by two variables. Age normally accompanies experience, which also accompanies a decrease in accident rate. Furthermore, there may be a selection effect—the more unsafe employees may leave the job.

It must also be pointed out that one does not know that all groups are doing the same task and exposed to the same chance of injury. The rates of women are lower because many were performing clerical and administrative tasks. It seems unlikely, however, that the great excess of accidents by the young male group was created by any special hazards of the work.

Health

It has been shown that accidents are significantly associated with one aspect of health. This aspect is number of visits to the dispensary because of sickness.[16] Figure 9-10 shows this relationship for 352 male metal-workers in an automobile plant. In this group, visits to the dispensary correlated significantly with accident rates. Holding age and experience constant does not materially alter the relationship between visits to the dispensary and accidents. Results were similar, but on the average slightly less positive, for five other groups of male and six groups of female workers. There is thus no doubt that there is a genuine positive relationship between accident frequency and visits to the dispensary because of sickness. The interpretation of the meaning of visits to the dispensary is another and more difficult matter. These apparently are not a measure of general health, for when sickness absences are studied they do not correlate significantly with accidents. The interpretation offered by the investigator is that dispensary visits are a mark of instability of personality, of wanting to avoid work, and that this instability is important in susceptibility to accidents.

Absenteeism

There appears to be a direct relationship between accidents and absenteeism (absenteeism being defined as absence without a cause satisfactory to the employer). Absence records of a company over a four-year period showed in a sample of 289 cases that 200 employees who had no accidents averaged fifteen absences, while the remaining 89 who had had accidents averaged twenty-four absences.[17] In a group of steel company employees, the absence rate for employees with accidents is higher than for the accident-free individuals.[18]

Psychological factors

Psychological factors have been reported to be associated with accidents in two studies. Nine Negro and nine Spanish-speaking teams in the

Figure 9-10. Relationship between Accidents Incurred by Metal Workers and Sickness Visits to Ambulance Room.

(Vernon, H. M., *Accidents and Their Prevention,* London: Cambridge University Press, 1936, p. 49; from Newbold, B. A., *A Contribution to the Study of the Human Factor in the Causation of Accidents,* Industrial Fatigue Research Board, No. 34, London: His Majesty's Stationery Office, 1926.)

224

finishing end of a steel mill hot strip were studied with reference to accident records and interpersonal preferences. Workers liked best by fellow workers tended to be accident-free, and high accident rates were experienced by workers who were most disliked by their associates.[19] Results from shop departments of a large tractor factory show evidence that such psychological and physical factors as comfortable shop environment and promotion possibility help to reduce accidents. Accidents were more frequent in crew-type work, where responsibility is less certain, than on individual-type job work.[20] It may be that in each of these three studies the important variable was morale. Where morale is high accidents are not so likely to happen.

INDUSTRIAL SAFETY PROGRAMS

Today American manufacturing plants place great stress on safety. Most managements practice some form of safety, but, like many personnel functions, it is extremely difficult to evaluate the results in terms of dollars. During the last thirty years there has been a steady decrease in both the severity and frequency rates of industrial accidents, although industrial employment has increased.

Organization Responsibility

Where there is an organized safety program, this is the responsibility of the Personnel or Industrial Relations Department in almost three companies out of four. In companies with over 1000 employees, five out of six have safety specialists who are engineers. Slightly less than half of smaller companies have a safety specialist.[21] The most common type of safety training attempts to make employees safety conscious and "safety-wise." This method uses psychology indirectly through the use of signs and contests.

Committees

More and more, safety committees are becoming the policy force behind safety programs. The two basic committees are management and joint union-management committees. The latter type is not used so frequently as management committees, but it is rapidly growing in popularity. Safety was a primary collective bargaining issue with John L. Lewis and the United Mine Workers in years past. Today the safety problem is seldom an issue in union-management contract negotiations. Both management and union officials realize its importance and are striving for improvements through joint safety committees.[22]

225

Prizes

One-half of the companies with industrial safety programs offer no rewards or special incentives to employees who have good safety records.[23] When there is an award, it is a group award, and only 10 per cent of the award-giving companies grant cash awards. This study reports also that most companies are conscious of accident-prone employees, and they help these employees by intensive training or by transferring them to a safer job. The companies supply safety equipment free, with the exception of shoes and prescription safety glasses.

Management support

In any type of safety program, success depends on the conviction of foremen and top management and their obtaining cooperation of rank-and-file employees. Safety is an integral part of a foreman's job. This best can be realized through group participation. Several safety studies, in which a group decision technique of problem solving has been used, have been made in the field of democratic supervision.

Safety consciousness by management appears to lower accident frequency rates. Over a five-year period one investigator visited sixty-two companies and studied accident records.[24] His study indicates that the accident frequency rate is less when classes in accident prevention are conducted on company time, and that, when top officials attend and lead the discussions, the rate is lower than when these officials fail to attend or participate.

Records

Procter and Gamble has had safety progress through "teamwork." There has been a program under which everyone "thought" safety and "worked" safety.[25] In 1930 the company had thirty-six disabling injuries for every million man-hours worked; in 1955 this accident frequency was 1. This corporation, like many others, is reducing accidents. An English plant, through training rules, use of safe clothing, and careful selection programs in the company, reduced the accident rate one-half.[26] Those companies which have demonstrated good safety records are those that have careful and comprehensive safety programs with a heavy emphasis on training.

Slogans with an appeal to fear attract attention 30 per cent longer than those with a positive appeal.[27] The relative training values of these appeals in decreasing accidents, however, has not been determined.

In England the results of safety organizations and education have been credited with the following decreases in the severity rates of accidents (severity rate is days lost per 1000 hours worked) : 9 per cent in one company, 38 per cent in a second company, and 70 per cent in a third.[28] These figures are not typical, but they are the most spectacular. There were other firms that profited materially from safety organizations and others that did not improve their accident rates at all.

It is unusual for a company to keep sufficient records of the expense either of training or of accidents to yield a balance sheet. An exception is shown in the case of the United States Steel Corporation, which spent $5 million dollars in eight years in a safety campaign including safety devices and measures.[29] "As a result, the accident rate was reduced 40 per cent during the last five years of the period, and during the last three years of it, the saving in the cost of accidents exceeded the amount spent on safety by 35 per cent."

The United States Steel Company, with its "3 C's of Safety" and "Single Objective Safety," is one of the leaders in a comprehensive program. The steel industry was successful in its initial efforts to reduce accidents, and it has continued to make progress. The Columbia-Geneva Steel division of United States Steel approached the safety program through the "Single Objective Safety." This approach calls for the reduction of *all* injuries to employees, whether minor or serious. The program involves four steps: (1) get the facts; know everything there is to know about an accident; (2) spot the critical situations from the facts; (3) single out objective and determine what correction is needed; and (4) take action. This is coupled with the "3 C's of Safety," which emphasizes a *comprehension* of the possibilities of injurious *contact* and their *control.* This over-all plan, which is designed to develop that awareness which leads to accident prevention, has reduced all accidents from a 1946–50 frequency of 463 to 71 per million man-hours in September, 1955. The disability dropped from a 1946-50 rate of 3.5 to 0.7 in 1955.[30]

Otis Elevator instituted a program of stopping minor injuries with a follow-up campaign.[31] From 1949 to the end of 1952 the rate of lost-time accidents dropped from 16.9 to 0.1. This simple program of having the nurse and foremen follow up minor accidents resulted in a tremendous saving for Otis.

Contests

Contests between one plant or one department or one driver and another may be effective for a time, but psychologically they are not believed to be good in the long run. The contestants lose interest. It is believed sounder to train to avoid accidents rather than to earn some extraneous reward; this is true of motivation in general—the reward should be a part of the activity and not foreign to it.

There are no outstanding instances of the use of psychological tests in the manufacturing industry to select persons who have traits that lead to safety at work. Still there appears to be considerable faith in some quarters that such traits do exist and that such tests should be used. Before a few studies in manufacturing are discussed, stock will be taken of just where the problem is with regard to a working hypothesis. Accidents appear to be due to several personal factors, some of the more important of which have been presented; they are age, possibly experience, and the causes of visits to the dispensary. In addition, a number of other causes of accidents have been presented. These are varying industrial hazards, conditions of work such as heating, light, and speed of work. Now it is quite possible, and even likely, that there will be more than one cause of a single accident. Low illumination, for example, may cause one worker to have an accident, while another worker who has been trained better or who is a better risk will avoid the same accident even though the illumination is below par. For psychological tests to be proved effective, it is necessary that the accident records be reliable as well as that the tests be valid.

A series of psychological tests was given to entering employees in one company, and the results were compared with later accident records.[32] The tests were for intelligence, reaction time, dotting, and pursuit meter. The scores of the last three were combined into a coordination score. The subjects were 414 apprentices. Intelligence tests did not correlate significantly with any of the groups or with the total group of apprentices. Coordination score correlated .33 with freedom from accidents for shipwrights and for electric fitters; .34 for the mechanics. It would appear worth while to use these tests in selecting workers for manufacturing industry, but such use has not been reported..

Vision

Accidents among steelworkers were clearly associated with visual functions.[33] Workers whose eyes turned in least from distance vision to near vision had the most accidents. At the extremes of the group those workers with the least convergence had twice as many accidents as those with the most convergence. The use of these results for selection is open to question, since some changes in convergence are due to age.

Personality

There are many claims that psychiatrists can determine a personality of accident proneness. A number of lines of evidence point to personality and attitudes as important in accidents caused by personal factors. Accurate diagnosis and prediction in the case of such persons are almost entirely lacking, as almost all the literature is in general rather than specific terms. A somewhat specific study is one in which psychiatric examinations were given to 130 industrial accident repeaters and something was found wrong with each one of them. The classifications were as follows: "revengeful attitude, unlucky, longing to be pampered, over-ambitious, over-fearful, alcoholics, feebleminded, organic diseases."[34] There was a control group of twenty persons who had none of the failings found in the accident repeaters. This is an interesting study, but it provides no application until and unless it receives confirmation. An indication of the need for caution with regard to medical diagnoses in the realm of personality is found in the striking study by the Civil Aeronautics Authority in which it was found that physicians who were examining candidates for pilots' licenses agreed on a diagnosis of psychoneurotic personality in only five out of one hundred cases.[35]

One psychiatrist's hypothesis of accident proneness, based on clinical observations, includes two points that are particularly interesting in that they are supported by suggestions from other independent investigations. The accident prone is called the impulsive person.[36] This is supported by an experiment in which the results suggest that workers with high accident rates are those who tend to act relatively more quickly than they can perceive. The second point is that the accident prone are unstable. There are several sources to support this. On the other hand, the accurate measurement of instability is not yet definitely established.

A psychiatrist suggested during World War II that a questionnaire for personality traits would be useful to assist in spotting the accident prone.[37] The items to be covered were: (1) previous accidents; (2) educational history, the hypothesis being that the accident prone is less likely to have finished an educational "unit"; (3) work record (irregular employment goes with tendency to accidents); and (4) "family relations" (background of a broken home on the part of parents is in the direction of accident proneness). This is an interesting questionnaire, but additional data are needed to show whether it will work.

In transportation industry

There has been a great deal more work on the psychological aspects of accident prevention in the transportation industry than in all other industries combined. This is not due to the danger to transportation employees, but rather to the companies' liability to their customers and possibly to the fact that the work of drivers is more related to what can be measured by psychological tests than is true of manufacturing jobs.

TABLE 9-III

Accidental Death of Workers by Major Industries, 1954

INDUSTRIAL GROUP	TOTAL DEATHS	DEATHS PER 100,000 WORKERS
Mining, quarrying, oil and gas wells	800	107
Construction	2,400	74
Agriculture	3,800	60
Transportation	1,200	41
Service	2,300	16
Public Utilities	200	14
Manufacturing	2,000	12
Trade	1,300	11
All industries	14,000	25

National Safety Council, *Accident Facts,* 1955, p. 23.

Transportation employees have neither the highest total number of deaths nor the highest death rates, as Table 9-III shows.

Claims for the value of psychological tests in the transportation field have far outdistanced their proved performance. Perhaps the explanation is that the driver tests look like effective gadgets and have been accepted as such even when their results have been shown to be of only moderate value. In many instances, tests have been used or have been advocated when there is no evidence of their validity. The following material will describe a few situations in which the validity of tests for selecting transport operators has been determined.

An elaborate study was made of the accident records of 482 street car motormen in comparison with seventy-six variables of a medical and personal nature. Accident records over a three-year period were corrected to compensate for nonpersonal factors, such as dangerous routes, dangerous times of day, day of week, season of the year, and mileage.[38]

No spectacular relationships were discovered between any of the seventy-six personal data, including age and experience and medical variables, and the corrected accident records. Confirmation was found for some of the existing medical standards—blood pressure and visual acuity.

A Motorman Selection Test has been found effective in Milwaukee.[39]

This is a work sample test in which the subject learns to operate controls in response to sounds and lights and to resist distracting noises. Only 0.6 per cent of the men selected by the test had to be discharged for accidents, in contrast to 14.1 per cent of operators who had not been selected by the Motorman Test. It was estimated that the use of the test saved $60,000 in a year's time.

Operators for the Boston Elevated Railway who had frequent accidents scored worse on a series of psychological tests than did operators whose records were better.[40] The tests were for speed, accuracy, oscillation, perseveration, and tapping. A comparison of test results with accident records is shown in Table 9-IV.

A combination of psychological tests and previous accident records was found predictive of accident records among London bus drivers.[41] These were dotting, coordination, interrupted pursuit meter, choice reaction time, and pursuit meter. The results, translated into percentages, are shown in Table 9-V. These are estimates. No follow-up has been reported to show that accidents were reduced.

By using the Otis Self-Administering Test of Mental Ability, the Bennett Test of Mechanical Comprehension, the Kuder Vocational Interest Test, the Bernreuter Personality Inventory, and the Minnesota Multiphasic Personality Inventory, a group of long-distance-hauling freight drivers were studied for a relationship between accidents and characteristics measured by these paper-and-pencil tests.[42] The authors concluded that accident rates were determined on the basis of miles driven per accident, but continued to follow the normal distribution when distance was held constant. Safe drivers tended to be more tense,

TABLE 9-IV

Comparison of Test Score with Accident Record of Elevated Railway Operators

GRADE ON TEST	HIGH ACCIDENT GROUP	LOW ACCIDENT GROUP
A (good)	16	20
B (medium)	19	21
C (poor)	8	2

Slocombe, C. S., and E. E. Brakeman, "Psychological Tests and Accident Proneness," *The British Journal of Psychology,* 1931, **21,** 29–38.

231

TABLE 9-V

Estimates of Accident Rate upon
Removing Bus Drivers with Many Accidents
or with Poor Coordination

	PERCENTAGE OF DRIVERS REMOVED	PERCENTAGE ACCIDENT RATE	PERCENTAGE REDUCTION
Accident rate of whole group for all years except first	—	100	—
1. Accident rate after removing drivers with three or more accidents in their first year	28	91	9
2. Accident rate after removing the worst 25 per cent in the tests	23	93	7
3. Combining methods 1 and 2	44	87	13

Farmer, E., and E. G. Chambers, *A Study of Accident Proneness among Motor Drivers,* Industrial Health Research Board, No. 84, London: His Majesty's Stationery Office, 1939.

less self-sufficient, and less dominant but had higher scores on the mechanical comprehension test. The accident rate was highest for drivers in the first six months of their employment.

SUMMARY

Industrial work has become considerably safer as accident rates have continued to fall. There are numerous examples of accident prevention reducing the number of accidents and increasing production and profit for management.

Accidents are related to many environmental, mechanical, and human conditions. There is usually a combination of mechanical ineffectiveness and human error. Seldom is there an accident where either mechanical or human error is completely missing.

Accidents can be the cause of poor morale and in turn low morale can be a cause of accidents.

Though there probably are some accident-prone individuals, accident proneness has become of secondary importance because the inter-pretation of accident statistics is becoming clearer. The best hope of accident prevention is through continual safety training, enlistment of the active participation of rank-and-file employees, and safer equipment design. Selection of safe employees is at a lower priority.

Psychological tests for picking safe employees have had some success in the transportation industry.

A well-developed safety campaign making employees safety conscious is often effective. In English coal mines an experimental group was compared with a control group; the situations were identical except that an accident prevention program was carried on with the experimental group. In nine months the experimental group had reduced its accident record 54 per cent below the other group.[43]

By using job analysis or step-by-step training procedures, accidents have been greatly reduced. In order to be successful, this training must make the purpose of each procedure understood.

RECOMMENDED READINGS

Thorndike, Robert L., "Human Factors in Accidents," U. S. Air Force School of Aviation Medicine Report No. 1, February, 1951. A thorough literature review of industrial and military accident studies.

Mintz, A., and M. L. Blum, "A Re-examination of the Accident Proneness Concept," *Journal of Applied Psychology,* 1949, **33**, 195-211. This shows that accident proneness is not nearly so important as it has been thought to be.

Van Zelst, R. H., "The Effect of Age and Experience upon Accident Rate," *Journal of Applied Psychology,* 1954, **38**, 313-317. Data presented show that immaturity and lack of training are responsible for a substantial number of industrial accidents.

10

Motivation

Human relations encompass the important reactions of a person to other people. The relations between individuals, between the individual and the group, and between groups constitute an important phase of industrial psychology in the United States today. Human relations are important in industry because they explain why one man works harder than another, why one employee quits his job much sooner than another, why one group of workers restricts its output and another works energetically, why one group strikes and another does not.

Motivation is the unifying concept for human relations; it cuts across all topics in industrial psychology. Employee motivation and attitudes may be positive or negative. An employer wishes to hire positively motivated people who want to work and will continue to try hard throughout the total years of employment. To determine these things is a major purpose of the employment interview. Methods of work which the engineer finds most efficient depend for their execution on motivation on whether the employees will accept the change. An essential requirement for safety is the attitude or motive of wanting to be safe. An essential requirement for learning is that an effective motive for the learner be present. The goal of supervision is to motivate employees toward their job, toward their company, and, incidentally, toward their supervisor.

Motivation and work

Men work for various reasons. One man works because he needs the money to feed his family. Another who has a million dollars works because he likes the power, the social position, or the self-respect that doing a useful job of work brings. From time to time motives for working change. One week the reason will be different from what it was the preceding week. It may no longer be financially necessary for a winner of the Irish Sweepstakes to continue to work, but he may do so because he is in the habit of working. Another man may gradually accumulate enough money to retire, but he may continue to work because he wants to beat a competitor. A third may not have to work for money, but he works because he enjoys it. It is necessary to consider the total situation at a given time to understand motivation. For example, the motive of hunger would be most prominent in explaining the actions of a starving man, but the motive would become relatively unimportant when the man is filled with food. The majority of industrial workers would not continue on their jobs but for the necessity of making money, whereas many professional persons and managers would.

The change, from time to time, of an individual's dominant motive to work is illustrated by an actual case.

Clark is still living with his friends, four to a room, and has given up his plan to marry. He still spends almost all his wages on clothes, liquor, and recreation. He still misses at least three days on the job out of every two weeks. During the four years he has been working, however, there have been three periods when he improved his work habits, his punctuality, and his motivation. The first was when he wanted to marry, and actually was buying furniture, and looking for a home. The second period of improvement occurred later, when Clark was trying to become a foreman, in order to convince his girl's mother that he was not an "ignorant bum," as she claimed. The third period followed his first visit to a meeting of his union, and his resultant interest in winning status within the union . . .[1]

For the most part Clark was motivated not by his job but by desire for recreation and relaxation. When his job performance was acceptable, Clark was motivated, not primarily by pay itself, but in his first period of improvement by sex—to buy furniture and rent a place for his bride to live in. His second period of highly motivated work habits was due to self-respect to convince his prospective mother-in-law that he would be a worth-while addition to the family. The third period of improvement can be attributed to wanting to win social approval of his fellow employees in the union.

Fundamentals of motivation

Clark's case illustrates three important motives to work: sex, self-respect, and social approval. Two other important motives in industry are activity, or work itself, and hunger. Hunger can operate as a powerful motive to work, but in the United States today it rarely does because few people suffer from hunger. Activity, however, frequently operates as a motive. A carpenter enjoys his part in building a house, a typist enjoys writing letters, a receptionist enjoys meeting people. It is easier to imagine a craftsman of former centuries obtaining pleasure from his work than to imagine a machine operator in a highly mechanized factory being motivated to work because of the activity of his job. The fact is that, as a group, industrial workers like their jobs less than do other employees whose work is more varied. Judging by their answers to questions, American employees in general are motivated by their work. This is particularly true in the professions and in business, but it is not true in general of the textile industry and mining and probably of many other highly mechanized jobs.

Motives are based on physiological drives such as the innate tissue conditions of the organism to avoid pain, to need food, water, rest, sleep, sex activity, and activity in general. In addition to the motives that are readily traceable to basic physiological drives there are several social motives that are more remote. The most important of these in our industrial society are social approval and self-respect; both of these were operative in Clark's case. The desire for self-respect or recognition in industry includes the desire for prestige, for feeling important, for having one's work appreciated. The motives of social approval and self-respect in combination largely explain the employee's need for participation in the decisions and plans affecting him.

Internal versus external motives

Industry frequently offers the employee external incentives such as pay and reprimands. These, however, are less successful than incentives which motivate people internally. Katz and Likert have suggested that there is a difference between external and internal motives.[2] External motivation stimulated by pay, praise, or punishment is effective only if it is internalized. Internal motivation is that which starts from the ego needs of the person. The status or prestige that an employee attaches to his job, a sense of "accomplishment in doing a job well," the need to be employed at work in which one is interested, "the illusion of self-determination and freedom"—these are examples of internal motivation. Another example of internal motivation, which has had limited study but which appears to be important, is the identification an employee has in being a member of a group and the satisfaction this identification sometimes brings.

There are complications in the determination of the relative value of external motivation, since each employee interprets the external stimuli in a personal way and this may differ from one person to another.[3] These interpretations are based on the "frame of reference" of the employee and on his personality. An employee's frame of reference for the adequacy of his wages may depend on pressure from his wife rather than on whether the wages are in line with a fair job evaluation. The employee's personality may have a hand in shaping his ambitions, which depend on his expectation and level of aspiration.

Motivation cannot be made effective merely by the application of external incentives such as money. Whether the incentives offered by industry will be effective depends in part on the internal state of the organism—his level of aspiration, what a man expects of himself.

Frustration

Just as it is often important to give motives full expression, so is it important not to frustrate motives by blocking such expression. Frustration behavior is behavior without a goal. For example, employees may have a need for social approval and self-respect, but, if they are not allowed to participate in the decisions that affect them, their blocked motivations may produce frustration, which shows itself as antagonistic behavior.

An explanation of strikes and other labor trouble can be found in large part in frustration. This frustration may be shown either by the leader or by the rank-and-file workers. A group of rank-and-file employees may suddenly form a union or strike when management believes that they have everything they deserve. Perhaps economically the employees do have all that under the circumstances they need to satisfy physical wants, but they may still be frustrated by not being allowed a voice in decisions regarding policies or practices that affect them.

The results of frustration in industry have been reported in a number of case histories and clinical reports. An unusual example of the result of frustration is that of the railroad engineer who, after thirty-two years of running dinky switch engines no farther than the yards of the city, finally went wild, climbed into the most elegant cross-country engine, opened up its throttle, then jumped out while it wrecked itself.[4]

Frustration may have been built up largely in childhood, and so a company cannot necessarily be blamed for employee frustration, but the company can safeguard itself by keeping in touch through supervisors who recognize and respond to conditions of frustration. Management provides many incentives to motivate people to work. Several motives and several incentives may be operating at once. When a motive is present in a person, it will become active when there is some appealing incentive. Management's problem is to induce employees to express their motives in productive work, and to prevent frustration resulting from blocked expression of these motives. For example, if an employee's most insistent motive is the need for self-respect, and management permits him to participate in job decisions, the employee may express this motive by productive work. If management does not allow him to participate, but tries to motivate him with a pay increase, the employee may be unproductive and frustrated.

IMPORTANT INCENTIVES

The important motives to work are activity, self-respect, social approval, sex, and hunger. These motives are stimulated by the incentives of pay, competition, praise and punishment, participation, and various ways of assuring security.

Pay

Money is the incentive most commonly used in American industry to get people to work. Management generally has the attitude that what the worker wants most is more money. It therefore is interesting that interview and questionnaire studies of employees almost never show higher pay at the top of the list of items that workers want most. A large nation-wide study concluded that differences in pay are less often related to morale than human factors such as relations with supervisor, handling of grievances, being given credit for suggestions.[5] Another national study found similar results where workers rated pay less important than management predicted and rated several human factors, "fair credit, appreciation, and counsel," higher than management expected.[6]

In spite of the fact that numerous studies show that workers do not rate higher pay at the top of the list of things wanted most, it is still necessary to consider how employees respond to more or less pay. In one study in which the employees stated that they valued "variations in social contact" higher than pay, there was evidence that pay differences were important. These people had all had at least two jobs. Each person was asked which of the two jobs he liked more than the other. In four out of five cases the preferred job was the one which carried higher pay as well as more responsibility and variety.[7]

A study of labor turnover showed that the most frequent reason given for employees' quitting in a department store and in six metal-trades establishments was dissatisfaction with pay.[8] There is other evidence that one of the strongest attractions to an applicant is high pay. High pay is less effective as an incentive for keeping a person on a job than in luring him to the job in the first place.

Wanting more pay is the reason most often given for strikes, but it is frequently claimed that this is only a superficial reason. It is asserted that there are frequently psychological or social factors causing dissatisfaction that cannot be expressed. The workers know no other way of expressing their dissatisfaction than through demands for higher wages.

The assumption that employees respond only to money has been called the "rabble hypothesis" because workers are, under this wrong assumption, treated as a group of unorganized rabble insensitive to the social motives of approval and self-respect.[9] If a pay increase is granted, employee motivation toward productive work may not be stimulated because the source of dissatisfaction has not been removed. The result is frustration. Nonproductive work continues, as do additional demands for pay.

Pay is an important incentive to work, but its incentive value varies from situation to situation and from person to person. While some people want to make more money no matter how much they are making, there is a definite trend toward satisfaction with one's income if it is high.[10] This can be illustrated by a study which is summarized in Table 10-I. The interviewee was asked what his income was and then was asked, "About how much more money than that do you think your family would need to have the things that might make your family happier or more comfortable than it is now?" The higher the income, the more

TABLE 10-I

Income Satisfaction and Income Aspiration

WEEKLY INCOME	CASES	DIS-SATISFIED	SATISFIED	NO OPINION	NO. SPECIFYING AMT. MORE INCOME WANTED	PERCENTAGE INCREASE IN INCOME WANTED
National	1165	56%	32%	12%	581	86%
Under $20	163	68	16	16	100	162
$20–$29.99	170	72	19	9	116	97
$30–$39.99	207	67	20	13	129	66
$40–$49.99	310	54	35	11	147	59
$50–$99.99	191	43	49	8	73	52
$100 and over	124	20	66	14	16	100

Centers, Richard, and Hadley Cantril, "Income Satisfaction and Income Aspiration," *Journal of Abnormal and Social Psychology,* 1946, **41,** 64–69. Reprinted by permission of the American Psychological Association.

likely it was for people to be satisfied and not to want more income. In 1946, $100 per week was enough for most people. The lower-income groups wanted a larger percentage increase. This study showed that there was a trend for satisfaction with income to be associated with high occupational status, but, when amount of income was held constant, these occupational differences largely disappeared. Dissatisfaction with earnings also varies with education, but, when earnings are held constant, the differences disappear. The only important cause of dissatisfaction with earnings that was found was low earnings. The sample studied was representative of the national population, 18 years of age and older.

English coal miners reduced their voluntary absenteeism considerably

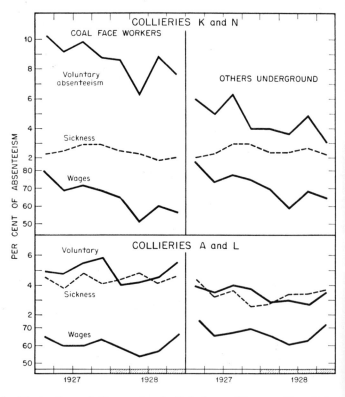

Figure 10-1. Fluctuations of Absenteeism in Relation to Wages at Two Pairs of Collieries.

Vernon, H. M., and T. Bedford, *Two Studies of Absenteeism in Coal Mines: No. 1, The Absenteeism of Miners in Relation to Short Time and Other Conditions,* Industrial Health Research Board, No. 62, London: His Majesty's Stationery Office, 1931.)

240

when their wages were cut. The relation between wages and such absenteeism for two groups is shown in Figure 10-1. When pay becomes marginal, the dominant motives to work are those closely associated with the basic physiological drives, and the other motives such as activity, need for self-respect, and social approval become less powerful. On some jobs people work mainly because of money, on others because of interest in their work. What was true of miners might not be true at all of persons in occupations that yield satisfactions in addition to pay.

This illustration demonstrates the impossibility of finding exactly the relative incentive value of money as compared with other incentives, because money gratifies various motives in different situations. Money may represent security for old age, it may act as a reward to secure greater social approval of the group or to increase one's self-respect. A second illustration showing the limited importance of pay as an incentive to some hourly paid workers was shown in a study wherein six hundred families, both white and Negro, were interviewed.[11] This study shows why money is not always an effective incentive to attendance on the job. The reason is that among certain groups the lack of money is no stigma; workers can live off their friends and relatives without feeling ashamed. Other pleasures, those of the flesh, are more satisfying than what additional money will buy. The importance of the home as an incentive is shown in this situation. The home operates as an incentive, both as a physical object to purchase which requires steady work habits and also as a place where family pressures often motivate a worker to regular work habits. Workers are motivated so strongly on occasions by social pressures outside the plant that the foreman is limited in the effectiveness of motivation that he can exert on the worker. The importance of pay, then, depends on an internalized system of motivation.

WAGE-INCENTIVE SYSTEMS

Management is interested in increased production, and many companies offer additional pay incentives that are tied to greater output. Wage-incentive systems in their operation do not always bear out the apparently justifiable assumption that workers will work harder to make more pay because it is to their advantage to do so. Industries vary in their utilization of wage-incentive plans, and some industries are more adaptable to their use than others.

Extensive use of wage incentives depends on both the type of industry and the appropriateness of piecework or other forms of measurable output, and on the willingness of labor. Wage incentives are not feasible in public utilities, but they are widely used in textiles. For example, a 1948 study of incentive wage systems used in Wisconsin showed that 91

241

per cent of the textile workers received incentive pay.[12] The second factor in the use of wage incentive systems, the willingness of labor, is important because of widespread employee fear of change, rate cutting, and speedup.

Management emphasizes the opportunity to earn more money through a wage-incentive plan. This incentive is effective to the degree that money satisfies employee motives to work and does not cause him to fear rate cutting, speedup, or working himself out of a job. There are other possible advantages for the employee producing under a wage-incentive system: (1) the boredom and monotony of a repetitive job may be reduced if the worker can make a game of trying to reach the production goal; (2) an employee can escape supervisory pressure if he produces more than his standard output, and he can even express his freedom from close control by loafing on his own time after producing the standard; (3) the goal offered by standard production and the incentive of greater earnings can reduce fatigue which may result on a repetitive job that is compensated for by a flat hourly rate. All three of these supplementary advantages depend on realistic production goals that are challenging but attainable.[13]

One employee expressed his attitude toward daywork and piecework in this way: "On piecework I hear that time clock behind me go 'clock, click,' clicking off the minutes. But on daywork I know it's no use looking around to see what time it is, because the hands won't have moved any."[14] Management offered two incentives to this man: one, a pay incentive; two, a goal that incited his interest in work activity. These incentives do not motivate every employee in the same way. The work group may exert pressure on rate busters and have their own informal production standards. Conformity results because of strong social motives of approval and self-respect. The high producer may be popular with management, but rejected by the group.

The force of production standards set by the group and not by management can be illustrated by the production record of a woman employee, a presser, at the Harwood Manufacturing Company.[15] When the employee learned the job, she was working in a group that had set an informal production standard. When she surpassed this standard during her second week of work, the group exerted pressure until she slacked off to the acceptable standard; however, when she was removed from the group and was made an individual worker, her production almost doubled, as shown in Table 10-II. While she was a member of the group, the motivational force of social approval exerted more pressure than the incentive offered by management.

Employee groups do not always set low production standards, and

TABLE 10-II

Production Record of an Employee
as a Group Member and as an Individual Worker

IN THE GROUP		BECOMES SINGLE WORKER	
DAYS	PRODUCTION AVERAGE	DAYS	PRODUCTION AVERAGE
1–3	46	21–24	83
4–6	52	25–28	92
7–9	53	29–32	92
10–12[a]	56	33–36	91
13–16	55	37–40	92
17–20	48		

[a] Group pressure begins to reduce production to the acceptable standard.

Coch, Lester, and John R. P. French, Jr., "Overcoming Resistance to Change," *Human Relations*, August, 1948, pp. 519–520.

if they are allowed to participate in setting their goals they may set higher standards than management anticipated. Eight women employees of the Hovey and Beard Company, a wooden toy manufacturing concern, painted the toys by removing them from a hook on a moving line, spraying them, and replacing them on the hook.[16] The job had been engineered for efficiency, and the girls were given a learner's bonus until they could reach standard production. The girls did not learn as quickly as anticipated and they complained that the job was messy, the hooks moved too fast, the standard was too high, and the work was too hot and hard. Finally a consultant, working through the foreman, tackled the problem. A series of group discussions centering on the job, working conditions, and the resultant frustrations finally produced the complaint that the hooks were moving too fast and the suggestion that the speed be adjustable so the girls could control the speed. This suggestion was worked out and a dial with three settings, low, medium, and fast, was installed. The girls spent a number of lunch hours discussing dial settings and several days experimenting before the group settled into a pattern. "The first half hour of the shift was run on what the girls called medium speed (a dial setting slightly above the point marked 'medium'). The next two and one-half hours were run at high speed; the half hour before lunch and the half hour after lunch were run at low speed. The rest of the afternoon was run at high speed with the

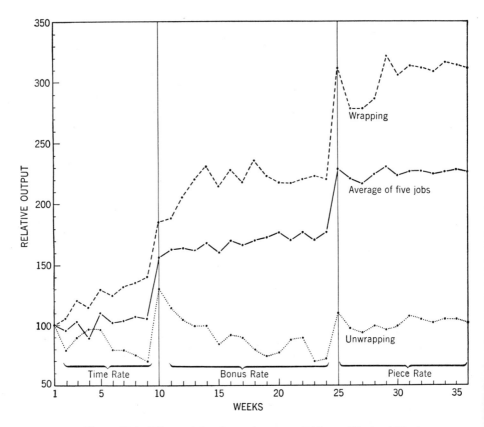

Figure 10-2. Effects of Pay Incentives upon Different Kinds of Work.

(Wyatt, S., *Incentives in Repetitive Work,* Industrial Health Research Board, No. 69, London: His Majesty's Stationery Office, 1934, pp. 5, 24.)

exception of the last forty-five minutes of the shift, which was run at medium."

Work satisfaction and production increased enormously. The girls gained partial control over their jobs, and still the group was earning large incentive payments. Unfortunately this created dissatisfaction among other workers, and this pressure plus the pile-up of production coming off the paint line resulted in a return to the old system of a one-speed hook line. After a month, six of the eight girls left their jobs, and the foreman also eventually left the company. For an incentive system to work, management must consider the effects throughout the plant and coordinate wage payments in order to maintain smooth production and fair differentials among employees.

Management offers a variety of wage incentives to employees. They include straight-time payment, piece rates, numerous formula rates based on production above a specified standard, bonus systems, and profit sharing. Little is known about their comparative effectiveness. One study (see Figure 10-2) showed that piece rates were more effective than bonus payments, and bonus incentives were more effective than straight-time payment.[17] The group studied was small and the employees were rotated among five jobs, and their production on each job was recorded under three types of payment—time, bonus, and piece. An important variable was the preference workers expressed for various jobs. They responded more fully to the changes in wage payments when working at the interesting jobs, such as wrapping. When they were working on the job of least interest, unwrapping, no effect resulted from changes in wage payment.

Employees, therefore, do not respond neatly and consistently to wage incentives. Their response depends on: (1) the degree of fear of speedup, rate cutting, and working themselves out of a job; (2) the fun of achieving a challenging goal, freedom from close supervision, and diminished fatigue, which are corollary incentives; (3) the group pressure and informal production standards and the employees' individual conformance to the group; (4) the satisfaction of participating in setting production standards; (5) the interest in the specific work activity.

Competition

Competition is another important incentive offered by industry. Competition may motivate an individual to achieve a personal goal; it may exist between or among employees who want to attain a group objective; it may be consistent with or contrary to management's goals. This incentive force affects individuals and industry.

It is generally held that the competitive system of American industry is mainly responsible for American preeminence in world industry. This competitive system, in which every industrialist decides for himself the product he will manufacture, and the quantity and quality of it, is believed to be superior to a planned economy of socialism in which the individual enterprise of the industrialist cannot be so active. The American business system is much more competitive than business in a planned state such as Russia. Despite the high regard that businessmen express for competition or free enterprise, they are characteristically trying to reduce competition. For example, competitors are prevented from using patented processes, troublesome competitors may be bought out so that they can no longer compete, or there are other procedures, some of which are less legal, such as combinations which become monopolies.

The effects of competition on performance, as found in a number of laboratory studies, can be summarized briefly. Competition increases speed of performance and decreases accuracy or quality of work. Competition between groups raises performance speed, but in the laboratory studies individual competition is more effective than competition between groups. Competition among persons of nearly equal skill produces better results than among persons of unequal skill. Contests often take the competitor's attention from the main task of performing a job well and focus attention on an outside goal—the contest. Interest in the contest reward often wanes, and then performance slumps considerably. Consequently the best motivation is one that interests the employee in excelling in the task to be performed; motivation that comes from the outside is not nearly so effective.

Very few clear results have been reported on the effectiveness of competition as an incentive for rank-and-file industrial workers. There have been contests that have shown improvement in safety over a relatively short period of time. Notifying a worker of his progress is probably conducive to competition with self, if not with others. When competition has been introduced in industry, there have usually been other new factors present, so that it is impossible to determine the net effect of competition. In a broad sense there is a great deal of competition among factory workers for jobs, for continuity of employment, and, among some of them, for advancement. The opportunity to advance to a better job has no doubt been important to the success of United States industry. Several bases support the general upward mobility of employees either within individual working lifetimes or from generation to generation: (1) the economy continues to expand, creating more room at the top; (2) the movement from the farm to the city and the previous relatively low fertility of upper-income urban families; (3) the increase of years of education and attainment; (4) the aspiration of wage earners to the middle class and their absorption by it.[18]

Labor unions have been accused of trying to do away with competition among factory workers by several means. These include: insistence that employees become members of the union, restriction of output to the average of the group or to the output of the slowest member of the group, and promotions and layoffs based on seniority. It is true that all these practices tend to reduce competition, but not all labor unions are guilty of them. The motives of labor unions do, however, have specific goals different from those of management. Both labor unions and management want security for themselves through competition with the other.

246

Praise and punishment

Among the other incentives offered employees by industry is the daily opportunity for praise and punishment. The incentives of praise and punishment are so prominent in industrial practice that it is worth while to study some of their effects. From studies of school children it is clear that praise or reward is more effective than punishment. Results of several studies are summarized in Table 10-III. In industry as well as in the school and elsewhere, people respond better to praise than to punishment. Punishment should be limited to the few worst things a person might do; it should not be given for small infractions. Even though punishment may apparently be effective initially, it has a long-range bad effect because it fosters resentment against the person doing the punishing. Despite all this, punishment is still more frequently used in industry than praise. One reason is that it is easier to punish. Punishment also gratifies the frustrations of the supervisor. There are occasions when punishment will have to be used, but its careful use should challenge the

TABLE 10-III

Comparison of Positive and Negative Incentives
in Studies of School Children

| | | PERCENTAGE SHOWING | | |
INCENTIVE	ORDER OF MERIT	BETTER RESULTS	SAME RESULTS	POORER RESULTS
Public commendation	1	87.5	11.5	.5
Private reprimand	2	66.3	22.3	10.7
Public reprimand	3	34.7	28.3	36.7
Private ridicule	4	32.5	33.0	34.5
Private sarcasm	5	27.9	27.2	44.8
Public ridicule	6	17.0	35.0	47.3
Public sarcasm	7	11.9	22.8	65.1

Briggs, T. H., "Praise and Censure as Incentives," *School and Society,* 1925, **26**, 596–598; "Sarcasm," *School Review,* 1928, **36**, 685–695; Laird, D. A., "How the High School and College Students Respond to Different Incentives to Work," *The Pedagogical Seminary,* 1923, **30**, 358–371.

best thinking of top executives. This does not imply, however, that discipline should be ignored. One study showed that "the effective supervisor does not avoid taking disciplinary measures when the occasion demands; he will not permit people to get away with violation of regulations; he can be firm in dealing with people when necessary; he will not put up with poor work in order to avoid disciplining a subordinate."[19]

The activities shown in Table 10-IV are among those which most often bring on punishment by discharge in industry. In addition to this punishment, there are lesser punishments, such as loss of time for such

TABLE 10-IV

Most Frequent Causes for Discharge of Hourly Workers

CAUSE FOR DISCHARGE	PER CENT OF COMPANIES
Insubordination, disobedience	47.0
"Flagrant disregard of" or "serious infraction of" rules	42.5
Inefficiency, incompetence	42.1
Irregular attendance	33.2
Intoxication—drinking on the job	32.8
Dishonesty	20.6
Misconduct	13.8
Any "reasonable" or "just" cause	10.1
Carelessness, gross neglect (other than safety)	8.5
Malicious damage or destruction	6.9
Fighting or causing disturbance	6.9
Breaking safety rules	6.1
Lack of cooperation	4.9
Excessive tardiness	2.8
Failure to join union or pay dues	1.2
Punching time clock for another employee	0.8
Lack of work	0.8
"Any except union activity"	0.4
"Disloyalty"	0.4
TOTAL REPLIES	247

The Management Almanac, New York: National Industrial Conference Board, 1944, p. 175.

infractions as tardiness. For such an offense as intoxication on the job, for example, the most common punishment for the first offense is discharge; the second most common punishment is one warning, and then discharge.[20] The ideal psychological procedure would be to discover the cause of the offense and to treat the cause rather than the symptom.

In general, industry offers rewards to the relatively few persons who are promoted, but it secures obedience to rules from the bulk of workers by punishment or by the threat of punishment. It is usually easier to punish than reward, but punishment often is not effective in producing the desired result because it merely frustrates employees rather than motivating for adaptive behavior. When an employee is reprimanded, he often reacts in an irrational way instead of correcting his behavior.

The most effective rewards in industry are probably intangible ones, which are consequently difficult to administer—such as praise for a job well done, recognition for outstanding work, or, even more fundamentally, interest in doing the job and being rewarded by the knowledge that it is well done and is appreciated. An employee merit rating system can effectively supplement the daily contacts between the supervisor and the worker, especially if the rating is fully discussed with the employee. More familiar are the tangible rewards for punctuality and attendance; about one company in five gives such rewards. The most common types of rewards are time off or bonuses.

Knowledge of results

Knowledge of results has been shown to be an effective incentive for persons in laboratory studies, and occasionally there have been demonstrations of its effectiveness in industry. A clear-cut example showed superior mental work when college students had knowledge of their results.[21] The mental work was arithmetic, cancellation, and substitution tests. One group that was shown its results improved more than a control group on each of the types of work. Then a switch was made. The group that had been shown its results was kept in ignorance of its progress. The original control group was shown its results, and then it excelled over the other group.

Participation

Participation means being active in pursuit of a goal which involves the ego. The incentive of participation of workers is becoming more and more prominent as one of the most important incentives for improving production, for causing job satisfaction, and consequently for reducing labor disputes. In terms of the fundamental motives discussed above, participation appears to incorporate an application of the two strongest motives, the social motives of self-respect and social approval. Self-respect comes into play when the worker is doing a job which he understands and which he approves. Social approval acts when employees participate as a group in such a way that each knows he is obtaining the approval of the other members of the group by doing his assigned task.

Using the incentive of participation sometimes conflicts with the traditional outlook of scientific management. It has been pointed out that, on hourly jobs, management often wants employees to do what they are told rather than to use their initiative.[22]

There is no disagreement with the point that an employee should not spend unnecessary time in, for instance, reaching a perfection that is not required. On the other hand, the fact that hourly workers are supposed to do what they are told implies that they are not to participate in working out methods for their jobs. The application of scientific management, whereby the worker is told exactly what he is to do and how to do it, frustrates participation.

There are a number of examples from industry to show the effect of participation, although as a rule the examples are complicated by other factors which may be partly responsible for the results. Such examples are found in the labor-management committees that were given credit for stimulating war production, and in the multiple-management system of the McCormick and Company Spice and Tea House, which are described below. The Relay Assembly study in the Western Electric Company presented in Chapter 8 is an example of participation. So to a large extent are profit-sharing systems, although pay and other incentives are present. Part of the value of suggestion systems, plant papers, and contests to tell about the good features of one's job lies in participation. Participation in research, in discussion, and in decision was effective in changing the opinions of supervisors from the stereotype that younger workers, in a garment plant, were better than older workers.[23] Persuasion through argument on this point had failed even though the evidence for that particular plant was clear.

Clear and spectacular results of participation on production have been shown in an example where group decision raised production sharply. The results of this group decision are shown in Figure 10-3. The workers were paid before and during the study on a piece-rate plan based on time and motion study. A group of workers representing the total group met with a psychologist three times to decide on their production goals. The first goal decided on was to raise production to 85 units per hour within five days. This was reached as shown in Figure 10-3. The second goal set by the workers was 95, and the third was 90. Although

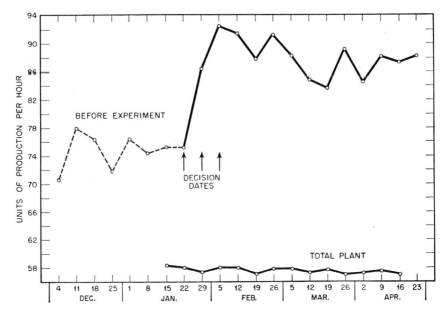

Figure 10-3. Effect of Team Decision. When a team of workers decided to attain a specific goal, their production showed a sharp increase, which was maintained despite the fact that the team's performance was already above the average of the plant.

(Maier, Norman R. F., *Psychology in Industry,* Boston: Houghton Mifflin Co., 1946, p. 265, reference to Bavelas, Alex, unpublished study.)

the goal of 95 was never met, production did reach 92 and leveled off at about 87 units; whereas, before the group decisions, the highest possible production had been regarded as 75 units. By securing group participation, goals can be reached that theretofore were regarded as unattainable. Two control groups of workers were used to test the value of group decisions. These groups of workers were similar to the earlier group, and they also had weekly meetings for three weeks with a psychologist and were urged to increase production. These groups were not asked to reach a decision about a production goal and, as shown in Figure 10-4, their production did not show a material rise as it did where a group decision was made. At the place of "double assurance" on the curve, the workers were assured that their rates would not be cut if their production rose and that any higher production that was attained would not be held as a standard for the future. It is clear that effective participation requires group decision.

Employees are conscious of the need of participation, as shown by

251

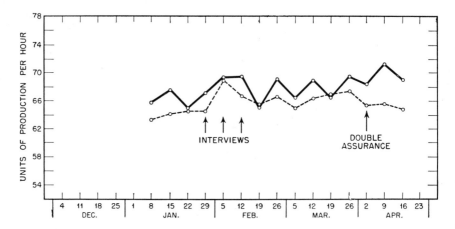

Figure 10-4. Effect of Team Discussion without Decision. Two teams held discussions but did not decide on a specific production goal. The discussions alone had little if any effect on production.

(Maier, Norman R. F., *Psychology in Industry,* Boston: Houghton Mifflin Co., 1946, p. 266, reference to Bavelas, Alex, unpublished study.)

the listing of two items relating to participation among the twelve most important things that workers wanted in a national study of a large sample of employees.[24] The two items were "being encouraged to offer suggestions and to try out better methods" and "being given information about important plans and results which concern the individual's work."

A group of women textile workers improved their morale through greater participation.[25] Low morale was evidenced by the women's being unresponsive, having a great deal of trouble with supervision, and not fitting into the community, which was new to them. Management, at least in the lowest levels, attributed this condition to the fact that the women were irresponsible. A social scientist was called in as adviser and trouble shooter. After he had talked with all parties, his diagnosis was that greater participation was needed by the workers. This antagonized management, which in this case represented benevolent paternalism, for in its opinion it was doing all for the workers that they deserved. Because of the antagonism of management toward this first adviser, a second adviser was called in. The second adviser, after surveying the situation, operated so as to allow management to participate in allowing greater participation by the workers. The second adviser pointed out to management that, since these girls were new to the community, management must help them by providing successful social adjustment. The second adviser went to the dormitory where the girls were living and conducted group interviews to obtain their complaints. They were not unresponsive. They had many complaints. The root of the matter seemed to be that they were not trusted by management and were not accepted in the community. At first some of their complaints and suggestions were too extreme, but these became milder after the catharsis of self-expression. They showed some loyalty to the company by not wanting to quit in spite of all their dissatisfaction. A number of suggestions were made about working conditions, conditions in their dormitory, and relations in the community. Later the women elected a committee by means of which they participated with management in handling things, and morale appeared to improve.

AROUSING ENTHUSIASM

Arousing the enthusiasm that employers want in their employees is usually a by-product of the incentive of participating, but there are some separate considerations. There is evidence that many employees are not so enthusiastic about their work as management thinks they should be. In 1946 a majority of employers in a poll reported that "a general indifference on the part of labor is a major factor in the lower labor efficiency in their plants."[26] "This general indifference on the part of labor" was, in the opinion of management, by far the most common factor responsible for a supposed decline in labor productivity after World War II. Immediately after the war 70 per cent of management thought that labor was less efficient than before the war, although production figures to support this idea are not available. In management's opinion the main reason for this lessened efficiency was "less interest in work."[27] The lack of enthusiasm prevailing among industrial workers is in contrast to the positive enthusiasm sought by employers.

Employers want their employees to be sufficiently zealous to carry on in the face of obstacles.[28] Some of the devices that have been advocated to produce enthusiasm, if presented properly, are awards that are deserved, arousing a "we attitude," emphasizing each person's importance in production, appreciation, recognition, fairness, and sharing responsibility with employees for making decisions.

SUGGESTION SYSTEMS

Suggestion systems are used primarily to obtain valuable suggestions from employees, but they also provide a means of having employees participate. Suggestion systems are in effect in 32 per cent of the companies in America and in 70 per cent of those having over 5000 employees.[29] The majority of companies make a cash award for a useful suggestion—usually 10 per cent of the net saving during the first year.[30] Labor, on the other hand, as represented by spokesmen for the CIO United Steel workers, has stated a belief that labor should have half of the total net benefits of a suggestion.[31]

Suggestion systems can do harm by antagonizing supervisors. The use of a suggestion system is an admission that the ordinary channels of communication through supervisors are not thoroughly effective. The suggestion system is adopted in part perhaps because employees will not make suggestions when they believe that supervisors will not give them credit for the ideas. When supervisors see the suggestion adopted, they may be antagonized. It would be more effective to have successful relations in the first place so that employees will make suggestions to their supervisors and receive full credit from them.

REPRESENTATION OF WORKERS IN INDUSTRY

Worker participation on committees deciding company policies and practices is most prominent in war years, when there is a recognized need for maximum production. During World War II the War Production Drive included not only "joint labor-management committees to push production and devise ways to do the job better" but three other features which might have been responsible for some of the successes reported.[32] These were: (1) production schedules with score boards for each shift— these made use of the incentives of competition and knowledge of results; (2) awards for workers who had done something unusual to promote production—these made use of the incentive of reward; and (3) reports by soldiers on the performance of the weapons the workers had produced —these were calculated to motivate through patriotism.

In addition to the four specific features of the War Production Drive, there were several other psychological procedures which helped production. These were: (1) training programs, especially the program of Training Within Industry, (2) selection and placement procedures, and (3) counseling.

The fact that production drives were started in both world wars suggests that peace-time motivation methods are not considered to provide peak production; and the fact that labor-management committees were used in both wars further suggests that additional participation by labor is considered effective for raising production. In 84 per cent of companies management considered the War Production Drive successful, and 79 per cent believed that the committees had helped. Management had feared that the committees of World War II would be an entering wedge for labor to obtain power in running business, but after the committees were in operation 93 per cent of management found no evidence of this. The most successful committees were those which had labor representatives chosen directly by employees rather than by the labor union or by management.

An active labor-management committee in the Coleman Lamp and Stove Company was given credit by the president of the company for the following outstanding accomplishment: "Reduction in absenteeism from an average of 7 per cent to 3 per cent, a 40 per cent increase in the number of suggestions submitted, a 50 per cent reduction in spoilage, an increase in production of 125 per cent, and creation of 'safety consciousness' in employees."[33]

The success of labor-management committees during wartime makes it seem strange that such arrangements are not continued to promote production in times of peace. Perhaps the reason is that management still fears that labor will take some of its prerogatives, or perhaps labor does not want to enter into agreements which will keep unions from aggressively pursuing additional union gains.

One company which has successfully used a representation plan during peace time is McCormick and Company, the biggest spice-and-tea house in the world.[34] In 1946 a system of representation called Multiple Management had been in successful operation in this company for fourteen years. Throughout this time, production, sales, and dividends rose, and there was no labor dispute. A junior board of directors was appointed from young executives in the company to provide participation. In addition, a group of employee managers were appointed within the plant to represent each group of workers in running the business. There were other changes in the organization, but the essential one appears to have been that of encouraging participation from the lowest level of employees. Impressive success in profits, wages, and labor peace have resulted from the participation in the company.

SUMMARY

Viewing all the studies and examples of motivation in industry together leads to the conclusion that participation is a key incentive. Participation is more likely to take place under conditions of successful leadership and cooperative team spirit. Other conditions include an atmosphere of good faith and trust, of having one's ego involved in a production goal.

The worker cannot participate effectively unless his status is acceptable to his self-respect. The importance of status will be discussed in more detail in Chapter 11. The importance of the group in determining participation in a profit-sharing plan will be discussed in Chapter 12. Motivation and participation continually recur under new themes in the remaining chapters.

Group relations

Work in industry is almost always done as a member of a small group or team and the contacts with other people at work can be an important incentive. Each work group usually develops an organization separate from the formal organization. After becoming established this informal organization remains relatively stable so long as the membership of the group remains the same. Many people do not wish to be transferred because they like the people with whom they work. Man is a social animal who gets pleasure out of friendly relations. Often these relations have not been planned or anticipated by management. Just how far management should attempt to go in providing or maintaining successful group relations is not completely clear, although some general principles do exist.

Management should realize that it is to be expected that any work group will build up cohesiveness, if it is well selected, well trained, and well managed. It is therefore to be expected that employees will often be reluctant to leave a work group—at times even when there is more pay or a more important job elsewhere. Management should accept as part of its responsibility the building of successful group relations on the job by group problem solving and by consideration for the individual. The responsibility of management for building group relations off the job by picnics, recreation, and other means is a more controversial matter and one which can easily lead to the dangers of paternalism.

SUMMARY

The central problem of motivation is complicated by the fact that motives differ from person to person and within the same person from time to time.

Social motives are more important in American industry than physiological drives. The most important social motives are social approval and self-respect.

American employees in professions and business management are highly motivated, but the factory worker, the miner, and other unskilled workers are not.

Pay has been assumed by business executives to be the most important incentive, and, at times, to be the only incentive that needs to be considered. The viewpoint of business executives toward pay is changing. It is coming to be believed that the worker wants several things more than he wants higher pay. An evaluation of the effectiveness of pay is difficult. High pay is effective in many situations in attracting persons to new jobs, but it is less effective in holding them on jobs. Pay serves as a symbol of prestige. It also cuts across security which, according to a number of surveys, is what workers say they want most. American adults are more likely to be satisfied with their income the higher it is. On the other hand, when a person is dissatisfied with his income, the absolute amount of increase in money that he wants in addition to what he has increases with the size of his income. Aspiration for money is controlled more by what a person is making in money than by his occupation or his education. There are, of course, individual differences. The results of certain wage-incentive plans have caused a re-examination of the effectiveness of pay as an incentive.

Praise should be given for work well done wherever possible. Punishment, if it is a reprimand, should be given in private; in any event, it should be used only when necessary.

Obtaining the participation of the individual worker is important for motivation. When practical, letting the group make decisions on matters of interest to the group is effective motivation.

RECOMMENDED READINGS

Viteles, Morris S., *Motivation and Morale in Industry,* New York: W. W. Norton & Co., Inc., 1953. A thorough review of studies of what employees want.

Whyte, W. F., *Money and Motivation,* New York: Harper & Brothers, 1955. Sociological studies and essays showing the importance of incentives other than money in industry.

11

Attitudes and job satisfaction

INTRODUCTION

This chapter, like Chapter 10, is concerned with motivation. It is focused on job or work satisfaction and on the measurement of attitudes in relation to such satisfaction. An attitude is "a set to action with an emotional overtone." Attitudes are learned, and some are changed frequently. A change of attitude cannot be forced upon a person; he must be willing and ready to change. One should therefore not expect fast results in trying to change another's attitudes. Several employee attitudes are important to productivity and morale. In the chapter to follow, the composition of attitudes which constitute employee morale will be explored.

METHODS OF FINDING EMPLOYEE ATTITUDES

Ideally, management should learn the attitudes of employees through supervisors. In medium- and large-sized companies, however, management at times does not trust the reports it obtains from supervisors, and it turns to other methods. Trends in number of grievances and turnover are sometimes studied as indications of attitudes. More direct methods are the interview and the questionnaire.

Alert executives frequently try to find employee attitudes through conversation with supervisors and other employees. A valid account of employee attitudes cannot be obtained through supervisory channels except in a thoroughly democratic organization where there is such a climate of permissiveness that supervisors and other employees are not afraid to speak freely. Otherwise, as in the majority of companies, attitudes are not communicated up through extended supervisory channels. A plant may be faced with employee dissatisfaction sufficient to cause a strike, while top management remains in ignorance because supervisors learn to tell the boss what he wants to hear. They learn that he wants to hear good news, and they are afraid that it will be a reflection on themselves to bring bad news.

258

THE SUGGESTION COMMITTEE
ASKS FOR
YOUR OPINION

In an effort to improve the suggestion system in our plant, we are asking for your answers to these questions.

Read each question below and then answer it by drawing a circle around "Yes," "No," or "?".

Do not put your name on this sheet.

1. Have you ever turned in a suggestion?...................... Yes No ?

2. Have you ever received a suggestion award?........... Yes No ?

3. Do you feel that suggestions are adopted or rejected promptly enough?.. Yes No ?

4. If you have a suggestion rejected, would you like to have your supervisor explain the reason for the rejection? .... Yes No ?

5. Do you think the awards for suggestions are fair?.... Yes No ?

6. Has one of your suggestions been adopted but not installed? .... Yes No ?

7. Does your supervisor encourage you to turn in suggestions? .... Yes No ?

8. Have you ever had a suggestion that you didn't turn in because you didn't know how to write it up?........ Yes No ?

Please give below any other ideas you have about the improvement of the suggestion system.

....

....

....

My department is...

Check the following concerning yourself:

( ) Male
( ) Female

Years of Service with Owens-Illinois:

( ) Under 1 year
( ) 1 to 5 years
( ) 5 years or over

Figure 11-1. Suggestion Questionnaire.

("How To Conduct a Survey," Industrial Relations Division, Owens-Illinois Glass Co., Toledo, January 1, 1947, pp. 1–9.)

Questionnaires and interviews have been used to determine attitudes toward job, toward company, and toward boss. In 1954 only 15 per cent of a sample of American companies had carried out such systematic studies, but this was double the percentage of eight years earlier.[1] The advantage of the questionnaire is that the answers can be made definite and consequently are easy to tabulate. It is also much cheaper than an

259

interview, and it avoids errors of memory that are damaging to interviewing unless immediate records are made. Some investigators think
that there is a tendency for employees to express themselves more freely
in an interview than on a questionnaire. There is no evidence on the
point. A questionnaire that has been used by the Owens-Illinois Glass
Company is shown in Figure 11-1. It is an example of a well-constructed,
simple questionnaire for finding out clearly something on which administrative action can be taken.

A serious objection to the attitude survey is that it bypasses supervision. Management implicitly admits, when it uses a questionnaire, that
it cannot obtain reliable information concerning employee attitudes from
supervisors. It is important to know employee attitudes, and realistic to
admit that reports through supervisory channels are too favorable and
unreliable. It might be better to attempt to clear the supervisory channels
through training in democratic leadership. Interesting information has,
however, been obtained through attitude surveys, and the popularity of
the method is increasing.

FACTORS RELATING TO JOB SATISFACTION

Job satisfaction is derived from and is caused by many interrelated factors. Although these factors can never be completely isolated from one
another for analysis, they can, by the use of statistical techniques, be
separated enough to give an indication of their relative importance to
job satisfaction. The discussion of the factors is hampered by a general
lack of complete information. Furthermore, the importance of the various factors appears to change from one situation to another. Hence a
study of the factors leading to job satisfaction must be discussed in
general terms. There are many factors, but only those considered most
important will be discussed here.

Personal factors

SEX

Most investigations on the subject have found that women are more
satisfied with their jobs than are men. In a study of 635 white-collar
workers it was found that 55 per cent of men and only 35 per cent of
women were dissatisfied with their jobs.[2] This is so despite the fact that
women are generally discriminated against in job competition and pay.
Quite possibly the reason is that women's ambitions and financial needs
are less.

NUMBER OF DEPENDENTS

Results of a study of white-collar workers indicate that, the more dependents one has, the less satisfaction he has with his job.[3] Perhaps the stress of greater financial need brings about greater dissatisfaction with one's job. The difference in satisfaction among employees with different numbers of dependents is, however, small.

AGE

Studies have found different results in different groups on the relationship of age to job satisfaction. There was higher intrinsic job satisfaction among older white-collar employees, but lower financial and job status satisfaction among this group.[4] From the consensus of other studies, age has little relationship to job satisfaction for all employees, but it is important in some job situations. In some groups job satisfaction is higher with increasing age; in other groups job satisfaction is lower; and in others there is no difference.

TIME ON JOB

Several investigations have indicated that job satisfaction is relatively high at the start, drops slowly to the fifth or eighth year, then rises again with more time on the job.[5] The highest morale is reached after the twentieth year.

INTELLIGENCE

The relation of intelligence to job satisfaction no doubt depends on the level and range of intelligence and the challenge of the job. Intelligence accounted for a tiny fraction of the variation in work attitude among Procter and Gamble clerical employees, the brightest having slightly poorer work attitudes.[6] An English investigation showed that the most intelligent girls employed in a chocolate factory were most easily bored.[7] At the Kimberly-Clark Corporation, however, there was no relation between attitude scores and intelligence.[8]

EDUCATION

There is a great deal of conflicting evidence on the relationship between education and job satisfaction. One study of white-collar workers indicated that those who had not completed high school were the most satisfied.[9] Other studies have shown no relationship whatever.[10] Certain variables, such as company advancement policies in relation to education, would have to be considered before any generalization could be made.

Personality has been suggested as a major cause of job dissatisfaction. One difficulty which has led to many inconclusive results is the comparative lack of true measures of personality. One criterion of personality is the existence of neurotic behavior. In an investigation of female employees of the Kimberly-Clark Corporation it was found that "of the 25 most neurotic, 16 were more dissatisfied than the average; of the 25 most stable, only 3 are this dissatisfied."[11] Neurotic tendency, in another study, accounted for a slight degree of the variability in work attitudes among women employees of a bank.[12] In both these studies the evidence is that neurotic tendency leads to job dissatisfaction only when the job itself is one of "greater" strain.

Another possible criterion of personality is general satisfaction with nonjob conditions. One such study indicated a fairly high correlation between general and job satisfaction; this would indicate the possibility that some job dissatisfaction is caused by the personality traits that made these employees unhappy off the job.[13]

In yet another study it was found that persons who were rated high in interpersonal desirability by their fellow employees were the most satisfied with their jobs.[14] Again, there is an implication of a general personality pattern of happiness. It is likely that personality maladjustment is the source of some job dissatisfaction, but it is not clear how strong the relationship is.

Factors inherent in the job

TYPE OF WORK

The most important factor inherent in the job is type of work. Several studies have shown that varied work brings about more job satisfaction than does routine work.[15] Another study found that about 60 per cent of the factory workers were dissatisfied with their jobs, whereas only 30 per cent of the professionals were dissatisfied.[16] Job satisfaction varies almost from 0 to 100 per cent, depending on the job.[17] Ninety-five per cent of a group of teachers have expressed feelings of satisfaction with their jobs, while 98 per cent of a group of textile operatives expressed dissatisfaction with their jobs.

It is difficult to separate the importance of type of work, skill, pay, and status, since they usually go together, but one or more of these variables could explain the results of two studies. In a study of a sample of employed people in St. Paul, street car motormen were least satisfied with their jobs and employers were most satisfied.[18] Approximately one hundred men of each of seven occupational groups were interviewed on each of two occasions. The occupational goals of these adults were unrealistic. Street car operators, city firemen, and clerical workers—all in considerable numbers—aspired to professional and managerial work or did not know to what they would shift if they had the chance, but they would want to change jobs if they were young enough. Tabulations of responses to the Vocational Interest Test show that 90 per cent or more of professional people like their occupations, but only 39 per cent of office clerks like their jobs.

SKILL REQUIRED

Skill in relation to job satisfaction has a bearing on several other factors: kind of work, occupational status, responsibility, and possibly others. A study of the relation of skill to job satisfaction concluded that "where skill exists to a considerable degree it tends to become the first source of satisfaction to the workman. Satisfaction in conditions of work or in wages becomes predominant only where satisfaction in skill has materially decreased."[19]

OCCUPATIONAL STATUS

Occupational status is related to, but not identical with, job satisfaction. Almost half of a group of clerks and manual workers stated that they were very happy with their occupations, but only 17 per cent said that they would like to enter their present occupation again.[20] The occupations which they wanted most often to enter were those of a higher status, their own business, professions, and other independent work. This status depends not only on the way the employee regards the status of his job, but also on the way it is regarded by others whose opinion he values. Student concept of the status of occupations remained almost constant in the United States from 1925 to 1948. Table 11-I shows the ranking, by students, of twenty-five occupations for social standing in 1925, 1946, and 1948. The white-collar jobs are prominently at the top of the list at all times. An indication that occupational status does not depend entirely on the job itself is shown by the rankings by Russian school children. In 1927 Russian children ranked the occupation of peasant first, aviator second, and physician fourth. Three occupations that have high status in America were given very low status by the Russian children: banker, forty-second; prosperous businessman, forty-fourth; and minister, forty-fifth. Occupational status shows a very high correlation with intelligence, income, and years of education, ranging from .87 to .97.[21]

TABLE 11-1

Social Status of Occupations as Ranked by Students in 1925, 1946, and 1948

OCCUPATIONS	1925	1946	1948
Banker	1	2.5	2
Physician	2	1	1
Lawyer	3	2.5	3
Supt. of Schools	4	4	4
Civil Engineer	5	5	5
Army Captain	6	6	8
Foreign Missionary	7	7	6
Elem. School Teacher	8	8	7
Farmer	9	12	10
Machinist	10	9	12
Traveling Salesman	11	16	14
Grocer	12	13	11
Electrician	13	11	13
Insurance Agent	14	10	9
Mail Carrier	15	14	15
Carpenter	16	15	16
Soldier	17	19	19
Plumber	18	17	17
Motorman	19	18	20
Barber	20	20	18
Truck Driver	21	21.5	21
Coal Miner	22	21.5	22
Janitor	23	23	23
Hod Carrier	24	24	24
Ditch Digger	25	25	25

Deeg, Maethel E., and Donald G. Paterson, "Changes in Social Status of Occupations," *Occupations,* 1947, **25,** 205–208; Welch, M. K., "The Ranking of Occupations on the Basis of Social Status," *Occupations,* 1949, **27,** 237–241.

Almost all the studies in which occupations have been rated by prestige or status have had students as the raters, although one investigation had laborers, and another had miners, rank occupations for prestige. The main differences when rankings by laborers were compared with those by students are that manager of a business and foreman are ranked higher by laborers and real estate and insurance agent is rated lower by them.[22] The ranks are very similar otherwise, and this indicates that the prestige values of occupations are rather general in a community. The rating of mining by miners is in the same relative position as students have placed it.[23] Miners, like students, placed it only above janitor when called upon to rate five occupations including carpenter, machinist, and farmer. Other studies have demonstrated that students in different parts of the country express almost the same values of occupational status.

It has been shown that employees are more dissatisfied in jobs that have less social status and prestige. These values are rather constant within a country, but they do vary among some countries and they probably vary from time to time within a country under some conditions, although this time variation has not been demonstrated. It seems plausible that the status of a worker in an airplane factory and that of a private in the Army are significantly higher during wartime. Exactly how much business managers can do about improving the status of a job is not known. It is possible to point out the importance of a job no matter how humble it is, but the effect of such in-plant communication is bound to be limited. No matter how skillfully a foreman points out to a sweeper that sweeping is essential, persons outside the plant will know that his status is low. Another point to be considered in efforts to change the status of jobs within a plant is the effect on the whole system of occupational status. If one job is raised in status, another is bound to be lowered. In spite of these qualifications each manager should try to show the importance of every job to all employees.

GEOGRAPHY

The section of the United States in which a person lives has a slight bearing on whether he wants to change jobs.[24] People on the Pacific Coast are the most satisfied and those in the mountain states are the least satisfied.

Workers in large cities are less satisfied with their jobs than are those in smaller cities and towns. Factory workers, as well as a separate group of the representative public in twelve cities, were asked the question: "Tell me, is this a good place to work in? In your opinion, is it a place where workers seem happy in their factory work and the wages they get . . . ?"[25] There are extreme differences between cities, as judged

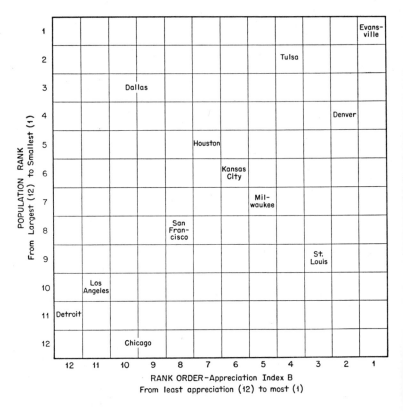

Figure 11-2. Relation between Worker's Rating of Plant and Population of His City.

(Adapted by Harrell, M. S., from Stedman, G. E., "An Appreciation Index," *The Personnel Journal,* 1945, **24,** 64–72.)

by both factory workers and the public. Seventy-eight per cent of the public say that Evansville, Indiana, is a good place to work, but only 18 per cent say that Detroit is a good place to work. Among the factory workers the difference in work satisfaction in cities is equally extreme. Factory workers and the public are in substantial agreement as to which cities are the best and which the worst places to work. Size of city is the most important factor that has been found to account for differences in work satisfaction among these cities. The relation between size and satisfaction is shown in Figure 11-2.

Size of city was also found to be of some importance by the "Fortune Survey": "in cities over a million restlessness is greatest, in rural villages least"; but the difference in satisfaction was not over 10 per cent between the largest and the smallest living places.[26] The greater job satisfaction in small towns is due, no doubt, to the difference in psychological environment rather than to size as such. Everyone in a small town knows better what his place is in the scheme of things. The father-son tradition is one aspect of the psychologically stabilizing effect of the small town.

SIZE OF PLANT

Morale, a combination of attitudes, in small companies has been found to be 6 per cent above that in large companies.[27] The favorable attitudes in small plants are based specifically on optimism about advancement, opportunity for making suggestions, treatment of employees, and respect for the ability of management. In an extensive Sears, Roebuck study the size of the operating branch was found to be very important in influencing employee attitudes.[28] It was felt that this relationship resulted because in a small branch individuals know each other better and are therefore more cooperative. The formal organization in a large branch becomes more impersonal and policies become more arbitrary, creating a feeling of less participation.

FACTORS CONTROLLABLE BY MANAGEMENT

Security

A summary of all the studies that can be compared (Table 11-II) shows that industrial employees say that what they want most is steady work, although in more recent studies security is rated lower, perhaps because of the time that has elapsed since the depression. The big depression made security important to employees. The desire for steady work by American factory workers was apparently being met to the satisfaction of the great majority of them in 1947.[29] A national cross section of factory workers was asked, "Do you think you can have your present job as long as you want it, except for temporary layoffs, or do you think there is a good chance that the job won't last as long as you want it to?" Eighty per cent answered: "Can have job as long as I want it"; 9 per cent: "Job may end before I want it to"; and the remainder expressed no opinion.

Many factory workers do not believe that they will have financial security when their working days are over. They were asked this question in 1947: "As it looks now, do you think it is likely or unlikely that you'll be able to retire from work when you are sixty-five and live the rest of

TABLE 11-II

Ranks of What People Say They Want in a Job

| | UNION AND NONUNION 1934[b] | WOMEN FACTORY WORKERS 1937[c] | JOB APPLICANTS (1945–1947)[d] | | | | EMPLOYEES, 6 COMPANIES, 1947[e] | GENERAL MOTORS "MY JOB" CONTEST, 1947[f] |
| | | | WOMEN | MEN | | | | |
			TOTAL	SALES	CLERICAL	MECHANICAL		
Advancement	4	5	3	2	2.5	2	5	8
Benefits[a]	5	—	9	9	9	8.5	2	2
Company	—	—	5	3	4	4	7	3
Co-workers	—	3	5	7	6	5	—	4
Pay	2	6	8	5	5	7	4	1
Personnel Policies	—	—	—	—	—	—	1	10
Security	1	1	2	4	2.5	1	3	6
Supervisor	6	4	5	6	7	6	6	5
Type of work	—	—	1	1	1	3	8	7
Working conditions	3	2	7	8	8	8.5	9	9
N	250	325	378	222	259	2252		174,854

[a] Includes vacation, sick pay, insurance, etc.

[b] Hersey, Rexford, "Psychology of Workers," *The Personnel Journal*, 1936, **14**, pp. 291–296.

[c] Wyatt, S., and J. N. Langdon, *Fatigue and Boredom in Repetitive Work*, Industrial Health Research Board, No. 77, London: His Majesty's Stationery Office, 1937, p. 44.

[d] Jurgensen, Clifford, "What Job Applicants Look for in a Company," *Personnel Psychology*, 1948, **1**, No. 4, 433–445.

[e] Adapted from National Industrial Conference Board, *Factors Affecting Employee Morale*, Studies in Personnel Policy No. 85, 1947, p. 12.

[f] Adapted from Evans, C. E., and La V. N. Laseau, "My Job Contest," *Personnel Psychology*, *Monograph No. 1*, Washington, D. C.: Personnel Psychology Inc., 1950, pp. 46–48.

your life in reasonable comfort on your savings, pensions, and social security payments?" Forty-two per cent answered "likely"; almost the same number, 41 per cent, answered "unlikely"; and the remainder had no opinion. When the answers to this question are combined with those to the one above, whether it is thought that the job will last, it appears that a large percentage of factory workers believe that, though they can work until they are sixty-five in their present jobs, they still will not be financially able to retire and are therefore lacking in economic security.

Security for old age was one of five factors significantly related to job satisfaction in a survey of factory workers throughout the United States.[30] The other four were "interest in the job," "not being overworked," "ability to advance," and belief "that individual merit is rewarded."

TABLE 11-III

Morale in Relation to Satisfaction with Job and Company

(Interviews with a National Cross Section of Factory Workers)

Factory workers who possess:	SATISFACTION WITH OWN COMPANY			SATISFACTION WITH KIND OF JOB			DEGREE OF ADJUSTMENT[a]	
	Own Company Good	Other Companies Better	No Opinion	Would Choose Same Occupation	Would Choose Different Occupation	No Opinion	Ideally Adjusted	Miserably Adjusted
Five factors[b]	92%	4%	4%	52%	41%	7%	49%	3%
Four factors	86	8	6	38	53	9	35	5
Three factors	80	14	6	32	58	10	27	9
Two factors	65	22	13	26	63	11	17	15
One factor	49	29	22	15	70	15	10	23
None	29	39	32	9	63	28	4	30
All factory workers	72	17	11	31	57	12	26	12

[a] Those who are both satisfied with their firm and their kind of work are called "ideally adjusted." Those who are satisfied with neither firm or work are called "miserably adjusted."

[b] The five morale factors are (1) interest in the job; (2) not being overworked; (3) security for old age; (4) ability to advance; (5) belief that individual merit is rewarded.
"The Fortune Survey," *Fortune*, June, 1947, Pt-2, pp. 5, 6, 10. Copyright, Time, Inc.

The importance of these five factors to job satisfaction is shown in Table 11-III, which shows that among factory workers whose jobs satisfy all five factors 52 per cent would choose the same occupation even if they were young enough to enter a different one, but only 9 per cent would choose the same occupation when none of the five factors is satisfied.

The five factors are even more important numerically for satisfaction with company than for satisfaction with job, as seen in Table 11-III. Factory workers who are interested in their jobs, are not overworked, feel secure about old age, and believe that they have ability to advance and that individual merit is rewarded think that their own companies are as good as any other in ninety-two cases out of one hundred. Where none of these five factors is present only twenty-nine factory employees out of one hundred say that their company is as good as any other.

Only about one factory worker out of four is satisfied with both his job and his company, as shown in Table 11-III. If the five factors are completely absent, it is almost certain that the worker will not be satisfied with either his job or his company. On the other hand, even if these five factors are present, there is no certainty that the factory worker will be satisfied with both his job and his company. The importance of security varies with the marital status and number of dependents. It seems logical that a man who has others depending on him for support would feel the need for security more strongly than would a single man.

Security is of less importance to the better-educated person, perhaps because there is not so much fear of layoff in the kind of jobs that the highly educated obtain, or the highly educated are justifiably more confident of being able to find other jobs if necessary.[31] One study revealed that college graduates ranked security third, below pay and opportunity for advancement.[32]

Pay

The importance of pay as a factor in job satisfaction has been greatly overemphasized by management. Many companies feel that a pay raise is a "cure-all" which will make everyone in the plant happy. As shown in Table 11-II, most studies have found that pay ranks well below security, type of work, and opportunity for advancement, although it was the factor mentioned most frequently in letters by General Motors employees as what they liked best about their jobs. In one study the feeling of importance of pay decreased slightly with an increasing number of dependents and increased with those better educated.[33] The relative importance of pay will probably change with the labor market, with economic conditions, and with employees' beliefs about the job situation.

Fringe Benefits

Benefits have been emphasized by both management and unions as something employees want, but the results of most of the studies listed in Table 11-II show benefits in a rather low position of importance. They were, however, second in the two most recent studies. In one survey, as Table 11-IV shows, employees ranked benefits fourth. Executives predicted that employees would put benefits in eighth position, but labor leaders did not expect them to be among the first ten factors selected by employees. Like pay, benefits have generally been misunderstood. Perhaps one reason is that some benefits are substitutes for security. Sick pay and insurance are examples. Another possible reason is that it would be difficult for employees to strike for "more opportunity for advancement" or "good working companions."

Opportunity for advancement

Table 11-II shows that opportunity for advancement, except among the General Motors employees, consistently ranks above average in importance among workers. One study found that this factor was most important to sales, clerical, and skilled personnel, and least important to the unskilled.[34] Another study revealed that older workers were less interested in advancement than younger ones, perhaps because a man does most of his advancing in his earlier years and settles in one or two jobs in his last twenty years of working.[35]

Belief that individual merit is rewarded would appear to be closely related to belief that there is chance to advance. Even where a person does not believe that he deserves a promotion, it is still highly important to him that the best man be promoted. He might not believe that he is the best candidate for promotion, but if the best man were not promoted, as in the case of nepotism, there would be an unfavorable attitude in terms of belief that individual merit is not rewarded. In a study of 100,000 employees of large corporations, one in twelve items found important was "certainty of promotions going to best-qualified employees."[36] If the company leads employees to expect advancement and then promotions do not come, attitudes are highly unfavorable.

Working conditions

As indicated by the results of studies shown in Table 11-II, working conditions rank variously from second to ninth in importance. There seems to be a tendency for working conditions to be ranked lower, perhaps because they have been improved. It seems plausible that the prestige value applied to the white-collar occupations is the result of more desirable conditions of work.

Co-workers

One's associates have frequently been mentioned as a factor in job satisfaction. Certainly this seems reasonable, because people like to be near their friends. The ranking of this factor in various studies, as shown in Table 11-II, indicates that it is of intermediate importance.

Responsibility

Responsibility is usually enmeshed with several other important determinants of job satisfaction in a way that makes it difficult to determine the relative contribution of each to job satisfaction. Responsibility usually goes with time on the job, age, salary, type of work, and participation, and it may have some relation to interest. One study of employees all over the United States showed that morale scores were higher for employees who had more responsibility.[37] Unemployed persons rated responsibility as one of a few things that had been a characteristic of the job they had preferred.[38] In neither of these studies, nor, as a matter of fact, in any study, has the effect of responsibility on job satisfaction been separated clearly from the other important influences mentioned.

Supervision

Good supervision ranks about average in importance of the first ten things people want in a job (Table 11-II). To the worker his supervisor is the company, hence a worker's feelings toward his supervisor are usually similar to his feelings toward the company.

An important part of the Hawthorne study was the changed attitudes of assemblers that accompanied a change in supervision.[39] Having a friendly rather than an oppressive supervisor changed attitudes greatly. The favorable attitude of employees toward their supervisor was believed to produce a climate in which attitudes of good team spirit were established.

Supervision was judged to be the most important single factor in determining employee morale scores in a series of investigations wherein comparisons were made of morale scores of groups of employees who had different supervisors.[40] This conclusion is also supported by what 100,000 employees said they wanted. Eight of the twelve most frequently mentioned items could be traced to supervision.[41] These eight items are:

Receiving help necessary to get results expected by management.
Being able to find out whether work is improving.

Reasonable certainty of being able to get fair hearing and square deal in case of grievances.

Encouragement to seek advice in case of real problems.

Being given reasons for changes which are ordered in work.

Not being actually hampered in work by superior.

Not getting contradictory or conflicting orders.

Being given to understand completely the results which are expected in a job.

A thorough study found supervision to be of greatest importance in the Kimberly-Clark Corporation.[42] "Comparison of two departments, which were practically identical except for the character of the supervision, revealed in one case 71 per cent of the girls more favorably inclined toward their jobs than the average of the mill and in the other case only 29 per cent so inclined . . ."

Supervision is, without question, one of the most important factors related to job satisfaction. Like other factors that bring about satisfaction or dissatisfaction with a job, supervision does not operate independently of the situation; it is correlated with factors that also are important. Chapter 15 explains in greater detail the qualities desired in a good supervisor.

Downward flow of information

Several studies have indicated a great desire of employees for information from management. They would like to know how they are doing and how they can improve.[43] They also want to know about the company—its plans, processes, whether their jobs will continue, and possibilities for promotion. Very few employees believe that they are getting more information than they want.

Understanding of employee attitudes
by executives and labor leaders

One study found that neither executives nor labor leaders had very accurate understanding of employee attitudes.[44] Employees in six companies ranked the factors most important to them in their job. Fifty executives in the same companies and forty-two labor leaders predicted what the employees' rankings would be. The first ten factors, as ranked by employees, executives, and labor leaders, are shown in Table 11-IV. Pay was ranked higher by both executives and labor leaders than by employees. Benefits were ranked higher by employees than by executives, who in turn ranked it higher than did labor leaders. Information on success or failure at job was important to employees but not recognized as such by either executives or labor leaders. Labor leaders understood employee attitudes less than did executives, rating highly several factors

TABLE 11-IV

Factors Affecting Employee Morale Selected by
Employees, Executives, and Labor Leaders

RANK	EMPLOYEE	EXECUTIVE PREDICTION	LABOR LEADER PREDICTION
1	Security	Pay	Pay
2	Advancement	Security	Security
3	Pay	Vacations	Hours
4	Benefits	Advancement	Working conditions
5	Information on success or failure at job	Working conditions	Unions
6	Type of work	Company attitude	Company attitude
7	Vacation and holiday practices	Type of work	Handling of grievances
8	Supervisor	Benefits	Vacations
9	Profit sharing	Supervisor	Union-management relations
10	Working conditions	Hours	Job evaluation programs

National Industrial Conference Board, Studies in Personnel Policy No. 85, *Factors Affecting Employee Morale,* New York, 1947, p. 21.

that were not important to employees: hours, working conditions, unions, company attitude, handling of grievances, vacation, union-management relations, and job evaluation programs.

INCREASING JOB SATISFACTION

Personal factors

Management cannot, of course, change the personal factors of employees. It should, however, appreciate the role of the personal factors in job satisfaction. Management should place workers where the personal factors of the individual will aid him in achieving job satisfaction. Chapters 3 to 6 have given some of the details about methods for selecting and placing employees so that they will be satisfied with their jobs.

Factors inherent in the job

In building a plant, a company should consider the role of location in job satisfaction. Likewise, in planning for expansion, job satisfaction should be considered in relation to the desirability of building one large plant or two small ones. In laying out the manufacture of a product, management should consider how to make the work less routine and, if possible, raise the occupational status of the workers. Several attempts have been made to accomplish this purpose, with mixed success. There has been success in showing each worker why his job is important. When this is done, a worker feels that he is a necessary part of the team and that he is making a definite contribution toward the goal of the company.

Factors controllable by management

These factors are most important for management to watch, for they include most of the differences between a well-satisfied group of employees and one whose collective morale is very low. Since security is most important to most workers, management should stress this as much as is financially feasible. If management were to leave pay at the same general level as for comparable jobs elsewhere and spend more money for pension plans and the leveling of seasonal peaks and troughs, job satisfaction should be much higher.

Promotion policies have been under fire from unions largely because it was suspected that companies were not fair in selecting employees for advancement. Workers should be assured that they will be promoted strictly on the basis of merit or seniority, and the promise should be kept.

Management should recognize that people generally like to work with others of similar background, and that they like to choose their associates. Therefore, if there is no sound reason for refusal, requests for transfer should be approved.

Adequate training of supervisors to make them capable democratic leaders is of utmost importance. A fuller discussion of this problem is given in Chapter 15.

Few, if any, organizations are guilty of giving too much information to their employees. As pointed out earlier, the workers want to know about their work situation and the company and its products. The service of giving information is cheap; its results in making better employees and citizens of its recipients is great. The workers do not want the information by way of the grapevine; if possible, they want to find out from their supervisors in person.[45] Information obtained through the grapevine is often erroneous and detrimental to the company, whereas correct information will help the company in the long run.

In discussing the factors related to job satisfaction, the stability of attitudes needs to be recognized. When an organization's employees are dissatisfied with their jobs, they tend to remain dissatisfied even after many of the factors involved are corrected. It is necessary, therefore, to be all the more diligent in correcting a poor situation. Likewise, high

275

morale will tend to persevere even after many of the factors leading to job satisfaction are removed.

CONDUCTING AN ATTITUDE SURVEY
WITHIN A COMPANY

The need

Many of the factors controllable by management are relative. For this reason it is well to find out exactly how the workers feel about various aspects of their jobs and surroundings. As pointed out at the beginning of the chapter, the most thorough method is to use the questionnaire or interview.

Prepared surveys

There is no single scale for measuring employee attitudes that provides adequate national norms, but several good prepared surveys are available to companies. The advantages of these are lower cost, proved reliability, and a saving of time.

SCIENCE RESEARCH ASSOCIATES
EMPLOYEE INVENTORY

The S. R. A. Employee Inventory has been developed to measure attitudes for any company. It is based on studies at the Hawthorne Works of the Western Electric Company, and at Sears, Roebuck, and by the University of Chicago's Industrial Relations Center in other companies.[46] The validity of the inventory has been verified by its use in thirteen large- and medium-sized companies in the United States. Instructions and work sheets are provided to conduct the survey and analyze the results. There are seventy-eight questions covering morale. In addition, there is space for twelve more questions which the particular company desires answered, and there is room for brief comments. Each question is answered on a three-scale rating by placing an "x" in the appropriate space. The questionnaire is unsigned. A very good estimation of employee attitudes can be obtained at fairly low cost with this survey.

THE TRIPLE AUDIT

The University of Minnesota Industrial Relations Center has devised the Triple Audit Employee Attitude Scale, which has had some use throughout industry. It is slightly shorter than the S. R. A. Employee

Inventory, and it uses a five-alternative answering system.[47] In order to assure anonymity it is administered by representatives from the University of Minnesota.

A short and simple type of attitude questionnaire is the Tear Ballot. No pencils are needed, as tears, rather than marks, are made at the appropriate places. There are only ten questions. It is claimed that only three minutes are needed to administer the "ballot." Several studies have indicated that it is valid in that its results agree with objective measures of morale.[48]

Development of attitude scales

Attitudes can be measured fairly accurately through scales that measure attitude to a single subject. For example, attitude toward job can be measured with a high degree of consistency if the proper questions are asked; or attitude toward company, or attitude to immediate supervisor. The statistical details of the method of constructing and standardizing an attitude scale go beyond the purpose of this book, but some of the essentials can be mentioned.

Several questions are needed to pinpoint attitude to any one topic, attitude toward job for example. A single question will not give accurate results.

Questions that are chosen initially need to be tried to make certain that they will work. They need to be pretested to make sure that employees interpret them as they are intended.

Interviews should be conducted to find the expressions that are used about a subject, so that the language employed will be natural.

Questions should be chosen that cover the range of attitudes that are held, and that express approximately equal intervals of intensity of feeling.

Company practice

Many companies have made up their own attitude surveys. These range from small questionnaires of two or three questions to elaborate studies, some of which are described below. Special surveys have the advantage of asking questions only in the areas in which information is desired. If very extensive, however, the cost can be high.

In order to get valid information, several rules have to be followed. Anonymity has long been considered necessary, as a worker might fear retaliation or discrimination if he were to criticize his supervisor or the company. Several studies have shown, however, that, if an independent organization conducts the study and the names of the participants are guaranteed to be strictly confidential, the answers are not appreciably different.[49] Questionnaires, however, should not be signed unless the identity of the individual is needed for future comparison or other necessary reasons. Questions should be so worded that their meaning will be absolutely clear, and so selected that the answers to the questions will give the organization the information it wants.

Two studies of employee attitudes that have been reported in detail are those of the Standard Oil Company of California and the General Motors Corporation. Each of these will be described.

STANDARD OIL COMPANY OF CALIFORNIA

In 1951 the California Institute of Technology conducted for the Standard Oil Company a survey of all its employees.[50] Response was voluntary, but return was very good—70 per cent. The unsigned questionnaire consisted of thirty-seven questions with a varying number of descriptive choices for answers to each. The questions covered personal information, the company in general, communication, benefit plans and personnel practices, and job satisfaction and working conditions. Space was made available for additional comment which was used by more than two-thirds of the persons returning the questionnaires. The responses to each question were tabulated and analyzed. Upon completion of the analysis a pamphlet written for the layman and containing the results and brief analyses was given to each employee. Some comments were admissions of need to improve; no facts were hidden from the employees. An attempt was then made to correct deficiencies as found in the survey. In the fall of 1955 a similar survey was made. The purposes were to find out what progress had been made, to gain new information on employee attitudes, and to test the reliability of the 1951 survey.

GENERAL MOTORS "MY JOB CONTEST"

General Motors decided upon an unusual technique for evaluating employee attitudes. An essay contest was used, with about 5000 prizes worth $150,000 offered for the best entries. The essay was used because the contest had the added purpose of helping "us all to appreciate the good things about our jobs."[51] Employees were asked to write about a hundred words on "My Job and Why I Like it." The reverse side of the blank provided space for suggestions for improving the job. The latter comments had no bearing on the grading of the essay.

There were about 175,000 returns; over 58 per cent of those eligible entered the contest. The essays were analyzed by listing the themes mentioned in each entry and adding them together.[52] Some of the themes mentioned most frequently are included in Table 11-II. When a theme was mentioned less than the average for the company in a particular plant or division, the executives concerned were to look into the cause of this deficiency and take appropriate action. As a method of finding out where deficiencies existed, General Motors was confident that the contest was a success.

Follow-up

The task of conducting an effective attitude survey is not complete with an analysis of the results. Where deficiencies are found, they should be corrected when it is appropriate and feasible. The employees should be informed of the results and the action taken or contemplated, for this will show them that management is really taking an interest in their opinions and problems. After appropriate action is taken and the personnel have had an opportunity to become accustomed to the changes, it would be interesting to have another attitude survey to find out what progress has been made.

SUMMARY

The most satisfactory way to gain information about employee attitudes is to use the questionnaire.

Job satisfaction is caused by, and is derived from, many interrelated factors. The personal factors are important to management because they have a relationship to job satisfaction, and because their use can result in better placement of workers. Management can use the factors inherent in the job to plan and administer jobs more advantageously for its workers.

Many of the factors controllable by management are quite significantly related to job satisfaction. The most important are security, opportunity for advancement, and working conditions. In recent years employees have been desiring much more information about the job and the company.

Several very good prepared attitude surveys are available for company use. Their advantages include low cost, proved reliability, and ease of administration. Tailor-made surveys, on the other hand, are made to fit the particular desires of the corporation.

Follow-up is essential after an attitude survey. It includes analysis of the results, informing employees of the results, and formation and execution of a corrective program.

279

RECOMMENDED READINGS

Morse, Nancy C., *Satisfactions in the White-Collar Job,* Ann Arbor: Institute for Social Research, University of Michigan, 1953. A clearly written account of a thorough study of job satisfaction and other attitudes among clerical employees.

Viteles, Morris S., *Motivation and Morale in Industry,* New York: W. W. Norton & Company, Inc., 1953, pp. 219-378. Methods and results of employee attitude surveys are comprehensively reviewed.

12

Morale and monotony

The subject of morale was introduced in the preceding chapter, but the term, which has had many meanings, was not defined. The dictionary definition of morale is "Prevailing mood and spirit conducive to willing and dependable performance." High morale is defined as "a confident spirit of wholehearted cooperation in a common effort." High morale then would imply perseverance at work, which is important to the objective of management. From the standpoint of measurement a useful definition of employee morale is that which has emerged from the University of Michigan studies: the combination of attitudes toward job, company, and immediate supervisor.[1] This definition is in terms of the individual, whereas some writers prefer to define morale in terms of the group. One's fellow workers do influence morale. Many other variables affect morale, some of which were listed in the previous chapter.

In this chapter the relation between morale and objective measures of turnover, absenteeism, and productivity will be traced. The causes and correlates of monotony will be presented. Attempts to raise morale and lower monotony will be described.

Aside from a brief presentation of some points relating to the morale of foremen, this chapter is concerned exclusively with issues concerning the morale and monotony of rank-and-file employees. Problems of morale and monotony are relatively much rarer among managers and executives than among rank-and-file employees. Monotony among managers and executives can result from misplacement or mismanagement, but it has not been a serious problem because the basis for monotony is repetitive work and almost all management jobs include sufficient variety so that they are not highly repetitive.

Low morale can exist in a manager or in a group of managers, and companies occasionally make separate morale surveys with questions for managers and supervisors different from those for rank-and-file employees. Morale is almost always higher among managers than among rank-

1. Generally speaking, how does *(company name)* compare as a place to work with other companies that you know about or have worked for? (Check **only one** answer)

( ) It is one of the **very worst.**
( ) **Worse** than average.
( ) Just **average.**
( ) **Better** than average.
( ) One of the **very best.**

2. How much does the management of the company care about the welfare of people in jobs such as yours?

3. Are there other companies in which you would rather work at the same earnings if you could get a job for which you feel equally qualified?

( ) I would rather work in **any** of the others.
( ) I would rather work in **almost any** of the others.
( ) **Some** of the others.
( ) **Very few of the others.**
( ) **None** of the others.

4. If you have ever been dissatisfied with your job here, how often was it the company's fault?

5. How much does the management do to have good working relationships between you and the people with whom you work?

6. To what extent are you made to feel that you are really a part of the organization?

7. How fair do you feel the top management of the company is with people in jobs such as yours?

( ) **Rarely** fair.
( ) **Occasionally** fair.
( ) **About half** the time fair.
( ) **Usually** fair.
( ) Practically **always** fair.

8. How fair do you feel that the people immediately above you are in their treatment of you?

9. In your opinion, are there other companies which treat their employees better than *(company name)* does?

10. Are you reasonably sure of being able to keep your job as long as you do good work?

( ) Doing good work doesn't have anything to do with holding my job.
( ) Holding my job depends a **little** on how good work I do.
( ) If I do good work I can be **fairly sure** of holding my job.
( ) As long as I do good work I can be **almost certain** of holding my job.
( ) As long as I do good work I can be **very sure** of holding my job.

Figure 12-1. Morale Questionnaire.

(Hull, Richard L., and Arthur Kolstad, "Morale Questionnaire," in Watson, Goodwin, *Civilian Morale,* New York: Reynal & Hitchcock, Inc., 1942, pp. 351–352.)

and-file employees. Consequently the results of management morale are not presented in detail herein.

MEASUREMENT OF MORALE

The attitude questionnaire is the method most used to measure the morale of employees. In analyzing the results, interdepartmental and inter-plant comparisons may be made, or plant profiles may be developed over a period of time. Where a standard instrument is used, for example, the S. R. A. Employee Inventory or the Triple Audit of Industrial Relations, norms can be compiled against which each company can compare its own findings. The Houser Associates, a consulting company, has developed an instrument for measuring morale shown in Figure 12-1.[2]

The morale scores resulting from the ten questions yield an average that is significantly above the theoretical average. Weights were applied in such a way that, if the middle alternative were selected for each of the ten questions, a person would make a score of 50. Scores could range from 0 to 100. A score of 50 was consequently considered the theoretical average. The actual average of all employees studied turned out to be 20 points higher than the theoretical one. There are two explanations for this difference. One is that the companies studied were not representative of American industry but were more progressive and had more enlightened industrial relations. Otherwise they would not have been among the minority of companies that have made systematic studies of employee morale. The second and more important explanation is that persons form a loyalty that makes them rate their company higher than it statistically deserves. Analogies would be the loyalty for home town or college.

SOME FACTORS AFFECTING MORALE

Studies of morale among approximately 12,000 English employees have emphasized, as in America, psychological and social influences.[3] The most prominent causes of poor morale were found in the occupational life of the worker rather than in his home life. The main causes of faulty cooperation were frustrations resulting from lack of recognition and from the belief that promotions were unfair, from jealousies between departments and between persons, and from fear of being inefficient. The last cause, fear of being inefficient, is nourished by the industrial practice of using blame so much more frequently than praise. It appears typical that during one day eighteen foremen had reprimanded employees, while only two had praised an employee.

Morale of foremen

The foreman, who stands in the precarious position between the ordinary worker and higher levels of management, has his morale raised when he is allowed to act and feel like a member of management.[4] It is not so much the title by which he is called as it is the actual position and power he is given which determine his morale. Management must provide the supervisor with visible symbols of dignity and authority such as office space, a desk, and a telephone. Differences in pay between supervisors and rank-and-file workers are important to the morale of the supervisors. A managerial climate which places the supervisor in the position of making and implementing decisions is perhaps most important to the supervisor's morale, especially now when union representatives have taken over so many in-plant functions. The Bell Telephone Company of Pennsylvania has worked out a coordinated program of group discussions and improved up-and-down communication in order to implement these ideas and raise the morale of supervisors. This democratic leadership is probably the most important step that can be taken to raise morale, and it should include rank-and-file employees as well as supervision.

Organization

In a very extensive study of employee morale at Sears, Roebuck & Co., the organizational structure of the company was found to be an important variable.[5] An attitude questionnaire was used to get the "feeling tone" of employees in general areas of inquiry, and interviewing was used to probe for specific sources of discontent. It was found that the work processes had been oversimplified and that the size and rigidity of the organization conflicted excessively with individual self-expression and maximum morale. In smaller, less complex, and more decentralized industrial plants, employee morale is higher. More will be said about this later, in connection with the monotony of assembly-line jobs.

Equipment

Another factor affecting morale is equipment.[6] A study in two plants, a metalworking plant and a company manufacturing electromechanical assemblies, found equipment to be an important cause of grievances, ill-humor, absenteeism, and turnover. Among workers on the ten poorest machines in one plant there were arguments and noncooperation; on the ten best machines, joking and mutual assistance. Over a one-year period, grievances from operators of poorly maintained machines ran 5:1 over grievances on good machines. In exit interviews this factor came out as an important reason for leaving the company. When a company continues to run an old or defective machine, the workers assume that management does not care enough about the workers to have it fixed or get a new one, and this in turn causes lowered morale.

EXTERNAL CORRELATES OF MORALE

There has been considerable interest but a lack of understanding of the extent to which morale causes desirable behavior. Behavior studies center on a measure of the extent to which employees will persevere at work. Measures of such perseverance are freedom from turnover and from absenteeism, return to company after war, lack of grievances and strikes, and production. Most of the correlation studies have reported results that are insignificant, or only slightly positive.

No single external measure of morale, such as freedom from turnover, or a combination of external measures is entirely satisfactory. There is no objective measure of morale that will demonstrate conclusively that workers in an industrial plant actually possess good morale in the sense that they want to persevere at work. With respect to the external measures mentioned above, each has some plausibility, but there is also some objection to each as a conclusive measure.

Turnover

High turnover can at times be traced to low morale, although the correlation is low between turnover and morale.[7] In a study of two electronics factories the most important causes of turnover were found to be financial and psychological.[8] Slightly higher turnover was found in departments which were rated by union officials as having low morale and in departments which had a wage-incentive plan.

In a study of forty-eight nationally representative companies, employee reasons for quitting were assessed by exit interview.[9] They were, in this order, dissatisfaction with pay, transportation, promotion, working conditions, poor health, job security, friction with co-workers, poor housing or excessive rents, personal happiness as affected by job experience, ability of supervisor, confidence in management, company interest in employee welfare, freedom of communication with higher levels, recreation, method of wage payment, and other problems. Grievances over pay were mentioned twice as often as any other reason.

Another study which shows the relationship between morale and turnover was made among 600 Michigan Bell Telephone operators and service representatives.[10] Neurotic personality, attitudes toward wages, and supervision did not show any significant relationship in this study. Rather, the worker's feeling of ego-involvement in the day-to-day operations of the plant was found to be the most important difference between those who stayed on and those who left. The former, much more than the latter, felt that they could make decisions on the job and that they were making an important contribution to the company. This finding suggests that, if the employee feels his is an important job, there will be a reduction in the cost and inconvenience of high turnover.

In a study of turnover and morale in a metals factory, the Kerr Tear Ballot for Industry was used on 894 employees.[11] Turnover was highest in departments with the least opportunity for conversation. Where there was an opportunity for conversation, there were also other desirable job features such as small departments, variety of work, and attractive work.

Absenteeism

Absenteeism as a morale problem appears to be related to turnover in both causes and manifestations. Both are symptoms of low morale, or little perseverance at work, as demonstrated by the worker's staying away from work. Some studies have shown a moderate relation between morale and absenteeism; in other groups there has been no relation.[12] The use of absenteeism as a measure of morale requires a knowledge of the total situation, including the number of absences due to illness, or to other reasons, that could not be avoided. There are situations, however, in which it has been shown that some absenteeism is traceable to low morale.

In a study in 1950 of employees of the Detroit Edison Company, it was found that low absence rates are correlated with satisfaction with supervision, work associates, wages and promotional opportunities, one's job, and the company as a whole.[13] There are fewer absences in the work groups of supervisors who encourage discussion of work problems and hold group meetings to solve them. A sense of group belonging, pride, and solidarity went with low absenteeism. People who can use their skills in their job and people who feel that there are good opportunities for promotion stay away from work less frequently. Satisfaction with present wages or the possibility of improving them leads to less absenteeism. For white-collar men, absences were mainly related to: attitudes toward supervision, work associates, financial and job status, and the company in general. For blue-collar workers, attitudes toward supervision, work associates, and satisfactions with the job itself were most important.

Production

Although it is commonly assumed that high morale usually causes high productivity, the consensus of the evidence does not support the assumption.[14] When the morale of individual employees was correlated with their production record or rating of production, the results were essentially zero in thirteen of fifteen different work groups. In the other two work groups the results were slightly positive, showing a small relationship between high morale and high production. Comparisons among groups have been more positive. These group comparisons are made by averaging the production for an entire work group and averaging the morale for the entire work group. A series of comparable work groups are correlated to determine the relationship between productivity and morale. The results have generally shown the groups high in morale to be high in production. Differences in production have, however, not been great, regardless of the size of the differences in morale.

Production in a Philadelphia spinning plant after introduction of rest pauses rose from approximately 70 per cent to 80 per cent, as the result, it was thought, of an improvement in morale.[15] A bonus plan for production of 75 per cent and over was in effect before and during the study. In this situation, morale, rather than pay, was believed to be effective in improving production.

Certain studies have shown an absence of relationship between productivity and attitudes toward the job. One study of machine operators showed that "efficiency ratings of employees had no relationship to their attitudes."[16] In fact, the most unfavorable attitudes were held by the most productive girls. Later studies of this sort also point to an absence of relationship between scores on a job satisfaction index and individual performance.

"Group analysis" studies have been made in which a group average based on individual attitudes is related to group production estimates by departments. In such a study by Likert (1941), morale among insurance agents was significantly related to the operational efficiency of the agency for which they worked.

In a study of worker morale and productivity in the shipyards, answers to the question, "Have you ever felt like quitting the yards?" agreed well with a productivity measure.[17] Production differences were great, morale differences were small, among the shipyards.

ATTEMPTS TO IMPROVE MORALE

A number of attempts to improve morale have been implied in the material presented; others will be suggested in connection with monotony and in later chapters. Stock purchase plans have been adopted by a number of companies in an effort to stimulate morale through identification with the objectives of management. These stock purchase plans have been generous in that the company usually pays one or two dollars for each dollar the employee invests. There is no objective evaluation of their effectiveness for improving morale. Profit sharing is another method which has had as one of its objectives the improvement of morale.

Profit sharing

Successful profit-sharing plans have increased employee morale in addition to increasing production and profits. Although profit sharing has important economic aspects, it is also psychological in nature. The most obvious of the psychological aspects is the importance of the friendly move by management in giving the employees an opportunity to participate in the profits. In the case histories of the most successful examples of profit sharing, the value of money as an incentive has been subordinated to the effect of the plan on morale or team spirit, and it is for that reason that profit sharing is discussed in relation to morale. The substantial increases in production that occur under successful profit sharing demonstrate that motivation was not adequate prior to the time when profit sharing began.

DEFINITION

Profit sharing, as used here, is a plan whereby arrangements are made in advance to distribute a definite percentage of the profits. Plans whereby bonuses are given but the basis for their determination is not fixed or known in advance by the employees participating are not included in this discussion. This discussion of profit sharing is limited to plans which include a large number of employees; it does not extend to the more numerous plans, particularly in the United States, that have been restricted to managerial participation.

OBJECTIVES

Profit sharing has had as its primary objectives "greater output and efficiency," "elimination of industrial unrest," "development of cooperation," "greater economic security for the employees," "reduction of labor turnover," "prevention of the growth of unions," and "social justice."[18] An objective of profit sharing is to provide a goal which can be shared by management and labor. More than half of American workers think that hard work does not pay.[19] Profit sharing is a system designed to convince them that it does.

PRO AND CON

A study has been reported of 168 profit-sharing plans which were discontinued and the reasons for their termination.[20] These reasons, as reported by managements of forty-three companies, are: too small profit or no profit; change in ownership or control; failure as group incentive; and workers' preference for wage increases. The median duration of these plans studied was twelve years. The median year of termination was 1934, and 29 per cent of the terminations occurred between 1930 and 1934. Profit sharing, which works best in small, nonunionized plants, should never be used to offset substandard wages or working conditions. Of the sixty-three reasons given by management for setting up these profit-sharing schemes, the most important were to encourage a sense of partnership, to provide a group production incentive, and to provide employee security. Other reasons were to increase interest in company profit, to reduce turnover, to improve morale, and to encourage employee thrift.

ADAMSON COMPANY

One example of a successful profit-sharing plan presents facts that pertain to morale. The Adamson Company, East Palestine, Ohio, employed approximately one hundred persons.[21] The company was unionized by the CIO Steelworkers. Its product was welded gasoline-storage tanks. Conditions of supply and demand, pay, and prices did not differ before and for a year or two after a profit-sharing plan was put into effect. The plan was to split profits fifty-fifty between employees and management. Profit sharing brought much better morale. Skilled workers, such as welders, began to help out on routine jobs when they had no welding to do. Everyone worked as an effective team. As a result, there was a 500 per cent increase in profits, or more than twice as much profit to management after the workers had their 50 per cent of the profits; there were no strikes at a time when steelworkers elsewhere in the country were striking; production efficiency increased 54 per cent; and earnings from profit sharing resulted in an increase of $42 per person on the average the first month.

The gain in efficiency was due to several factors at the Adamson Company. One, as mentioned above, was that workers helped out when they had nothing to do on their own jobs. Another was the suggestions that resulted in improved methods.

This example of successful profit sharing demonstrates what proponents of profit sharing stress, that it is not the system by itself that will succeed, but how it is put across to assure workers of the good faith of management. In the Adamson Company there was one unusual aspect that might be important. The head of the company had a close relationship to his employees that made him more one of them than heads of companies usually are. He was a working head who could work skillfully with his hands and with his employees. His relationship to the employees was probably partly responsible for the ease with which cooperative attitudes were established.

Some proponents of profit sharing look upon it as not merely a pay plan, but also as a crusade. Some view it as a moral reformation, others as a way of saving America for capitalism by instilling successful morale among workers and ensuring cooperation between labor and management. When it is accepted fully, it brings high morale to management.

SUMMARY

Results of successful profit sharing show that motivation and morale are not nearly so high as they might be among rank-and-file employees in American industry. Profit sharing is highly effective, at least for a time, when it is properly applied with frequent payments and a clearly understood system, and especially in a small company where one's efforts can be observed on the over-all total. In successful profit-sharing plans there always seems to have been participation. Workers become interested in production goals, and their egos become involved in the activity to attain these goals.

Other methods

Other methods used to improve morale are grievance procedure, recreational programs, contests such as "Why I Like My Job," and suggestion programs. There has been little or no evaluation of these methods to show positive effects on morale. No specific technique can take the place of a thoroughgoing personnel program endorsed by line management which aims at building attitudes of satisfaction toward immediate supervisor, job, and company.

MONOTONY

Monotony of work is a frequently mentioned basis for low industrial morale. A job is monotonous or boring when it is not interesting. Monotony is a characteristic, not of a particular job, but of the relationship between the job and the worker at a particular time. A job that may look very monotonous to a bystander may have considerable interest for the man who is doing the work. The situation and the meaning of the work determine to a large extent whether or not monotony occurs.

The primary cause of monotony in jobs is repetition, or lack of variety. There is no case known where a job with variety is monotonous. There are situations in which repetitious work is not considered monotonous. During wartime, for instance, workers were doing routine, repetitive jobs which were considered interesting because of their meaning.

With the increasing mechanization of industry, jobs have been becoming more and more repetitive, making the matter of monotony one of increasing importance. This trend to more repetitive work is changing with the advent of automation. Some of the most routine work is being done by machine, so that the skill level of work is being upgraded.

In some situations shifting jobs from time to time is a good way to combat monotony. The Capital Transit Company, operator of buses and street cars in Washington, D. C., has found that allowing operators to shift jobs every several months works well. Bus drivers and street car motormen are given an opportunity to trade jobs if they wish to do so.

Individual differences in susceptibility to monotony are so pronounced that they deserve study and consideration during placement.

TABLE 12-1

Variety of Work and Intrinsic Job Satisfaction

CHARACTERISTICS OF OWN JOB LIKED	DEGREE OF INTRINSIC JOB SATISFACTION			*N*
	LOW	MEDIUM	HIGH	
Employees who mention variety	14%	45%	41%	159
Employees who mention other characteristics[a]	36	33	31	55
Employees who do not mention any specific job characteristics	38	36	26	366
			TOTAL	580
CHARACTERISTICS OF OWN JOB DISLIKED				
Employees who mention lack of variety	63%	29%	8%	130
Employees who mention other characteristics[b]	24	44	32	152
Employees who do not mention any specific job characteristics	21	39	40	298
			TOTAL	580

[a] "Other characteristics" include: liking to be on one's own, feeling of accomplishment from work, and a few respondents said, "opportunity to make decisions."

[b] "Other characteristics" include primarily: "having to meet deadlines," "too much work to be done," but also include some cases of people who mention: supervision, overtime, lack of advancement, working conditions, social climate, no opportunity to make decisions, and no feeling of accomplishment.

Morse, Nancy C., *Satisfactions in the White-Collar Job,* Ann Arbor: University of Michigan, 1953, p. 62.

Some people express satisfaction in doing extremely routine jobs. Dissatisfaction on routine jobs is due to more than the matter of routine. Almost everyone wants to be important. It is recognized that a routine job is seldom an important one. It does not give the gratification of frequent personal contacts, as jobs carrying more responsibility do. To a certain extent no job in itself is psychologically fatiguing or monotonous. It is the situation or the reaction of the employee that determines whether the job is monotonous to him.

Clerical work

Monotony is a problem in clerical work as well as in the manufacturing plant. Employee attitudes have been shown to be affected by the nature of the clerical job.[22] A study of a white-collar population in a large organization shows the need for variety and the opportunity to use one's skills and abilities on the job. Those in the more varied, skilled jobs are more satisfied with their jobs than those having monotonous, routine jobs. However, the level of aspiration of the individual worker is also very important in this respect. His job satisfaction depends on the degree of variety and responsibility in his job, relative to what he wants. The attitude toward the job may be colored by strong satisfactions or dissatisfactions in other areas, for example, concerning pay. Table 12-I shows the relationship between variety of work and intrinsic job satisfaction.

TABLE 12-II

Decisions on Job and Intrinsic Job Satisfaction

| | DEGREE OF INTRINSIC JOB SATISFACTION | | | |
	LOW	MEDIUM	HIGH	*N*
Employees who report making decisions	25%	39%	36%	344
Employees who report making no decisions	39	38	23	234
Not ascertained				2
			TOTAL	580

Morse, Nancy C., *Satisfactions in the White-Collar Job,* Ann Arbor: University of Michigan, 1953, p. 63.

TABLE 12-III

Aspiration Related to Achievement Level in Decision Making and Intrinsic Job Satisfaction

	DEGREE OF INTRINSIC JOB SATISFACTION			
	LOW	MEDIUM	HIGH	*N*
Employees making some decisions who would not like to make more	14%	36%	50%	70
Employees making no decisions who would not like to make any	10	52	38	58
Employees making some decisions who would like to make more	29	40	31	248
Employees making no decisions who would like to make some	49	32	19	161
Not ascertained				43
			TOTAL	580

Morse, Nancy C., *Satisfactions in the White-Collar Job*, Ann Arbor: University of Michigan, 1953, p. 64.

Variety in work is seen to be important, and its lack can determine attitudes toward one's job.

Table 12-II shows how decision making in the job, which lessens the monotony and routine, affects intrinsic job satisfaction. Those who make decisions are more satisfied. Table 12-III shows how decision making and job satisfaction are relative to the individual worker's aspirations.

Manufacturing

Another study also shows that mechanized, routine work leads to feelings of dissatisfaction.[23] A sample of workers was studied in an automobile-manufacturing plant, an auto-assembly plant, and six metal mills. The general level of satisfaction was considerably lower in auto assembly, possibly because of the greater degree of mechanization there. Employees who did nonmechanized work were more satisfied than those doing mechanized work. About 75 per cent of those doing nonmechanized work were "very and moderately satisfied with their jobs" compared to 54 per cent of those who were satisfied with mechanized work.

One study has explored the effects of mass-production industrial techniques on the worker.[24] Fundamental to mass-production methods are standardization and interchangeability of parts, as well as mechanical pacing of work. A man's work is brought to him mechanically and taken to the next worker mechanically. On the assembly line itself, the human being feeds the machine and must time his own movements to the mechanical, ever moving line. He must adapt his own rhythm to the rhythm of the machine. The work is broken down into a series of simplified motions which require little skill and are easily learned. There is no choice of tools or methods, and the individual worker usually has very little relationship to the whole finished product. Furthermore, only surface attention is required on most of these jobs; some attention is required, but not deep mental absorption. Obviously these conditions of work must have an effect, and often an undesirable effect, on the worker in mass-production industries. In one plant a substantial number of grievances centered on job standards, for example, mechanical pacing and other mass-production characteristics. Grievances of this nature were much more numerous than those concerning pay or seniority. "A majority specifically stated that they liked their jobs to the degree to which they lacked repetitiveness, mechanical pacing, or related characteristics. On the other hand, they disliked them to the degree to which they embodied these mass production characteristics."[25] In the same plant more absenteeism was found on highly repetitive, mechanized jobs. Likewise, twice as many workers left the highly mechanized jobs as left jobs with moderate mass-production characteristics. Thus, in attitudes and behavior, the workers showed their hostility to the assembly-line techniques affecting their working lives.

Personality traits affecting monotony

People who perform repetitive work without finding it monotonous are older than average, prefer regularity in their daily routine, are not restless in their leisure-time activities, and are generally satisfied with their personal life as well as with their home life and life on the job.[26]

Several personality traits which have been believed to be causes of monotony are not found to influence it, as shown by the latest and best evidence. Monotony is not associated with high intelligence, with extroversion, with freedom from daydreaming, or with lack of ambition.[27]

294

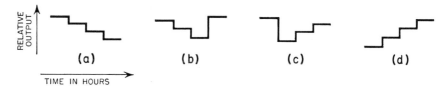

RELATIVE OUTPUT

(a)   (b)   (c)   (d)

TIME IN HOURS

Figure 12-2. Output Curves for Different Degrees of Fatigue and Boredom. Curve (a) represents what is expected to happen from fatigue; curve (d) represents what is expected to happen from boredom; curves (b) and (c) represent what is expected under conditions of mixed fatigue and boredom.

(Wyatt, S., and J. N. Langdon, *Fatigue and Boredom in Repetitive Work,* Industrial Health Research Board, No. 77, London: His Majesty's Stationery Office, 1937.)

Monotony curve

The output curve typical of monotony has been contrasted with an output curve said to be expected in the presence of fatigue.[28] In the theoretical monotony curve, output will increase throughout the work span as relief from the monotonous work approaches. This is the opposite of the theoretical fatigue curve in which output drops as fatigue sets in. When the output curves of sixty-eight women workers doing fairly monotonous work were examined, some curves approximated each of the theoretical monotony and fatigue curves, but the majority were of a mixed type similar to types b and c in Figure 12-2. Type b is closer to what would be expected under the hypothesis of monotony, and type c to what would be expected under the hypothesis of fatigue. Each output curve over a period of several months was classified separately for each of the sixty-eight workers. These were compared with appraisals of boredom based on what the girls said about their feelings in an interview. The curve assessments agreed with the boredom assessments in 51 out of 68 cases, whereas chance would have yielded 17 out of 68. In this situation, then, there was a high correlation between feeling of monotony and the shape of the output curve.

Methods of reducing monotony at work

JOB ENLARGEMENT

One development for reducing the monotony of overspecialized, mass-production jobs is job enlargement. In 1943 IBM's president realized that machine operators could save a lot of time and gain variety in their jobs by setting up their own machines and checking the results of their work, thus eliminating the setup men and inspectors, who could be transferred to other jobs. This type of job enlargement brings more

295

pride in work and less specific strain and fatigue, as well as less monotony.

One report gave job enlargement credit for cutting overtime in half despite an increase in work volume, reducing absenteeism 10 per cent, cutting a full day off the schedule for setting up new accounts, increasing pay for many employees, increasing interest in jobs, and lowering overall costs for the company.[29] In a study of 122 electric utility companies, billing costs per customer were highest in the companies having the most specialization, lowest in those having the least. There was a 40 per cent difference in costs. At Detroit Edison, where job enlargement was being put into effect in some departments, morale was found to be higher and overtime dropped 50 per cent as a result, it was thought, of job enlargement.[30]

Connected with job enlargement is the idea of giving the worker more say in organizing his work. Monotony at work has been reduced by changing the job in some situations, and in some instances merely by changing the mental set of the worker. Mental set can be changed by seeing new meaning in a task, or by breaking up the task into a series of subgoals to give a more frequent sense of accomplishment. Breaking up the job so that a more interesting element is added can relieve monotony. To the engineer this is inefficient, being contrary to the simplification of work. To the psychologist it is effective because it prevents work from being a meaningless, unending flow which causes extreme boredom.

MUSIC

Music has been used to counteract the monotony of mass-production work. Some studies have indicated that the use of music resulted in increased production and improved employee attitudes. In one study, music had no effect on production, but was liked and felt to be beneficial by the workers questioned.[31] This study was made of 142 women workers employed in "setting" in rug manufacturing. On a questionnaire the women said that music decreased the monotony of the work, made time pass more rapidly, and made the work easier. Fifty-nine per cent of them felt that they got more work done with music, although the objective measure showed no increase in production. Supervisors who were questioned agreed that music had a good effect on the morale of the workers as well as on their own morale.

In one study of approximately 1000 employees, almost all of them (98 per cent) thought that music during working hours would be at least "mildly pleasant," and 74 per cent thought that it would be "extremely pleasant."[32]

Music in relation to production was studied on a highly repetitive assembly-line operation which was on incentive pay. Two separate shifts with an average of twenty-one employees on each shift were studied simultaneously for twelve weeks. The results showed that production under varying conditions of music increased 4 to 25 per cent. The average increase on the day shift was 7 per cent, on the night shift, 17 per cent. The increases were statistically significant and large enough to be of economic importance.

The results of the effect of music are varied in that in some studies production was increased, whereas in one study no significant improvement was shown. All studies agree that employees on routine jobs generally prefer music.

OTHER METHODS

More rest periods and more "banks" were recommended by the workers in the study of assembly-line work mentioned previously. Rest periods have been discussed in Chapter 8. "Building a bank" means piling up a quantity of the product, small subassemblies of door handles, for example, and thus varying one's pace. In this way the person who brings materials, and not the moving conveyor belt, determines the pace; the worker has a little more freedom. Also, by "working up the line," that is, by working very fast on four or five units, then taking a breather, the worker can alter his pace a little, and the job may seem less monotonous. Job rotation and job enlargement are the two main suggestions for increasing the variety of the job in a mass-production industry. The system of rotating an employee from one machine to another has good effects in relieving the monotony of mass-production work.

SUMMARY

Employee morale can be thought of as attitudes toward job, company, and immediate supervisor, and can be ascertained through attitude questionnaires and interviews.

Being recognized for one's work, being understood by one's supervisor, receiving the pay and status one expected to receive, getting need-fulfillments from the work itself—all these factors tend to create high morale.

High turnover, sometimes indicative of low morale, is attributed to dissatisfactions with pay, a lack of involvement with the company, and highly regimented work situations. Absenteeism and, at times, low productivity also accompany dissatisfaction with the company in general or with specific aspects of the work situation, although morale and productivity are often not related.

297

Profit sharing has been used in small and medium-sized companies to improve morale and give the workers a sense of participating in the company.

Monotony in American repetitive factory and office work is far from universal, but it is a prominent factor in causing a decrease in morale. Workers who are older than average, prefer regularity in daily routine, are not restless, and are generally satisfied with life are less likely to find repetitious work monotonous. There are variations in interest in jobs that objectively seem to be approximately the same. Monotony is less when the job seems to be important, when work is varied from time to time, and when it is divided into segments that can be completed.

Work should be broken up into segments that can be completed in a day or so. Workers should be allowed to change jobs every few months if they wish to do so.

Music is preferred by a great majority of workers who are doing repetitive work, and in some situations it has increased production.

Highly mechanized repetitive jobs cause absenteeism and high turnover as well as dissatisfaction.

RECOMMENDED READINGS

Brayfield, Arthur H., and Walter H. Crockett, "Employee Attitudes and Employee Performance," *Psychological Bulletin,* 1955, **52**, 396-424. A thorough review of studies relating attitudes and morale to productivity, turnover, and absences.

Walker, Charles R., and Robert H. Guest, *The Man on the Assembly Line,* Cambridge, Mass.: Harvard University Press, 1952. A major study of dissatisfaction and satisfaction with assembly line work in an automotive plant.

13

Personnel counseling

Personnel counseling is a method of understanding and helping people who are upset emotionally. It is important because every student will need to employ counseling techniques at one time or another in his business career. This is not a subject which is to be used only in certain situations; it represents a point of view toward people that can be used constantly. Counseling will remain a basic part of business psychology as long as people work with other people.

OBJECTIVE

The objective of counseling is to help solve some emotional problem. Serious mental illness is beyond the scope of this book, although the theory and method are not different from those which apply to upset people. The problems here may not seem to be very significant or complex. They are, however, important to the people who have them, and consequently the productive efficiency of these people and their performance on the job will be affected. Their problems interfere with their adjustment in all phases of their lives. Everyone will benefit if these people can be helped to solve their problems. They will benefit, their families will benefit, and their supervisors will obtain more effective working groups.

Counseling is effective for a wide range of problems, as determined by the needs of the person being counseled. Some idea of the problems presented in industrial counseling may be gathered from the following cases. These problems were run-of-the-mill cases for counselors at the Hawthorne Works of the Western Electric Company.[1]

1. An employee who feels that his progress is too slow and who cannot see any chance for further progress in his department.
2. An employee in a group which expects to be transferred soon is disturbed by the insecurity of the situation.
3. A woman disturbed by her supervisor's criticism of her work.

4. An employee who has been offered a higher paid job elsewhere but cannot decide whether to accept it.
5. Friction with other workers on the job.
6. A young woman having difficulties with parents over getting married.
7. A man with a neurotic wife.
8. A young woman whose husband had deserted her.

The first five cases are ones which line supervisors should be qualified to counsel; the other three might also be. Circumstances in each of the latter three cases would certainly affect the supervisor's decision as to whether he felt qualified to counsel. If the line supervisor were qualified, he would be the most desirable person for counseling the employee.

LINE MANAGEMENT

Counseling of employees with industrial problems is within the capabilities of line management in almost all companies. Such counseling responsibility should not be shunted off to special staff counselors. It is desirable for line management to assume responsibility for aiding in the solution of problems which it may have caused. This approach strengthens the relationship between supervisor and worker. Clearly, this procedure places greater responsibility on line supervisors and emphasizes the necessity for good supervisory techniques.

When a staff member acts as counselor, he encounters disadvantages which do not exist for the line supervisor as a counselor. The supervisor may suspect that an employee is criticizing him while talking to the counselor, and often he may be right. Although this might help the employee by giving him a chance to express his criticism of his supervisor, it would not solve the employee-supervisor problem if the supervisor were antagonized by the employee-staff relationship. The staff role also presents an industrial counselor whom some employees would be embarrassed to contact.

The risk of a supervisor's doing harm as a nondirective counselor is slight. There would be a great danger if partially trained supervisors attempted directive counseling. Bad advice can make upset people's problems much worse. Since to take part in nondirective counseling means to give no advice, but to listen to and thus help a person to see and solve his own problem, it is not dangerous even if not done professionally.

It would be desirable to engage staff counselors for counseling on a full-time basis only if a company could justify devoting a fair amount of time and expense to helping individual employees with nonbusiness problems. Most companies would find it more appropriate to refer employees with such problems as cannot be handled by line managers to

300

counseling services in the local community. Line management's function is to counsel employees with minor problems and provide referral information to employees with problems which line management is not qualified to handle.

EXTENT OF COUNSELING

In 1951 a survey by the American Management Association indicated that approximately 300,000 workers were employed by thirty-five firms having rather extensive counseling services for their employees.[2] The counseling was provided for the employees' welfare, for its expected beneficial effect on employee efficiency, and for its value in producing better employer-employee relations. In other words, counseling was provided because the companies felt that it was benefiting them.

The counseling services dealt with a wide scope of problems. The services offered centered around individual interviews and dealt with a variety of problems. Counseling to management was almost as widespread as to rank-and-file employees.

Nearly all the counseling programs were recent innovations. Twenty-two of the firms had installed their counseling services during the war, and seven had instituted programs since the war. While the data above are by no means complete, the survey suggests a growing recognition of the importance of counseling in industry.

HISTORY

Historically, the counseling viewpoint described in this chapter began a short time before World War II. The studies at Hawthorne are directly responsible for industrial counseling; another source of modern counseling concepts have been the writings of Carl R. Rogers. Wartime demands for all-out production caused a rapid growth of interest in the potentialities of counseling, and it is now a significant part of the psychological scene. The first results of intensive studies of the counseling process, using statistical techniques, have shown that counseling is effective.[3] Some of these results will be summarized later in this chapter.

FORMS OF COUNSELING

Counseling may be divided into directive counseling and nondirective counseling. Directive counseling, or the giving of advice, used to be standard practice with social agencies and workers in the field of personal relations.[4] It was found, however, that people did not wish to follow advice, no matter how good it might be. One writer compared directive and nondirective counseling by saying that directive counseling tells a patient what to do, which he frequently already knows.[5] His trouble is that he does not wish to do it. Nondirective counseling brings him to decide to do what is reasonable.

Strange as it seems, one has to know more in order to talk less. The training of a person who provides information and advice is the opposite of the orientation of a nondirective counselor. Therefore, any information services provided by a company should be separated from its nondirective counseling services. Since a supervisor must perform both functions, he must keep clearly in mind which hat he is wearing. He must be conscious that in an employee interview or informal contact the employee may change his viewpoint rapidly from objective questions to subjective emotions. Therefore the supervisor-counselor must be prepared to shift methods when necessary.

Nondirective

Nondirective counseling is a counseling relationship which provides an interested listener to a person with worries. For that reason, it is also known as client-centered counseling. In other words, anyone performs one of the functions of nondirective counseling when he is an interested listener. In a good conversation, where the listener does not block the conversation with questions, there is a beginning of nondirective counseling. This is why counseling is a practical technique for anyone in business. Every listener already has some conception of counseling fundamentals.

The nondirective counseling contact allows the person with troubles to talk about his troubles as long as he wishes, without interruption, and with an understanding and appreciative audience. Although the counselor does not provide sympathy, he does demonstrate empathy. Such an opportunity for expression of this kind was allowed few people before the advent of counselors.

One author has made a neat comparison of counseling with other procedures which seek to accomplish the same purpose.[6]

The three methods of individual trouble shooting in industrial personnel work are: advice, which considers the surface crisis and dictates the solution; guidance, which considers the surface crisis, guesses at the cause, offers a number of possible solutions, and lets the employee make the deciding choice; and counseling, which goes to the underlying cause, the real crisis, and leads the employee to an emancipating understanding of his trouble. Advice is quick and ineffective. Guidance is, in all respects, the middle way. Counseling takes time but does the job.

If the counselor is careful to offer no advice, he cannot give bad advice. The counselor operates with a deep respect for the person in difficulty.[7] He is confident that the person is best qualified to solve his own problems, and he directs his actions toward helping the person reach that goal. The goal is one which the person may reach with the assistance of any other person who has been trained in the principles of counseling, whether that person is a supervisor or a fellow employee.

In nondirective counseling the supervisor or counselor allows the interviewee to guide the interview, to talk about anything the interviewee chooses—no matter how unrelated to the original subject the topic may *seem* to be. The counselor will need an agile and acceptant mind for this. The counselor does not offer advice, but mirrors the interviewee's feelings so that the interviewee solves his own problem. The counselor aids the interviewee in fully talking out the problem. The interviewee perhaps gains courage in expressing his thoughts to an acceptant other person. The counselor also helps in that he provides an incentive for the interviewee to concentrate his thoughts on his problem, rather than let his thoughts stray away from it. In the course of counseling, the interviewee's principal topic may change from the immediate problem at hand to deeper problems which fundamentally are responsible for the surface problems. This change in the interviewee's thoughts is exactly the opposite of straying away from the problem. An important third function of the counselor is to release the inherent desires within the interviewee to tend toward the normal, or toward acceptance of other persons and himself.

THEORY

Turning from this introduction to nondirective counseling techniques, the theory of nondirective counseling has been briefly summarized by Rogers, who originally developed the method in the clinic.[8]

... Within the client reside constructive forces whose strength and uniformity have been either entirely unrecognized or grossly under-estimated ... In most, if not all, individuals there exist growth forces, tendencies toward self actualization ... The individual has the capacity and the strength to devise, quite unguided, the steps which will lead him to a more mature and more comfortable relationship to his reality ... All of these capacities ... are released in the individual if a suitable psychological atmosphere is provided.

It seems that client-centered counseling releases dynamic forces in a manner achieved by no other counseling relationship.

In other words, almost everyone can think for himself better than another person, or better than any psychologist can think for him, provided that he is placed in the right psychological atmosphere. Even though a psychologist could reach the same correct decision as the client about a course of action, it would still be better for the client to reach the decision for himself, even though it takes longer, because no one will follow a course of action unless he has become convinced in his own mind that it is the thing to do. All of this fits in with antiauthoritarian beliefs.

Nondirective counseling thus fits into the theory of democratic or participative leadership and, in fact, is the keystone of the theory. For a supervisor to be nondirective with a subordinate he must endorse the theory that the employee is important enough to be able to solve his own problems, and that he, the supervisor, is not the only one who can make the right decision. It would be unrealistic to expect an employee to feel free to talk to an autocratic supervisor about many personal problems. The same skills and attitudes are necessary for the nondirective counselor as for the effective conference leader. Consequently each one reinforces the other. To the extent that the supervisor can learn to be an effective nondirective counselor, he will be a better conference leader.

STEPS IN THE COUNSELING PROCESS

The counseling process is an exceedingly individual experience, which varies widely from person to person. Nonetheless, certain characteristic steps are encountered in counseling. Some of these will be illustrated later in this chapter. Of the steps in nondirective counseling, the two most significant are the release of expression and the achievement of insight. These concepts will be explained below.

Counseling is needed when a supervisor becomes aware that an employee is disturbed by a problem or irritated by a situation. The supervisor seeks to express tacitly the conditions under which he may provide help, and to listen to the employee's problems. The supervisor does not have the answers, but the counseling situation offers the employee an opportunity to work out the solution to his own problems.

The employee is encouraged to express his feelings about his problems at the outset of counseling. The counselor provides a receptive attitude, and listens intently. The employee usually is eager to explain his problems under those circumstances, and proceeds to do so.

In doing so, the employee finds "emotional release from the feelings he has previously repressed, increasing awareness of the basic elements in his own situation, and increased ability to recognize his own feelings openly and without fear. He also finds his situation clarified by this process of exploration and begins to see relationships between his various reactions."[9] This experience thus forms the beginning of, and the basis for, achieving insight.

As the employee expresses himself to an understanding listener, he will begin to see what his problem really is in a way that is new to him.[10] As he continues to talk, he will see his problem more clearly and begin to understand why it arose. This will lead to his seeing himself in a different light. Whereas in the beginning he was hostile and frustrated, he will come to recognize his responsibility for his trouble. After there is accurate perception of a problem, the next step for the employee will be to think of what he should do about it. This will lead him to list the various courses of action that he could take with the advantages and disadvantages of each. At this stage the employee will decide what, under the circumstances, is the best thing for him to do. He will not need advice or direction from the supervisor.

When the employee decides definitely what he is going to do about his problem, he is approaching the time when he no longer needs his supervisor's counseling.[11] The employee should make up his own mind when he no longer wants to talk further with his supervisor. The latter should not suggest that he carry on alone. When the employee does decide that he has had enough help, the supervisor should invite him back anytime he would like to come and talk again.

The length of time over which these counseling experiences take place may vary from a short while to an extended period of interviews. The supervisor's concern is with counseling employees with relatively minor problems, which may be expected to be resolved within a few sessions. If it appears from a preliminary interview that the employee is in need of extended counseling, he should be presented with the opportunity of discussing his problems with a professional counselor. This ensures that responsibility for decision remains with the employee. If he desires, he may be given the name of a counselor or social service agency providing counseling.

WHO CAN BENEFIT FROM COUNSELING?

Nondirective counseling is advocated for relatively normal people with personal-social-emotional problems whose personality integration is such that they can come back to reality with the little help that the counselor gives. Treatment of people with severe mental illnesses cannot be considered within the scope of this book. The great majority of problem individuals in business situations will be persons with those minor difficulties previously mentioned. If they are helped, their productive energies will be released so that they may become more effective on the job.

Persons with personal or social problems who are employed in business and industrial activities usually have a background favorable to nondirective counseling because they generally meet the qualifications listed below. Nondirective counseling is likely to be successful if the individual:

1. Has some capacity to cope with life. He possesses adequate ability and stability to exercise some control over the elements of his situation. He is not a victim of uncontrollable circumstances from which there is no escape.
2. Is reasonably independent, either emotionally or spatially, of close family control.
3. Is reasonably free from excessive instabilities, particularly of an organic nature.
4. Is able to express his tensions and conflicts. A conscious desire for help is advantageous, but not entirely necessary.[12]

TECHNIQUES

In the foregoing pages the rationale of nondirective counseling has been discussed. There are several important techniques. Illustrations and explanatory material together can give the reader an idea of the process, but no printed matter can ever replace the experience of actual counseling.

Put yourself in the place of Bill Smith, a foreman, who is faced with a somewhat disgruntled employee by the name of Jim Jones. Jim feels that he should have been given a raise, when in fact his work does not warrant it. A common reaction would be to tell Jim that he didn't deserve a raise. With nondirective counseling, something like this might result:

JIM: Smitty, I've been wanting to ask you why I didn't get a raise last week when all of the other fellows got raises.

SMITH: Jim, why don't we go down to the cafeteria and talk about this over a cup of coffee?

JIM: O. K.

(They go to the cafeteria.)

SMITH: Well, Jim, as I understand it, you feel you should have gotten a raise last week.

JIM: Yes, I feel as if I haven't been making any progress here. Everything seems to be going wrong. I work and work and don't seem to get anywhere. My wife picks on me, and tells me to get on the ball. Then I come down here and I run into Max and he tries to take all the good jobs from me. Well, Max, he makes me so mad that I start spoiling work; and well, you know, that just doesn't do a fellow any good. I just have to do something to ease the strain, so I stop off with the boys on the way home, and then she nags me for coming home late and making such a bad example for the kids. What can a guy do?

SMITH: Everything seems pretty hopeless, doesn't it?

JIM: It's gotten me so that I hardly know what to do about it, and then, when Bill and John got new rates I just seemed to be further behind than ever. Mind you, I'm not kicking that they got the raises because they've really turned out the work. But it does seem pretty discouraging.

(Jim pauses for half a minute.)

Do you think it would make a difference if I could match what they're doing? You know, sometimes I get so tied up just thinking about the other guys that I really don't keep up with my own work. . . . I'm really going to try to do a good job on that new run we're setting up for; it means a lot to me to get that extra money. Smitty, the next time I'm up for that higher rate, I'll be worth it!

SMITH: (Smiling) Well, Jim, I'm glad you feel you have the answer. It seems to help when there's a chance to talk about problems, and I hope that any time you feel there's something wrong, you'll tell me about it.

(They finish their coffee, and talk about various other things.)

In this little incident the actual counseling process has been fore-shortened, but the feelings and process would be similar under actual conditions. By listening, we have learned that Jim's problems were of his own making, and that things were not really so bad as he originally described them. It turns out that only two men in his department have had raises. Jim is an ordinary person with some problems which temporarily have gotten the better of him.

Let's consider what happened in this conversation. Jim had a chance to say what was actually on his mind, and he did not leave the cafeteria with the feeling that his boss was an ogre who lost his temper at every opportunity. In the interview the decisions were made entirely by Jim; since he made them, he is much more likely to live up to them than if he had been given a stern lecture on his vices. With Jim's realization of his problem there comes an internal change in his thinking; the effects of counseling will persist beyond the counseling period. Jim is likely to continue evaluating his problems, in an attempt to solve them, even though he receives no more counseling.

Both persons gained respect for each other, and so the way was paved for better working relationships. Better communication between boss and employee was the result.

Certain elements of the interview contributed to its success.[13] For one thing, Jim's supervisor was attentive. He was interested and friendly. He was permissive. The interview was free from distraction by telephone calls or urgent requests for administrative action because Jim and the supervisor were in the cafeteria. Jim talked in an atmosphere of psychological privacy. That is to say, Jim felt that he could talk privately, although he was not talking in a private room or office. Psychological privacy may be obtained in locations where conversations cannot be overheard and in places where the counselee does not feel that someone is staring at him. Jim was put at ease in the cafeteria so that he could talk freely.

Structuring is another element of counseling. Structuring consists in explaining the functions of the counseling interview, the extent to which the interview is confidential, and the amount of time available for the interview. In our example, Jim's supervisor suggested that they spend perhaps twenty minutes over a cup of coffee. He might have found it necessary to suggest that anything Jim said would be regarded as confidential and would not be entered in his record.

At the end of the interview, Jim was urged to return if he wished to do so. Jim, however, was not asked to return. His supervisor had structured his closing remarks so that "the door was always open for Jim," if Jim needed it.

The counselor listens

The counselor having provided proper conditions and clarified his role, his most important contribution to the counseling process is listening.[14] Release of expression is one of the most important purposes of listening. The counselee should do the great majority of the talking. Had the supervisor talked as much as the employee in the example above, he would have failed. The supervisor made only two remarks during the actual counseling. Jim said a great deal more.

It seems that, if you go to someone for advice, you want that person to do more than merely sit and listen to you. Why shouldn't the interviewer yield to the urge to help by advice? In a few words, the answer is that advice is cheap. Many people will gladly give advice. Psychologically, the answer is that most people have sufficient mental ability to solve their own problems or to avoid difficulties. Intelligence, however, is not all that is required. When upset, people do not really want to talk to someone to obtain information or to have the supervisor solve their problems. People seek counseling because they seek to understand themselves. They are confused and do not actually know what their real problem is and, consequently, cannot decide what to do.

An upset person is not ready to accept advice because he is frustrated and not motivated. Teaching or directive counseling will not aid him; he must learn for himself. The nondirective counselor encourages the person to get rid of his frustration and become motivated to see what he wants. The counselor listens acceptantly and expresses neither approval nor disapproval as the person seeks his way toward a solution. The person himself must decide what values are important to him.

In the course of listening, the counselor will almost unconsciously indicate that he is listening. He will have given his whole-hearted attention to the employee, and he probably will make an occasional affirmative "uh-huh," to show that he is following the employee's line of thought. For example:

EMPLOYEE: Last week everyone was saying we would be transferred to Department C, and I've been wondering about it.

COUNSELOR: Uh-huh.

EMPLOYEE: I'd rather not work there because I don't like to work with the old lathes they have there.

COUNSELOR: Uh-huh.

EMPLOYEE: I can't see why the company just transfers us around any time it pleases; they ought to work out some system to give us older fellows a break ...

Focus on feeling

Since the counselor is concerned with the emotional problems of the person rather than the person's intellectual problems, it follows that, when the counselor does speak, he should be concerned with feelings rather than facts.[15] The counselor responds to encourage further expression of the employee's feelings. To put it another way, the counselor focuses his attention on the feelings and attitudes expressed by the interviewee rather than on the content of the interviewee's remarks.

The counselor's responses to feelings might be considered to mirror what the interviewee says. This is done for several reasons. The counseling experience will be more meaningful to the employee if the counselor uses the employee's own terms and symbols so that the employee finds it easier to think.[16] The "mirroring" also is useful to the employee because it returns his own thoughts to him. He may then realize that the words he has used or the ideas he has expressed have been designed to justify, or to conceal from himself, the feelings that are the real determinants of his behavior. If, on the other hand, the counselor attempts to interpret the interviewee's thoughts, or to lead the employee to a conclusion which seems obvious to the counselor, the employee will be distracted from his chain of reasoning and the interview will be unsuccessful.

Interrogatory question-and-answer procedures will lead the employee to believe that the counselor's purpose is to solve the problem for the interviewee. Hence the counselor seeks to phrase his replies so that the responsibility for the problem remains with the interviewee. Moments of silence may be expected. Often in those intervals the employee is doing his deepest thinking, and at those times the counselor would merely be interrupting if he were to speak.

One example of focusing on feelings follows:

EMPLOYEE: I think I want a transfer to X department. Two friends work there and say it's nice, even if it wouldn't pay as well as my present job. In our department everyone is out for himself.

COUNSELOR: It would be pleasant to be with your friends, even if the job isn't as good. It seems as if nobody cares much about you here, just about how much work they can turn out.[17]

Emotional detachment

One of the counselor's most difficult problems is to achieve emotional detachment during the counseling session. The counselor who has mastered the attitude and skill necessary will be detached so that he will be neutral to any remarks that an upset employee makes. Only when this situation is present can counseling be most effective. The disturbed person must be completely free to express his feelings, whatever they are. They may be antagonistic to the supervisor, or they may contradict his firm beliefs about company policy or morality or ethics. The successful counselor must not disagree. Even if he feels like disagreeing but tries to play the agreeable role, it is likely that he will not succeed because attitudes often can be perceived. If the counselor is looking for feelings rather than having a mental set that allows disagreement, he will find his task easier and at the same time interesting and rewarding.

Detachment will be a problem to the line supervisor who performs counseling functions. He may wonder how he can reconcile his two roles. Should he permit his workers to criticize his company, its executives, and policies? How can he be "boss" if such actions are permitted? The problem will be especially acute for authoritarian supervisors who permit no insubordination.

310

Probably the best compromise in this difficulty is to recognize that persons who are disturbed by problems will be prone to complain, and that such complaints heard in confidential counseling contacts should not be held against the employee. This sets high ethical standards for the supervisor.

If the employee has complained about the company and later sees that he is the cause of the problem, he will later regret having made the unfavorable remarks and will be glad that his supervisor was sufficiently broadminded to forget them. If the employee complains to his supervisor about a correctable shortcoming of the company or his supervisor, the supervisor may be able to change the situation itself by taking action in the matter. Counseling will enable the supervisor to learn of the difficulty. If there is no justifiable reason for the employee's complaint, and the complaint continues after competent counseling, the company probably would be as well off without the employee. The company would not be the loser if such an employee were to quit.

The best remedy for an unjustified complaint is to forestall the problem altogether by preventing it through high morale. A supervisor may be unable to alter his employees' home problems, but he can greatly reduce the problems on the job by techniques of democratic supervision.

The supervisor who counsels also faces the problem of detaching himself from feelings with which in an ordinary conversation he would agree.[18] Agreement in the counseling process is as much out of place as is disagreement. This is particularly true when an employee states his personal beliefs and attitudes. The supervisor should merely show that he understands rather than show agreement.

There will be times when an employee praises the supervisor who is counseling him and shows deep positive personal feelings toward him. It is important for the supervisor to recognize the fact, but it is necessary that he not react emotionally to the feeling. The supervisor needs to see that positive feelings are present which represent progress over frustrated feelings of hostility. The supervisor should keep clearly in mind that his goal is to help the employee see his problem clearly and to solve it. This purpose will not be served if he becomes diverted by accepting or reciprocating the feelings of the upset employee. This would only lead into a blind alley as far as solving the employee's problem is concerned. Therefore the counselor must be able to remain emotionally detached from the grateful employee, although permissive in his outlook. For example:

EMPLOYEE: Thanks so much for your time. You're the only person who has really got to know me.

SUPERVISOR: You feel that I've come to understand you pretty clearly.

311

To summarize, the feelings that the employee expresses toward the supervisor in a counseling relationship should depend mainly on the employee's needs. They are the interpretation of the supervisor in terms of the employee's needs where these needs are more prominent than what the supervisor has done. If the employee becomes angry at the supervisor, this should be because of the employee's feelings of hostility rather than because of what the supervisor has done. Similarly, if the employee expresses deep appreciation to the supervisor, this is a reflection of the inner feeling of the employee which the supervisor has helped bring to the surface, rather than a logically deserved reaction. The supervisor must continue to stay neutral and not react either positively or negatively to the feelings of the employee. By maintaining this detachment he will help the employee to understand himself better.

One final idea should be considered under the topic of emotional detachment. The beginning counselor often is perplexed when he is asked a direct question by the employee. The counselor may lose his emotional detachment and attempt to give advice if he is not prepared for such a possibility. For example, what should the counselor do in the following situations?

EMPLOYEE: Now that I've told you the facts, I wonder what you'd recommend.

                            or

EMPLOYEE: What would you do?

These situations often result because of a lack of proper structuring at the beginning of the interview; in other words, the employee has entered counseling under the impression that the counselor does have the answers. The best solution for these situations is to return the question to the employee:

COUNSELOR: You'd like me to tell you what to do.

                            or

COUNSELOR: You'd like me to give you some advice about this.

Generally, these comments will stimulate the employee to further elaboration of his problem, during which time he may begin to achieve insight.

Ending the interview

The supervisor sometimes has the problem of ending an interview smoothly.[19] He may have another appointment. Even if the supervisor has unlimited time, it is better to end the sessions so that no one lasts more than an hour or so. For example, an employee might spend half an hour or more reciting his problems to a supervisor, and yet desire to continue longer. Closure could not be achieved under those circumstances.

The employee's failure to obtain closure is not so much of a problem as it might seem to be. Lack of a definite conclusion at the end of the interview will stimulate the employee to think more about his problem. The employee's comments at a subsequent interview are likely to reveal that he has done much to solve his problem in the time between interviews. Therefore it is desirable to indicate in advance the time available for an interview, and to adhere to the expected time no matter how unresolved the employee's problems seem to be. It should, of course, be understood by the employee that he is welcome to return at a future time (which might even be scheduled) to continue the discussion. Many employees will expect some remarks which suggest that the interview is at an end even if they have not solved their problems.

RESEARCH STUDIES ON NONDIRECTIVE COUNSELING

A thoroughgoing research report has been published on the initial experimental results of a program to test the hypotheses of nondirective counseling. Experimental and control groups were employed, and as many variables as possible were eliminated from the experimental tests.[20] Tests of the significance of statistical results were employed. The individuals studied were of both sexes, and engaged in various occupations. The problems of the individuals probably were more complex than those arising solely from industrial situations.

This discussion does not pretend to summarize all the major conclusions of the report. However, one conclusion does stand out above all the rest. The personality characteristics of persons who underwent client-centered therapy tended to show significant changes from characteristics of borderline psychoses, severe neuroses, and severe discomfort. The changes were in the direction of milder problems or toward the characteristics of essentially well-functioning persons. The changes tended to be maintained through the period following therapy. No similar changes were discovered in the control individuals studied. Thus experimental validation has been given to this aspect of the theory of nondirective counseling.

SUMMARY

Nondirective counseling is a skill in which all supervisors in business and industry should be competent. It is a technique which is advocated for all persons who feel emotionally disturbed. While supervisors are not qualified to handle complex cases, they definitely can do much to help people with minor problems arising in the business environment.

The two major aspects of nondirective counseling are the release of expression and the achievement of insight. The responsibility for the solution of the disturbed employee's problem rests with the employee in nondirective counseling. The counselor serves only to guide the employee in counseling by attentive listening, reflection of feelings, and suitable structuring of the interview.

This chapter has presented only the bare fundamentals of counseling. Skill in counseling is something which can be learned by any supervisor who has sincere interest and an opportunity to practice helping other people solve their own problems.

RECOMMENDED READINGS

Black, John D., *Some Principles and Techniques of Employee Counseling,* Chicago: The Dartnell Corporation, 1955. This is a useful presentation of the essential steps for anyone who is learning to counsel, together with a number of clear examples of each step.

Rogers, Carl R., and Rosalind F. Dymond (eds.), *Psychotherapy and Personality Change,* Chicago: University of Chicago Press, 1954. Evidence is presented to show the effectiveness of counseling in the clinic.

14

Psychological aspects of labor relations

The psychological aspects of labor relations are made up of group as well as individual relationships. Studies of individual personality are insufficient to explain the major happenings in industrial cooperation and conflict. Concentration of study on the group, however, often leads back to the individual as the most important aspect of group relations in the interaction of individuals. For example, the most important relationship in an industrial group, from the standpoint of the worker, is the relationship between each worker and his boss. The boss is much more important to the worker than the worker is to the boss.

The term group dynamics, or group relations, has already appeared several times previously in this book, but in this chapter it will be given more thorough study. The group or team was important in bringing about a low rate of absenteeism in an aircraft plant. Group decision has been shown to be effective in several production problems.

Team spirit appears to be best in groups that have been together for some time and that are relatively homogeneous. This would mean that groups should be left together when they are working smoothly, if that is practical. It seems likely that people of the same racial extraction, religion, marital status, and approximate age will work together more harmoniously than groups whose members vary widely in these characteristics. The legal and social requirements for fair employment practices may prevent the full use of social and psychological findings on the advantages of homogeneous groups.

The legal rather than the human aspect of labor relations has at times received too much emphasis. It is not proposed that one can supplant the other, but a balance is desirable. Through laws, management has sought to force labor to abide by certain rules. Since these laws have often been frustrating, the reaction of labor has been aggressive and not always logical. At times it would be more advantageous in the long run for management to forget the law during labor disputes and to be generous. Studies of firms that have been successful in maintaining industrial peace have shown that the absence of the legalistic approach is one of the major characteristics of the relationship.[1]

What the psychologist, or, for that matter, any person, can do about group dynamics and industrial cooperation and conflict is limited. When management and a labor union want to fight, there is no magic in the psychologist's bag of tricks that will ensure peace and cooperation. When one or both want to cooperate, then they probably do not need any assistance. It is possible, however, to describe some of the aspects of group dynamics and their relationship to labor relations. Many of the concepts are only partially developed. This chapter attempts to furnish information concerning methods of improving cooperation between labor and management and areas that will be the subject of continued research.

GROUP DYNAMICS

Group dynamics is an expression that describes the situation in which people acting together in a group accomplish certain things, either positively or negatively, in a way that cannot be explained adequately in terms of the individual acting separately. The recognition of group dynamics, or team spirit or *esprit de corps,* has an extensive history in military units and among athletic teams, but its application in industry is fairly recent. Concepts of the informal group and the place of personal and written communications in group relations will be discussed.

Informal groups

The recognition of the social organization of informal groups was first made in industry in the studies at the Hawthorne plant of the Western Electric Company,[2] referred to in Chapter 8. These studies were initiated to evaluate the effect of factors such as lighting, temperature, and wages on the output of the group. Informal group relationships emerged which focused attention on the social organization and the effect of group relationships.

The first of these studies, the Relay Assembly study, was concerned with a group of five girls who had been placed in a special location apart from the normal production workers. This created a small group in which an informal leader developed and took charge of the group. The girls were consulted concerning the various aspects of the experiment as it progressed. The participation resulted in a change of attitude of the group toward their work. The conditions of work, such as rest periods and lighting, were varied; however, the significant finding was that the production continued to increase even when conditions were returned to their original condition. This study is an example of the possibility of developing cooperation through teamwork—or what is elsewhere emphasized as participation.

Participation is commonly denied in industry because specialized staff organizations, such as time and motion study departments, independently develop new methods and force them on the group. Opposition to this procedure is evidenced by restriction of output to a standard unofficially decided by the work group and by oral expressions of hostility.

Another Hawthorne study, that of the Bank Wiring Room, also showed that informal organization and unappointed leadership developed. The formal supervisors recognized the operation of the informal group, but were unable to assert themselves even when rules were disobeyed. The social organization resisted change, and informal leaders dealt with enforcement of the group code and dealt with outsiders. The group relationship that developed effectively exerted pressure on employees which resulted in the curtailment of production.

Communications

In large industrial organizations as in large military organizations, there is customarily a breakdown in communications between the top and the bottom layers. Rank-and-file workers do not know the objectives of management, while top management does not know what is on the worker's mind. In short, there is a lack of understanding between workers and management. Supervisors are not trained to communicate the attitudes of employees up the line. They learn that their bosses want to hear good tidings. If a supervisor at the middle or top of the organization hears from the low-ranking supervisors that employees are restricting output, the low-ranking supervisor is blamed. Consequently, the low-ranking supervisor learns that he had better not tell his supervisor about such things. Organizations are directed by the management group whose primary interest in communications is to design procedures to facilitate the one-way flow of technical information and orders to subordinates.

A study at the Western Electric Company was perhaps the first to emphasize the importance of communications and, at the same time, to point out the difficulty of communications in a large industrial plant.[3] After the first study with a Relay Assembly group showed the importance of the feelings and attitudes of workers, it was decided to find out what attitudes were important to a large number of employees in the Haw-

317

thorne plant. At the start a list of questions was prepared dealing with such topics as supervision, conditions of work, and pay. The purpose of the interview was to obtain answers to questions about these definite topics. When this method was used, the interviewers found that it was difficult to keep an employee on the track. Frequently he would want to talk about something of particular concern to him and spend all his time on that. When some unfavorable situation was reported by an employee, such as objection to the ventilation in a particular part of the plant, an effort was made to correct the situation. Often when this attempt was made to locate the trouble, it was found that there was no objective basis for the complaint.

The complaints were expressions of sentiment rather than of fact. These experiences led to a change in the interviewing program. It was decided to let the employee talk. The function of the interviewer was to get him started and keep him talking by showing interest in what he had to say. Even though the interviewers had no power to do anything about what was found out in the interview, still the employees enjoyed the experience. They reported that it was the finest thing that the company had ever done. Their attitudes changed with their recognition by management and their chance for expression, as had been found earlier by psychoanalysts in clinical situations.

One case was cited of a new supervisor, Brown, who built up successful communication in a few days such as had not been approached by his predecessor, Jones, who had had a long time to try.[4] The successful method was to ask in a group meeting how the department should be run. When employees brought in their suggestions, they learned that Brown was really interested. This made them react with enthusiasm and then they felt free to talk to him about many things.

PERSONAL COMMUNICATION

Two-way communication cannot be established until a channel is made available to both parties. The status relationship existing in organizations must be recognized as a condition that inhibits the free flow of information. Recognizing that organization is necessary in our complex society, we must create an "atmosphere of approval" in which the subordinate and worker will feel free to express problems and offer suggestions. Ideally, the communication should be carried out face to face in order to get the true feelings of the individuals or group. This requires the skill of "listening," as discussed in Chapter 13, which is the ability to recognize the feelings that underlie the words. The perception of the true attitudes is a requirement for successful communications because the attitudes form the "frame of reference" of the other party.

Knowledge of the attitudes should help prevent common failures in communications: evaluating the remarks of another without actually understanding his feelings, and making a reply that is not adequate.

The exchange of information between supervisors and subordinates can act as a two-way chain carrying information both to the worker and upward to top management. Exchange of information and discussion at each level allows participation and aids the free flow of information. It should be recognized that these two-way communication methods represent a clear departure from the common method, which without regard to feelings attempts to convince the other party.

WRITTEN COMMUNICATION

Management should attempt to find out what to communicate, how to do it, and then evaluate the results. Improved personal communications should certainly improve management's knowledge of the interests and the problems of subordinates.

Timely checks on the interests and the needs of the worker are necessary if communications are to be effective. A survey to ascertain employee interest found that employees were primarily interested in the company product, company services, and computation of wages.[5] On the other hand, management personalities, business in general, and company history ranked low. The employees were interested in the things that affected them personally.

One method of evaluating written communication is the Flesch reading-ease scale, which measures both difficulty and human interest.[6] The difficulty factor is based on the number of words per sentence and the number of syllables per 100 words. The human interest is derived from the percentage of personal words and sentences. The value of this type of analysis can be seen in a study of employees' handbooks.[7] The evaluation rated 91.6 per cent of the handbooks too difficult for the intended readers. Also the human interest failed to achieve the desired level of "very interesting."

One sample of what can be done to increase the effectiveness of communications by improving readability is shown in Figures 14-1 and 14-2. Figure 14-1 is part of the actual information sheet that was given to applicants for employment. It has been analyzed for reading level and is at the "Hard to Read" level of difficulty for high-school or college students. The first section of Figure 14-1 is so difficult that it requires college reading skill for understanding. Several things have been done to make Figure 14-2 easier to read than the original. The words are shorter and the sentences are shorter. There is more use of the personal pronouns "we" and "you," which increases interest. These changes make

---

APPLICANTS** GENERAL INFORMATION—FORM A

Before completing your application it would be advantageous for each applicant to know something about our Company, the products we manufacture, and the employment opportunities for both experienced and inexperienced persons.

Type of Work—Our Company manufactures a very high quality line of women's and children's underwear, women's nightwear and slips.

Is it necessary to have experience—Many organizations follow the policy of employing only experienced operators. Although it is desirable that applicants have had some training, our records indicate that many of our highest-paid operators have had no previous experience or training before they entered our employ. Sincere interest in this type of work is much more important than previous experience in some other organization.

Can anyone learn this work—We do not encourage everyone who makes application to enter this industry. We recognize that some applicants are not interested or suited for this work, just as there are women who are not suited by temperament to enter office work, nursing, or some similar vocation. It would be unfair to you as an applicant, and to the Company if we were to adopt a policy of hiring all applicants.

Figure 14-1. Part of an Information Sheet for Potential Applicants.

(Paterson, D. G., and J. J. Jenkins, "Communication between Management and Workers," *Journal of Applied Psychology*, 1948, **32**, 74–75. Reprinted by permission of the American Psychological Association.)

Figure 14-2 so easy to read that it can be read well by anyone with only fifth-grade reading skill.

It would be well for management to use such methods in the preparation of employee handbooks, financial statements, or other material that employees with limited educational opportunity are expected to read.

INFORMATION FOR APPLICANTS—FORM B

BEFORE YOU APPLY. We think you would like to know something about our Company. This page tells you what we make and how *you* will fit into the jobs we offer.

What do we make? We make a very high quality type of women's and children's underwear, women's nightwear and slips. We make these with electric sewing machines like those in many homes.

Do you need experience? Some companies only hire people who have done this kind of work before. Some companies demand experience. We do not. Why? Because our records show that many of our best-paid workers started work here without experience. Some had never worked before. Now they are very good workers. We like to hire trained workers but we know that real interest in sewing and real ability come first.

Can anyone learn this work? No. Some people are not interested in it or suited for it. You know some women who are not good bets for office work, nursing or other special jobs. In the same way, some women are not good bets for our jobs. It would not be fair to you if we hired you for a job you did not like or could not do. If we hire you, it means we think you are really fitted for this work.

Figure 14-2. Part of a Simplified Information Sheet for Potential Applicants.

(Paterson, D. G., and J. J. Jenkins, "Communication between Management and Workers," *Journal of Applied Psychology*, 1948, **32**, 76–77. Reprinted by permission of the American Psychological Association.)

The informative value of a checkup on communications is found in the results of an employee opinion survey concerning communication.[8] The survey showed that, although only 2 to 3 per cent of the personnel thoroughly read the annual report, 38 per cent liked it and wanted it every year. The survey found a partial list of sources of employee information to be the company magazine, 49 per cent; newspapers, 42 per cent; rumor and gossip, 41 per cent; friends with access to official information, 27 per cent; and supervisors, 6 per cent. This clearly shows that the supervisors were not an effective link in the communications area and that the company should take remedial action.

Summary

Management at all levels should be aware of the presence and nature of small groups so that they can deal effectively with them. The large organization derives its characteristics from the smaller work groups of which it is comprised. Informal work groups tend to resist change and as a result have been frequently discouraged by management, which believes that quick change in product and process is necessary to meet business conditions. Improved communications, sensitivity to feelings, participation, and knowledge of the effect of group pressures can contribute to better labor-management relations.

UNION-MANAGEMENT RELATIONS

Union organizations, when studied in regard to group concepts of human relations, offer a key to improved union-management contacts. Unions provide important human relations advantages to employees. One of the main functions of a union is to provide a channel of communication. In a large business organization this channel is often blocked in the upward direction. The union also provides an organization that is the worker's own. It is consequently more concerned with the worker's feelings and attitudes than is management. The union organization places the power generally in the hands of the membership, in contrast to the business organization, where the power comes down from the top. Unions are primarily political organizations, and the leaders must consider the wishes of the workers if they desire to stay in office.

Sources of conflict

It is possible to study the conflicts between unions and managements, but it is important to recognize that neither psychology nor any of the social sciences provides easy remedies for the conflict. By understanding the causes of the conflicts, however, it should be possible to improve situations in the future.

THE UNION AS AN INSTITUTION

One student of labor-management affairs interviewed sixty management leaders and sixty labor leaders in an effort to inquire into the future of labor-management relations.[9] He concluded that conflict is inevitable, because both management and labor want something that the other cannot give and still survive in the way it thinks it has to survive.

Among the conflicting objectives is the fact that management looks upon its industrial relations as representing only the workers who are employed by the company, while union leadership, on the other hand, must represent a number of companies. This causes conflict. The union takes on the quality of an institution. What the leaders do is often done in terms of what will benefit the institution of the union organization, not of what will benefit an individual company, nor even what is wanted by the individual union members of a single company. In other words, the selfishness of organizations as well as of individuals prevents cooperation.

MANAGEMENT PREROGATIVES

"Management prerogatives" is a fighting phrase. Management feels that, if it is to manage and to continue to do so, it must draw the line somewhere. With the advance of the labor movement, management has become irritated with delays and with restrictions in taking action on placement, hiring, firing, promotions, layoffs, work assignments, and other personnel decisions. Consequently, management attempts to limit the area of union participation so that additional areas will not be restricted. At one extreme, management has said that militant unionists are trying to take over management. In these interviews with union leaders, it was clear that there is no plot or plan to take over the running of business, but such a trend may follow from the pressures that exist in the present organizations. Union leaders want to have a voice in all management decisions that affect the welfare of union members. This includes just about all management decisions.

ATTITUDES OF LABOR AND MANAGEMENT LEADERS

This same question, whether labor and management must fight, has been explored in a questionnaire study of approximately 100 labor and management leaders.[10] Twice as many labor leaders as management leaders thought that World War II had increased understanding between labor and management. Some of the labor leaders might have been letting their optimism get the better of their judgment on this question, because a number of them could give no factual information to back up their answer. On both sides there were more favorable answers when the leaders had had contact with the other side. A common explanation on each side for their thinking that understanding was improving was the recognition of common problems. Eighteen per cent of labor leaders thought that the labor-management committees during the war had improved understanding. Not one management leader thought so.

This survey brought out a basic cause of industrial conflict, namely, that in 1946 management was not convinced that labor has the right to organize. "Only 2.8 per cent [of management leaders] believe there is no longer any controversy attached to the right to organize. . ."[10] The results might be greatly different today. It is clear, however, that some management leaders still oppose the right to organize.

When labor and management leaders talked about each other in this survey, their personal relations were emphasized. Almost all the leaders on each side were annoyed with those on the other side. These annoyances were not directed at policies, but at personalities. Management called union leaders "dishonest, unscrupulous, greedy, emotional, egotistical." Union leaders called management leaders "unintelligent, stubborn, arrogant, hypocritical." In general, management was more critical, and the union leaders were on the defensive and resented the fact that management had a poor opinion of them. Both labor and management relied for information on sources of their own group. The conflict was sharpened by the fact that neither side was willing to expose itself to the communications of the other side.

ATTITUDES OF MANUFACTURERS

Another example of a critical attitude is found in a group of manufacturers, 70 per cent of whom believed that labor was less efficient in 1945 than before World War II and, of these, 32 per cent blamed union activities for the decrease in efficiency.[11] The only results available suggest that productivity was higher rather than lower at this time.

SOCIAL CHANGES

A strike in a New England shoe factory has been traced to social rather than to economic causes.[12] The social causes were the breakdown in relationships between the employees and supervision. Supervision here means first-line supervision and also top management. Before machinery became so important to the manufacture of shoes, the factory made up a closely knit social group. The social status of the factory was on an age-grade system. Each man knew his place and how to work up to the next step. He respected the senior skilled craftsmen. The foreman was respected by the employee because he had some definite skill to teach, and this skill was highly regarded. The employees knew the owner and manager personally, and these top officials respected the skill of the

324

craftsmen. After the machine became all-important, the foreman merely had to enforce a set of rules; he no longer had any prized skill to teach the employee. There was greater social distance between the top and the bottom. Managers were imported from outside the city. There was less chance for workers to work their way up to the top of the factory. The strike was thought to be due largely to discontent with the social disorganization that had been brought about by the machine's taking away the skilled-craftsman social system. It is difficult to prove exactly the effect of social organization on a particular strike, but it sounds plausible that such a situation would lead to conflict and hostility.

Ways to peace

We have now seen sharp divergence in attitude, resistance to participation, failure to communicate, and lack of understanding, which appear to make the prospects for cooperation between labor and management quite dim. However, there are studies that show new insight into the problem where the application of human relations has led to a successful relationship. Truly scientific studies of union-management relationships have not been carried out, and it is not certain that they will be possible. The manipulation of working conditions that would be necessary to prove various theories might have unknown social effects when large groups of people are involved.

Characteristic of a number of successful firms which have enjoyed peaceful labor relations are acceptance of collective bargaining and the union, widespread participation, negotiations conducted in a problem-solving atmosphere, and an effective grievance procedure.[13] The managements gave unions the opportunity to participate by advance discussions of problems affecting the workers and by joint committees for such areas as safety, time studies, and seniority problems. The grievance procedure evolved into an excellent communication channel which improved mutual understanding and gave the union the opportunity to carry out its function of representing the workers.

A clash of goals has been stated as a lasting barrier to cooperation, but a recent study emphasizes a new approach.[14] Workers in this study discerned the role of unions as giving job protection and status, while the company provided job security. Despite these different roles, the workers did not side with one at the expense of the other, and 73 per cent of them had a dual allegiance. The worker wanted both institutions and did not want either one to exert pressure on the other one. The study also found that the grievance procedure was providing an excellent channel for two-way communications.

325

An example of the development of good relations from an historically unsatisfactory situation is that of S. Buchsbaum and Company, Chicago, makers of jewelry and plastics.[15] During World War II it converted to making raincoats and other articles for the military services. The company had a history of successful union "busting," having on two occasions, with the cooperation of its trade association, beaten down strikes and attempts to organize its employees into unions. The dislike of the president of the company for unions was based on his direct experience with racketeering by union leaders, on union organizers' encouraging restriction, and on the attitude passed on to him by the previous president, his father.

President Buchsbaum's attitude toward a 1941 strike was similar to the view he held regarding the one in 1935—that he should break it. On the other hand, he realized that, even though he might still hold unions in low esteem, the world around him had moved on with respect to the status of unionization. In 1935 his legal advisors had counseled him that the Wagner Act was unconstitutional. Law and order had to be defended, for otherwise the property rights that Mr. Buchsbaum valued so highly would be threatened.

The 1941 strike was in full swing and Buchsbaum had refused a couple of times to meet with union representatives until his lawyer advised him that he was violating the law. A meeting was held between Buchsbaum and Laderman, the president and manager of the local, and a business acquaintance of Buchsbaum, with whom Laderman's union had a contract. Buchsbaum, a lover of great music, discovered that Laderman was an opera lover; this made him believe that maybe, after all, Laderman was human. The main thing that made Buchsbaum agree to a union contract was that several union men made suggestions of improvements that Buchsbaum recognized would save money.

A contract was signed that was generous to the union. It granted the checkoff of union dues. Transfers and virtually all personnel actions were subject to union approval. As a matter of fact, this meant that the business agent of the union practically became the personnel director for the company, a dangerous thing in the eyes of a management consultant if trouble should develop.

Cooperation developed, on the whole, in a very successful manner, although there was some difficulty with employees and with foremen. Some employees refused to join the union, and by their loyalty to management expected favors in promotions as they had had in the past. Buchsbaum finally called them in one by one and suggested that they join the union. It was a little embarrassing when they quoted him to the effect that they would be victimized by racketeers. Almost all of them joined; the few who refused were fired. Foremen, or at least a few of them, found it hard to change their attitudes at once. Several tried to undercut the union, and one attempted to route materials away from a unionized department. The majority of foremen and nonunion employees were converted to the new order, but again one or two had to be fired because they could not adjust.

Discipline was completely turned over to the union, and this was the source of much of the trouble with the foremen. The foremen became "know-how, show-how" men. They were responsible for production and for training and methods. They were not responsible for firing, for disciplining men who were late, or for any discipline. This method of handling discipline worked out well.

Perhaps the outstanding contribution of the union was with respect to the assimilation of Negro employees. In order to expand from about 150 workers to about 1600, and in keeping with wartime provisions for fair employment practices, Negroes were brought into the plant, under the sponsorship of the AFL union, and assimilated mainly by them. At first, Negro supervisors were placed over only Negro employees, but later there was no segregation, and there was no racial problem. The union applied discipline to any white workers who objected. A few of these had to be fired, but almost all accepted the Negroes. As an expression of cooperation, there were dinners several times a year for top management and employees. There were speeches by the union and management leaders explaining their long-range and immediate aims. Each side also expressed faith in the other side.

In a number of instances it developed that the same person was both a union committee chairman and a supervisor.

The social system at the Buchsbaum Company was one that resulted in outstanding cooperation instead of the conflict that immediately preceded it. Results were pleasing to both management and workers. Profits continued to be ample, although they were not disclosed exactly in the report. (Workers, through their union, could examine the books.) It was said that workers were producing about three times as much in dollar value per man, but this did not take into account increase in prices and changes in methods, both of which were important through this period. Workers' wages increased 100 per cent, but they were still not so high as in several other industries, the automobile industry for example.

This case is said to be typical of those in which the University of Chicago Committee on Human Relations found satisfactory union-management relations.[16] It is typical in that both union and management adopted the other's goal in addition to its own. The union became cost-minded. Management cooperated in the spirit of the contract, and beyond its letter.

There are, no doubt, many representatives of management who believe that the Buchsbaum Company went too far in its cooperation by firing employees who did not join the union and by turning over many important personnel functions to the union. For some this question may be a matter of values that cannot be studied by science. Employees would rather deal directly with their employers, but the majority of industrial employees do not trust their employers. When a majority of the employees favor a union, there is evidence that the employer will obtain cooperation from the employees if he adopts some of the union objectives and does not try to break the union.

This company demonstrates that a radical change of attitude from resistance to complete acceptance of both union and collective bargaining can be successful. A follow-up study showed that the acceptance of the union was paralleled by union acceptance of management.[17] This shows that mutual respect can lead to cooperative relations.

COOPERATION

A final optimistic note is found in the recent statement of Meany, head of the merged CIO-AFL labor organization: "The interests of labor and management are interdependent rather than inimical. The earnings of both are keyed to the continuing prosperity of a particular business, and the nation as a whole. Neither can produce without the other."[18]

The General Foods Corporation has attempted to secure industrial peace through a definite personnel policy.[19] Part of a summary of the policy follows.

. . . each operating executive, manager, and supervisor who directs the work of others will be held responsible for the whole-hearted and effective execution of the principles of personnel administration and employee relations set forth here. We want, and need, the cooperation, interest, and loyalty of all employees. We want employees to be happy in their work relationships and well informed regarding the enterprise in which we all are engaged. We want this business to be conducted in an efficient manner and in a spirit of friendliness to the mutual advantage of employees, management, stockholders, and consumers.

The principles of the policy were written out in some detail. Each level of management was trained in them. Attempts were made to find improvements. There was reported to be less friction, reduced turnover, better morale, and lowered unit costs as a result.

SUMMARY

Group dynamics emphasizes the influence of group attitude on the behavior of the individual.

In some cases it is possible to improve motivation by establishing or continuing congenial work groups. In general, people are more likely to be congenial if they are of approximately the same age, marital status, and race. Friction within a group interferes with production. It is recognized that practical industrial demands often preclude giving first priority to maintaining a working group, but the point is still worth the foreman's consideration. Will these people work together? When they are working together and are congenial, it is unwise to break up the group unless necessary, just as it is unwise to break up a winning ball team.

Much of the conflict and dissatisfaction within industrial America is the result of our not knowing how to develop and continue small cooperating groups.

Effective communication from the workers to top management in a large industrial organization does not exist, and communication from top management is poor.

The factory is a status system; it has an important informal as well as formal organization; and the equilibrium of the social system of the factory is important in explaining cooperation and conflict.

Interpersonal relations is the key to human relations in industry, and particularly important is the relationship of the worker to his immediate boss.

Conflict between American labor and management may be inevitable because neither management nor unions can survive if they behave the way the other wants them to. Although this is true in many situations, it is not universal. If labor and management are to get along, each has to adopt the point of view of the other as well as his own.

Several case studies have been presented to show that successful human relations and effective business operations go together. There has been as yet, however, no clear study predicting in advance what would have to be done to produce successful labor relations, with a follow-up to show that events happened as predicted.

RECOMMENDED READINGS

Kornhauser, Arthur, Robert Dubin, and Arthur M. Ross (eds.), *Industrial Conflict,* New York: McGraw-Hill Book Company, Inc., 1954. The psychological, sociological, and economic causes of and possible cures for industrial conflict are presented.

329

Golden, Clinton S., and Virginia D. Parker, *Causes of Industrial Peace under Collective Bargaining for Committee on Industrial Peace,* New York: Harper & Brothers, 1955. The results of a survey by the National Planning Association show the conditions that are present in United States companies that have enjoyed industrial peace.

Purcell, Theodore V., *The Worker Speaks His Mind on the Company and the Union,* Cambridge: Harvard University Press, 1953. Employees of the Swift Packing Company were interviewed, and apparently they talked very freely about their views of the company and the union.

15

Supervision

INTRODUCTION

The relationship between an employee and his supervisor is the most important human relation in industry from the standpoint of the employee. Consequently, it is necessary to look for ways of improving this relationship if employees are to be effectively adjusted to their work. After the meaning of supervision has been examined, the job of supervision will be evaluated. How people react under different types of leaders will be discussed, with primary emphasis on participatory supervision, in which the people affected by a decision participate in making it. Closely related is the conference, which is growing in importance as a means of decision making in business today. In an attempt to isolate some of the practices of high-producing supervisors, recent research in this field will be examined. The only two studies showing behavior measurements after human relations training will be reported with their results, which suggest that example is stronger than theory.

MEANING OF SUPERVISION

Since a supervisor works through people and is a leader, it is well to examine briefly some concepts of leadership. At first leadership was thought to consist of various personality traits, such as energy, verbal facility, and drive. As a result, the goal of early research was to develop a list of traits to differentiate leaders from followers. A review of this work revealed a long list of traits.[1] There is an absence of consistent personality traits characteristic of all leaders. This finding has an important effect on leadership. Leadership appears to be a relationship between an individual and a group in a certain situation.[2] Different situations will require different attributes in the leader.

While the trait approach generally has been discarded, research is being conducted on deeper personality traits of the leader. Two characteristics that appear to increase the leader's effectiveness are social sensitivity and behavioral flexibility.[3] Social sensitivity, or empathy, is the accuracy with which one person perceives, or understands, another. Behavioral flexibility is the leader's ability to behave appropriately in respect to his insight into the other person. Some research results suggest that the lack of these two characteristics is related to unresolved personality problems within the individual. However, in the light of present research it does not necessarily follow that every leader is a well-adjusted person. The approach to deeper personality traits suggests an answer to the question, "What enables military leaders to transfer successfully to industry and an industrial leader to transfer with success from one industry to another?"

The supervisor must be able to recognize a problem when one exists, decide what additional information is needed, realize what is pertinent, and make a decision. If the situation permits, he may elect to utilize the powers of a group decision, which will be discussed later in the chapter. In any event, he should consider the effect of his decision on the continuing cooperation of his work group.

EVALUATION

The evaluation of supervision, like that of any other job, can be considered conveniently in terms of evaluation of the job and evaluation of the man. Evaluation of the job of leadership, because of its complexity, is much less definite than the evaluation of the jobs of more routine workers. There is so much variation in the jobs of supervisors—the result of organizational levels, differences of company policies, and the changing times—that the difficulties of evaluation are apparent. The variety of duties is so great that a definite finding is difficult. Usually the lower levels of supervision have been evaluated most clearly. A study of a plant in 1954 showed that only 31 per cent of the foremen's time was being spent in direct supervision in their assigned areas. Some foremen were spending as much as 15 per cent of their time hunting men, materials, and equipment.[4] The results of this study suggest that companies should examine the activities of their foremen and aid them in better allocating their time to the important job of supervision.

Foremen

Although the foreman occupies an important position, his responsibility has been decreasing steadily over a period of years. In general, the absolute authority of the foreman to hire and fire is gone. His responsibility for setting work standards has been allocated to the industrial engineer. This withdrawal of authority has been caused both by the increased strength of unions and by management's assignment of many of the foreman's duties to staff personnel.

The foreman stands between management and employees. He must implement the decisions of higher management and still not be considered a stooge of management by the workers. He must translate into action the principles of good human relations, strike a balance between consideration and the demands of the time, and adapt rapidly to technological and social changes.

ATTITUDES

In a study where a representative sample of foremen were questioned, the following attitudes were revealed. Eight out of ten foremen were satisfied with their chances for advancement.[5] Twenty-six per cent considered themselves more like workers than management, 65 per cent identified themselves with management, while the remainder occupied an intermediate position. Twenty-five per cent of the foremen believed that management does not understand their problems. This number is large enough to cause management serious concern. Foremen believe that their salaries are fair when compared with the earnings of people over them, but decidedly not fair with respect to the pay of men under them. Three out of four foremen thought that workers were better off in unions. A desire was expressed for a social organization for foremen so they could get together and discuss their problems.

A lengthy questionnaire was administered in 1951 to the 2500 employees of a midwestern manufacturing company.[6] In 1952, when twenty-three of the original workers had been promoted to foremen and thirty-five had been elected union stewards, the questionnaire was repeated. By comparing specific answers to factual questions on age, birthplace, and similar items, it was possible to match both questionnaires and to give group comparisons without disclosing individual identities. Generally the tests showed that future foremen and future stewards have much in common. Both were significantly different from the rank-and-file workers when they were a part of that group. Selected results of the survey are shown in Table 15-I.

An analysis of the data in the table reveals, in part, that the future foreman or steward, while still a regular worker, is likely to be more dubious about the interest of both management and labor leaders in the welfare of the workers than the ordinary worker. He is less satisfied with his current job, and ready to change jobs more quickly than other workers. He is willing to take either a foreman's or a steward's job, whichever is offered him. The future foreman or steward is likely to be the more ambitious, less satisfied, and more skeptical employee.

A reduction of work force in 1954 made it possible to determine what the demoted foreman or steward thought after he returned to the ranks.[7] Demoted foremen generally returned to their preforeman atti-

TABLE 15-1

Attitudes of Future Foremen and Union Stewards

	FUTURE FOREMEN	FUTURE STEWARDS	TOTAL WORKFORCE
High-school education	61%	43%	33%
Under 40 years of age	91	89	57
Married	96	89	73
Highly skilled or semiskilled	91	89	69
Would rather have another job	74	63	51
Willing to take foreman job	78	57	31
Willing to take steward job	30	40	19
Feel they have good understanding of management-union contract	17	20	33
A good place to work (test company)	35	26	46
Management officers care a lot about workers	4	9	14
Union officers care a lot about workers	22	20	38
Most unions are good	48	43	61
Seniority should count more in promotion to foreman	0	14	14

Larke, Alfred G., "How Foremen Get That Way," *Dun's Review and Modern Industry*, January, 1955, **65**, 44–50. Copyright, 1955 by Dun & Bradstreet Publications Corporation.

tudes, and the ex-stewards generally retained their stronger prounion attitudes. The foremen and stewards who retained their positions were those who most strongly held to the beliefs of management and labor, respectively.

PARTICIPATORY SUPERVISION

The extent to which supervisors allow their subordinates to participate in the company's affairs is important and influential. Some examples of motivating employees through participation were given in Chapter 10. The effects of participatory supervision have been studied intensively and have been shown to affect worker productivity, job satisfaction, morale, and attitudes.

Effects of different types of supervision on children

An experimental study of children's groups was made to determine the effects of individual and group behavior under three types of leadership: democratic, authoritarian, and laissez-faire.[8] Because the definition of these terms differs from conventional political definitions, the differences between the methods are shown in Table 15-II.

The subjects of the study were four groups of five boys each, which met after school to engage in hobbies. All boys were 10 years old and the groups were roughly matched in intelligence, personality, physical characteristics, socioeconomic status, and social behavior. Four adult leaders were trained to be skilled in each of the three types of leadership. Every six weeks the leaders were rotated. Each leader changed his leadership technique when he was rotated; therefore, each group had a different type of leader for six weeks. Not only were the groups observed and interviewed, but also the boys' parents were interviewed concerning the child's feelings about the club.

Since there is a general tendency to attribute some of the undesirable results of laissez-faire to democracy, it is well to determine what behavior differences resulted in the two leadership types. In the laissez-faire situation there was less work and more play than in the democratic situation. The work was also of poorer quality. The boys liked the democratic leader the better of the two. The lack of an active leader often resulted in work failures, which sometimes led directly to aggression in the laissez-faire situation.

The quantity of work accomplished under autocracy was greater than under democracy. However, the interest in the work was higher in the democracy. Perhaps the best test of work interest was the behavior of the boys when the leader left the room. The groups under democratic leaders usually continued working, while the other two groups seemed glad to stop working. Creative thinking attained its highest level under democratic leadership.

Autocracy can create hostility and aggression, although they did not always occur. Perhaps the making of scapegoats which appeared in autocracies was aggression that could not be directed at the leader but could be directed at a member of the group. It appears that all the discontent caused by autocracy is not shown immediately. Four boys dropped out, all during the autocratic phase. Nineteen out of twenty

TABLE 15-II

Differences in Types of Leadership

DEMOCRATIC	AUTHORITARIAN	LAISSEZ-FAIRE
All policies a matter of group discussion and decision, encouraged and assisted by the leader.	All determination of policy by the leader.	Complete freedom for group or individual decision, with a minimum of leader participation.
Activity perspective gained during discussion period. General steps to group goal sketched, and, when technical advice was needed, leader suggested two or more alternative procedures from which choice could be made.	Techniques and activity steps dictated by the authority, one at a time, so that future steps were always uncertain to a large degree.	Various materials supplied by the leader, who made it clear that he would supply information when asked. He took no other part in the discussion.
The members were free to work with whomever they chose, and the division of tasks was left to the group.	The leader usually dictated the particular work task and work companion of each member.	Complete nonparticipation of the leader.
The leader was "objective" or "fact-minded" in his praise and criticism and tried to be a regular group member in spirit without doing too much of the work.	The dominator tended to be "personal" in his praise and criticism of the work of each member; remained aloof from active group participation except when demonstrating.	Infrequent spontaneous comments on member activities, unless questioned, and no attempt to appraise or regulate the course of events.

White, Ralph, and Ronald Lippitt, "Leader Behavior and Member Reaction in Three 'Social Climates,'" in Cartwright, Dorwin, and Alvin Zander (eds.), *Group Dynamics,* Evanston, Ill.: Row, Peterson and Company, 1953, p. 586.

members preferred the democratic leader, and more dissatisfaction was expressed in autocracy than in democracy. In the democratic groups there was a greater "we" feeling, more frequent mutual praise, and more readiness to share group property than in the other leadership situations.

Several conclusions are indicated by the results of this experiment. The poorest situation was laissez-faire, in terms of both productivity and member satisfaction. Although less work was accomplished in the democratic situation than in the autocratic, the greater originality, interest, and cooperation would give the democratic leadership the best over-all performance. The effect of the leader's behavior on the children's actions was demonstrated when the children behaved differently when the leadership situation changed.

Effects of participation on adults

Group decision was able to raise the consumption of fresh and imported milk by several groups of housewives. Groups experienced either a lecture or group discussion, and the same material was brought out in both methods. Four weeks after the group discussion 50 per cent of the mothers reported an increase in the consumption of fresh milk, while only approximately 18 per cent of those who had listened to the lecture reported an increase.[9]

During World War II a meat shortage developed. An experiment was conducted to persuade housewives to help alleviate the shortage by eating more beef hearts, sweetbreads, and kidneys.[10] In most people there are deep-seated aversions to eating these foods. Three groups of housewives were given an interesting 45-minute lecture in an attempt to urge them to increase their use of these foods. Three groups participated in discussions of 45 minutes which were led by a well-qualified leader. Only 3 per cent of the women in the lecture groups served one of the meats they had not served before, while 32 per cent of those who participated in the discussion groups served one of them.

INDUSTRIAL PRODUCTION

Production gains as a result of group decision were shown in Figures 10-5 and 10-6. The effect of group decision on production was shown for two additional groups of employees under controlled conditions.[11] The results for individuals and the groups are shown in Figures 15-1 and 15-2.

Although production increased for both discussion and decision-making groups, when compared to the control period the production of the latter groups was significantly greater than that of the former. An analysis of individual records showed that individual production increases were not correlated with age, salary, dexterity, intelligence, or

337

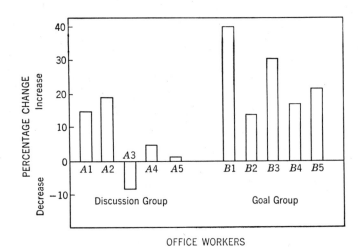

Figure 15-1. Production Change of Individual Office Workers after Group Discussion.

(Lawrence, Lois C., and Patricia Cain Smith, "Group Decision and Employee Participation," *Journal of Applied Psychology,* 1955, **39,** 335.)

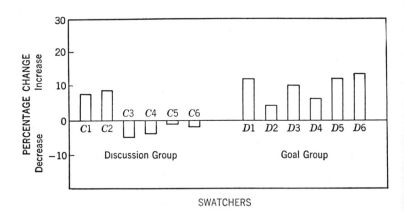

Figure 15-2. Production Change of Individual Swatchers after Group Discussion.

(Lawrence, Lois C., and Patricia Cain Smith, "Group Decision and Employee Participation," *Journal of Applied Psychology,* 1955, **39,** 335.)

length of employment. The significant variable was that one group made a decision and the other did not. On the basis of these two studies, it appears that effective participation requires group decision.

OVERCOMING RESISTANCE TO CHANGE

It is often necessary to change work standards, either for competitive or for technological reasons. Many workers resent changes in their jobs, or resent being transferred to another job. A study conducted at Harwood Manufacturing Corporation suggests what can be done about this cause of dissatisfaction. In one group of several hundred experienced operators whose jobs were changed, only 38 per cent regained their previous production record, even though the two jobs were of equal difficulty. The other 62 per cent either quit or became chronically substandard operators.[12] There was evidence that the inability to regain former production was due primarily to emotional causes.

Because of this resistance to change an experiment was made. Four groups of workers were selected whose jobs were to be changed and for whom new standards were to be set. All groups were about equal in efficiency, and each change represented about 10 per cent of the job.

One group was to have no participation, or the change was to be made in an autocratic method. A meeting was held with the workers, and management explained why the change was necessary. A time study man explained the new piece rate and answered the workers' questions. The meeting was dismissed. The workers knew that a transfer bonus would prevent them from losing money if they learned the new job at an average relearning rate.

Two groups had complete participation—the democratic process. At a group meeting the company explained why the change was necessary. However, all workers were asked to participate in the change. As a result, many suggestions were made. Each worker was studied by a time study man, who worked with him to establish the new job process and rates.

The fourth group did not have complete participation, but special operators were selected by the group to represent them. These operators received the same treatment as the democratic groups, and in addition they trained the other operators on the new job. The experiment results are portrayed in Figure 15-3.

The democratic groups recovered faster from the change than the other two groups. In the first forty days after the change, there were no acts of aggression against the supervisor. The group that participated partially had one act of aggression against the supervisor in the same period.

There were no "quits" in the three participatory groups in the first

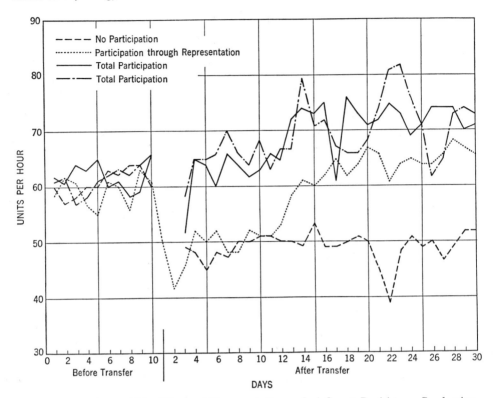

Figure 15-3. Effects of Representation and of Group Decision on Production.
(Coch, Lester, and John R. P. French, Jr., "Overcoming Resistance to Change,"
Human Relations, 1948, **1,** 522.)

forty days, but 17 per cent of the autocratic group did quit. In this group there was hostility toward the supervisor, deliberate restriction of production, conflict with the methods engineer, and grievances against the piece rate. This group was disbanded after thirty-two days and scattered throughout the plant. The group was later reassembled and had full participation in the new job change. The results were substantially the same as for the original democratic groups. That such different results were obtained with the same group indicates that the results were dependent on participation and not on the personality of group members. This experiment appears to indicate that participation by workers in changes that affect their jobs will reduce turnover and aggression due to the changes and will aid in the more rapid learning of the new job.

Characteristics of group decision

When democratic supervision is practiced, decisions obtained are those of the group. The leader does not attempt to impose his will on his subordinates, but encourages them to work together and have a common decision. When necessary, he acts as an expert to supply information the group may need. This is counter to the traditional concept of leadership where all decisions are made by the leader.

Area of freedom[13]

The supervisor and his workers can make decisions only in their area of freedom. This area represents the limit of authority that is invested in the supervisor by higher management. The supervisor's immediate superior may assume part of the supervisor's job. This would represent a restriction in the area of freedom. Obviously the work group cannot make decisions that are in conflict with company policies or practices, nor can they make decisions that are in conflict with the union contract. Some problems would be solved by experts. Problems that are free from these restrictions might be solved by the group.

Unanimity

A goal of group decision is unanimity. If the majority forces its decision on the minority, in effect it is acting autocratically. Hostility and aggression, which are common in groups led by autocratic leaders, are likely to appear. When all members participate and agree to the solution, they all feel important. This is a means for satisfying the motives discussed previously—self-respect and social approval.

There will be occasions when total agreement is not possible. Perhaps the group needs to make a decision rapidly and there is not enough time to obtain unanimity. Under the circumstances the action by the group is still preferred to a decision by the supervisor. The group will feel that the decision is theirs and recognize a responsibility for enforcing it. Perhaps one member of the group is stubborn and resists going with the group. He may come into line eventually.

Effect on channels of communication

Group decision, when properly applied, begins at the top of the organization and continues to the bottom. Below the top man the leader of one group is then a member of the next lower group, and so on down the line. This provides a direct line of communication upward from rank-and-file employees, as the feelings and attitudes of all ranks of workers and supervisors are reflected upward progressively as the groups meet. The lack of this channel of communication has resulted in various attempts to obtain upward communication through the personnel manager, attitude surveys, suggestion boxes, and the union office.[14] These means are often not satisfactory for the upper levels of management to ascertain the attitudes and needs of the employees at lower levels.

Group decision results

The person who has not experienced the power of group decision is likely to be skeptical of the results obtained by this method. Maier, one of the leading authorities on group decision theory and practice, has found from his experiences that group decisions have several general characteristics.[15]

The issue to be solved should be presented to the group as a problem rather than as a criticism. The attitude of the group is then constructive rather than defensive. This atmosphere encourages cooperative effort, a high degree of participation, and frankness and interest in the discussion. Issues might be raised in the discussion of which management has no previous knowledge. Although the time necessary to reach a decision will vary with the difficulty of the problem, it is usually short. This appears to indicate that the interests of a group of employees are not so diverse as many supervisors believe.

Not only is the quality of the group decision good, but also the goals are frequently higher than management would set. All members of the group are considered, so that unreasonable demands are not imposed on members whose skills or abilities are below the general group level. Since the people on the job know best what aspects of the job they can control, solutions are realistic. As shown by the studies referred to earlier in the chapter, workers can closely approach a production goal which they set, even though management may consider the goal unrealistic. The people who reached the decision assume the responsibility for making it work. There is a high degree of acceptance, and the solution is seen as "their solution." The decision seems to be maintained by the group for a long period of time. This is in contrast to an autocratically imposed solution, which tends to be forgotten when discipline to maintain the solution is withdrawn.

Supervisors who have used the group decision method generally like it. They do not feel that they have given up anything by using the method, but rather have experienced a gain. This is due partly to the better understanding they have of their work group.

Summary

The purpose of group decision is to make the job easier for the worker by removing forces of stress. It is not a method to gain increased production by a speedup. Nor is it a bag of tricks to enforce the will of the supervisor. Sincerity is essential. The supervisor must have faith in the group and must believe they can reach the best solution. He must allow them to implement their decision and do all that he can to back up his workers.

CONFERENCES

Conferences are becoming more important in industry. An indication of their importance to the executive is the time spent in conferences. One diversified group of executives reported spending an average of ten hours a week in conferences.[16] Conferences generally are called to aid in decision making or to communicate information.

Problem-solving conferences

A conference called to solve a problem represents a method of arriving at a group decision. If the leader wishes to impose his solution on the conferees, the conference is called merely for the purpose of conveying information. There are some people who believe that a skilled conference leader can so guide the group discussion as to arrive at his preconceived solution. Research to date is inconclusive on this belief. Few conference leaders appear to possess enough skill to do this and also the ability to cover up their feelings when the group refuses to pursue their course. The leader can attempt to stimulate critical thinking by general questions.

The conferee usually sharpens and refines his ideas before he presents them to a group. This process enables the group to obtain the best thinking of each member and is an aid in arriving at a decision of high quality. Perhaps the executives who call conferences are not aware that their subordinates are capable of reaching a quality decision. Only 15 per cent of a group of executives said that they called conferences because they believed the decision would be better as a result of group discussion.[17] The variety of experiences in a group makes a group less likely to make a big mistake than an individual.

Unless the conditions are conducive to a free interchange of ideas, the time for the conference may perhaps be better utilized otherwise. The atmosphere must be permissive, the conferees attempting to decide what is right rather than who is correct. The leader should also realize that some problems are more complex than others and will require more time to solve. Some problems may not warrant calling a conference but might be better solved by some individual work mixed with conferences.

Information conferences

If a decision has been reached by higher authority, a conference to communicate the decision may be helpful. All aspects of the decision can be discussed. Ways of putting the decision into action, as well as anticipated difficulties, are aired. The conference may be for the purpose of learning the attitudes of subordinates so they may be taken into consideration

343

when the decision is made at a higher level. However, the purpose of the meeting must be made clear to the conferees to avoid misunderstandings. Again, the conferees must feel free to talk or only favorable opinions will be expressed.

Leading a conference

The job of a leader in a democratic problem-solving conference is not easy. He does not merely sit back and let the discussion go off on a tangent and then conclude the conference when the allotted time is up. There are certain techniques which make his job easier and the conference more productive.

PREPARATION

The leader should be well prepared. This does not mean that he should have the solution he wants the group to adopt, but it does mean that he should have all the information on the subject that he believes he will need. In his role as an expert, the group will ask the leader to supply certain information. He should therefore anticipate questions the group may ask. If the problem will also require preparation by the conferees, they should be notified of the conference topic.

STATING THE PROBLEM

To open the discussion the leader needs to explain the problem, which should be expressed in situational terms and with a view to obtaining the interest of the group. The group may wish to refine the objectives or may accept them as stated. The group should know definitely what the objectives are. It is helpful to have them listed on a blackboard or perhaps have the leader write them on a chart on an easel.

USE OF QUESTIONS

By the skillful use of questions directed at the group, the leader attempts to determine the views of all conferees and obtain complete participation. The results of one study suggest that the possibility of participation is more important than whether the conferee actually participates.[18] This study showed that the satisfaction with the conference and the decisions reached is related to whether or not the member felt that he was free to participate if he so desired and not to how much he actually participated. This is another reason for a permissive atmosphere in a conference.

MAINTAINING NEUTRALITY

The leader should be neutral and should not attempt to influence the decision. However, he should protect the minority and allow their

344

opinions to be expressed. In order to reduce the time spent in the conference, tangents should be avoided. This requires a great deal of judgment. A member should not be rudely cut off but may be asked how his contribution relates to the objectives the group has decided upon. There is a possibility that the tangent may be related to the objective, and a discussion of it may be helpful to the group.

KEEPING TRACK OF IDEAS

Ideas brought out by the group may be written down by the leader and each explored if the group feels they are important. Frequent summarization is useful in helping the group to see where they stand and what they have accomplished. As ideas are accepted and rejected, the group will move forward to a decision or decisions. Each solution is recorded by the leader to prevent misunderstanding.

THE SUMMARY

To conclude the conference the leader should again state the conference objectives, review the major ideas which have been discussed, and summarize the decisions which the group reached. These remarks by the leader tie the conference together so that the members have a feeling of accomplishment.

PRACTICES OF HIGH- AND LOW-PRODUCING SUPERVISORS

The University of Michigan has conducted one of the more important research programs of recent years to determine the conditions and causes of employee productivity and employee morale. Studies have been conducted in the home office of an insurance company, in section gangs on a railroad, in a utility company, in an automotive manufacturing concern, in a tractor company, in an appliance-manufacturing organization, and in two agencies of the federal government.[19] The research findings suggest four supervisory practices which are consistently related to the productivity of a group. Each of these practices is discussed below.

Differentiation of supervisory role

Supervisors whose groups were above average in productivity performed more of the functions commonly associated with leadership. They did not do the same work as the rank-and-file worker. In contrast, the lower-producing supervisors were more likely to spend their time doing what the workers were doing, or in paper-work aspects of their jobs. High-producing foremen of the railroad section gangs and the tractor company devoted more of their time to the planning aspects of the job than foremen of low-producing sections. Their men also considered the quality of planning better than that in most other groups. The same was also true of supervisors of high-producing sections in an insurance company.[20]

Supervisors who spent the most time in supervising had higher morale as well as higher productivity in their work groups. In the tractor company the workers with the highest morale were those who perceived their supervisors as performing a number of broad, supportive functions. Almost all workers said that their supervisors enforced the rules and kept production up. The supervisors of high-morale employees were also reported to perform other supervisory functions, such as on-the-job training, trying to obtain promotions and transfers for their subordinates, and keeping their subordinates informed about their duties and pertinent company matters.[21]

Differentiation of duties could be either one or both of two separate kinds of supervisory practices. It could be planning, or the engineering leadership of laying out the work. It could be the interpersonal contacts of motivating employees. Both practices are not necessarily found in the same supervisor's work.

Closeness of supervision

High-producing supervisors generally did not supervise as closely as low-producing supervisors. Close supervision consists in frequently checking up on workers, giving workers frequent and detailed instructions, and in general limiting their freedom to do the work in their own way. Close supervision may have negative morale and motivation implications. Conversely, more freedom may increase motivation to produce. It appears that close supervision can interfere with the gratification of some strongly felt needs.[22]

The closeness of supervision which the first-line supervisor employs may well be determined by the style of supervision he receives from his supervisor. This was borne out by the results of both the tractor and the insurance companies. It has the implication that the best way to improve foremen's practices is to have good practices existing at all organizational levels. If a foreman is given little freedom or authority by his superiors, he will be ineffective in dealing with employees, regardless of his human relations skills. Since his intended supportive actions encouraged worker expectations which the foreman could not meet, these actions had a negative effect on their attitudes where the supervisor had little authority.

Employee orientation

Employee orientation means being interested in employees and showing this interest by spending time in motivation. High-producing foremen were more likely to take a personal interest in their men, to be more understanding, to punish them less often when mistakes were made, and to groom them for promotion by teaching them new skills.[23] Low-producing supervisors in the insurance company thought of people as a means to get the work done instead of primarily as individuals. Low-producing supervisors were mostly management-identified, while high-producing supervisors were mainly employee-identified.[24] Being identified with employees meant siding with them and speaking up for them in disagreements with higher management. However, it does not follow that, merely because a supervisor sides with his employees and identifies himself with them, the morale and productivity of the employees will rise. These actions will tend to raise morale only if the supervisor has enough influence in his department to translate his feelings into actual gains for his employees.[25]

Table 15-III indicates how workers in a tractor factory perceived the actions of their foreman. While the response between employees of different productivity groups are statistically significant, there is not a large absolute difference in many instances. An analysis of the table shows that the higher-producing employees are more likely to have a better over-all relationship with their foreman than lower-producing groups. They felt that the foreman was interested in them on the job and that he let them know how they were doing. When they had a problem, it was easy to talk to the foreman, the talk was a help, and the foreman would take action promptly.

The extent to which supervisors were oriented toward their employees, as well as the closeness of their supervision, was probably determined

TABLE 15-III

Relation of Employee Perceptions
of Supervisory Behavior to Productivity

(Workers in a Tractor Factory)

	EMPLOYEES WITH PRODUCTIVITY OF				
	100–119%	90–99%	80–89%	70–79%	40–69%
"On the whole, how would you say you get along with your foreman?"					
Better than most	24%	21%	17%	16%	14%
About the same as most	71	73	77	76	78
Not as good as most	4	5	5	7	7
Not ascertained	1	1	1	1	1

Continued

TABLE 15-III (Cont.)

EMPLOYEES WITH PRODUCTIVITY OF

	110–119%	90–99%	80–89%	70–79%	40–69%
"How much interest does your foreman take in you on the job?"					
Great deal or quite a lot	47%	45%	46%	40%	38%
Little or none	50	54	52	59	61
Not ascertained	3	1	2	1	1
"Does your foreman let you know how you're doing? Do you know where you stand with him?"					
Always or usually know	59%	60%	54%	49%	55%
A lot of times I don't know or hardly ever know	39	39	45	50	45
Not ascertained	2	1	1	1	0
"If you have a problem you would like to talk over with your foreman, how easy is it to talk to him?"					
Easy to talk to about most things	78%	76%	78%	67%	70%
Hard to talk to about many things	22	22	22	33	29
Not ascertained	0	2	0	0	1
"If you talk over a problem with your foreman, does it do any good?"					
Usually or always does some good	54%	47%	47%	38%	44%
Sometimes does some good	30	34	35	40	33
Usually does no good or hardly ever does any good	16	18	16	22	22
Not ascertained	0	1	2	0	1
"If there is something that needs to be taken care of, will your foreman do it right away or will he let it go?"					
Takes care of things right away	55%	52%	51%	43%	52%
Sometimes takes care of things right away, sometimes doesn't	28	30	28	32	27
Lets things go	16	17	20	25	20
Not ascertained	1	1	1	0	1
	327	762	452	269	275

Kahn, Robert L., and Daniel Katz, "Leadership Practices in Relation to Productivity and Morale," in Cartwright, Dorwin, and Alvin Zander (eds.), *Group Dynamics,* Evanston, Ill.: Row, Peterson and Company, 1953, p. 616.

348

in part by the example of higher management. For example, the supervisors in the tractor company who regularly explained to their employees the changes that were coming in the job said that their superiors kept them informed in the same way [26]

Group cohesiveness

The forces which attract and hold members to a group are those of group cohesiveness. One factor that helps develop group cohesiveness is how the group members evaluate the production of their group in relation to other groups. In the insurance company, railroad gang, and tractor factory, members of high-producing groups more often felt that their group was producing more than other groups.[27] This was true even when objective work records were not available to the workers. Foremen also had similar perceptions. It is possible that the feeling of belonging to a high-producing group increased the members' regard for the prestige of their own jobs. The degree of prestige ascribed by group members to their own jobs is positively related to group cohesiveness.[28]

It appears that high-producing sections have high group cohesiveness. However, the converse is not necessarily true. Unless management is able to obtain the employees' confidence, group cohesiveness may tend to decrease production. Before management attempts to develop group cohesiveness, it should ascertain that the employees believe that the company is interested in them.

TRAINING SUPERVISORS

While the evidence is fairly clear from those few studies that have been reported that democratic supervision brings not only better morale but also higher productivity, there is unfortunately no evidence that supervisors can be trained in the classroom to be more democratic. Numerous attempts have been made, and are being made in increasing numbers, to try to train supervisors to be more democratic in the sense of being more considerate and less bossy and to enlist more active participation in problem solving. Some of these training efforts may be highly effective, but in the only two studies where there have been rigorous controls to measure the behavior of the supervisors before and after training, as their behavior was perceived by their subordinates, the results have not been positive. The explanation has been in both instances that higher management was providing an example that was different from the formal training, and that this example was more powerful than the classroom theory. One of these studies was made by the University of Michigan at the Detroit Edison Company and the other by Ohio State University at the International Harvester Company.[29, 30]

349

Detroit Edison

The Detroit Edison training program was conducted in two divisions of the company by Maier, who is one of the most experienced experts in this field. The training consisted of a series of lectures on the psychological principles basic to democratic leadership, the training of line supervisors as discussion leaders, and the opportunity for these line supervisors to apply the principles they had learned to actual job situations by leading discussions on the job.

The design of the study was to make a measurement just before training began, to make a second measurement one year later, and a third measurement two years later. The third measurement has not yet been reported, and consequently this account is based on only the first two measurements. The second measurement was made three months after the completion of training. There was a control group which had no training but which was given the same before-and-after tests. The tests measured employee satisfaction with supervisors. A number of hypotheses were tested, most central of which was "Training foremen in human relations will result in greater employee satisfaction with the foremen."

The results showed improved satisfaction with supervision for employees in one division and less satisfaction for those in the other division. When the two groups were combined, there was no significant change in satisfaction on the part of employees whose supervisors had been trained as compared to employees in the control group.

It was thought that the failure of the training in the one division was due mainly to the fact that higher management in that division was acting contrary to the objectives of the human relations training. It was found, furthermore, that many personality factors and other personal factors of foremen were partly responsible for whether or not there was a change in behavior after training.

International Harvester

The attempt at International Harvester to find changes in behavior after human relations training for management was similar to the Detroit Edison study both in method and in very broad results. The method was similar for part of the Harvester study in that: one measure of training success was the reaction of employees under the trained supervisors; measures were taken before and after training; and a control group of untrained supervisors was also studied. The broad results again failed to show any favorable effects of training once the supervisor returned to the job. Again, as with the Detroit Edison study, the main explanation of the lack of effectiveness of the training was in terms of the leadership climate at the plant. There were other interesting parts of the Harvester study which should be considered in more detail.

The Ohio State students who made the Harvester study decided that the two characteristics of leadership that should be measured were "Consideration" and "Initiating Structure." These they defined as follows:

Consideration. Items with high positive loadings on this factor were associated with behavior indicative of friendship, mutual trust, respect, and certain warmth between the leader and his group. High negative loadings appeared on items which suggest that the leader is arbitrary and impersonal in his relations with group members.

Initiating structure. Items with high positive loadings on this factor imply that the leader organizes and defines the relationship between himself and the members of his group. He tends to define the role which he expects each member to assume, and endeavors to establish well-defined patterns of organization, channels of communication, and ways of getting the job done.[31]

Questionnaires were developed for Consideration, and for Initiating Structure, that could be scored numerically. The factors were almost, but not quite, independent. There was some tendency for a supervisor who was high in Consideration to be low in Initiating Structure, and for one who was low in Consideration to be high in Initiating Structure. For the most part, however, one could not predict one type of behavior from knowledge of the other factor. One set of questionnaires was developed for the supervisor to describe his own attitude to Consideration and Initiating Structure, and another set was constructed with slight changes in wording for superiors and subordinates to describe the behavior of supervisors.

The Harvester supervisors who were being evaluated were given a two-week training course at Central School in Chicago. These supervisors were from a truck assembly factory in Ohio. The training looked similar to that of many companies today and included a heavy emphasis in human relations that would be expected to make supervisors more considerate and perhaps to initiate structure on the job less often.

During training, attitudes changed slightly in the directions expected on both the factors. These shifts are shown in Figure 15-4. The differences immediately after training are probably not due to chance. Training did not make the supervisors more homogeneous, or conforming. In fact, there was a wider range of attitude about Initiating Structure after the training than there had been before. There was no significant change in Consideration.

The effects of training disappeared once the supervisors returned to the plant, and, in fact, the net effect on the Consideration factor was in the opposite direction from that intended. Scores on both Consideration

351

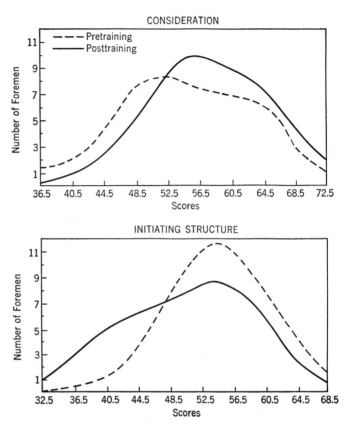

Figure 15-4. Foremen's Scores on Leadership Opinion before and after Training.

(Fleishman, Edwin A., Edwin F. Harris, and Harold E. Burtt, *Leadership and Supervision in Industry,* Monograph No. 33, Bureau of Educational Research, Columbus: The Ohio State University, 1955, p. 42.)

and Initiating Structure were compared for groups of untrained foremen and for those who had been through training and had been back on the job. The analysis was made by separating foremen into those whose training was 2 to 10 months ago in one group, 11 to 19 months ago in a second group, and 20 to 39 months ago in a third. The foreman's Consideration Behavior was less desirable shortly after training than it had been before training. These results are shown in Figure 15-5. Behavior was measured by asking subordinates how their foremen acted on the job. There was no significant change in Initiating Structure behavior after training compared to what it was before training.

Although the attitudes of foremen were more considerate immediately after training, this change quickly disappeared on the job and behavior was even less considerate than before training. The investigators speculated on an explanation for this in terms of foremen becoming more aware of their place as a leader during training. They felt that they were members of management, whereas before training they may have identified more with their subordinates.

REFRESHER TRAINING

Refresher training was given to one of the groups of foremen several months after training at the Central School. The average for the group showed no significant change in either Consideration or Initiating Structure as compared to a control group who did not receive the refresher training, but who had, like the experimental group, attended the Central School. Although the group average had not changed significantly, another type of analysis showed that training had had some effect. Attitudes were less stable in the group that had refresher training than in the group who did not. It had been noted in a previous group in the Central School that their leadership attitudes had been less stable than those of a control group who did not receive the training. In other words, although there was no average change for the trained group in Consideration, some members of the group after training became more considerate,

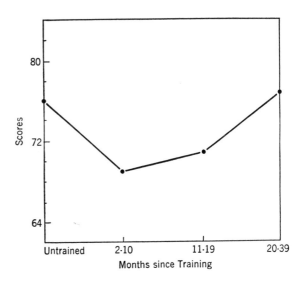

Figure 15-5. Consideration Behavior Scores of Untrained and Trained Groups of Foremen Back in the Plant.

(Fleishman, Edwin A., Edwin F. Harris, and Harold E. Burtt, *Leadership and Supervision in Industry,* Monograph No. 33, Bureau of Educational Research, Columbus: The Ohio State University, 1955, p. 47.)

some became less considerate. It was thought that these varying effects on members of the group were due to a combination of personality differences and differences in the situation in which supervisors found themselves on the job.

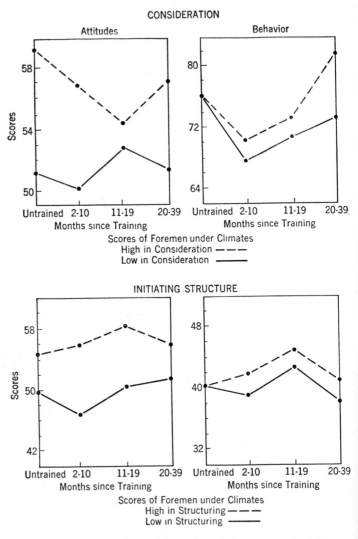

Figure 15-6. Leadership Attitudes and Behavior of Foremen under Different Leadership Climates Back in the Plant.

(Fleishman, Edwin A., Edwin F. Harris, and Harold E. Burtt, *Leadership and Supervision in Industry*, Monograph No. 33, Bureau of Educational Research, Columbus: The Ohio State University, 1955, p. 56.)

Leadership climate was found to be more closely related to the behavior and attitudes of foremen than whether or not they had been trained. Leadership climate was measured in four ways, all of which appeared to be equally good: (1) foremen rated the behavior of their bosses, just as the subordinates of the foremen rated them; (2) foremen rated how they thought their bosses expected them to act; (3) foremen's bosses answered the way that they expected their subordinate foremen to lead; (4) attitudes of the foremen's bosses.

Four groups of foremen were divided for comparison according to the leadership climate provided by their bosses. One group had had no training, and each of the other three groups of foremen had been trained but at different time intervals. Each of these groups was divided into halves, those foremen whose bosses were above average in Consideration and those whose bosses were below average in Consideration. Foremen were similarly analyzed in terms of the leadership climate provided by their bosses on Initiating Structure. The results are shown in Figure 15-6. The attitudes and behavior of foremen correspond in Consideration and in Initiating Structure to the leadership climate. Some or all of the differences in Figure 15-6 are significant except in behavior of Initiating Structure, that is, being bossy. Here, while the foremen are more likely to initiate structure if the leadership climate is in that direction, the difference is not great enough to be statistically significant. The difference between the untrained foremen and those trained at any time interval is not significant in any of the curves in Figure 15-6. Leadership climate is therefore more important in determining the leadership behavior or the leadership attitudes of foremen than is training.

RELATION TO MORALE

The final analysis of the International Harvester foremen was an attempt to find out whether it was desirable to train or instill a leadership climate with more Consideration and less Initiating Structure. Morale, as determined by the preferences of subordinates, gave clear results. Rank-and-file employees definitely preferred those foremen who were high in Consideration. They were more likely to prefer foremen who were low in Initiating Structure to those who were high in this behavior.

RELATION TO BOSSES' RANKINGS

The question of the desirability of Consideration and undesirability of Initiating Structure receives less clear-cut answers from a study of bosses' rankings of the proficiency of foremen in relation to four objective measures of their proficiency. The findings for production foremen differ

TABLE 15-IV

Leadership Behavior Related to Performance
in Production and Nonproduction Departments

	CONSIDERATION		INITIATING STRUCTURE	
	PRODUCTION	NONPRODUCTION	PRODUCTION	NONPRODUCTION
Proficiency	$-.31^a$	.28	$.47^a$	$-.19$
Absenteeism	$-.49^a$	$-.38$	$.27^b$	.06
Accidents	$-.06$	$-.42^b$	.15	.18
Grievances	$-.07$	.15	$.45^a$	.23
Turnover	.13	.04	.06	$.51^b$

^{a} Significant at or beyond the 1 per cent level of confidence.

^{b} Significant at or beyond the 5 per cent level of confidence.

Fleishman, Edwin A., Edwin F. Harris, and Harold E. Burtt, *Leadership and Supervision in Industry: An Evaluation of a Supervisory Training Program,* Monograph No. 33, Bureau of Educational Research, The Ohio State University, 1955, p. 85.

from those for nonproduction foremen. Table 15-IV shows the results; the clearest of these findings is that, among nonproduction foremen, high Initiating Structure is accompanied by high turnover and high Consideration is accompanied by freedom from accidents; and, among production foremen, high Initiating Structure is accompanied by high absenteeism. Also significant among the results, but not quite so clear, are several other relations. Among production foremen, highly considerate foremen have fewer absentees but are rated as less proficient by their bosses; those who are high in Initiating Structure are rated as more proficient by their bosses, but have more grievances.

PROFICIENCY AND MORALE

Among production foremen there is an apparent conflict between proficiency and morale. Bosses rate as superior those foremen who are high in Initiating Structure and low in Consideration. Rank-and-file employees prefer the opposite and show it by lower absenteeism with highly considerate foremen and more grievances with foremen who initiate structure more than the average. The question arises, but cannot be answered, whether, in the long range, turnover, grievances, absenteeism, and accidents might be so expensive as to prove that, after all, high Consideration and low Initiating Structure are desirable.

The fact that superintendents in production divisions rate foremen high who are high in Initiating Structure and low in Consideration while these relations do not apply with superintendents in nonproduction divisions is interpreted as due to more pressure for quick results in production jobs. Independent analyses supported this explanation.

CONCLUSIONS

This thorough study of training International Harvester foremen leads to several conclusions and several questions. Foremen's attitudes are changed during training in which human relations are stressed. Back on the job, there is no lasting effect in the direction intended by the training; in fact, the opposite effect occurs. Some time after the conclusion of training, foremen are less considerate and initiate structure more than before they were trained. The leadership climate as established by the foremen's boss clearly influences the leadership behavior of foremen more than whether they have had formal training or not. There is some question whether the goals of human relations training, higher Consideration and lowered Initiating Structure, are consistent with the objectives of a production organization. They do, however, result in lower turnover, fewer grievances, less absenteeism, and fewer accidents.

SUMMARY

Successful supervision means getting work done through people. Personal relationship is the key to successful supervision. However, the leadership climate is established from the top down, and the supervisor may have little opportunity to practice sound human relations principles. All levels of supervision should be taught human relations. There has been considerable emphasis on this teaching to the first-line supervisors, but the value of this training would be increased greatly if it were also given to intermediate and top management.

Top management needs to be aware of the extent to which the first-line supervisor is in the middle. To be effective, the first-line supervisor has to be considerate of the attitudes of the working group as well as of the wishes of top management. In large industrial organizations the channel of communications in each direction is often ineffective. The proper application of group decision and the conference is a big help in alleviating the communications problem.

Allowing workmen to participate in changes and decisions which affect them has been beneficial to the worker and to the company. To have an effective conference, everyone must feel free to participate. The leader must strike a middle ground between domination and letting the conference wander. He has a difficult job.

High-producing supervisors were found to have four characteristics:

they differentiated the supervisory role, did not supervise too closely, were employee-oriented, and developed group cohesiveness.

While great emphasis is being put on human relations training, much of which may be effective, the only two studies of supervisors' behavior after training show disappointing results. In neither instance had behavior on the job improved. The lack of improvement seemed to be due to the more powerful force of the example of autocratic leadership by higher management.

RECOMMENDED READINGS

Haire, Mason, *Psychology in Management,* New York: McGraw-Hill Book Company, Inc., 1956. A general presentation of the principles of psychology for managers.

Shartle, Carroll L., *Executive Performance and Leadership,* Englewood Cliffs, N. J.: Prentice-Hall, Inc., 1956. Presents some of the results of the extensive research on leadership that has been done for ten years at Ohio State University.

References and Index

References

CHAPTER 1

1. Canter, Ralph R., "Psychologists in Industry," *Personnel Psychology,* 1948, **1,** 145–162.
2. Ruch, Floyd L., *Psychology and Life,* 4th ed., Chicago: Scott, Foresman & Company, 1953, pp. 30–31.
3. Krech, David, and Richard S. Crutchfield, *Theory and Problems of Social Psychology,* New York: McGraw-Hill Book Company, Inc., 1948, pp. 76–109.
4. *Ibid.,* p. 84.
5. *Ibid.,* p. 94.
6. Ruch, *op. cit.,* pp. 105–122.
7. Maier, Norman R. F., *Frustration,* New York: McGraw-Hill Book Company, Inc., 1949.
8. Argyris, Chris, *Personality Fundamentals for Executives,* rev. ed., New Haven: Labor and Management Center, Yale University, 1953, p. 76.
9. Kahn, Robert L., and Daniel Katz, "Leadership Practices in Relation to Productivity and Morale," in Cartwright, Dorwin, and Alvin Zander (eds.), *Group Dynamics,* Evanston, Ill.: Row, Peterson & Company, 1953, pp. 612–627.

CHAPTER 2

1. Spriegel, William R., and Alfred G. Dale, Personnel Study No. 8, *Personnel Practices in Industry,* Austin: The University of Texas, 1954, p. 46.
2. Shartle, Carroll L., *Occupational Information,* 2nd ed., Englewood Cliffs, N. J.: Prentice-Hall, Inc., 1952, pp. 25–56.
3. Flanagan, John C., "Critical Requirements: A New Approach to Employee Evaluation," *Personnel Psychology,* 1949, **2,** 419–426.
   ———, "Defining the Requirements of the Executive's Job," *Personnel,* 1951, **28,** 28–35.
4. Trattner, Marvin H., Sidney A. Fine, and Joseph F. Kubis, "A Comparison of Worker Requirement Ratings Made by Reading Job Descriptions and by Direct Job Observation," *Personnel Psychology,* 1955, **8,** 183–194.

5. Spriegel and Dale, *op. cit.,* p. 46.
6. Rupe, Jesse C., "Research into Basic Methods and Techniques of Air Force Job Analysis—I," *Human Resources Research Center, Technical Report 52–16,* San Antonio, Texas: Lackland Air Force Base, December, 1952, p. iii.
7. Gomberg, W., "A Trade Unionist Looks at Job Evaluation," *Journal of Applied Psychology,* 1951, **35,** 1–7.
8. Martucci, Nicholas L. A., "Case History of a Joint Management-Labor Job Evaluation Program," *Personnel,* 1946, **23,** 98–105.
9. National Industrial Conference Board, Studies in Personal Policy No. 62, *Principles and Application of Job Evaluation,* New York, 1944.
10. Jones, Alice M., "Job Evaluation of Nonacademic Work at the University of Illinois," *Journal of Applied Psychology,* 1948, **32,** 15–19.
11. Spriegel and Dale, *op. cit.,* p. 47.
12. Lawshe, C. H., Jr., Edmund E. Dudek, and R. F. Wilson, "Studies of Job Evaluation VII. A Factor Analysis of Two Point Rating Methods of Job Evaluation," *Journal of Applied Psychology,* 1948, **32,** 118–130.
13. ———, and G. A. Satter, "Studies in Job Evaluation I. Factor Analysis of Point Ratings for Hourly-Paid Jobs in Three Industrial Plants," *Journal of Applied Psychology,* 1944, **28,** 189–199.
    ———, "Studies in Job Evaluation II. The Adequacy of Abbreviated Point Ratings for Hourly Paid Jobs in Three Industrial Plants," *Journal of Applied Psychology,* 1945, **29,** 177–185.
    ———, and A. A. Maleski, "Studies in Job Evaluation III. An Analysis of Point Ratings for Salary Paid Jobs in an Industrial Plant," *Journal of Applied Psychology,* 1946, **30,** 117–129.
14. ———, and R. F. Wilson, "Studies in Job Evaluation VI. The Reliability of Two Point Rating Systems," *Journal of Applied Psychology,* 1947, **31,** 355–365.
15. Davis, M. K., and J. Tiffin, "Cross Validation of an Abbreviated Point Job Evaluation System," *Journal of Applied Psychology,* 1950, **34,** 225–228.
16. Miles, M. C., "Studies in Job Evaluation IX. Validity of a Check List for Evaluating Office Jobs," *Journal of Applied Psychology,* 1952, **36,** 97–102.
17. Lawshe, C. H., Jr., and R. F. Wilson, "Studies in Job Evaluation V. An Analysis of the Factor Comparison System," *Journal of Applied Psychology,* 1946, **30,** 426–434.
18. Spriegel and Dale, *op. cit.,* p. 46.
19. Shartle, *op. cit.,* p. 113.
20. Rothe, Harold F., "Matching Men to Job Requirements," *Personnel Psychology,* 1951, **4,** 291–302.
    Gaiennie, L. Rene, "An Approach to Supervisory Organization Control in Industry," *Personnel Psychology,* 1950, **3,** 41–52.
21. Rothe, *op. cit.,* p. 292.
22. Gaiennie, *op. cit.*

CHAPTER 3

1. McClelland, David C., *Personality,* New York: William Sloane Associates, 1951, p. 69.
2. *Ibid.,* p. 216.
3. National Industrial Conference Board, *Management Almanac,* New York, 1944.
4. Brown, Clarence W., and Edwin E. Ghiselli, "Age of Semi-skilled Workers in Relation to Abilities and Interests," *Personnel Psychology,* 1949, **2,** 497–511.
5. Hull, Clark L., *Aptitude Testing,* Yonkers, N. Y.: World Book Company, 1928, p. 49.
6. Beckham, Albert Sidney, "Minimum Intelligence Levels for Several Occupations," *The Personnel Journal,* 1931, **9,** 309–313.
7. Guilford, J. P., "The Discovery of Aptitude and Achievement Variables," *Science,* 1947, **106,** 279–282.
8. *Ibid.*
9. Guilford, J. P. (ed.), "Printed Classification Tests," *AAF Aviation Psychology Program Research Reports No. 5,* Washington: U. S. Government Printing Office, 1947, p. 89.
10. Harrell, Thomas W., "A Factor Analysis of Mechanical Ability Tests," *Psychometrika,* 1940, **5,** 17–33.
11. Hathaway, S. R., and J. C. McKinley, *Minnesota Multiphasic Personality Inventory Manual,* rev. ed., New York: The Psychological Corporation, 1951.
12. Strong, Edward K., Jr., *Vocational Interests 18 Years after College,* Minneapolis: University of Minnesota Press, 1955, pp. 62–66.
13. Darley, John G., and Theda Hagenah, *Vocational Interest Measurement,* Minneapolis: University of Minnesota Press, 1955, p. 83.
14. Strong, Edward K., Jr., *Vocational Interests of Men and Women,* Stanford, Calif.: Stanford University Press, 1943, p. 161.
15. Bittner, Reign, "Developing an Employee Merit Rating Procedure," in Dooher, M. Joseph, and Vivienne Marquis (eds.), *Rating Employee and Supervisory Performance,* New York: The American Management Association, 1950, p. 25.
16. *Ibid.,* p. 26.
17. Driver, R. S., "Employee Performance Evaluation," *Personnel Series,* 1945, **93,** 16–23.
18. Spicer, L. G., "A Survey of Merit Rating in Industry," *Personnel,* 1951, **28,** 517.
19. National Industrial Conference Board, Studies in Personnel Policy No. 39, *Employee Rating,* New York, 1942.
20. National Industrial Conference Board, Studies in Personnel Policy No. 86, *Personnel Activities in American Business,* rev. ed., New York, 1947.
21. Mahler, W. R., *Twenty Years of Merit Rating 1926–1946,* New York: The Psychological Corporation, 1947.

363

22. Tiffin, Joseph, "Merit Rating: Its Validity and Techniques," in Dooher and Marquis, *op. cit.,* p. 11 ff.
23. *Management Record,* September, 1953, p. 322 ff.
24. Flanagan, John C., *Personnel,* 1952, **29,** 376 ff.
25. Sisson, E. Donald, "Forced Choice—The New Army Rating," *Personnel Psychology,* 1948, **1,** 370.
26. *Industrial Relations Memos,* No. 119, p. 9.
27. *Ibid.,* p. 19.
28. Driver, Randolph S., "A Case History in Merit Rating," *Personnel,* 1940, **16,** 137–162.
29. Ewart, Edwin, S. E. Seashore, and Joseph Tiffin, "A Factor Analysis of an Industrial Merit Rating Scale," *Journal of Applied Psychology,* 1941, **25,** 481–486.
30. Bolanovich, D. J., "Statistical Analysis of an Industrial Rating Chart," *Journal of Applied Psychology,* 1946, **30,** 23–31.
31. Van Zelst, Raymond H., and Willard A. Kerr, "Workers' Attitudes toward Merit Rating," *Personnel Psychology,* 1953, **6,** 162.
32. Armstrong, T. O., "Talking Your Ratings," in Dooher and Marquis, *op. cit.,* p. 150.
33. National Industrial Conference Board, Studies in Personnel Policy No. 121, *Appraisal of Job Performance,* New York, p. 15.
34. Van Zelst and Kerr, *op. cit.,* p. 162.
35. "Rate Jobs and Establish Wage Brackets," *Factory Management and Maintenance,* August, 1944, pp. 97–104.
36. "Union Contracts Rate Employees," *American Machinist,* September, 1941, pp. 913–914.
37. Stackman, Harvey A., Jr., "A Case Report on Employee Rating," *Personnel,* 1947, **23,** 410–424.

CHAPTER 4

1. Scott, Walter D., Robert C. Clothier, and William R. Spriegel, *Personnel Management,* 5th ed., New York: McGraw-Hill Book Company, Inc., 1954, Appendix A, p. 620.
2. Bingham, Walter Van Dyke, and Bruce Victor Moore, *How To Interview,* 3rd ed., New York: Harper & Brothers, 1941, p. 1.
3. *Ibid.,* p. 14.
4. Gobetz, Wallace, Harold Cash, and Florence Schumer, "Behavioral Aspects of the Employment Interview," *Personnel,* 1953, **29,** 332–334.
5. Scott, Walter Dill, "The Scientific Selection of Salesmen," *Advertising and Selling,* 1915, **25,** 5–6, 94–96.
6. Snow, A. J., "An Experiment in the Validity of Judging Human Ability," *Journal of Applied Psychology,* 1924, **8,** 339–346.
7. McMurry, Robert N., "Validating the Patterned Interview," *Personnel,* 1947, **23,** 2–11.
8. Fear, Richard A., and Byron Jordan, *Employee Evaluation Manual for Interviewers,* New York: The Psychological Corporation, 1943, Appendix.

9. McMurry, *op. cit.*

———, and Dale L. Johnson, "Development of Instruments for Selecting and Placing Factory Employees," *Advanced Management,* September, 1945, pp. 113–120.

10. O'Rourke, L. J., *A New Emphasis in Federal Personnel Research and Administration,* United States Civil Service Commission, Washington: U. S. Government Printing Office, 1930, p. 21.

11. Bingham and Moore, *op. cit.,* p. 25.

12. Scott, Clothier, and Spriegel, *op. cit.,* p. 620.

13. National Industrial Conference Board, Studies in Personnel Policy No. 38, *Employment Procedures and Personnel Records,* New York, 1941.

14. Bills, Marion A., "Selection of Casualty and Life Insurance Agents," *Journal of Applied Psychology,* 1941, **25,** 6–10.

15. Tiffin, Joseph, B. T. Parker, and R. W. Habersat, "The Analysis of Personnel Data in Relation to Turnover on a Factory Job," *Journal of Applied Psychology,* 1947, **31,** 615–616.

16. Gifford, Walter S., "Does Business Want Scholars?," *Harper's Magazine,* May, 1928, pp. 667–674.

17. Bridgman, D. C., "Success in College and Business," *The Personnel Journal,* 1930, **9,** 1–19.

18. Gowin, E. B., *Selection and Training of the Business Executive,* New York: The Macmillan Company, 1918.

19. Starch, Daniel, *How To Develop Your Executive Ability,* New York: Harper & Brothers, 1943, pp. 22–23.

20. Sorokin, P. P., "Leaders of Labor and Radical Movements in the United States and Foreign Countries," *American Journal of Sociology,* 1927, **33,** 382–411.

21. Ohmann, O. A., "A Report of Research on the Selection of Salesmen at the Tremco Manufacturing Company," *Journal of Applied Psychology,* 1941, **25,** 18–29.

CHAPTER 5

1. National Industrial Conference Board, Studies in Personnel Policy No. 145, *Personnel Practices in Factory and Office,* New York, 1954, pp. 12, 69.

2. Wilkinson, B., "Validity of Short Employment Tests," *Personnel Psychology,* 1953, **6,** 419–425.

3. Kornhauser, Arthur, "Replies of Psychologists to Several Questions on the Practical Value of Intelligence Tests," *Educational and Psychological Measurement,* 1945, **5,** 181–189.

4. "Bosses Should Fire Nosy Psychologists," *Labor,* Sept. 11, 1954, p. 4.

5. Cohen, Leonard, "To Test or Not To Test," *The Personnel Journal,* 1946, **25,** 72–75.

6. Van Zelst, Raymond H., Otto J. Kroh, and Willard A. Kerr, "Workers' Attitudes toward Employment Tests," *Personnel Psychology,* 1951, **4,** 261–270.

7. Taylor, Calvin W., "Pre-testing Saves Training Costs," *Personnel Psychology,* 1952, **5,** 213–239.
8. Stromberg, Eleroy L., "Testing Programs Draw Better Applicants," *Personnel Psychology,* 1948, **1,** 21–29.
9. American Bankers Association, Customer and Personnel Relations Department, *Clerical Testing in Banks,* New York: American Bankers Association, 1952, p. 4.
10. Doppelt, Jerome E., and George K. Bennett, "Reducing the Cost of Training Satisfactory Workers," *Personnel Psychology,* 1953, **6,** 1–8.
11. "Basics of Personnel Testing," *Personnel,* 1956, **32,** 548–561.
12. "Better than Chance," *Test Service Bulletin* No. 45, New York: The Psychological Corporation, May, 1953, pp. 1–5.
13. Jackson, R. W. B., and A. J. Phillips, "Prediction Efficiencies by Deciles for Various Degrees of Relationship," *Educational Research Series* No. 11, Department of Educational Research, Ontario College of Education, University of Toronto, as reported in "Better than Chance," *op. cit.*
14. Tiffin, Joseph, and C. H. Lawshe, Jr., "The Adaptability Test: A Fifteen Minute Mental Alertness Test for Use in Personnel Allocation," *Journal of Applied Psychology,* 1943, **27,** 152–163.
15. Ghiselli, E. E., "The Measurement of Occupational Aptitude," *University of California Publications in Psychology,* 1955, **8,** No. 2.
16. Dvorak, Beatrice J., "The New USES General Aptitude Test Battery," *Journal of Applied Psychology,* 1947, **31,** 372–376.
17. Greene, Edward B., in Buros, Oscar K. (ed.), *The Fourth Mental Measurements Yearbook,* Highland Park, N. J.: The Gryphon Press, 1953, pp. 690–691.
18. Haire, Mason, "Use of Tests in Employee Selection," *Harvard Business Review,* 1950, **28,** 42–51.
19. "Choosing Better Foremen," *Factory Management and Maintenance,* November, 1952, p. 113.
20. Standard Oil Company (New Jersey), Employee Relations Department, *Made to Measure,* New York, 1951, pp. 40–41.
21. ———, *Employee Relations Research in Standard Oil Company (New Jersey) and Affiliates,* No. 1, Vol. 1, New York, 1956, pp. 107–110.
22. Wesman, Alexander G., "Faking Personality Test Scores in a Simulated Employment Situation," *Journal of Applied Psychology,* 1952, **36,** 112.
23. Heron, Alastair, "The Effects of Real Life Motivation on Questionnaire Response," *Journal of Applied Psychology,* 1956, **40,** 65–68.
24. Ferguson, Leonard, "The Effects of a Second Administration of an Employment Test," *Journal of Applied Psychology,* 1943, **27,** 170–175.
25. Seashore, Harold G., "The Improvement of Performance on the Minnesota Rate of Manipulation Test," *Journal of Applied Psychology,* 1947, **31,** 254–259.
26. Longstaff, Howard P., "Practice Effects on the Minnesota Vocational Test for Clerical Workers," *Journal of Applied Psychology,* 1954, **38,** 18–20.

27. Faubion, Richard W., Earle A. Cleveland, and T. W. Harrell, "The Influence of Training on Mechanical Aptitude Test Scores," *Educational and Psychological Measurement,* 1942, **2,** 91–94.
28. Churchill, Ruth D., et al., "Effect of Engineer School Training on the Surface Development Test," *Educational and Psychological Measurement,* 1942, **2,** 279–280.
29. Hay, E. N., and A. N. Blakemore, "The Relationship between Clerical Experience and Scores on the Minnesota Vocational Test for Clerical Workers," *Journal of Applied Psychology,* 1943, **27,** 311–315.

CHAPTER 6

1. Ghiselli, Edwin E., and Clarence W. Brown, *Personnel and Industrial Psychology,* New York: McGraw-Hill Book Company, Inc., 1955, pp. 225–245.
2. Shuman, J. T., "The Value of Aptitude Tests for Supervisory Workers in the Aircraft Engine and Propeller Industries," *Journal of Applied Psychology,* 1945, **29,** 185–190.
3. Harrell, Thomas W., "Testing Cotton Mill Supervisors," *Journal of Applied Psychology,* 1940, **24,** 31–35.
   ———, "Testing the Abilities of Textile Workers," *Georgia State Engineering Experiment Station Bulletin,* No. 5, 1940.
4. Uhrbrock, R. S., and M. W. Richardson, "Item Analysis the Basis for Forecasting Supervisory Ability," *The Personnel Journal,* 1933, **12,** 141–154.
5. Ghiselli and Brown, *op. cit.*
6. Shuman, *op. cit.*
7. Thurstone, L. L., *A Factorial Study of Perception,* Chicago: University of Chicago Press, 1944.
8. Sartain, A. Q., "The Use of Certain Standardized Tests in the Selection of Inspectors in an Aircraft Factory," *Journal of Consulting Psychology,* 1945, **9,** 234–235.
9. Bennett, George K., and Richard A. Fear, "Mechanical Comprehension and Dexterity," *The Personnel Journal,* 1943, **22,** 12–17.
10. Lawshe, C. H., Jr., I. A. Semanek, and J. Tiffin, "The Purdue Mechanical Adaptability Test," *Journal of Applied Psychology,* 1946, **30,** 442–453.
11. Jurgensen, C. E., "Extension of Minnesota Rate of Manipulation Tests," *Journal of Applied Psychology,* 1943, **27,** 164–169.
12. Barnette, W. Leslie, Jr., "Clerical Personnel," in Fryer, Douglas H., and Edwin R. Henry (eds.) *Handbook of Applied Psychology,* New York: Rinehart & Company, Inc., 1950, I, 197–207.
13. Ghiselli and Brown, *op. cit.*
14. Hay, Edward N., "Postscript to Predicting Success in Machine Bookkeeping," *Journal of Applied Psychology,* 1947, **31,** 235.

15. ———, "Predicting Success in Machine Bookkeeping," *Journal of Applied Psychology,* 1943, **27,** 483–493.
16. Gottsdanker, R. M., "Measures of Potentiality for Machine Calculation," *Journal of Applied Psychology,* 1943, **27,** 233–248.
17. Fraser, John M., "An Experiment with Group Methods in the Selection of Trainees for Senior Management Positions," *Occupational Psychology,* 1946, **20,** 63–67.
18. Williams, Stanley B., and Harold J. Leavitt, "Group Opinion as a Predictor of Military Leadership," *Journal of Consulting Psychology,* 1947, **11,** 283–291.
19. Ghiselli, Edwin E., and Richard P. Barthol, "The Validity of Personality Inventories in the Selection of Employees," *Journal of Applied Psychology,* 1953, **37,** 18–20.
20. Martin, Howard G., "Locating the Troublemaker with the Guilford-Martin Personnel Inventory," *Journal of Applied Psychology,* 1944, **28,** 461–467.
    Dorcus, Roy M., "A Brief Study of the Humm-Wadsworth Temperament Scale and the Guilford-Martin Personnel Inventory in an Industrial Situation," *Journal of Applied Psychology,* 1944, **28,** 302–307.
21. Harrell, Thomas W., "Humm-Wadsworth Temperament Scale and Ratings of Salesmen," *Personnel Psychology,* 1949, **2,** 491–495.
22. Meyer, Henry D., and Glenn L. Pressel, "Personality Test Scores in the Management Hierarchy," *Journal of Applied Psychology,* 1954, **38,** 73–80.
23. Meyer, Herbert H., "Factors Related to Success in the Human Relations Aspect of Work-Group Leadership," *Psychological Monographs,* 1951, **320,** 29 pp.
24. Tobalski, Francis P., and Willard A. Kerr, "Predictive Value of the Empathy Test in Automobile Salesmanship," *Journal of Applied Psychology,* 1952, **36,** 310–311.
25. Rundquist, E. A., "Personality Tests and Prediction," in Fryer and Henry, *op. cit.*
26. Demaree, Robert G., in Buros, Oscar K. (ed.), *The Fourth Mental Measurements Yearbook,* Highland Park, N. J.: The Gryphon Press, 1953, p. 116.
27. Sarbin, Theodore R., and Hedwin C. Anderson, "A Preliminary Study of the Relation of Measured Interest Patterns and Occupational Dissatisfaction," *Educational and Psychological Measurement,* 1942, **2,** 23–36.
28. Brayfield, Arthur H., "Clerical Interest and Clerical Aptitude," *The Personnel and Guidance Journal,* 1953, **31,** 304–306.
29. Strong, Edward K., Jr., *Vocational Interests 18 Years after College,* Minneapolis: University of Minnesota Press, 1955, pp. 42, 89.
30. Bills, Marion A., "A Tool for Selection That Has Stood the Test of Time," in Thurstone, L. L. (ed.), *Applications of Psychology,* New York: Harper & Brothers, 1952, pp. 131–137.
31. Strong, Edward K., Jr., *Manual for Vocational Interest Blank for Men,* Stanford, Calif.: Stanford University Press, 1938, p. 10.

32. Tiffin, Joseph, and S. Edgar Wirt, "The Importance of Visual Skills for Adequate Job Performance," *Journal of Consulting Psychology*, 1944, **8**, 80–89.
33. Ayers, Arthur W., "A Comparison of Certain Visual Factors with the Efficiency of Textile Inspectors," *Journal of Applied Psychology*, 1942, **26**, 812–827.
34. Halsey, George D., *Selecting and Inducting Employees*, New York: Harper & Brothers, 1951, p. 173.
35. Maloney, Paul W., "Reading Ease Scores for *How Supervise?*," *Journal of Applied Psychology*, 1952, **36**, 225–227.
36. Wickert, Frederic R., "Relation between *How Supervise?*, Intelligence and Education for a Group of Supervisory Candidates in Industry," *Journal of Applied Psychology*, 1952, **36**, 301–303.
37. Weitz, Joseph, and Robert C. Nuckols, "A Validation Study of *How Supervise?*," *Journal of Applied Psychology*, 1953, **37**, 7–8.

CHAPTER 7

1. Spriegel, William R., and Alfred G. Dale, Personnel Study No. 8, *Personnel Practices in Industry*, Austin: The University of Texas, p. 39.
2. Urwick, Lyndall F., *Management Education in American Business, Part I, General Summary*, New York: American Management Association, 1954, p. 29.
3. Mahler, W. R. and W. H. Monroe, *How Industry Determines the Need for and Effectiveness of Training*. A contract research report to Personnel Research Section, Adjutant General's Office. New York: The Psychological Corporation, 1952.
4. Biggane, Robert J., "How We Determined Training Needs," *Personnel Journal*, 1950, **29**, 13–16.
   Trickett, Joseph M., *A Survey of Management Development, Part II, The Quantitative Aspects*, New York: American Management Association, 1954, p. 33.
5. Mahler and Monroe, *op. cit.*, pp. 70–78.
6. Rood, Joseph E., "How Foremen Trainees Learn by Doing: A Company Program," *Personnel*, 1956, **32**, 409–422.
7. Mahler and Monroe, *op. cit.*, pp. 87–88.
8. "Training Manpower," *Fortune*, April, 1951, p. 154.
9. Smith, P. C., and R. A. Gold, "Prediction of Success from Examination of Performance during the Training Period," *Journal of Applied Psychology*, 1956, **40**, 83–86.
10. McGehee, William, "Cutting Training Waste," *Personnel Psychology*, 1948, **1**, 336.
11. ———, and Dwight H. Livingstone, "Persistence of the Effects of Training Employees To Reduce Waste," *Personnel Psychology*, 1954, **7**, 33–39.
12. Wallace, S. Rains, Jr., and Constance M. Twichell, "The Purdue Study," *Manager's Magazine*, 1953, **28**, 7 ff.

CHAPTER 8

1. Taylor, F. W., *The Principles of Scientific Management,* New York: Harper & Brothers, 1911, pp. 42, 71.
2. Gomberg, William, *A Trade Union Analysis of Time Study,* Chicago: Science Research Associates, 1948.
3. Golden, Clinton S., and Harold J. Ruttenberg, *The Dynamics of Industrial Democracy,* New York: Harper & Brothers, 1942, pp. 269–272.
4. Chapanis, Alphonse, Wendell R. Garner, and Clifford T. Morgan, *Applied Experimental Psychology,* New York: John Wiley & Sons, Inc., 1949.
5. Warren, Neil D., "Automation, Human Engineering and Psychology," *The American Psychologist,* 1956, **11,** 531–536.
6. Fitts, Paul M. (ed.), *Army Air Forces Aviation Psychology Program Research Report No. 19, Psychological Research on Equipment Design,* Washington: U. S. Government Printing Office, 1947, p. 265.
7. Morgan, Clifford T., "Human Engineering," in Dennis, Wayne (ed.), *Current Trends in Psychology,* Pittsburgh: University of Pittsburgh Press, 1947, pp. 169–195.
8. Institute of Applied Experimental Psychology, Tufts College, *Handbook of Human Engineering Data,* 2nd ed., Medford, Mass.: Tufts College, 1952.
9. Bello, Francis, "Fitting the Machine to the Man," *Fortune,* November, 1954, pp. 134–135, 148–158.
10. Warren, *op. cit.*
11. Bello, *op. cit.*
12. McFarland, Ross A., *Human Factors in Air Transport Design,* New York: McGraw-Hill Book Company, Inc., 1946.
13. Dunlap, Jack W., "Human Engineering—Another Management Tool," *Proceedings of the Fourth Annual Meeting, Social Science for Industry, Social Science Research and Policy Decisions,* Menlo Park, Calif.: Stanford Research Institute, 1956, pp. 27–35.
14. Hunt, L. I., "A Study of Screwdrivers for Small Assembly Work," *N. I. I. P. Journal,* 1934, **8,** 70–73.
15. Nadler, Gerald, and J. Wray Wilkes, "Studies in Relationships of Therbligs," *Advanced Management,* February, 1953, pp. 20–22.
16. Simon, J. Richard, and Robert C. Smader, "Dimensional Analysis of Motion: VIII. The Role of Visual Discrimination in Motion Cycles," *Journal of Applied Psychology,* 1955, **39,** 5–10.
17. Myers, C. S., *Industrial Psychology in Great Britain,* London: Jonathan Cape Ltd., 1926, pp. 87–88.
18. Barnes, Ralph M., and Marvin E. Mundel, *A Study of Simultaneous Symmetrical Hand Motions,* University of Iowa Studies in Engineering, Bulletin 17, 1939.
19. ——— and ———, *A Study of Hand Motions Used in Small Assembly Work,* University of Iowa Studies in Engineering, Bulletin 16, 1939.

20. *Ibid.*
21. Koepke, Charles A., and Lee S. Whitson, "Summary of a Series of Experiments To Determine the Power and Velocity of Motions Occurring in Manual Work," *Journal of Applied Psychology,* 1941, **25,** 251–264.
22. Farmer, E., and R. S. Brooke, *Motion Study in Metal Polishing,* Industrial Fatigue Research Board, Bulletin No. 15, London: His Majesty's Stationery Office, 1921.
23. Morrow, R. L., *Time Study and Motion Economy, with Procedures for Methods Improvement,* New York: The Ronald Press Company, 1946, p. 248.
24. Ryan, Thomas Arthur, *Work and Effort,* New York: The Ronald Press Company, 1947, pp. 213–229.
25. Rogers, Winston, and J. M. Hammersley, "The Consistency of Stop-Watch Time-Study Practitioners," *Occupational Psychology,* 1954, **28,** 61–76.
26. Barnes, Ralph M., *Work Measurement Project,* Industrial Engineering Bulletin No. 102, State University of Iowa, 1948, p. 55.
27. Lifson, Kalman A., "Errors in Time-Study Judgments of Industrial Work Pace," *Psychological Monographs,* 1953, **355,** 1–14.
28. Cohen, Leonard, and Leonard Strauss, "Time Study and the Fundamental Nature of Manual Skill," *Journal of Consulting Psychology,* 1946, **10,** 146–153.
29. Barnes, Ralph M., "Stop-Watch Time Study vs. Standard Data for Elementary Motions," *Modern Management,* July, 1948.
30. "Productivity of Labor," *Mill and Factory,* August, 1946.
31. Mathewson, Stanley B., *Restriction of Output among Unorganized Workers,* New York: The Viking Press, Inc., 1931.
32. Williams, Whiting, *Mainsprings of Men,* New York: Charles Scribner's Sons, 1925.
33. Mathewson, *op. cit.*
34. Collins, Orvis, Melville Dalton, and Donald Roy, "Restriction of Output and Social Cleavage in Industry," *Applied Anthropology,* 1946, **5,** No. 3, 1–14.
35. Roethlisberger, F. W., and William J. Dickson, *Management and the Worker,* Cambridge, Mass.: Harvard University Press, 1939, pp. 379–447.
36. Gardner, B. B., *Human Relations in Industry,* Homewood, Ill.: Richard D. Irwin, Inc., 1945.
37. Roethlisberger and Dickson, *op. cit.,* pp. 3–188.
38. Whitehead, T. N., *The Industrial Worker,* Cambridge, Mass.: Harvard University Press, 1938, Vol. II.
39. ———, *The Industrial Worker,* Cambridge, Mass.: Harvard University Press, 1938, I, 198.
40. Whiting, Helen Francis, and Horace Bidwell English, "Fatigue Tests and Incentives," *Journal of Experimental Psychology,* 1925, **8,** 33–49.
41. Katzell, Raymond A., "Fatigue and Its Alleviation," in Fryer, Douglas H.,

and Edwin R. Henry (eds.), *Handbook of Applied Psychology,* New York: Rinehart & Company, Inc., 1950, I, 74.

42. Poffenberger, A. T., *Principles of Applied Psychology,* New York: Appleton-Century-Crofts, Inc., 1942, pp. 110–111.
43. Bills, A. G., *The Psychology of Efficiency,* New York: Harper & Brothers, 1943, p. 111.
44. ———, "Blocking: A New Principle in Mental Fatigue," *American Journal of Psychology,* 1931, **43**, 230–245.
45. Poffenberger, *op. cit.,* pp. 109–112.
46. Miles, G. H., and A. Angles, "The Influence of Short Time on Speed of Production," *Journal of the National Institute of Industrial Psychology,* 1925, **2**, 300–302.
47. Kossoris, Max D., "Hours of Work and Output," *Monthly Labor Review,* 1947, **65**, 5–14.
48. *Ibid.*
49. Bartley, S. Howard, and Eloise Chute, *Fatigue and Impairment in Man,* New York: McGraw-Hill Book Company, Inc., 1947, p. 175.
50. Best, Ethel L., *A Study of a Change from 8 to 6 Hours of Work,* U. S. Department of Labor, Bulletin of the Women's Bureau, No. 105, Washington: U. S. Government Printing Office, 1933.
51. U. S. Public Health Service, *Comparison of an Eight-Hour Plant and Ten-Hour Plant,* Bulletin No. 106, Washington: U. S. Government Printing Office, 1920.
52. Kossoris, *op. cit.*
53. *Ibid.*
54. U. S. Public Health Service, *Fatigue and Hours Service of Interstate Truck Drivers,* Bulletin No. 265, Washington: U. S. Government Printing Office, 1941.
55. Vernon, H. M., and T. Bedford, *The Influence of Rest Pauses on Light Industrial Work,* Industrial Fatigue Research Board, No. 25, London: His Majesty's Stationery Office, 1924.
56. National Industrial Conference Board, Studies in Personnel Policy No. 145, *Personnel Practices in Factory and Office,* New York, 1954, p. 18.
57. Hersey, R. B., "Rests—Authorized and Unauthorized," *Journal of Personnel Research,* 1925, **4**, 37–45.
58. Manzer, C. W., "An Experimental Investigation of Rest Pauses," *Archives of Psychology,* 1927, No. 90, p. 29.
59. Wylie, H. L., "10 Ways To Save Fatigue," *American Business Magazine,* April, 1954, pp. 16–17.
60. ———, "The Coffee Break Is No Fad," *Modern Sanitation,* September, 1952, pp. 17–20.
61. ———, "10 Ways To Save Fatigue," *op. cit.*
62. Pollock, K. G., and F. C. Bartlett, *Two Studies in the Psychological Effects of Noise, I. Psychological Experiments on the Effects of Noise,* Industrial Health Research Board, No. 65, London: His Majesty's Stationery Office, 1932.

63. Laird, D. A., and K. Coye, "Psychological Measurements of Annoyance as Related to Pitch and Loudness," *Journal of Acoustical Society of America*, 1929, **1**, 158.

64. ———, "Influence of Noise on Production and Fatigue as Related to Pitch, Sensation Level and Steadiness of the Noise," *Journal of Applied Psychology*, 1933, **17**, 320–330. Also Pollock and Bartlett, *op. cit.*

65. Harmon, F. L., "The Effects of Noise upon Certain Psychological and Physiological Processes," *Archives of Psychology*, 1933, No. 147.

66. Morgan, J. J. B., "The Overcoming of Distraction and Other Resistances," *Archives of Psychology*, 1916, No. 35, 1–84.

67. Davis, R. C., *The Muscular Tension Reflex and Two of Its Modifying Conditions*, Indiana University Publication, Science Series, No. 3, 1935.

68. Kemp, E. H., "A Critical Review of Experiments on the Problem of Stimulation Deafness," *Psychological Bulletin*, 1935, **32**, 325–342.

69. Stannard, Fred, "Shiny Shops," *Wall Street Journal*, Dec. 14, 1955.

70. *Ibid.*

71. Bartley, S. H., "A Factor in Visual Fatigue," *Psychosomatic Medicine*, 1942, **4**, 369–375.

72. Stannard, *op. cit.*

73. *Ibid.*

74. Mackworth, N. H., "Effects of Heat on Wireless Telegraphy Operators Hearing and Recording Morse Messages," *British Journal of Industrial Medicine*, 1946, **3**, 143–158.

75. New York State Commission on Ventilation, *Ventilation*, New York: E. P. Dutton and Co., 1923, p. 96.

76. Vernon, H. M., and T. Bedford, *The Relation of Atmospheric Conditions to the Working Capacity and the Accident Rate of Miners,* Industrial Fatigue Research Board, No. 39, London: His Majesty's Stationery Office, 1927.

77. Wyatt, S., J. A. Fraser, and F. G. L. Stock, *Fan Ventilation in a Humid Weaving Shed,* Industrial Fatigue Research Board, No. 37, London: His Majesty's Stationery Office, 1926.

78. Vernon, H. M., *Accidents and Their Prevention,* Cambridge: Cambridge University Press, 1934, p. 76.

79. *Heating, Ventilating, Air Conditioning Guide, 1948,* New York: The American Society of Heating and Ventilating Engineers, 1948, p. 212.

80. Mackworth, N. H., "High Incentives versus Hot and Humid Atmospheres in a Physical Effort Task," *British Journal of Psychology*, 1947, **38**, 90–102.

CHAPTER 9

1. National Safety Council, *Accident Facts,* Chicago, 1955, p. 40.

2. Webb, Wilse B., "The Statistics of Accident Records and Accident Proneness," U. S. Naval School of Aviation Medicine, A. A. A. S. National Meeting, December, 1954.

3. Mintz, Alexander, and Milton L. Blum, "A Re-examination of the Accident Proneness Concept," *Journal of Applied Psychology,* 1949, **33**, 195–211.
4. Greenwood, Major, and Hilda M. Woods, *A Report on the Incidence of Industrial Accidents upon Individuals with Special Reference to Multiple Accidents,* Industrial Fatigue Research Board, No. 4, London: His Majesty's Stationery Office, 1919.
5. Brown, Clarence W., and Edwin E. Ghiselli, "Accident Proneness among Street Car Motormen and Motor Coach Operators," *Journal of Applied Psychology,* 1948, **32**, 20–23.
6. Johnson, H. M., "Born To Crash," *Collier's,* July 25, 1936, pp. 28, 58, 60.
7. Newbold, B. A., *A Contribution to the Study of the Human Factor in the Causation of Accidents,* Industrial Fatigue Research Board, No. 34, London: His Majesty's Stationery Office, 1926.
8. Dunbar, Flanders, "Medical Aspects of Accidents and Mistakes in the Industrial Army and in the Armed Forces," *War Medicine,* 1943, **4**, 161–175.
9. *Accident Facts, op. cit.,* pp. 26, 29.
10. Hambly, W. D., and T. Bedford, *Preliminary Notes on Atmospheric Conditions in Boot and Shoe Factories,* Industrial Fatigue Research Board, No. 11, London: His Majesty's Stationery Office, 1921.
11. Vernon, H. M., *Accidents and Their Prevention,* London: Cambridge University Press, 1936, pp. 78–84.
12. Davies, E., *Transactions of the Institute of Mining Engineering,* 1922, **63,** 326.
13. Tolman, Wm. H., and L. B. Kendall, *Safety: Methods for Preventing Occupational and Other Accidents and Disease,* New York: Harper & Brothers, 1913, p. 80.
14. Osborne, Ethel E., and H. M. Vernon, *The Influence of Temperature and Other Conditions on the Frequency of Industrial Accidents. Two Contributions to the Study of Accident Causation,* Industrial Fatigue Research Board, No. 19, London: His Majesty's Stationery Office, 1922.
15. Van Zelst, R. H., "Experience and Accident Rate," *Journal of Applied Psychology,* 1954, **38,** 313–317.
16. Newbold, *op. cit.*
17. Hill, J. M. M., and E. L. Trist, "Changes in Accidents and Other Absences with Length," *Human Relations,* 1955, **8,** 121–152.
18. ———, "A Consideration of Industrial Accidents as a Means of Withdrawal from the Work Situation," *Human Relations,* 1953, **6,** 357–380.
19. Speroff, Boris, and Willard Kerr, "Steel Mill Hot Strip Accidents and Interpersonal Desirability Values," *Journal of Clinical Psychology,* 1952, **8,** 89–91.
20. Keenam, V., and W. Kerr, "Psychological Climate and Accidents in an Automotive Plant," *Journal of Applied Psychology,* 1951, **35,** 108–111.
21. Bureau of National Affairs, "Company Safety Programs," Personnel Policies Forum Survey No. 29, Washington, D. C., Feb., 1955.

22. Strickland, Jack, "Union, Management, and Industrial Safety," *Institute of Labor and Industrial Relations Bulletin Series,* Vol. 5, No. 2, Urbana: University of Illinois, June, 1951.
23. Bureau of National Affairs, *op. cit.*
24. Walker, Stanley M., "Safety Consciousness—an Evaluation," *Information Circular* 7595, Washington, D. C.: Bureau of Mines, March, 1951.
25. Ewell, J. M., *Safety Bulletin,* Cincinnati, Ohio: Procter and Gamble, January, 1956.
26. Vernon, H. M., "Prevention of Accidents," *British Journal of Industrial Medicine,* 1945, **2,** 1–9.
27. Vernon, H. M., *Accidents and Their Prevention, op. cit.,* p. 263.
28. *Ibid.,* p. 269.
29. *Ibid.,* p. 270.
30. "Single Objective Safety," San Francisco: Columbia Geneva Steel Company, 1948.
31. "Stopping Little Injuries Stops Big Ones," *Factory Management and Maintenance,* May, 1953, pp. 67–69.
32. Farmer, E., E. G. Chambers, and F. J. Kirk, *Tests for Accident Proneness,* Industrial Health Research Board, No. 68, London: His Majesty's Stationery Office, 1933.
33. Tiffin, Joseph, and S. Edgar Wirt, "The Importance of Visual Skills for Adequate Job Performance in Industry," *Journal of Consulting Psychology,* 1944, **8,** 80–90.
34. Adler, Alexandra, "The Psychology of Repeated Accidents in Industry," *The American Journal of Psychiatry,* 1941–1942, **98,** 98–101.
35. Brimhall, R., and Raymond Franzen, *Problems of Consistency Arising from CAA Medical Examinations,* Washington, D. C.: Division of Research, Civil Aeronautics Administration, Department of Commerce, 1942.
36. Dunbar, *op. cit.*
37. *Ibid.*
38. Kraft, Merwyn, and Theodore W. Forbes, "Evaluating the Influences of Personal Characteristics on the Traffic Accident Experience of Transit Operators," *Proceedings of the Twenty-Fourth Annual Meeting, Highway Research Board,* 1944, pp. 278–289.
39. Shellow, Sadie Meyers, "Selection of Motormen," *Journal of Personnel Research,* 1926–1927, **5,** 183–188.
    Viteles, Morris S., "Research in the Selection of Motormen," *Journal of Personnel Research,* 1925–1926, **4,** 173–199.
40. Slocombe, C. S., and E. E. Brakeman, "Psychological Tests and Accident Proneness," *The British Journal of Psychology,* 1931, **21,** 29–38.
41. Farmer, E., and E. G. Chambers, *A Study of Accident Proneness among Motor Drivers,* Industrial Health Research Board, No. 84, London: His Majesty's Stationery Office, 1939.
42. Moffie, D. J., Andrew Symmes, and Charlotte R. Milton, "Relation be-

tween Psychological Tests and Driver Performance," *Road-User Characteristics Bulletin* 60, Highway Research Board, January, 1952, pp. 17–24.
43. Paterson, T. T., and F. J. Willett, "An Anthropological Experiment in a British Colliery," *Human Organization,* 1951, **10,** No. 2, 19–25.

CHAPTER 10

1. Davis, Allison, "The Motivation of the Under-Privileged Worker," in Whyte, William Foote (ed.), *Industry and Society,* New York: McGraw-Hill Book Company, Inc., 1946, p. 211.
2. Katz, Daniel, and Rensis Likert, "A Long-Range Program for the Study of Group Motivation, Group Morale, and Group Performance," paper at meetings of the American Psychological Association, Boston, September 7, 1948.
3. *Ibid.*
4. *Time,* June 17, 1946, pp. 29–30.
5. Hull, Richard L., and Arthur Kolstad, "Morale on the Job," in Watson, Goodwin (ed.), *Civilian Morale,* New York: Reynal & Hitchcock, Inc., 1942, pp. 362–364.
6. Watson, Goodwin, "Work Satisfaction," in Hartmann, George W., and Theodore Newcomb (eds.), *Industrial Conflict,* New York: The Cordon Company, Inc., 1939, pp. 118–119.
7. *Ibid.,* pp. 114–124.
8. Brissenden, P. F., and E. Frankel, *Labor Turnover in Industry,* New York: The Macmillan Company, 1922, pp. 96–101.
9. Mayo, Elton, *The Social Problems of an Industrial Civilization,* Division of Research, Graduate School of Business Administration, Harvard University, Boston, 1945.
10. Centers, Richard, and Hadley Cantril, "Income Satisfaction and Income Aspiration," *Journal of Abnormal and Social Psychology,* 1946, **41,** 64–69.
11. Davis, Allison, "The Motivation of the Under-Privileged Worker," in Whyte, *op. cit.,* p. 211.
12. Britton, Charles E., *Incentives in Industry,* Esso Standard Oil Company, Employee Relations Department, Research and Compensation Division, p. 27, reproduced from: Mayer, Wm. H., and Wm. H. Keown, *The Prevalence of Incentive Wages in Wisconsin,* Madison: University of Wisconsin, 1948.
13. Whyte, W. F., *Money and Motivation,* New York: Harper & Brothers, 1955, pp. 37–38.
14. *Ibid.,* p. 32.
15. Coch, Lester, and John R. P. French, Jr., "Overcoming Resistance to Change," *Human Relations,* August, 1948, pp. 512–532.
16. Whyte, *op. cit.,* pp. 394–395.
17. Wyatt, S., *Incentives in Repetitive Work,* Industrial Health Research Board, No. 69, London: His Majesty's Stationery Office, 1934, p. 24.

18. Caplow, Theodore, *The Sociology of Work,* Minneapolis: University of Minnesota Press, 1954, p. 62.
19. Comrey, A. L., J. M. Pfiffner, and W. S. High, *Factors Influencing Organizational Effectiveness, A Final Report,* for Office of Naval Research, Los Angeles: University of Southern California, 1954, p. 54.
20. National Industrial Conference Board, Studies in Personnel Policy No. 145, *Personnel Practices in Factory and Office,* 5th ed., New York, 1954, p. 60.
21. Book, W. F., and L. Norvell, "The Will to Learn: An Experimental Study of Incentives in Learning," *The Pedagogical Seminary,* 1922, **29,** No. 4, 305–362.
22. National Industrial Conference Board, Studies in Personnel Policy No. 62, *Principles and Application of Job Evaluation,* New York, 1944.
23. Marrow, Alfred J., and John R. P. French, Jr., "Changing a Stereotype in Industry," *Journal of Social Issues,* 1945, **1,** No. 3, 33–37.
24. Watson, Goodwin, "Work Satisfaction," in Hartman and Newcomb, *Industrial Conflict, op. cit.,* p. 118.
25. Sutherland, J. D., and I. E. Menzies, "Two Industrial Projects," *Journal of Social Issues,* 1947, **3,** No. 2, 51–58.
26. "Productivity of Labor," *Mill and Factory,* August, 1946.
27. "Can Industry Raise Wages without Increasing Prices?," *Mill and Factory,* November, 1945.
28. Heyel, Carl, *How To Create Job Enthusiasm,* New York: McGraw-Hill Book Company, Inc., 1942.
29. National Industrial Conference Board, Studies in Personnel Policy No. 145, *op. cit.,* p. 55.
30. ———, *Management Almanac,* New York, 1944, pp. 186–187.
31. Golden, C. S., and H. J. Ruttenberg, *Fundamentals of Industrial Democracy,* New York: Harper & Brothers, 1946.
32. *Management Almanac, op. cit.,* pp. 184–185.
33. *Ibid.*
34. Lear, John, "House of a Hundred Bosses," *The Saturday Evening Post,* Sept. 28, 1946, pp. 28–29, 93–94, 97.

CHAPTER 11

1. National Industrial Conference Board, Studies in Personnel Policy No. 145, *Personnel Practices in Factory and Office,* 5th ed., New York, 1954, p. 55.
2. Morse, Nancy C., *Satisfactions in the White-Collar Job,* Ann Arbor: Institute for Social Research, University of Michigan, 1953, p. 72.
3. *Ibid.,* pp. 72–73.
4. *Ibid.,* pp. 58, 70.
5. Hull, Richard L., and Arthur Kolstad, "Morale on the Job," in Watson,

Goodwin (ed.), *Civilian Morale,* New York: Reynal & Hitchcock, Inc., 1942, pp. 349–354.

Morse, *op. cit.,* p. 78.

6. Uhrbrock, R. S., "Attitudes of 4430 Employees," *Journal of Social Psychology,* 1934, **5,** 365–377.

7. Wyatt, S., and J. N. Langdon, *Fatigue and Boredom in Repetitive Work,* Industrial Health Research Board, No. 77, London: His Majesty's Stationery Office, 1937.

8. Kornhauser, A. W., and A. A. Sharp, "Employee Attitudes: Suggestions from a Study in a Factory," *The Personnel Journal,* 1932, **10,** 393–404.

9. Morse, *op. cit.,* p. 86.

10. Fryer, Douglas, "Industrial Dissatisfaction," *Industrial Psychology,* 1926, **1,** 29.

Hoppock, Robert, *Job Satisfaction,* New York: Harper & Brothers, 1935, p. 129.

11. Kornhauser and Sharp, *op. cit.,* pp. 393–410.

12. McMurry, R. N., "Efficiency, Work-Satisfaction and Neurotic Tendency, a Study of Bank Employees," *The Personnel Journal,* 1932, **11,** 201–210.

13. Weitz, Joseph, "A Neglected Concept in the Study of Job Satisfaction," *Personnel Psychology,* 1952, **5,** 201–206.

14. Van Zelst, Raymond H., "Worker Popularity and Job Satisfaction," *Personnel Psychology,* 1951, **4.**

15. Morse, *op. cit.,* p. 60.

16. "The Fortune Quarterly Survey XI," *Fortune,* January, 1938, p. 88.

17. Hoppock, *op. cit.,* p. 166.

Bell, Howard M., *Youth Tell Their Story,* Washington: American Youth Commission, 1937, p. 135.

18. Paterson, Donald G., and C. Harold Stone, "Dissatisfaction with Life Work among Adult Workers," *Occupations,* 1942, **21,** 219–221.

19. Fairchild, M., "Skill and Specialization, a Study in the Metal Trades," *The Personnel Journal,* 1930, **9,** 28–71, 128–175.

20. Form, William H., "Toward an Occupational Social Psychology," *Journal of Social Psychology,* 1946, **24,** 85–99.

21. Cattell, Raymond B., "The Concept of Social Status," *Journal of Social Psychology,* 1942, **15,** 293–308.

22. *Ibid.*

23. Deeg, Maethel E., and Donald G. Paterson, "Changes in Social Status of Occupations," *Occupations,* 1947, **25,** 205–208.

24. "The Fortune Quarterly Survey XI," *op. cit.,* p. 88.

25. Stedman, Gerald Eldridge, "An Appreciation Index," *The Personnel Journal,* 1945, **24,** 64–72.

26. "The Fortune Quarterly Survey XI," *op. cit.,* p. 88.

27. Benge, Eugene J., "How To Learn What Workers Think of Job and Boss," *Factory Management and Maintenance,* May, 1944, pp. 101–104.

28. Worthy, James C., "Factors Influencing Employee Morale," *12 Studies*

on *Communications and Management Skills,* Boston: Harvard Business Review, 1950, p. 102.

29. "The Fortune Survey," *Fortune,* May, 1947, Pt. 2, p. 6.
30. "The Fortune Survey," *Fortune,* June, 1947, Pt. 2, pp. 5, 6, 10.
31. Blum, M., *Readings in Experimental Industrial Psychology,* Englewood Cliffs, N. J.: Prentice-Hall, Inc., 1952, p. 107.
32. Stanford Research Institute, "Tomorrow's Manpower," *Research for Industry News Bulletin,* May, 1955, pp. 8–9.
33. Blum, *op. cit.,* pp. 109 ff.
34. *Ibid.*
35. *California Institute of Technology Bulletin* No. 25, "Fantasies and Facts in Corporations," 1955, p. 11.
36. Watson, Goodwin, "Work Satisfaction," in Hartmann, George W., and Theodore Newcomb (eds.), *Industrial Conflict,* New York: The Cordon Company, 1939, p. 118.
37. Watson, Goodwin (ed.), *Civilian Morale, op. cit.*
38. Hartmann and Newcomb (eds.), *op. cit.*
39. Roethlisberger, F. W., and William J. Dickson, *Management and the Worker,* Cambridge, Mass.: Harvard University Press, 1939.
40. Watson, Goodwin (ed.), *op. cit.*
41. Hartmann and Newcomb (eds.), *op. cit.,* p. 118.
42. Kornhauser and Sharp, *op. cit.*
43. California Institute of Technology, "Project 5, Surveys of Employee Opinion," *Summary of Annual Report, 1953–1954,* p. 4.
44. National Industrial Conference Board, *Factors Affecting Employee Morale,* Studies in Personnel Policy No. 85, 1947, pp. 21–22.
45. "Project 5, Surveys of Employee Opinion," *op. cit.*
46. The Industrial Relations Center, University of Chicago, *The Employee Inventory Survey Recommended Program,* p. 1.
47. Industrial Relations Center, University of Minnesota, "Triple Audit Employee Attitude Scale," Bulletin No. 11, August, 1951.
48. Kerr, Willard A., "Summary of Validity Studies of the Tear Ballot," *Personnel Psychology,* 1952, **5,** 105–112.
49. McIntosh, Vergil M., "Anonymity as a Factor in Attitude Measurement," Research Notes 51–4, Project 21–07–003, San Antonio, Texas: Lackland Air Force Base, Human Resources Research Center, Air Training Command, pp. 1–8.
    Hamel, La Verne, and Hans G. Reif, "Should Attitude Questionnaires Be Signed?," *Personnel Psychology,* 1952, **5,** 87–91.
50. Standard Oil Company of California, *Here's Your Opinion,* 1952.
51. Evans, Chester E., and La Verne N. Laseau, "My Job Contest—An Experiment in New Employe Relations Methods, Part I," *Personnel Psychology,* 1949, **2,** 1–16.
52. Evans, Chester E., and La Verne N. Laseau, "My Job Contest—An Experiment in New Employe Relations Methods, Part II," *Personnel Psychology,* 1949, **2,** 185 ff.

379

CHAPTER 12

1. Kahn, Robert L., and Daniel Katz, "Leadership Practices in Relation to Productivity and Morale," in Cartwright, Dorwin, and Alvin Zander (eds.), *Group Dynamics,* Evanston, Ill.: Row, Peterson & Company, 1953, p. 616.
2. Hull, Richard L., and Arthur Kolstad, "Morale on the Job," in Watson, Goodwin (ed.), *Civilian Morale,* New York: Reynal & Hitchcock, Inc., 1942, p. 350.
3. Raphael, Winifred, "A Study of Some Stresses and Strains within the Working Group," *Occupational Psychology,* 1947, **21,** 92–101.
4. Viteles, Morris, "What Raises a Man's Morale?," *Personnel,* 1954, **30,** 302–313.
5. Worthy, James C., "Organizational Structure and Employee Morale," *American Sociological Review,* 1950, **15,** 169–179.
6. Odiorne, George S., "Some Effects of Poor Equipment Maintenance on Morale," *Personnel Psychology,* 1955, **8,** 195–200.
7. Brayfield, Arthur H., and Walter H. Crockett, "Employee Attitudes and Employee Performance," *Psychological Bulletin,* 1955, **52,** 396–424.
8. Kerr, Willard A., "Labor Turnover and Its Correlates," *Journal of Applied Psychology,* 1947, **31,** 366–371.
9. Smith, F. J., and W. A. Kerr, "Turnover Factors as Assessed by the Exit Interview," *Journal of Applied Psychology,* 1953, **37,** 352–355.
10. Wickert, Frederick R., "Turnover and Employees' Feelings of Ego-Involvement in the Day-to-Day Operations of a Company," *Personnel Psychology,* 1951, **4,** 185–198.
11. Kerr, Willard A., George J. Koppelmeier, and James J. Sullivan, "Absenteeism, Turnover, and Morale in a Metals Fabrication Factory," *Occupational Psychology,* 1951, **25,** 50–55.
12. Brayfield and Crockett, *op. cit.*
13. Mann, Floyd, and Howard Baumgartel, *Absences and Employee Attitudes in an Electric Power Company,* Ann Arbor: Survey Research Center, University of Michigan, December, 1952.
14. Brayfield and Crockett, *op. cit.*
15. Mayo, Elton, *The Human Problems of an Industrial Civilization,* New York: The Macmillan Company, 1946, pp. 48–50.
16. Kornhauser, A. W., and A. A. Sharp, "Employee Attitudes," *Personnel Journal,* 1932, **10,** 393–404.
17. Katz, D., and H. Hyman, "Morale in War Industries," in Newcomb, T., and E. Hartley (eds.), *Readings in Social Psychology,* New York: Henry Holt and Company, 1947, pp. 437–447.
18. *Profit Sharing,* Industrial Welfare Division, Department of Labour and National Service, Commonwealth of Australia, 1947.
19. Roper, Elmo, *New York Herald Tribune,* Feb. 13, 1947.
20. Knowlton, P. A., "Studies in Profit Sharing," Evanston, Ill.: Profit Sharing Research Foundation, 1952–1953.

21. Chamberlain, John, "Every Man a Capitalist," *Life,* Dec. 23, 1946, pp. 93–94, 97–100, 103.
22. Morse, Nancy C., *Satisfactions in the White-Collar Job,* Ann Arbor: University of Michigan, 1953.
23. Walker, J., and R. Marriott, "A Study of Some Attitudes to Factory Work," *Occupational Psychology,* 1951, **25,** 181–191.
24. Walker, Charles R., and Robert H. Guest, *The Man on the Assembly Line,* Cambridge, Mass.: Harvard University Press, 1952.
25. *Ibid.*
26. Smith, P. C., "The Prediction of Individual Differences in Susceptibility to Industrial Monotony," *Journal of Applied Psychology,* 1955, **39,** 322–329.
27. Bills, A. G., *The Psychology of Efficiency,* New York: Harper & Brothers, 1943, pp. 68–71.
28. Wyatt, S., and J. N. Langdon, *Fatigue and Boredom in Repetitive Work,* Industrial Health Research Board, No. 77, London: His Majesty's Stationery Office, 1937, p. 29.
29. Wharton, Don, "Workers Don't Have To Be Robots," *The American Mercury,* October, 1954.
30. "Broadening the Job. An Answer to Specialization and Boredom," *Time,* April 12, 1954.
31. McGehee, William, and James E. Gardner, "Music in a Complex Industrial Job," *Personnel Psychology,* 1949, **2,** 405–418.
32. Smith, Henry Clay, "Music in Relation to Employee Attitudes, Piece-Work Production and Industrial Accidents," *Applied Psychology Monograph No. 14,* 1947.

CHAPTER 13

1. Dickson, W. J., "The Hawthorne Plan of Personnel Counseling," *American Journal of Orthopsychiatry,* 1945, **15,** 345.
2. Eilbert, Henry, "Management Policy Aspects of Employee Counseling," *Personnel,* 1951, **27,** 519–523.
3. Rogers, Carl R., and Rosalind F. Dymond (eds.), *Psychotherapy and Personality Change,* Chicago: University of Chicago Press, 1954, pp. 3–434.
4. ———, *Counseling and Psychotherapy,* Boston: Houghton Mifflin Co., 1942, pp. 22–25.
5. Snyder, William U., "Dr. Thorne's Critique of Non-Directive Psychotherapy," *Journal of Abnormal and Social Psychology,* 1945, **40,** 336–339.
6. Shepherd, William G., "Advice, Guidance and Counseling," *The Personnel Journal,* 1946, **25,** 167–170.
7. Rogers, Carl R., "Effective Principles for Dealing with Individual and Group Tensions and Dissatisfactions," *Executive Seminar Series on Industrial Relations, Session X,* Chicago: University of Chicago, 1947, p. 5.

8. ———, "Significant Aspects of Client-Centered Therapy," *American Psychologist,* 1946, **1,** 415–422.
9. Rogers, *Counseling and Psychotherapy, op. cit.,* p. 173.
10. *Ibid.,* p. 216.
11. *Ibid.,* p. 237.
12. *Ibid.,* pp. 76–77.
13. Black, John D., *Some Principles and Techniques of Employee Counseling,* Chicago: The Dartnell Corporation, 1955, p. 1.
14. *Ibid.,* pp. 2–3.
15. *Ibid.,* p. 3.
16. Rogers, *op. cit.,* p. 205.
17. Black, *op. cit.,* p. 3.
18. *Ibid.,* pp. 3–4.
19. *Ibid.,* p. 6.
20. Rogers and Dymond (eds.), *op. cit.,* p. 420.

CHAPTER 14

1. Committee on the Causes of Industrial Peace under Collective Bargaining of the National Planning Association, *Fundamentals of Labor Peace— A Final Report—Case 14,* Washington, D. C.: National Planning Association, December, 1953.
2. Roethlisberger, F. J., and William J. Dickson, *Management and the Worker,* Cambridge, Mass.: Harvard University Press, 1939.
3. *Ibid.*
4. Gardner, Burleigh B., and William F. Whyte, "The Man in the Middle: Position and Problems of the Foreman," *Applied Anthropology,* 1945, **4,** No. 2.
5. Kirchner, Wayne K., and Jerry Belenker, "What Employees Want To Know," *Personnel Journal,* March, 1955, **33,** 378–379.
6. Flesch, R., *The Art of Plain Talk,* New York: Harper & Brothers, 1951.
7. Davis, Keith, and James O. Hopkins, "Readability of Employee Handbooks," *Personnel Psychology,* 1950, **3,** 317–326.
8. Householder, Frank R., Jr., "A Railroad Checks on Its Communications," *Personnel Journal,* April, 1954, **32,** 413–415.
9. Bakke, E. Wight, *Labor and Management Look Ahead,* New York: American Management Association, Personnel Series No. 98, 1946, pp. 9–25.
10. *Must Labor and Management Fight?* New York: Nejelski and Company, Inc., 1946.
11. "Can Industry Raise Wages without Increasing Prices?," *Mill and Factory,* November, 1945.
12. Warner, Lloyd, *The Social System of a Modern Factory,* New Haven: Yale University Press, 1947.
13. Golden, Clinton S., and Virginia D. Parker, *Causes of Industrial Peace under Collective Bargaining for Committee on Industrial Peace,* New York: Harper & Brothers, 1955.

14. Purcell, Theodore V., *The Worker Speaks His Mind on the Company and the Union*, Cambridge: Harvard University Press, 1953.
15. Buchsbaum, Herbert J., et al., "From Conflict to Cooperation," *Applied Anthropology*, 1946, **5**, No. 4, 1–31.
16. Harbison, Frederick H., "The Basis of Industrial Conflict," in Whyte, William F., *Industry and Society*, New York: McGraw-Hill Book Company, 1946, Chapter IX.
17. Gottlieb, Bertram, and Willard A. Kerr, "An Experiment in Industrial Harmony," *Personnel Psychology*, 1950, **3**, 445–453.
18. Meany, George, "Meany Looks into the Future," *New York Times*, Dec. 4, 1955, Magazine Section, p. 6.
19. Francis, Clarence, "The Causes of Industrial Peace," speech delivered before the 52nd Annual Congress of American Industry, December, 1947, New York, N. Y.

CHAPTER 15

1. Stogdill, Ralph M., "Personal Factors Associated with Leadership: A Survey of the Literature," *Journal of Psychology*, January, 1948.
2. Gibb, Cecil A., "The Principles and Traits of Leadership," *Journal of Abnormal and Social Psychology*, 1947, **42**, 267–284.
3. Tannenbaum, Robert, "Helping Managers Become More Effective Leaders," speech given at Third Seminar on Social Science for Industry, 1955, arranged by the Stanford Research Institute.
4. Allen, Louis A., "Making the Foreman a Manager," National Industrial Conference Board, *Management Record*, 1954, **16**, 294–296.
5. Robinson, Claude, *Foreman Attitudes*, American Management Production Series No. 154, New York: American Management Association, 1944.
6. Larke, Alfred G., "How Foremen Get That Way," *Dun's Review and Modern Industry*, January, 1955, **65**, 44–50.
7. *Ibid.*
8. White, Ralph, and Ronald Lippitt, "Leader Behavior and Member Reaction in Three 'Social Climates'," in Cartwright, Dorwin, and Alvin Zander (eds.), *Group Dynamics*, Evanston, Ill.: Row, Peterson & Company, 1953, pp. 585–611.
9. Radke, Marian, and Dana Klisurich, "Experiments in Changing Food Habits," *Journal of the American Dietetics Association*, 1947, **23**, 403–409.
10. Lewin, Kurt, "Forces behind Food Habits and Methods of Change," *Bulletin of the National Research Council*, 1943, **108**, 35–65.
11. Lawrence, Lois C., and Patricia Cain Smith, "Group Decision and Employee Participation," *Journal of Applied Psychology*, 1955, **39**, 334–337.
12. Coch, Lester, and R. P. French, Jr., "Overcoming Resistance to Change," *Human Relations*, 1948, **1**, 512–532.
13. Maier, Norman R. F., *Principles of Human Relations*, New York: John Wiley & Sons, Inc., 1952, pp. 24–25.

14. *Ibid.,* pp. 28–29.
15. *Ibid.,* pp. 254–256.
16. Kriesberg, Martin, "Executives Evaluate Administrative Conferences," *Advanced Management,* March, 1950, pp. 15–17.
17. *Ibid.*
18. Marquis, D. G., Harold Guetzkow, and R. W. Heyns, "A Social Psychological Study of the Decision-Making Conference," in Guetzkow, Harold (ed.), *Groups, Leadership and Men,* Pittsburgh: Carnegie Press, 1951, pp. 55–67.
19. Kahn, Robert L., and Daniel Katz, "Leadership Practices in Relation to Productivity and Morale," in Cartwright and Zander (eds.), *op. cit.,* pp. 612–627.
20. Katz, Daniel, Nathan Maccoby, and Nancy C. Morse, *Productivity, Supervision and Morale in an Office Situation,* Part I, Ann Arbor: Survey Research Center, University of Michigan, 1950, p. 17.
21. Kahn and Katz, in Cartwright and Zander, *op. cit.,* p. 616.
22. *Ibid.,* p. 618.
23. Katz, Daniel, Nathan Maccoby, Gerald Gurin, and Lucretia G. Floor, *Productivity, Supervision and Morale among Railroad Workers,* Ann Arbor: Survey Research Center, University of Michigan, 1951, p. 23.
24. Pelz, Donald C., "Influence: A Key to Effective Leadership in the First Line Supervisor," *Personnel,* 1952, **29,** 216.
25. Katz, Maccoby, and Morse, *op. cit.,* p. 20.
26. Kahn and Katz, *op. cit.,* p. 622.
27. *Ibid.,* p. 624.
28. Seashore, Stanley E., *Group Cohesiveness in the Industrial Work Group,* Ann Arbor: Survey Research Center, University of Michigan, 1954, pp. 98–99.
29. Hariton, Theodore, "Conditions Influencing the Effects of Training Foremen in New Human Relations Principles," Ph.D. Dissertation, The University of Michigan, 1951.
30. Fleishman, Edwin A., Edwin F. Harris, and Harold E. Burtt, *Leadership and Supervision in Industry; An Evaluation of a Supervisory Training Program,* Monograph No. 33, Bureau of Educational Research, The Ohio State University, 1955.
31. *Ibid.,* p. 27.

Name Index

387

Subject Index